Hiking
California's
Desert Parks

by
Bill Cunningham
and
Polly Burke

FALCON
HELENA, MONTANA

CAUTION

Outdoor recreational activities are by their very nature potentially hazardous. All participants in such activities must assume the responsibility for their own actions and safety. The information contained in this guidebook cannot replace sound judgment and good decision–making skills, which help reduce risk exposure, nor does the scope of this book allow for disclosure of all the potential hazards and risks involved in such activities.

Learn as much as possible about the outdoor recreational activities in which you participate, prepare for the unexpected, and be cautious. The reward will be a safer and more enjoyable experience.

 Text pages printed on recycled paper.

CONTENTS

CONTENTS

CONTENTS

DEDICATION

To the thousands of citizens from California and elsewhere, past and present, who laid the groundwork for protection of a large portion of the California Desert, to those who helped secure passage of the California Desert Protection Act, and to the dedicated state and federal park rangers and naturalists charged with the stewardship of California's irreplaceable desert wilderness.

ACKNOWLEDGMENTS

The help of many individuals was essential in writing this hiking guide. At each park staff members generously shared their knowledge by contributing data, ideas and advice. The following deserve special thanks: Homer Townsend, chief ranger, and Mark Jorgensen, associate resource ecologist at Anza-Borrego Desert State Park; Charlie Callagan, ranger and one of the leading authorities on the wilderness of Death Valley, and Corky Hays, chief of interpretation, Death Valley National Park; Esy Fields, director of the Death Valley Natural History Association; Joe Zarki, chief of interpretation, Thomas M. Gavin, backcountry ranger, Joshua Tree National Park and Sue E. Alexander, director of the Joshua Tree Natural History Association; Kirsten Talken, district interpreter, at Mojave National Preserve; and Ramon Sanchez and Thom Thompson, interpretive rangers at Providence Mountains State Park/Mitchell Caverns Natural Preserve. We'll never forget the hot shower Ramon provided for us during our visit to Providence, our first in several weeks of desert exploration. The amazing dedication of these professionals to resource protection and visitor education gives us great optimism for the future of California's magnificent desert parks. Our thanks also to all the hospitable folks who provided advice and insights to us during our treks in the desert. In some cases it was a simple act of kindness, such as when a wonderful couple from Alberta replaced our lost Death Valley map. Please know that you are not forgotten.

OVERVIEW MAP

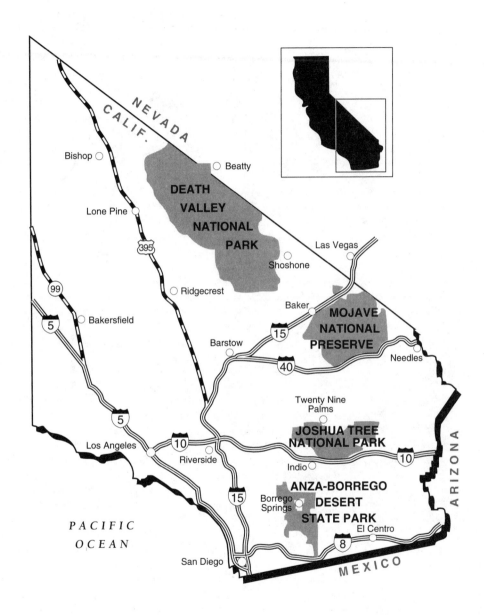

NEVADA

CALIF.

Bishop ○

○ Beatty

DEATH
VALLEY
NATIONAL
PARK

Lone Pine ○

395

○ Ridgecrest

Las Vegas ○

Shoshone

99

5

○ Bakersfield

Baker ○

MOJAVE
NATIONAL
PRESERVE

15

Barstow

40

Needles

5

Twenty Nine
Palms

JOSHUA TREE
NATIONAL PARK

Los Angeles ○

10

Riverside ○

Indio ○

10

ARIZONA

15

Borrego
Springs ○

ANZA-BORREGO
DESERT
STATE PARK

El Centro
○

PACIFIC

OCEAN

8

San Diego ○

MEXICO

SUB-REGIONS OF CALIFORNIA DESERT

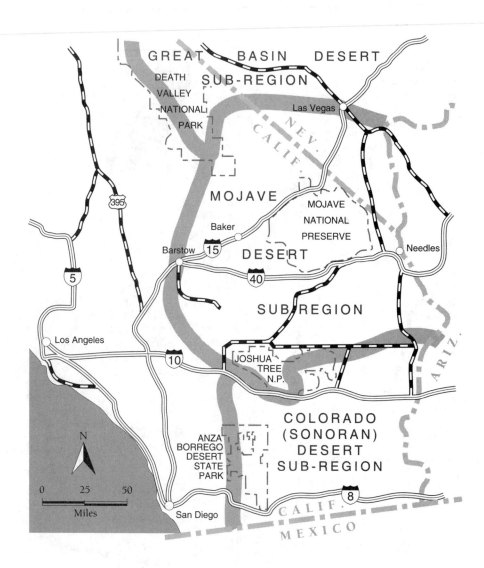

MAP LEGEND

Interstate	(00)	Campground	▲
US Highway	(00)	Cabins/Buildings	▪
State or Other Principal Road	(000)	Peak	9,782 ft.
National Park Route	(00)	Hill	
Interstate Highway	⟹	Elevation	9,782 ft. ✕
Paved Road	⟹	Gate	•—•
Gravel Road	⟹	Mine Site	⚒
Unimproved Road	= = = = = = =▷	Overlook/Point of Interest	◻
Trailhead	◯	Sand Dunes	
Main Trail(s)/Route(s)	- - - - -	National Forest/Park Boundary	
Alternate/Secondary Trail(s)/Route(s)	- - - - -		
Parking Area	Ⓟ	Map Orientation	N
River/Creek		Scale	0 0.5 1
Spring	⚲		Miles
One Way Road	One Way		

Hiking the serpentine ridge of the swirling Panamint Dunes—Death Valley National Park.

INTRODUCTION

The California Desert covers the southeastern quarter of our most populous and most ecologically diverse state. And the four huge desert parks featured in this book encompass about a quarter of the California Desert—from its southern to northernmost extent. Incredibly, three of the four desert subregions that make up most of the arid southwest corner of North America are found within the California Desert. These subregions—the Colorado (called the Sonoran in Mexico), Mojave, and Great Basin deserts—differ by climate and distinct plant and animal communities.

The geographer's definition of a desert as a place with less than 10 inches average annual rainfall says little about what a desert really is. Deserts are regions of irregular and minimal rainfall, so much so that for most of the time scarcity of water is limiting to life. Averages mean nothing in a desert region that may go one or two years without *any* rain only to receive up to three times the annual average the following year.

In the desert, evaporation far exceeds precipitation. Temperatures swing widely between night and day. This is because low humidity and intense sun heat up the ground during the day, but almost all of the heat dissipates at night. Daily temperature changes of 50 degrees Fahrenheit or more are common—which can be hazardous to unprepared hikers caught out after dark.

Sparse rainfall means sparse vegetation, which in turn means naked geological features. Most of the California desert is crisscrossed with mountain ranges, imparting an exposed, rough-hewn, scenic character to the landscape. Rather than having been uplifted, the mountains were largely formed by an east-west collision of the earth's tectonic plates, producing a north-south orientation of the ranges. Some would call the result stark, but all would agree that these signatures on the land are dramatic and, at times, overpowering. This very starkness tends to exaggerate the drama of space, color, relief, or sheer ruggedness.

Despite sparse plant cover, the number of individual plant species in the California Desert is amazing. At least 1,000 species are spread among 103 vascular plant families. Equally amazing is the diversity of bird life and other wildlife on this deceptively barren land. Many of these birds and animals are active only at night, or are most likely seen during the hotter months at or near watering holes. Hundreds of bird species and more than sixty kinds of reptiles and amphibians fly, nest, crawl, and slither in habitat niches to which they have adapted. Desert bighorn sheep and the rare mountain lion are at the top of the charismatic mega-fauna list, but at least sixty other species of mammals make the desert their home—from kit foxes on the valley floors to squirrels on the highest mountain crests. The best way to observe these desert denizens is on foot, far from the madding crowd, in the peace and solitude of desert wilderness.

Anza-Borrego Desert State Park is within the Colorado (Sonoran) Desert, which extends deep into Arizona and Mexico. This is the hottest and lowest of the desert types, with elevations from below sea level to 4,500 feet. Temperatures are among the highest in the United States, with summer highs of 120 degrees Fahrenheit. or more. Characteristic plants include jumping cholla, creosote bush, ocotillo, and ironwood.

Joshua Tree National Park is in the transition zone between the Colorado and Mojave deserts, accounting for much of its rich diversity of plant and animal life. The Mojave Desert is the smallest of the four North American deserts and lies mostly in southeastern California. Elevations range from below sea level to around 4,000 feet, with average elevations of 3,000 feet in the rugged eastern portion, which includes the Mojave National Preserve. The hottest temperature ever recorded in the United States—134 degrees—took place in the Mojave Desert at Death Valley. Summer temperatures usually exceed 100 degrees, but winter can bring bitter cold, sometimes dropping near zero in valleys where dense, frigid air settles at night. Plant cover is typified by Joshua trees, creosote bush, white bursage, and indigo bush.

Much of Death Valley National Park is on the southwestern edge of the vast Great Basin desert region, which also encompasses most of Nevada, much of Utah, and portions of Oregon, Idaho, and Wyoming. This is high, cold desert, largely above 4,000 feet, with snow and freezing temperatures during winter. The Great Basin is distinguished by sunken interior drainage basins bounded by hundreds of mountain ranges, created by shifting along fault lines. Rubber rabbitbrush, blackbrush, and big sagebrush characterize the plant cover.

Death Valley, Joshua Tree, and Anza-Borrego were included within the Colorado and Mojave Desert Biosphere Reserve, which was internationally designated in 1984. There are more than 265 biosphere reserves worldwide that protect lands within each of the earth's biogeographic regions. The parks are within the core of the biosphere reserve where human impact is kept to a minimum. The core is surrounded by a multiple use area where sustainable development is the guiding principle. In Death Valley the "human connection" of the reserve is represented by members of the Timbisha Shoshone Indian tribe who live within the park.

Each of the desert parks receives many international visitors who are drawn to the desert because there is no desert in their homeland. Many come during the peak of summer to experience the desert at its hottest. Regardless of whether the visitor is from Europe, a nearby California town, or someplace across the nation, the endlessly varied desert offers something for everyone. Unlike snowbound northern regions, the California Desert is a year-round hiker's paradise. There is no better place in which to actually *see* the raw, exposed forces of land-shaping geology at work. Those interested in history and paleoarcheology will have a field day. And the list goes on. This book is designed to enhance the enjoyment of all who wish to sample the richness of California's desert parks on their own terms. Travel is best done on foot, with distance and destination being far less important than the experience of getting there.

THE CALIFORNIA DESERT PROTECTION ACT OF 1994

The California Desert Protection Act of 1994 was one of the last measures passed by the 103rd Congress. More than eight years of vigorous lobbying by a huge alliance of local concerned citizens, the California Desert Coalition, and national environmental groups culminated in this monumental legislation, the largest wilderness designation since the 1980 Alaska Lands Bill, and the largest ever in the Lower Forty-eight. The law upgraded Death Valley and Joshua Tree National Monuments to national park status, and

The view straight down to Badwater (282 feet below sea level) from Dante's View with the snowy summit of 11,048 foot Telescope Peak in the background—Death Valley National Park.

enlarged the territory of each of them. Death Valley National Park, at 3.3 million acres, is now the largest national park outside of Alaska. Joshua Tree was likewise enlarged to 793,955 acres from its original 560,000 acres. The 1.4 million acres of the East Mojave National Scenic Area became the Mojave National Preserve, and was transferred from the commodity-oriented Bureau of Land Management to the preservation-minded National Park Service. Wilderness areas were designated within these new national parks and preserve, and sixty-nine new wilderness areas were established on nearby BLM, national forest, and wildlife-refuge lands in the California desert.

The California Desert Protection Act had both friends and foes. To gain passage, it was necessary to compromise often. Thus, while federal wilderness protection was provided for 6 million acres, many pre-existing uses are also permitted to continue under the act. Pre-existing mining, grazing, and military overflights are allowed in Mojave National Preserve and in the expansion regions of Death Valley and Joshua Tree. A major last-minute concession to gain passage involved hunting in Mojave; thus, this region is not a national park (where hunting is not allowed), but instead, to permit continued hunting, was named a national preserve.

While passage of the Desert Protection Act was widely hailed both in California and throughout the nation, pockets of opposition to the new status of these desert wildlands continue. In the 104th Congress, local congressional hostility to the new regulations threatened to severely reduce funding for the Mojave National Preserve. Instead, political stalemate over the federal budget resulted in providing no funds for Mojave under the National Park Service's continuing resolution. During 1995 operations at Mojave were brought to a standstill, halting the implementation of the Desert Protection Act in one of the largest federally protected wilderness areas in the Lower Forty-eight states.

The 1994 law proclaimed that "federally owned desert lands of southern California constitute a public wildland resource of extraordinary and inestimable value for this and future generations." It is indeed noteworthy that it is in the nation's most populous state—and one of the fastest growing states as well—that the recognition of wilderness protection as essential to preserve the quality of life for all citizens resulted in passage of this law. These desert lands are close to huge and rapidly expanding urban areas; this is exactly what makes these vast desert spaces even more valuable as protected wildlands.

Changing from national monument to national park status represents a gigantic step. While both monuments and parks are administered by the National Park Service and thus appear to be identical to the visitor, the permanence of these entities is different. A national monument is designated by executive order of the president. The original 1.6 million-acre Death Valley National Monument was created by President Herbert Hoover in 1933. Joshua Tree National Monument, 825,000 acres, was created by President Franklin Roosevelt's executive order in 1936. But what can be created by the stroke of a pen can also be removed, as the history of Joshua Tree illustrates. In 1950 and again in 1961 Joshua Tree's acreage was reduced by acts of Congress in response to demands of the mining industry. Now, as a national park, its boundaries are both expanded and more sacrosanct.

Although funding will always be a concern, these desert wildlands are safer from development and exploitation with park or preserve status. The proponents of desert protection worked for decades to achieve their goal. Much of the California desert, which took many thousands of years to form, is now assured a protected future. What Congress designates, however, Congress can also take away. Only through the continued support of the American people will these fragile lands remain protected.

THE MEANING AND VALUE OF WILDERNESS

With millions of acres of California desert parks designated as Wilderness in both the state and federal systems, visitors to these wildlands should appreciate the meaning and values of wilderness, if for no other reason than to better enjoy their visits with less impact on the wildland values which have attracted them in the first place. Nearly 14 percent of California (almost 14 million acres) is designated federal Wilderness, making the Golden State the premier wilderness state in the continental United States. The California Desert Protection Act of 1994 doubled the wilderness acreage in the state and tripled the amount of wilderness under National Park Service jurisdiction, increasing from 2 million to 6 million acres.

Those who know and love wild country have their own personal definition of wilderness, heartfelt and often unexpressed, which varies with each person. But since Congress reserved to itself the exclusive power to designate Wilderness in the monumental Wilderness Act of 1964, it is important that we also understand the *legal* meaning of Wilderness. The California Wilderness Act, which applies to much of Anza-Borrego Desert State Park, is patterned largely after the federal statute, so the following applies to both federal and State of California Wilderness.

The most fundamental purpose of the Wilderness Act is to provide an *enduring* resource of Wilderness for this and future generations so that a growing, increasingly mechanized human population does not occupy and modify every last wild niche. Just as important as preserving the land is the preservation of natural processes, such as naturally ignited fire, erosion, landslides, and other forces that shape the land. Before 1964 the uncertain whim of administrative fiat was all that protected wilderness. During the 1930s the "commanding general" of the wilderness battle, Wilderness Society cofounder Bob Marshall, described wilderness as a "snowbank melting on a hot June day." In the desert the analogy might be closer to a sand dune shrinking on a windy day. Declassification of much of Joshua Tree National

View to the north from the east ridge of Monument Mountain—Joshua Tree National Park.

Monument prior to its present park status certainly illustrates lack of permanancy for land lacking statutory protection.

The act defines Wilderness as undeveloped federal lands (or state lands in the case of the California Wilderness System) "where the earth and its community of life are untrammeled by man, where man is a visitor who does not remain." In old English the word "trammel" means a net, so "untrammeled" conveys the idea of land that is unnetted or uncontrolled by humans. Congress recognized that no land is completely free of human influence, going on to say that Wilderness must "generally appear to have been affected primarily by the forces of nature, with the imprint of man's work substantially unnoticeable." Further, a Wilderness must have outstanding opportunities for solitude or primitive and unconfined recreation, and be at least 5,000 acres in size, or large enough to preserve and use in an unimpaired condition. Also, Wilderness may contain ecological, geological, or other features of scientific, educational, scenic or historical value. The various stretches of California desert parks wilderness described in this book meet and easily exceed these legal requirements. Any lingering doubts are removed by the distant music of a coyote beneath a star-studded desert sky, or by the soothing rhythm of an oasis waterfall in a remote canyon.

In general, Wilderness designation protects the land from development such as roads, buildings, motorized vehicles, and equipment, and from commercial uses except pre-existing livestock grazing, outfitting, and the development of mining claims and leases validated before the 1984 cutoff date in the federal Wilderness Act. The act set up the National Wilderness System and empowered three federal agencies to administer Wilderness: the Forest Service, the Fish and Wildlife Service, and the National Park Service. The Bureau of Land Management was added to the list with passage of the 1976 Federal Land Policy and Management Act. These agencies can and do make wilderness recommendations, as any citizen can, but only Congress can set aside Wilderness on federal lands, or the State of California in the case of Anza-Borrego Desert State Park. This is where politics enters in, epitomizing the kind of grassroots democracy that eventually brought about passage of the landmark California Desert Protection Act. The formula for wilderness conservationists has been and continues to be "endless pressure endlessly applied."

But once designated the unending job of wilderness stewardship is just beginning. The managing agencies have a special responsibility to administer wilderness in "such manner as will leave them (wilderness areas) unimpaired for future use and enjoyment *as wilderness.*" Unimpairment of wilderness over time can only be achieved through partnership between concerned citizens and the agencies.

Wilderness is the only truly biocentric use of land. It is off-limits to intensive human uses with an objective of preserving the diversity of nonhuman life, which is richly endowed in the California Desert. As such, its preservation is our society's highest act of humility. This is where we deliberately slow down our impulse to drill the last barrel of oil, mine the last vein of ore, build a parking lot on top of the last wild peak. The desert wilderness explorer can take genuine pride in reaching a remote summit under his or her power, traversing a narrow serpentine canyon, walking across the uncluttered expanse of a vast desert basin. Hiking boots and self-reliance replace motorized equipment and push-button convenience, allowing us to find something in ourselves we feared lost.

HAVE FUN AND BE SAFE

Wandering in the desert has a reputation of being a dangerous activity, thanks to both the Bible and Hollywood. Usually depicted as a wasteland, the desert evokes fear. With proper planning, however, desert hiking is not hazardous. In fact, it is fun and exciting, and is quite safe.

An enjoyable desert outing requires preparation. Beginning with this book, along with the maps suggested in the hike write-ups, you need to be equipped with adequate knowledge about your hiking area. Carry good maps and a compass, and know how to use them.

Calculating the time required for a hike in the desert defies any formula. Terrain is often rough; extensive detours around boulders, dryfalls, and dropoffs mean longer trips. Straight line distance is an illusion. Sun, heat, and wind likewise all conspire to slow down even the speediest hiker.

Therefore, distances are not what they appear in the desert. Five desert miles may take longer than ten woodland miles. Plan your excursion conservatively, and always carry emergency items in your pack (See Appendix B).

While you consult the equipment list (Appendix B), note that water ranks the highest. Carrying water is not enough—take the time to stop and drink it. This is another reason why desert hikes take longer. Frequent water breaks are mandatory. It's best to return from your hike with empty water bottles. You can cut down on loss of bodily moisture by hiking with your mouth closed and breathing through your nose; reduce thirst also by avoiding sweets and alcohol.

Driving to and from the trailhead is statistically far more dangerous than hiking in the desert backcountry. But being far from the nearest 911 service requires knowledge about possible hazards and proper precautions to avoid them. It is not an oxymoron to have fun and to be safe. Quite to the contrary—if you're not safe, you won't have fun. At the risk of creating excessive paranoia, here are the *treacherous twelve*:

DEHYDRATION

It cannot be overemphasized that plenty of water is necessary for desert hiking. Carry 1 gallon per person per day in unbreakable plastic screw-top containers. And pause often to drink it. Carry water in your car as well so you'll have water to return to. As a general rule, plain water is a better thirst-quencher than any of the colored fluids on the market, which usually generate greater thirst. It is very important to maintain proper electrolyte balance by eating small quantities of nutritional foods throughout the day, even if you feel you don't have an appetite.

CHANGEABLE WEATHER

The desert is well known for sudden changes in the weather. The temperature can change 50 degrees in less than an hour. Prepare yourself with extra food and clothing, rain/wind gear, and a flashlight. When leaving on a trip let someone know your exact route, especially if traveling solo, and your estimated time of return; don't forget to let them know when you get back. Register your route at the closest park office or backcountry board, especially for longer hikes that involve cross-country travel.

HYPOTHERMIA/HYPERTHERMIA

Abrupt chilling is as much a danger in the desert as heat stroke. Storms and/or nightfall can cause desert temperatures to plunge. Wear layers of clothes, adding or subtracting depending on conditions, to avoid overheating or chilling. At the other extreme, you need to protect yourself from sun and wind with proper clothing. The broad-brimmed hat is mandatory equipment for the desert traveler. Even in the cool days of winter, a delightful time in the desert, the sun's rays are intense.

VEGETATION

You quickly will learn not to come in contact with certain desert vegetation. Catclaw, Spanish bayonet, and cacti are just a few of the botanical hazards that will get your attention if you become complacent. Carry tweezers to extract cactus spines. Wear long pants if traveling off trail or in a brushy area. Many folks carry a hair comb to assist removal of cholla balls.

RATTLESNAKES, SCORPIONS, TARANTULAS

These desert "creepy crawlies" are easily terrified by unexpected human visitors, and they react predictably to being frightened. Do not sit or put your hands in dark places you can't see, especially during the warmer "snake season" months. Carry and know how to use your snake bite venom extractor kit for emergencies when help is far away. In the event of snakebite seek medical assistance as quickly as possible. Keep tents zipped and always shake out boots, packs, and clothes before putting them on.

MOUNTAIN LIONS

The California desert is mountain lion country. Avoid hiking at night when lions are often hunting. Instruct your children on appropriate behavior when confronted with a lion. Do not run. Keep children in sight while hiking; stay close to them in areas where lions might hide.

MINE HAZARDS

The California desert contains thousands of deserted mines. All of them should be considered hazardous. Stay away from all mines and mine structures. The vast majority of these mines have not been secured or even posted. Keep an eye on young or adventuresome members of your group.

HANTA VIRUS

In addition to the mines, there are often deserted buildings around the mine sites. Hanta virus is a deadly disease carried by deer mice in the Southwest. Any enclosed area increases the chances of breathing the airborn particles that carry this life-threatening virus. As a precaution, do not enter deserted buildings.

FLASHFLOODS

Desert washes and canyons can become traps for unwary visitors when rainstorms hit the desert. Keep a watchful eye on the sky. Never camp in flashflood areas. Check at a ranger station on regional weather conditions before embarking on your backcountry expedition. A storm anywhere upstream in a drainage can result in a sudden torrent in a lower canyon. Do not cross a flooded wash. Both the depth and the current can be deceiving; wait for the flood to recede, which usually does not take long.

This old mine door below the Keane Wonder Mine spells danger—for the sake of safety—resist the temptation to enter—Death Valley National Park.

LIGHTNING

Be aware of lightning, especially during summer storms. Stay off ridges and peaks. Shallow overhangs and gullies should also be avoided because electrical current often moves at ground level near a lightning strike.

UNSTABLE ROCKY SLOPES

Desert canyons and mountainsides often consist of crumbly or fragmented rock. Mountain sheep are better adapted to this terrain than us bipeds. Use caution when climbing; the downward journey is usually the more hazardous. Smooth rock faces such as in slick-rock canyons are equally dangerous, especially when you've got sand on the soles of your boots. On those rare occasions when they are wet, the rocks are slicker than ice.

GIARDIA

Any surface water, with the possible exception of springs where they flow out of the ground, is apt to contain *Giardia lamblia*, a microorganism that causes severe diarrhea. Boil water for at least 5 minutes or use a filter system. Iodine drops are not effective in killing this pesky parasite.

LEAVE-NO-TRACE DESERT ETIQUETTE

The desert environment is fragile; damage lasts for decades—even centuries. Desert courtesy requires us to leave no evidence that we were ever

A no trace hiking ethic is indeed emphasized at the trailhead for Crystal Spring— Providence Mountains.

there. This ethic means no grafitti or defoliation at one end of the spectrum, and no unnecessary footprints on delicate vegetation on the other. Here are seven general guidelines for desert wilderness behavior:

Avoid making new trails. If hiking cross-country, stay on one set of footprints when traveling in a group. Try to make your route invisible. Desert vegetation grows very slowly. Its destruction leads to wind and water erosion and irreparable harm to the desert. Darker crusty soil that crumbles easily indicates cryptogamic soils, which are a living blend of tightly bonded mosses, lichens, and bacteria. This dark crust prevents wind and water erosion and protects seeds that fall into the soil. Walking can destroy this fragile layer. Take special care to avoid stepping on cryptogamic soil.

Keep noise down. Desert wilderness means quiet and solitude, for the animal life as well as other human visitors.

Leave your pets at home. Most parks have regulations forbidding dogs on trails; check with park authorities before including your dog in the group. Share other experiences with your best friend, not the desert.

Pack it in/pack it out. This is more true in the desert than anywhere. Desert winds spread debris, and desert air preserves it. Always carry a trashbag, both for your trash and for any that you encounter. If you must smoke, pick up your butts and bag them. Bag and carry out toilet paper (it doesn't deteriorate in the desert) and feminine hygiene products.

Never camp near water. Most desert animals are nocturnal, and most, like the bighorn sheep, are exceptionally shy. The presence of humans is very disturbing, so camping near their water source means they will go without water. Camp in already used sites if possible to reduce further damage. If none is available, camp on ground that is already bare. And use a campstove. Groundfires are forbidden in most desert parks; gathering wood is also not permitted. Leave your campsite as you found it. Better yet, improve it by picking up litter, cleaning out fire rings, or scattering ashes of any inconsiderate predecessors. Contradictory though it be, remember that artifacts fifty years old or older are protected by federal law, and must not be moved or removed.

Treat human waste properly. Bury human waste 4" deep and at least 200 feet from water and trails. Pack out toilet paper and feminine hygiene products; they do not decompose in the arid desert. Do not burn toilet paper; many wildfires have been started this way.

Respect wildlife. Living in the desert is hard enough without being harrassed by human intruders. Remember this is the only home these animals have. They treasure their privacy. Be respectful and use binoculars for long-distance viewing. Especially important: Do not molest the rare desert water sources by playing or bathing in them.

Beyond these guidelines, refer to the regulations of the individual park areas for their specific rules governing backcountry useage. Enjoy the beauty and solitude of the desert, and leave it for others to enjoy.

HOW TO USE THIS BOOK

This guide is THE source book for those who wish to experience on foot the very best hikes and backcountry trips the vast and varied California desert has to offer. A broad array of hikes is presented here for each of California's four major desert parks. Hikers are given many choices from which they can pick and choose, depending on their wishes and abilities. The guide is designed to be used with the applicable detailed topographic maps, which are listed for each of the following 111 desert hikes.

For a general geographic orientation begin with the overview map of southeastern California near the front of this book. Here you'll find the relative sizes and locations of the four parks—from Anza-Borrego, just north

Blair Valley trailhead—Anza Borrego Desert State Park.

Badlands surround the middle stretch of Golden Canyon—Death Valley National Park.

of the Mexican border, northward to Death Valley. The book is divided into four chapters, one for each of the four major parks. The parks are presented from south to north, beginning with Anza-Borrego Desert State Park, followed by Joshua Tree National Park, Mojave National Preserve, and Death Valley National Park. The numbering of the individual hikes in each park also generally runs south to north, although this is sometimes altered by the clustering of hikes sharing common access. This south to north presentation roughly parallels the progression of seasons. For example, spring comes earlier in Anza-Borrego as compared to Death Valley, due to its lower average elevation. Thus, the desert hiker seeking comfortable hiking weather can start the season earlier in Anza-Borrego and work gradually to the more northern desert parks as the season advances.

After selecting the park you'll be visiting, refer to the hike locator map at the beginning of the applicable section, along with the "Hikes at a Glance" matrix for a quick overview of all of the hikes presented for the park. After making your selections turn to the specific hike descriptions for added detail. Each hike is numbered and named, and begins with a *general description*. This overview briefly describes the type of hike and highlights the destination and key features.

Hike *length* is given in total miles for the described route and may be broken down between the basic route and additional suggested side trips. The distance is either point-to-point, which usually requires a car shuttle, loop, or round-trip for an out-and-back route. Mileages were calculated in

14

the field and double checked as accurately as possible with the most detailed topographic maps.

The *general location* is the approximate road distance from a nearby city or town to the trailhead, along with its rough location in both the park and the state of California. The idea is to give you a mental picture of where the hike is in relation to your prospective travels.

Trail conditions are evaluated based on well-defined trail standards. Clear trails have no obstructions and are easy to follow. Good trails may be partially blocked by slides, rocks, or debris but are generally obvious and easy to find. Primitive trails are faint, rough, and rocky and may have disappeared completely in places. In the desert some of the best hiking takes place on old four-wheel-drive mining roads that are now closed to vehicular use because of wilderness designation or to protect key values, such as wildlife watering holes. These old two-tracks are a cross between a road and a trail and are thus referred to as "troads" in many of the hike descriptions. Look at a troad as a wide trail which, over time, will gradually revert to a single path trail through lack of vehicular use. Admittedly, this will take a long time in the desert. Many of the desert hikes are off-trail in washes, canyons, ridges, and fans. "Use trails" may form a segment of the route. A use trail is simply an informal, unconstructed path created solely by the passage of hikers.

Special attractions highlight the more notable features seen during the hike, such as canyon narrows, arches, waterfalls, or unusual plants and animals.

The *difficulty* rating is necessarily subjective, but it is based on the authors' extensive backcountry experience with folks of all ages and abilities. Easy hikes present no difficulty to hikers of all abilities. Moderate hikes are challenging to inexperienced hikers. Moderately strenuous will tax even experienced hikers. Strenuous hikes are extremely difficult and challenging, even for the most seasoned hikers. Distance, elevation gain and loss, trail condition, and terrain were considered in assigning the difficulty rating. There are, of course, many variables. The easiest hike can be sheer torture if one runs out of water in extreme heat—a definite no-no.

The *best season* is based largely on the moderate temperature months for the particular hike, and is greatly influenced by elevation. Additional consideration is given to seasonal road access at higher altitudes. The range of months given is not necessarily the best time for wildflowers, which is highly localized and dependent on elevation and rainfall. Nor is it necessarily the best time to view wildlife, which may be during the driest and hottest summer months near water sources.

Starting and maximum elevations were measured to the nearest 10 feet with an altimeter, adjusted whenever possible at known points of elevation. An added check was made on 7.5-minute topographic maps with 40-foot contour intervals. *Elevation gain/loss* is a cumulative total of the ups and downs encountered during the hike. For an out-and-back hike where elevation is gained with no loss in elevation to the destination or turnaround point, the loss is shown as "none." For the return trip simply reverse the

The largest known joshua tree in the park reaches 35 feet in height near the Covington Flat Backcountry Board—Joshua Tree National Park.

numbers. For example, a gain/loss of 3,000 feet/250 feet *to* a peak would be a gain/loss of 250 feet/3,000 feet *from* the peak. The gain/loss for both loop and point-to-point hikes are the cumulative total for the trip and need not be reversed.

The *maps* listed are the best available for route-finding and land navigation: the relevant 7.5-minute topographic map (1:24,000 scale or 2.6 inches = 1 mile) with a 40-foot contour interval. These U.S. Geological Survey maps can usually be purchased at the park visitor centers. They can also be purchased for $4 each (price as of this writing) directly from Map Distribution, USGS Map Sales, Box 25286, Federal Center, Bldg. 810, Denver, CO 80225. See Appendix C for a listing of other useful smaller-scale maps for each park.

For more information the park management agency is listed. See Appendix D for a complete listing of all agency addresses and phone numbers.

Finding the trailhead includes detailed up-to-date driving instructions to the trailhead or jumping-off point for each hike. To follow these instructions start with the beginning reference point, which might be the park visitor center, nearby town, or important road junction. In many cases an unsigned trailhead may be nothing more than a wide spot in the road for parking. Pay close attention to mileage and landmark instructions. American Automobile Association (AAA) map mileages are used when available, but in many instances we had to rely on our car odometer, which may vary slightly from other car odometers.

The *trail itinerary* is a quick reference for the hike, showing the mileages of key points along the route, such as trail junctions, canyon entrances, dryfalls, peaks, and historic sites.

An *elevation profile* is included for all hikes having an elevation gain or loss of at least 400 feet. This elevation-distance graph provides a schematic look at the major elevation gains and losses during the hike. Profiles for out-and-back hikes show only the first half of the route. Simply reverse the graph for the trip back to the trailhead. Profiles for both loop and point-to-point hikes show the ups and downs of the entire route.

The text following the *park/hike number* is a detailed narrative of the actual route with distances, elevations, and key features noted. In some cases interpretation of the natural and cultural history of the hike and its surroundings is included. The idea is to provide accurate route-finding instructions, with enough supporting information to enhance your enjoyment of the hike without diminishing your sense of discovery—a fine line indeed. These descriptions are augmented with photographs which preview a representative segment of the hike.

And last, please don't allow our value-laden list of "favorite hikes" (Appendix A) to discourage you from completing any of the other hikes. They're all worth doing!

ANZA-BORREGO DESERT STATE PARK

Anza-Borrego Desert State Park was set aside by the state of California in 1933, decades before the state's population expanded and desert junctions grew into cities. Anza-Borrego's irregular boundary encloses 600,000 acres, making it California's largest state park, 63 percent of which is protected in twelve wilderness areas. One thousand private inholdings are located within the park; the town of Borrego Springs is an island surrounded by it. The name Anza-Borrego, adopted in 1957, is a blend of the human and natural history of the San Diego desert: Anza for the Spanish explorer who traversed the region with a party of emigrants in 1774, and Borrego, a Spanish word meaning bighorn sheep, for those animals that still make these desert mountains and canyons their home.

Ten million years ago, the Anza-Borrego region formed the floor of a great inland sea. As the mountains rose and the Colorado River delta expanded, the area was eventually blocked from the sea, and the water diminished. A million years ago mastodons and saber-tooths roamed the savannahs around the receding estuary. Early man arrived in the region at least ten thousand years ago, and enjoyed the temperate climate of southern California. The rivers, lakes, and grasslands provided a bountiful environment for humans and animals. Gradual warming began eight thousand years ago. Rising mountains to the west, driven upward by faults and earthquakes as tectonic plates collided, blocked the moisture-laden oceanic winds. Ancient ice-age lakes became playas. The desert began to form.

The earth's dynamics that created the landscape at Anza-Borrego are still at work. Like many desert regions, the park is a geology lab in action. The San Andreas Fault, to the north and east of the park, is constantly shifting. Park elevations range from 15 feet near Travertine Point (NE corner of the park) to 6,193 feet at Combs Peak in the Bucksnort Mountains on the west. Vast valleys, badlands, canyons, oases, and mountain ranges are included in this varied geological wonderland.

NATURAL AND HUMAN HISTORY

Animals, plants, and man adapted to a changing climate as this southern California region became a desert. The endangered desert pupfish are well-known residents of Anza-Borrego that date from earlier times. As the prehistoric inland sea shrank and increased in salinity, this hardy member of the minnow family adapted to the new conditions. Pupfish can live within a broad range of temperatures (from 34 to more than 108 degrees) and in water twice as saline as sea water. Ponds at the park's visitor center and the Borrego Palm Canyon trailhead harbor pupfish schools.

Of the famed Peninsular bighorn sheep, only about four hundred of these rare animals remain. Researchers are actively engaged in finding the cause of their continued decline here in the park. Three groups live in the Santa

OVERVIEW MAP

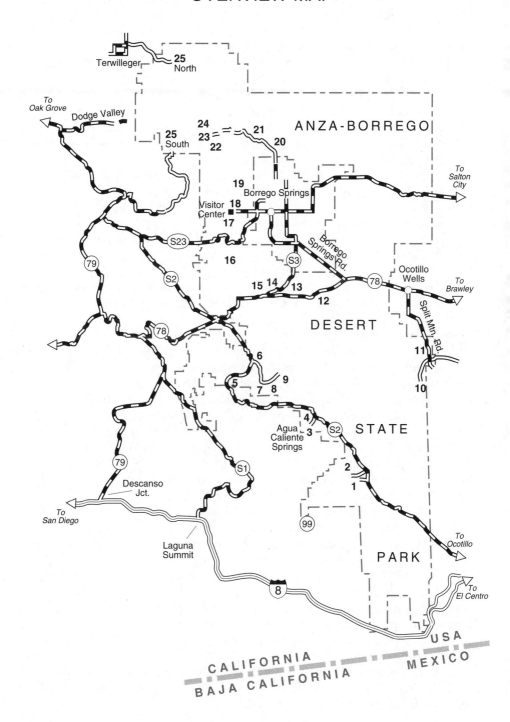

Terwilleger
25 North

To Oak Grove
Dodge Valley

25 South

24
23 **22** **21**
20

ANZA-BORREGO

To Salton City

19 Borrego Springs
Visitor **18** Center
17

Borrego Springs Rd.

79

S23

S2

16

S3

Ocotillo Wells

78

To Brawley

15 14 **13**
12

DESERT

Split Mtn. Rd.

78

6

5 **7 8** **9**

11

10

4
Agua **3**
Caliente **S2**
Springs

STATE

79

Descanso Jct.

S1

2
1

To San Diego

Laguna Summit

99

To Ocotillo

8

PARK

To El Centro

USA

CALIFORNIA

MEXICO

BAJA CALIFORNIA

Rosa Mountains, the Vallecitos Mountains, and Carrizo Gorge, while two more herds hang out in Coyote and Palm canyons. Hikers may spot these elusive denizens of the desert in the rocky, high backcountry. Sheep also drop down to canyon water sources every few days for an early morning drink. They can be seen in Borrego Palm Canyon or at other streams. Because the shrunken water sources of summer put pressure on the sheep population, Coyote Canyon is closed to all human visitors from June 1 through September 30 to protect the sheep's access to water there.

In addition to these two celebrity species, nearly 60 mammal species, 270 bird species, 27 snake species, and 31 lizard species call Anza-Borrego home, dispelling the myth that there is no life in the desert. An evening coyote chorus is evidence of a flourishing rodent food chain. It does take a sharp eye to spot desert creatures. Many are nocturnal, and most are very shy. Do not camp, therefore, within 200 yards of a water source to allow the animals a chance to drink. The twenty-five oases in the park are the most likely locations for viewing wildlife.

In the botanical kingdom, Anza-Borrego is in the Colorado (Sonoran) Desert. California fan palms (*Washingtonia filifera*), the only palm tree native to California, are numerous at the springs and oases and in the canyons of Anza-Borrego. The rare elephant tree (*Bursera microphylla*) exists here and nowhere else in California. Chaparral vegetation dominates the higher mountains on the western side of the park. At lower elevations, creosote bush and ocotillo are common. Twenty-two varieties of cacti, especially several of the ubiquitous cholla family, flourish, ranging from the 3-inch fishhook cactus to the barrel cactus, sometimes over 8 feet tall. Removing or disturbing any of these plants is forbidden by law.

The spectacular spring bloom of desert wildflowers attracts thousands of visitors annually. The flower season ranges from late February through April, depending on weather. Park naturalists will notify you of the anticipated peak bloom. Send a self-addressed stamped postcard to WILDFLOWERS, Anza-Borrego Desert State Park, 200 Palm Canyon Dr., Borrego Springs, CA 92004 if you would like to be notified about two weeks before the peak. The park also maintains a flower hotline, (619) 767-4684.

Man is a relative newcomer, arriving from ten thousand to six thousand years ago. These early inhabitants left few artifacts. They left no pottery, since they stored their food in rock-lined caches. They hunted with spears, not the more advanced bow and arrow. Beginning two thousand years ago, the Kumeyaay people from the Colorado River, and the Cahuilla people from the Great Basin, migrated to the Anza-Borrego region. These were semi-nomadic hunter-gatherers. Sites of their *morteros*, pictographs, and petroglyphs are numerous, as are their fire-rings and fire-pits, their ancient trails, campsite middens, and fragments of pottery. All artifacts are protected by law and must not be altered or removed by visitors. Please leave these traces of prior inhabitants for future generations to enjoy.

Beginning in the eighteenth century with the Anza expedition, Spanish and American groups have traveled through this desert, heading for the coastal areas of southern California. Several historical routes of emigrants and stages can be seen in the Blair Valley and Collins Valley areas. In the late nineteenth century, ranchers and farmers began to settle in Borrego Springs and the nearby valleys. Their efforts to make the desert productive had varied results. Today, stock watering tanks can be found in remote corners of the park, remnants of the defunct cattle industry, whereas the green orchards of Borrego Valley indicate greater success for the growers. Unlike the other desert parks of southern California, Anza-Borrego was never the scene of frenzied mining activity. Mine openings and tailings do not dot the mountainsides.

The palms of Mary's Grove are tightly clustered on the north end of the Mountain Palm Spring Loop.

HOW AND WHEN TO GET THERE

Anza-Borrego Desert State Park is 80 miles east of San Diego at the eastern border of San Diego County. Interstate 8 passes by the park's southern boundary on the way to El Centro. California Highway 78 is the major access route to the central region of the park. County Road S22 is the highway to Borrego Springs where the park visitor center is located.

The nearest commercial airports are in San Diego and Palm Springs, although an airport in Borrego Springs provides facilities for private aircraft and refueling.

Although the summer is typically sizzling in Anza-Borrego, with temperatures well over 100 degrees, the remainder of the year features highs from 70 to 85 degrees. Winter months may bring rain showers. The summer months also have occasional thunderstorms. Heavy rains at any season may result in flash flooding. Average annual rainfall at Park Headquarters is about 6 inches.

PARK REGULATIONS

Anza-Borrego Desert State Park has no entrance fee. It is also one of the few California parks that permits open camping. This policy has resulted in a tradition of care and consideration; roadside campsites are clean and well cared for. Vehicles must remain within one car-length of the road, and all fires must be enclosed in metal containers. Visitors should not camp within 200 yards of water sources to protect animals' access to water. Developed fee campgrounds are near the visitor center in Borrego Spring and at Tamarisk Grove; open camping is not permitted near these two sites. Nine undeveloped no-fee campgrounds are also located throughout the park.

All vehicles must be highway legal, and must stay on the 500 miles of established roads within the park. Drivers must be licensed. Ocotillo Wells State Vehicular Recreation Area is immediately west of the park on CA 78 for off-road vehicle driving, where a driver's license is not required

In Anza-Borrego, bicycles too must remain on the paved and dirt roads. There are more than 500 miles of roads in the park open to bicycles. The park has published a new mountain-biking guide, available at any ranger station.

No dogs are permitted on the trails of Anza-Borrego. On roadways and in campgrounds, dogs must be on leashes no longer than 6 feet. It is advised that you leave your pet at home. Coyotes, cactus, and rattlesnakes all make the desert inhospitable to pets.

Backcountry permits are not required for backpacking. However, registering your trip plan with the ranger at the regional ranger station is recommended for safety.

All cultural and natural contents of the park are protected by state law. No collecting of any kind is permitted. Carrying a loaded weapon of any kind and hunting are likewise forbidden in the park.

The visitor center just west of Borrego Springs is open daily 9 A.M. to 5 P.M. from October through May. From June through September it is open only on weekends and holidays, 9 A.M. to 5 P.M. Maps, publications, and video shows, and informational exhibits are available here. There also a signed nature trail featuring much of the variety of desert plants found in the Colorado (Sonoran) Desert. Check here for current regulations and road conditions. Several self-guided brochures are available at the visitor center, providing information for hikes and auto tours throughout the park.

ANZA-BORREGO DESERT STATE PARK HIKES AT A GLANCE

Hike (Number)	Distance	Difficulty	Feature	Page
Alcoholic Pass (20)	3.4 miles	M	Vista	65
Borrego Palm Canyon (19)	3.0 miles	E/M	Oasis	63
Box Canyon Overlook (5)	1.8 miles	E	Hist. Site	36
Cactus Loop Trail (14)	1.0 miles	E	Nature Trail	52
CA Riding & Hiking (17)	8.5 miles	MS	Vistas	57
Cougar Canyon (23)	3.0 or 11.0 miles	M	Canyon	73
Elephant Trees (11)	1.0 mile	E	Nature Trail	47
Foot and Walker Pass (6)	0.2 mile	E	Hist. Site	37
Ghost Mountain (7)	2.0 miles	M	Hist. Site, Vista	39
Indian Canyon (22)	4.5 or 12.5 miles	MS	Canyon	71
Kenyon Overlook Trail (13)	1.0 mile	E	Vista	50
Lower Willows/ Box Canyon (21)	7.0 miles	M	Stream, Canyon	68
Moonlight Canyon (3)	1.5 miles	M	Canyon	31
The Morteros (8)	0.5 mile	E	Arch. Site	42
Mtn. Palm Springs Loop (1)	6.5 miles	M	Oases	25
Narrows Earth Trail (12)	0.5 mile	E	Geology	49
Pacific Crest Trail S. (25)	5.0 miles	MS	Mountain Peak	78
Pacific Crest Trail N. (25)	5.0 miles	M	Mountain Peak	78
Panorama Overlook (18)	1.4 or 2.6 miles	M	Vista	61
Pictograph Trail (9)	3.0 miles	E	Arch. Site	43
Sheep Canyon (24)	3.0 or 11.0 miles	MS	Canyon, Oasis	75
Squaw Peak/Pond (4)	1.9 miles	E	Vista, Oasis	34
Torote Canyon (2)	4.0 miles	M	Elephant Trees	29
Wilson Trail (16)	11.0 miles	M	Vistas	55
Wind Caves (10)	2.0 miles	M	Geology, Arch. Site	44
Yaqui Well Nature Trail (15)	2.0 miles	E	Nature Trail	54

ANZA-BORREGO DESERT STATE PARK
TOPO MAP INDEX

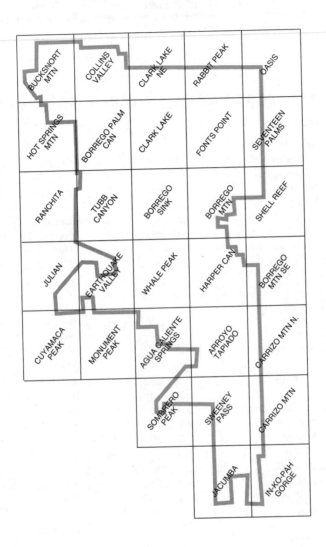

General description:	A loop trail with several short but steep climbs in the eastern Tierra Blanca Mountains, with two branches to six native palm groves, where springs provide excellent birding.
Length:	5.1-mile loop with an optional 1.4-mile out-and-back side trip to Indian Gorge.
General location:	About 52 miles south of Borrego Springs, in southern Anza-Borrego Desert State Park, south-central California.
Trail condition:	Mostly clear trail with several clear wash stretches along with short good sections of rocky cutoff trails.
Special attractions:	Hidden palm oases.
Difficulty:	Moderate.
Best season:	October through April.
Starting elevation:	750 feet (Mountain Palm Springs parking area).
Maximum elevation:	1,070 feet (high point on the loop); 1,190 feet (high point on the Indian Gorge Cutoff Trail).
Elevation gain/loss:	320 feet/320 feet (loop); additional 200 feet/60 feet for Indian Gorge Cutoff Trail.
USGS topo map:	Sweeney Pass-CA (1:24,000).
For more information:	Anza-Borrego Desert State Park (see Appendix D).

Key points:

0.0	Trailhead. Head west up the sandy wash.
0.8	Pigmy Grove.
1.0	Turn left next to a single palm tree and head up the main wash.
1.2	Fork in the trail; stay right.
1.5	Southwest Grove.
2.5	Surprise Canyon; turn left and walk up to Palm Bowl Grove.
3.0	Palm Bowl Grove; turnaround point.
3.3	Signed Indian Gorge Trail takes off to the left (north).
4.0	Indian Valley Road.
4.7	Back to Surprise Canyon for completion of 1.4-mile out-and-back side hike.
4.9	Back to Surprise Canyon Grove.
5.4	North Grove.
5.7	Mary's Grove.
6.0	Back to North Grove.
6.5	Completion of loop; trailhead.

MOUNTAIN PALMS SPRINGS LOOP
• TOROTE CANYON

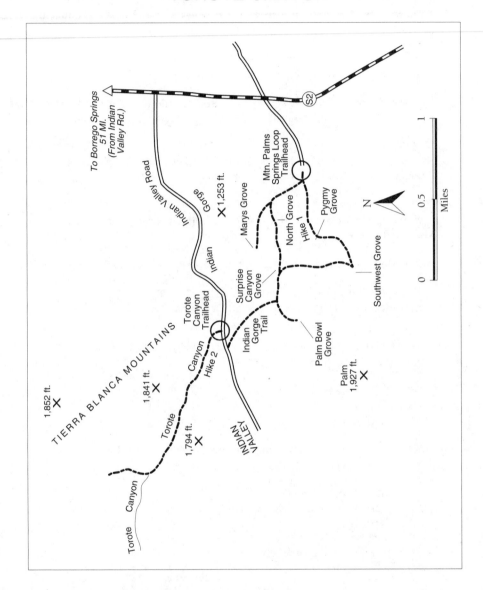

Finding the trailhead: From the park visitor center go 1.9 miles east on Palm Canyon Drive to Christmas Circle; from the circle take Borrego Springs Road, S3, south for 5.6 miles to the Y intersection, where you bear right. Continue on S3 7.4 miles to the Tamarisk Grove intersection with California Highway 78. Go right (west) on CA 78 for 7.4 miles to Scissors Crossing. Turn left (south) on Park Route S2. Drive 31.8 miles south on S2. Shortly after mile marker 47, turn right (west) onto the dirt road for the Mountain Palm Springs Campground. Continue 0.5 mile to the trailhead and parking area.

The hike: The Mountain Palm Springs oasis loop is really two separate hikes from the same trailhead to the end point of both hikes: the extensive Palm Bowl Grove. The two legs described below can easily be combined into a wonderful loop to all six of the captivating palm groves in the Mountain Palm Springs complex. Both trails lead up sandy washes, one westward and the other to the north. It makes little difference which way you hike the loop, except that if you plan to take a side trip on the Indian Gorge Trail it is preferable to begin on the south leg of the loop by heading west to the Pigmy Grove.

The native California fan palm derives its name from the shape of its leaves. As the tree produces new leaves at the top of its trunk, skirts of older leaves die and droop over the lower part of the tree, giving it the distinctive full look characteristic of these palms. These groves are remnants of ancient savannahs. Here water and shade attract scores of bird species, such as the hooded oriole, which weaves its nest on the underside of palm fronds. You may also catch a glimpse of a great horned owl, mourning dove, cactus wren, or western bluebird. In the fall, coyotes help regenerate the trees by eating their tiny fruits and leaving seed-laden droppings in new locations.

On the south end of the loop head west up a sandy wash to the first small grove of four large palm trees at 0.4 mile. Continue up the main wash another 0.4 mile to Pigmy Grove, named after the larger grove of short, fire-scarred trees. The third small grove consists of five trees in a tight cluster. From here a rocky ravine leads to the right another 0.2 mile to a single palm tree. Turn left up the main valley to a fork in the trail at 1.2 miles. Continue to the right another 0.3 mile to the sizable Southwest Grove, which can be seen straight ahead. Pools of water and nearby elephant trees make this peaceful oasis an enjoyable interlude during the loop hike.

From Southwest Grove take a fairly distinct trail northward over a rocky ridge 1 mile to Surprise Canyon. From here turn left and walk up the canyon another 0.5 mile to the largest and most luxuriant grove in the complex, Palm Bowl. On the way back down from Palm Bowl Grove look for the signed Indian Gorge Cutoff Trail leading to the north. This old Indian trail is signed "0.5 mile to Indian Gorge." The actual distance is closer to 0.7 mile. The narrow, rocky trail gains 200 feet to the top of the ridge then angles down left into Indian Valley. The round-trip distance from Surprise Canyon to Indian Valley is 1.4 miles, providing yet more variety and a short extension to this already diverse hiking loop.

To complete the loop from Surprise Canyon continue down the wash to the parking area/trailhead. North Grove is reached 0.5 mile down canyon, Mary's Grove is a 0.6-mile side trip to the left, and from this junction the trailhead is only another 0.5 mile.

The Surprise Grove on the Mountain Palm Springs Loop.

If you start the hike on the northern leg of the loop, the trail leads north from the parking area up a sandy wash or, if you prefer firmer footing, up the right bank of the wash. Straight ahead you can catch a glimpse of palm trees 0.2 mile ahead. The wash grows progressively rockier as you approach Mary's Grove, where huge 30- to 40-foot palms tower above the rocky gorge. Retrace your steps 0.3 mile back down the wash to the trailpost that marks the mouth of the wash that runs westward. The intersection is rocky, but this new wash becomes sandy as it gains slightly in elevation.

As you continue west up the new wash, you will pass North Grove, which consists of several clumps of palm trees, providing a delightful shady interlude in your journey. One spot to keep in mind for later is a distinctive row of palms (appropriately called Surprise Canyon Grove), for it is there that a marked cut-off trail climbs over the ridge to the south to the Southwest Grove. Meanwhile, however, keep moving west, because another lovely surprise awaits you: a huge array of majestic palms, arranged like an orchestra in an amphitheater valley. This is the Palm Bowl Grove. Plan on allowing ample time to enjoy this magical place before hiking back down the wash.

2 TOROTE CANYON

General description:	A half-day out-and-back hike through a sandy wash/ boulder canyon to a sizable "herd" of elephant trees and large, open valleys.
Length:	4 miles round-trip.
General location:	About 50 miles south of the visitor center, in southern Anza-Borrego Desert State Park, south-central California.
Trail condition:	A use trail follows the main wash with easy routes over and around boulders.
Special attractions:	Elephant trees (*torote* in Spanish), and wide, remote basins ringed by rugged rock ridges.
Difficulty:	Moderate.
Best season:	October through April.
Starting elevation:	1,060 feet.
Maximum elevation:	1,600 feet.
Elevation gain/loss:	540 feet/540 feet.
USGS topo maps:	Aqua Caliente Spr-CA; Arroyo Tapiado-CA; Sombrero Peak-CA; and Sweeney Pass-CA (1:24,000).
For more information:	Anza-Borrego Desert State Park (see Appendix D).

See Map on Page 26

Key points:

0.0   Trailhead at mouth of Torote Canyon (1,060 feet).
0.6   Sizable "herd" of elephant trees.
1.0   First wide basin.
1.5   Canyon junction; main Torote Canyon to left; turn right (north).
2.0   Low pass above a second wide valley (1,600 feet).

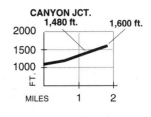

Finding the trailhead: From the park visitor center drive east 1.9 miles to Christmas Circle, turn right on Borrego Springs Road (S3) and drive south for 5.6 miles to the "Y" intersection; turn right (south) on S3 and drive 7.4 miles to the junction with California Highway 78. Turn right on CA 78 and drive another 7.4 miles to Scissors Crossing. Turn left (south) on Park Route S2 and drive 29.6 miles to the signed Indian Gorge Road. Turn right (southwest) and drive 1.8 miles up the sandy road to the mouth of Torote Canyon, which is marked with a small sign. A monument entitled "El Torote" faces away from the road into the canyon. Park and begin the hike here.

The hike: Hike up the sandy wash use trail of Torote Canyon which, for the most part, makes a good and easy-to-follow trail. At times you will need to scramble up and over an occasional boulder-clogged segment of the wash, but in general the going is easy enough to allow enjoyment of the remote surroundings of the canyon. You'll come to the first elephant tree on the left slope (south side) in less than 0.4 mile, but keep going for a good look at one of the densest "herds" of elephant trees in this bizarre tree's northernmost range.

The Spanish word *torote* means "twisted," referring to the gnarled growth pattern of the elephant trees, which are widespread in Mexico. At about 0.6 mile (1,180 feet) a large group of trees clings to the steep, rocky slopes above the canyon floor. Take time to get better acquainted with Borrego's rarest tree—feel its parchment-like bark, take note of its small, feathery leaves, and breathe deeply of its pleasant cedar-like aroma. At about 0.9 mile the canyon opens up into the first wide valley, which stretches a good half-mile to the northwest. At the head of the valley the main Torote Canyon continues up a bouldery draw to the northwest. Instead of continuing up the main canyon, follow what appears to be the main valley northward to the right. This leads to a short, tight canyon that opens after about 300 yards to the second wide valley. Continue up the valley to a low pass, straight ahead.

Although several cross-country routes are possible—eastward to Carrizo Valley or to the south toward the North Fork of Indian Valley—the upper end of this second wide valley is a good turnaround point for this pleasant 4-mile round-trip journey. But go back only after you've given yourself enough time to savor the remote upper canyon's magic.

3   MOONLIGHT CANYON

General description:	A short loop trip south through the canyon from a well-known desert hot springs.
Length:	1.5-mile loop.
General location:	About 43 miles southeast of Borrego Springs, in Agua Caliente Springs Regional Park, south-central Anza-Borrego Desert State Park, south-central California.
Trail condition:	Clear trail, clear wash.
Special attraction:	Colorful canyon.
Difficulty:	Moderate.
Best season:	October through April.
Starting elevation:	1,190 feet (Agua Caliente Springs parking area).
Maximum elevation:	1,540 feet.
Elevation gain/loss:	350 feet/350 feet.
USGS topo map:	Agua Caliente Springs-CA (1:24,000).
For more information:	Anza-Borrego Desert State Park (see Appendix D).

Key points:
0.0   Trailhead at campsites 39 and 40.
1.0   Trail enters main wash.
1.1   Junction marked by sign; short box canyon is a worthy sidetrip.
1.3   Open ocotillo forest as canyon broadens.
1.5   Return near campsite 63.

Finding the trailhead: From the park visitor center, drive east on Palm Canyon Drive 1.9 miles to Christmas Circle. Turn south at the circle on S3 (Borrego Springs Road) 5.6 miles to the Y. Bear right and continue south on S3 for 7.4 miles to its intersection with California Highway 78 just beyond the Tamarisk Grove Campground. Turn right (west) on CA 78, and go 7.4 miles to Scissors Crossing. At the crossing turn left (south) on S2 and drive 22.3 miles to the turnoff to Agua Caliente Springs and campground. Turn right and continue 0.5 mile to the trailhead at the parking area adjacent to the park gate. There is a daily $2 per person park entrance fee. The trailhead leaves from campsites 39 and 40, and returns near campsite 63.

The hike: Although this trail lies outside of the Anza-Borrego boundary, and there is an entry fee to the county park, it is definitely worth a visit. Interesting erosion formations, intermittent watery spots, and cozy side canyons combine for a series of discoveries as you follow the well-marked trail through its circular route in the canyon.

The trail begins inauspiciously by climbing to a low ridge; it quickly drops to the stream bottom, which goes up a rocky draw and into the canyon itself. Side washes and small canyons periodically invite further exploration as the main wash winds downward. There are occasional steep slopes

The Moonlight Canyon trail crossing a wash near its beginning.

MOONLIGHT CANYON
• SQUAW PEAK/POND

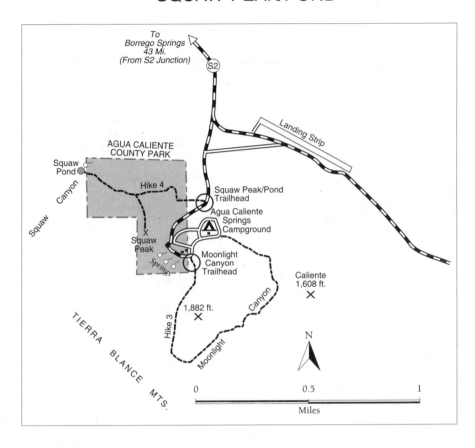

To
Borrego Springs
43 Mi.
(From S2 Junction)

S2

Landing Strip

AGUA CALIENTE
COUNTY PARK

Squaw
Pond

Squaw Canyon

Hike 4

Squaw Peak/Pond
Trailhead

Agua Caliente
Springs
Campground

X
Squaw
Peak

Springs

Moonlight
Canyon
Trailhead

Caliente
1,608 ft.
X

1,882 ft.
X

Hike 3

Moonlight Canyon

TIERRA BLANCE MTS.

N

0   0.5   1
Miles

requiring only simple scrambling on this otherwise easy hike. The rock formations, courtesy of centuries of water and earthquake activity, are endlessly fascinating. The variety of colors of the rocks is also noteworthy. Sudden splashes of greenery where water exists, tamarisk and willow patches, punctuate the trip.

The canyon empties into a wide dry wash, leading to a rock-lined trail that winds through an ocotillo forest and back to the campground at site 63, down the hill from your starting point.

4   SQUAW PEAK/POND

General description:	A short climb on the edge of the Tierra Blanca Mountains to a scenic overlook of the Carrizo Valley and Vallecito Mountains, combined with a sandy wash hike to a favored watering hole for wildlife.
Length:	0.7 mile round-trip to Squaw Peak plus an additional 1.2 miles round-trip to Squaw Pond.
General location:	About 43 miles southeast of Borrego Springs, in Agua Caliente Springs Regional Park, surrounded by the south-central portion of Anza-Borrego Desert State Park, south-central California.
Trail condition:	Clear trail.
Special attractions:	Scenic vista point; a lush desert spring oasis.
Difficulty:	Easy.
Best season:	November through April.
Starting elevation:	1,190 feet.
Maximum elevation:	1,450 feet (Squaw Peak overlook).
Elevation gain/loss:	260 feet/none (Squaw Peak); 140 feet/90 feet (Squaw Pond).
USGS topo map:	Agua Caliente Springs-CA (1:24,000).
For more information:	Agua Caliente Regional Park (see Appendix D).

See Map on Page 33

Key points:
0.0   Trailhead.
0.1   Trail junction-turn left to Squaw Peak overlook; right to Squaw Pond.
0.35 Squaw Peak overlook (1,450 feet).
0.6   Back to the trail junction (1,290 feet).
0.7   Squaw Canyon wash (1,240 feet).
1.2   Squaw Pond (1,280 feet).
1.9   Back to the parking area trailhead.

Finding the trailhead: From the Anza-Borrego visitor center head east on Palm Canyon Drive for 1.9 miles to Christmas Circle. Turn south at the circle on S3 (Borrego Springs Road) 5.6 miles to the Y; bear right at the Y and continue south on S3 for 7.4 miles to its intersection with California Highway 78 just beyond the Tamarisk Grove Campground. Turn right (west) on CA 78 and go 7.4 miles to Scissors Crossing. At the crossing turn left (south) on S2 and drive 22.3 miles to the turnoff to Agua Caliente Springs. Turn right and drive 0.5 mile to the trailhead at the parking area adjacent to the park entrance. The park entrance fee is $2 per person per day. The trailhead is directly north of the ranger station. Cross the parking lot to a low ridge on the right next to the campfire circle and take the path that leads to the campground amphitheater and Squaw Peak/Pond.

From Squaw Peak, an eagle's view of Agua Caliente County Park.

The hike: From the Agua Caliente Springs parking area pick up the Squaw Peak/Pond trail near the campfire circle just above the ranger station/park entrance. Climb 0.1 mile to the ridgetop trail junction. Take the left trail 0.25 mile to 1,450-foot Squaw Peak. From the junction the trail makes switchbacks up 150 feet to this overlook of the Carrizo Valley and Badlands and the more distant Vallecito Mountains.

To reach Squaw Pond drop back to the junction and continue left down to the sandy Squaw Canyon wash. Turn left up the well-traveled wash past clumps of honey mesquite, an important food staple for early-day Cahuilla Indians. Mesquite are adorned with cylindrical spikes of yellow flowers in late spring.

Squaw Pond is 0.5 mile up the wash. Tracks of coyote, bobcat, and a host of smaller animals tell the tale of their visitation to this desert spring oasis shaded by dense willow and a single palm tree. Include your binoculars for excellent bird watching at Squaw Pond. The surrounding hillsides are dotted with barrel and cholla cactus.

After savoring this tranquil setting, the most direct return to the trailhead is to simply walk all the way back down the wash, which intersects the road just below the parking area. In so doing, you'll avoid the additional climb back over the ridge to the trail junction.

After the hike you might enjoy a soak in the mineral hot springs of Agua Caliente. A shallow outdoor pool averages around 95 degrees F. and is open during the day. A larger indoor Jacuzzi pool is kept slightly warmer. The natural hot water source is an offshoot of the Elsinore Fault.

5   *BOX CANYON OVERLOOK*

General description: A short walk to an overlook of the Old Southern Emigrant Trail used by '49ers and other emigrants, with optional hike via winding path down to the trail itself and farther on to Park Route S2.

See Map on Page 38

Length: 250-foot walk to overlook; 0.4 mile round-trip to trail; 1.8-mile round-trip for exploring the trail to S2.

General location: 31.1 miles south of the park visitor center in Borrego Springs, south-central Anza-Borrego Desert State Park, south-central California.

Trail condition: Clear trail; clear wash.

Special attraction: Southern Emigrant Trail/Butterfield Overland Stage Route.

Difficulty: Easy.

Best season: October through April.

Starting elevation: 2,360 feet (trailhead on S2).

Maximum elevation: 2,360 feet.

Elevation gain/loss: None/160 feet.

USGS topo map: Earthquake Valley-CA (1:24,000).

For more information: Anza-Borrego Desert State Park (see Appendix D).

A boy scout group hiking the Southern Emigrant Trail in Box Canyon.

Finding the trailhead: From the Visitor Center, go east 1.9 miles to Christmas Circle in Borrego Springs; turn south on Park Route S3 and go 5.6 miles to the Y. Bear right and continue on S3 7.4 miles to intersection with California Highway 78. Turn right on CA 78 and go another 7.4 miles to Scissors Crossing. Turn left on Park Route S2, and continue south 9 miles. About 0.6 miles south of mile marker 25 on S2 is the Box Canyon parking pullout on the south side of the road.

The hike: Much Anza-Borrego history coincides at this spot! The Southern Emigrant Trail, the Mormon Battalion, and the Butterfield Overland Mail Route used this arduous low mountain pass. The historical marker is right by the highway; the overlook of the trail below is 250 feet farther east.

By following the path down to the trail itself, you quickly get a feeling for the obstacle that this rocky ridge represented for early travelers. The Mormon Battalion cut a detour around the box canyon; traces of its efforts are visible on the canyon walls. To follow a piece of the trail itself, follow the sloping trail down to the right to a wooden post marked "U.S. Mormon Battalion Trail." At this point, the trail coincides with the wash. The historic wash trail is marked with an occasional wooden post. Follow the gently graded wash down 0.7 mile to a pullout where S2 almost touches the wash. Your hike parallels the highway but is wholly hidden in the small canyon to provide a feeling of seclusion and communion with the hundreds of previous users of this trail segment.

Return to the overlook via the wash, not the highway. The narrow blind curves make it dangerous at this point.

6 FOOT AND WALKER PASS

General description:	A short hike to an overlook at Blair Valley, site of the Butterfield Stage Route over Puerta Pass.
Length:	0.2 mile up-and-back.
General location:	In the Blair Valley region of Anza-Borrego, 31 miles south of Borrego Springs, south-central California.
Trail condition:	Clear trail.
Special attraction:	Site of Butterfield Overland Stage Route.
Difficulty:	Easy.
Best season:	October through April.
Starting elevation:	2,480 feet.
Maximum elevation:	2,570 feet.
Elevation gain/loss:	90 feet/none.
USGS topo map:	USGS Earthquake Valley-CA (1:24,000).
For more information:	Anza-Borrego Desert State Park (see Appendix D).

BOX CANYON
• FOOT AND WALKER PASS

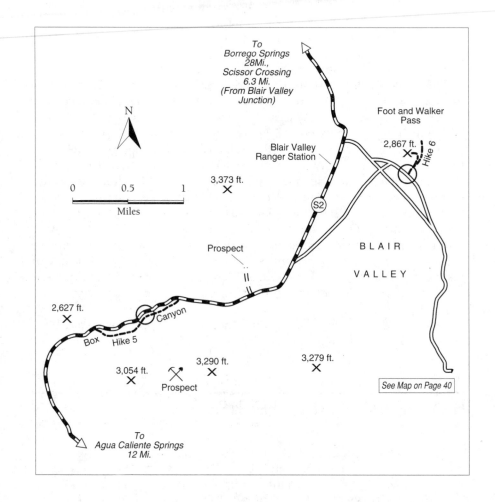

To
Borrego Springs
28Mi.,
Scissor Crossing
6.3 Mi.
(From Blair Valley
Junction)

N

Foot and Walker
Pass

2,867 ft.
✕

Hike 6

Blair Valley
Ranger Station

3,373 ft.
✕

0   0.5   1

Miles

S2

Prospect

B L A I R

V A L L E Y

2,627 ft.
✕

Canyon

Box   Hike 5

3,054 ft.
✕
Prospect

3,290 ft.
✕

3,279 ft.
✕

See Map on Page 40

To
Agua Caliente Springs
12 Mi.

Finding the trailhead: From the park visitor center go east 1.9 miles to Christmas Circle; turn south on Borrego Springs Road (S3) and go 5.6 miles to the Y. Bear right and continue on S3 7.4 miles to the intersection with California Highway 78. Turn right on CA 78 and go another 7.4 miles to Scissors Crossing. Turn left on S2 and go 6.3 miles to Blair Valley turnoff, on your left. The Foot and Walker Trail historical monument is 0.3 mile from the turnoff on the north side of the valley.

The hike: This short trail provides an excellent orientation to the Blair Valley region, with its layers of human use, from prehistoric (pictographs and morteros) to historic (routes through Box Canyon and Foot and Walker Pass) to recent (the south home on Ghost Mountain) times.

Here at the entrance to the valley, the Butterfield stage had difficulty with the pass, especially if the coach had a heavy load. Often passengers had to hop out and walk—hence the name of the pass.

From the pullout on the dirt road below the hill above you, a use trail goes up the rise to a historic marker. A second use trail goes through the pass itself. A brief hike in this area reminds us of the arduous conditions for nineteenth-century desert travelers.

7   GHOST MOUNTAIN
MARSHAL SOUTH HOME

General description:	Steep rugged trail to remains of adobe home built in 1932.
Length:	2 miles out-and-back.
General location:	Blair Valley region of Anza-Borrego Desert Park, 33 miles south of the park visitor center in Borrego Springs, south-central California.
Trail condition:	Clear trail.
Special attraction:	Historic site of primitive home, spectacular view.
Difficulty:	Moderate.
Best season:	October to April.
Starting elevation:	2,790 feet.
Maximum elevation:	3,210 feet.
Elevation gain:	420 feet/none.
USGS topo map:	Earthquake Valley-CA (1:24,000).
For more information:	Anza-Borrego Desert State Park (see Appendix D).

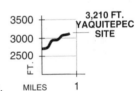

Finding the trailhead: From the visitor center, drive east 1.9 miles to Christmas Circle in Borrego Springs. Turn south on Park Route S3, then drive 5.6 miles to the Y; bear right at the Y and continue on S3 7.4 miles to the intersection with CA 78. Turn right on 78, and go another 7.4 miles to the intersection with Park Route S2 at Scissors Crossing. Turn south (left) on S2. 6.3 miles southeast of the Scissors Crossing on your left at mile 23 is Blair Valley. Turn left onto the dirt road. The road junctions in Blair Valley are clearly marked with signs. The Ghost Mountain parking area is 2.3 miles from S2.

The hike: Poet Marshal South was an early refugee from civilization, fleeing with his family in the 1930s to this remote desert mountaintop, named Yaquitepec. This hike is an interesting mixture of scenic splendor and devastating squalor—the South home was primitive at best. The remains of the family's attempt to live atop a mountain peak in this valley creates a striking contrast with the awesome views in every direction. No water is available; remains of a cistern system sit on the boulders near the cooking area. Fuel is also nonexistent. Living here was hard work.

The path snakes its way to the mountaintop with a series of steps and switchbacks. Marshal South built quite a trail; there are even steps on some of the steeper stretches. It is thought-provoking to imagine what it would be like to transport essentials up this hillside and rear three children in such a location. When you arrive at the house site, the ruins reveal how basic life was for the South family. This was no castle. Of course, the dwelling has fallen into severe disrepair.

GHOST MOUNTAIN • THE MORTEROS • PICTOGRAPH TRAIL

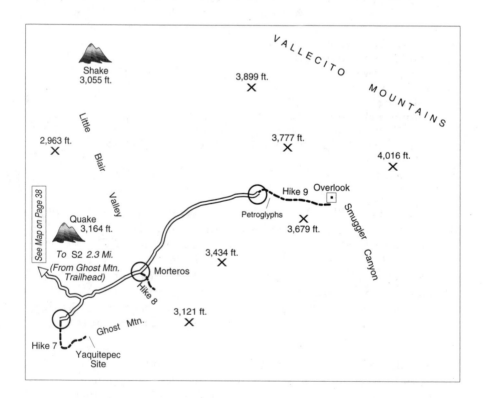

The stone remnants of the Marshal South home on Ghost Mountain.

Since both sunrise and sunset are spectacular from Ghost Mountain, campers have used the two or three sites available here, apparently with no trouble from the ghost. However, to protect the homesite, the park does not encourage camping there. The South family surely enjoyed the view. Many interesting tales exist among local residents about the family and its escapades. According to one source, Marshal South eventually left his family and the mountain, going to live with a lady librarian in a nearby town.

8   THE MORTEROS

General description:	An easy path to site of Indian grinding holes cut into granitic boulders.
Length:	0.5 mile out-and-back.
General location:	28.2 miles from the visitor center in Borrego Springs, in west-central Anza-Borrego Desert State Park, south-central California.
Trail condition:	Clear trail.
Special attractions:	Ancient grinding stones and habitation site.
Difficulty:	Easy.
Best season:	October to April.
Starting elevation:	2,700 feet (Morteros parking area).
Maximum elevation:	2,760 feet.
Elevation gain/loss:	60 feet/none.
USGS topo maps:	Earthquake Valley-CA (1:24,000) and Whale Peak-CA (1:24,000).
For more information:	Anza-Borrego Desert State Park (see Appendix D).

See Map on Page 40

Finding the trailhead: From the visitor center drive east on Palm Canyon Drive 1.9 miles to Christmas Circle. Turn south on Park Route S3. At 5.6 miles south of the circle bear right at the "Y" intersection and continue

Closeup of several morteros embedded high atop a large flat rock at the end of the Morteros Trail.

7.4 miles on S3 to intersection with California 78. Turn right on CA 78 and go 7.4 miles to Scissors Crossing. Turn left on S2 and go south 6.3 miles. At mile marker 23 is the Blair Valley road. Turn left and follow the dirt road 3.5 miles to the Morteros pullout.

The hike: A broad, sandy trail leads from the parking lot up the rise to the site of a prehistoric village set against the rock-strewn hillside. The slight elevation gain provides a sweeping view of Little Blair Valley, stretching to the northwest. Huge obelisk-like boulders frame large horizontal granite stones, in which the *morteros*, or mortar stones, were worn over a thousand years of grinding by the Kumeyaay Indians. Fortunately, the site has been respected by visitors and remains in the same condition as when the Indians departed, giving it a hallowed feeling.

9 PICTOGRAPH TRAIL

General description:	Short hike to a major pictograph site and an overlook of Vallecito Valley.
Length:	3 miles out-and-back.
General location:	28.2 miles from the visitor center in Borrego Springs, west-central Anza-Borrego Desert State Park, south-central California.
Trail condition:	Clear trail.
Special attractions:	Pictographs, overlook to Whale Peak.
Difficulty:	Easy.
Best season:	October through April.
Starting elevation:	3,120 feet.
Maximum elevation:	3,280 feet.
Elevation gain/loss:	160 feet/140 feet.
USGS topo map:	Whale Peak-CA (1:24,000).
For more information:	Anza-Borrego Desert State Park (see Appendix D).

See Map on Page 40

Finding the trailhead: From the visitor center drive east on Palm Canyon Drive 1.9 miles to Christmas Circle. Turn south on Park Route S3. At 5.6 miles south of the circle bear right at the "Y" intersection and continue 7.4 miles on S3 to intersection with California 78. Turn right on CA 78 and go 7.4 miles to Scissors Crossing. Turn left on S2 and go south 6.3 miles. At mile marker 23 is the Blair Valley road. Turn left (southeast) on the road to Blair Valley. Follow the dirt road 3.6 miles to the sign for Pictograph Trail; take this rough but passable road 1.5 miles to the parking area/trailhead.

The hike: Blair Valley has attracted human visitors for centuries. High above the desert, its temperatures are more moderate than those of its surroundings. Early inhabitants evidently found it comfortable, as do present-day hikers and campers.

A wide, sandy trail leads from the parking lot up a gradual slope to a saddle 160 feet higher than the parking area. The trail becomes more rocky as it climbs through pinyon-juniper vegetation. Over the saddle, at 0.4 mile on your right, is a large boulder with the mysterious pictographs (identified as petroglyphs on the topographic map) left by prehistoric residents of this high valley. These striking artifacts of an ancient culture have been well-preserved in spite of their remote, wild location. Hikers can pause to contemplate the meaning of these signs, which still puzzle archeologists.

About 0.5 mile farther down the sandy wash path is a sharply defined notch in a rocky ridge; through the notch is the overlook of Vallecitos Valley and the Vallecitos Mountains. Whale Peak (5,349 feet) is prominent to the northeast. There's an abrupt 100-foot precipice at the overlook, so keep an eye on overly adventurous members of your hiking party.

Your view of Little Blair Valley on the hike back to the parking area shows the value of this location to early desert dwellers. Residents enjoyed excellent visibility from this slope at the end of the valley. There's a sacred feeling about being in an area that was lived in so many centuries ago.

10 WIND CAVES

General description:	A long drive for a short hike to an interesting geologic and archaeological site on a ridgetop, with a sweeping view of the Carrizo Badlands.
Length:	1.5-mile loop; another 0.5 mile for exploring the caves.
General location:	11 miles south of Ocotillo Wells, on the eastern edge of Anza-Borrego Desert Park, south-central California.
Trail condition:	Clear trail.
Special attraction:	Geologic feature, archaeological site.
Difficulty:	Moderate.
Best season:	October to April.
Starting elevation:	480 feet (Wind Caves Parking Area).
Maximum elevation:	1,100 feet.
Elevation gain/loss:	620 feet/none.
USGS topo map:	Carrizo Mountain NE-CA (1:24,000).
For more information:	Anza-Borrego Desert State Park (see Appendix D).

Key points:

0.0   Trail climbs steeply from wash to plateau above.
0.3   Variety of trails, all heading northeast. Take any one.
0.7   Arrive at Wind Caves

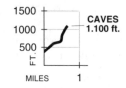

WIND CAVES • ELEPHANT TREES NATURE TRAIL

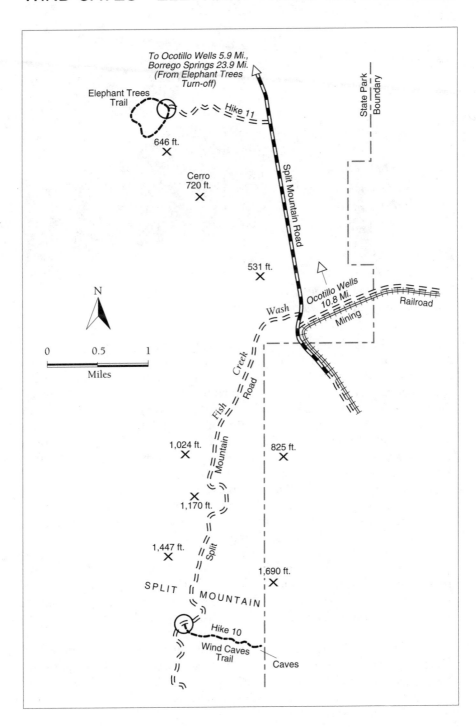

To Ocotillo Wells 5.9 Mi.,
Borrego Springs 23.9 Mi.
(From Elephant Trees
Turn-off)

Elephant Trees
Trail

Hike 11

Split Mountain Road

State Park Boundary

646 ft.
X

Cerro
720 ft.
X

N

0   0.5   1
Miles

531 ft.
X

Ocotillo Wells
10.8 Mi.

Wash

Railroad

Mining

Fish Creek Road

1,024 ft.
X

825 ft.
X

Mountain

X
1,170 ft.

1,447 ft.
X

Split

1,690 ft.
X

SPLIT MOUNTAIN

Hike 10

Wind Caves
Trail

Caves

45

The wind-eroded sandstone of Wind Caves forms an unearthly appearance high on the ridge above Split Mountain Wash.

Finding the trailhead: From the park visitor center in Borrego Springs, take Palm Canyon Drive 1.9 miles east to Christmas Circle; at the circle turn south on Borrego Springs Road (S3). In 5.6 miles, at the Y, continue straight on Borrego Springs Road 6.6 miles to intersection with California Highway 78. Turn left on CA 78; go 6.7 miles east to Ocotillo Wells. At the main intersection in town, turn right (south) onto Split Mountain Road. Drive south on Split Mountain Rd., past Elephant Trees, to the right turn onto Split Mountain wash at 10.8 miles. Drive up the sandy wash 5.1 miles to a very small Wind Caves sign indicating the trail on your left. The trailhead is just south of the narrows of Split Mountain wash. The wash is not difficult for a passenger vehicle, but should definitely be avoided in wet or threatening weather. This road often requires four wheel drive. Check conditions at the visitor center before taking this road.

The hike: The trip's excitement begins with the drive up the wash. Progressing upward from the valley floor, the wash approaches the rocky face of Split Mountain—then cuts through the mountain, with hardly any gain in elevation. The trailhead is beyond this narrow spot in the wash.

The first 0.2 mile of trail climbs from the floor of the wash to the ridge via a rocky but well-defined trail. The view of the Carrizo Badlands behind you is spectacular. A variety of worn footpaths lead from the edge of the wash into the lands above; some of these routes are believed to be remnants of prehistoric use of the area. They all converge on the caves, so it does not matter which one you choose.

Around 0.6 mile, the caves come into view. A lower, smaller set of these fascinating sandstone wind-sculpted formations lies slightly below the larger set. There is an extraterrestrial quality about the site, due to both its ethereal appearance and the evidence that early Indians made use of these natural shelters. On your return trip down Split Mountain wash, watch for additional wind cave formations high above the rim on the right.

11 ELEPHANT TREES NATURE TRAIL

General description:	An easy self-guided loop displaying the diverse plant community of an alluvial fan and desert wash, including several rare and unusual elephant trees.
Length:	1-mile loop.
General location:	22 miles southeast of Borrego Springs, in east-central Anza-Borrego Desert State Park, south-central California.
Trail condition:	Clear nature trail.
Difficulty:	Easy.
Best season:	November through April.
Starting elevation:	320 feet (Elephant Trees Parking Area).
Maximum elevation:	330 feet.
Elevation gain/loss:	10 feet/10 feet.
USGS topo map:	Borrego Mountain SE-CA (1:24,000).
For more information:	Anza-Borrego Desert State Park (see Appendix D).

See Map on Page 45

Finding the trailhead: From the park visitor center in Borrego Springs, go east 1.9 miles on Palm Canyon Drive to Christmas Circle. Take Borrego Springs Road south from the circle for 5.6 miles to Park Route S3. At the intersection with S3, go straight (southeast) on Borrego Springs Road towards Ocotillo Wells. Borrego Springs Road meets California Highway 78 in 6.6 miles. Go left (east) on CA 78 6.7 miles to Ocotillo Wells. Turn right (south) at the Ocotillo Wells intersection onto Split Mountain Road, and drive 5.9 miles to Elephant Trees Road. Turn right (west) and follow the dirt road 1 mile to the parking area/trailhead.

The hike: This well-signed self-guided nature trail climbs gently up a rock-lined wash to a small "herd" of elephant trees. An informative brochure is available at the trailhead.

The unusual elephant tree of the Sonoran Desert was not discovered and identified by botanists until 1937. This grove was long thought to be the northernmost group of elephant trees in California. However, in 1987 another grove of almost 200 elephant trees was discovered on the western slopes of the Santa Rosa Mountains, 21 miles farther north. Numbering

Elephant trees—Anza Borrego's most unusual plant.

only in the hundreds, they cling precariously to boulders and steep side slopes. Desert Indians used their red sap as medicine and to bring good fortune. Elephant trees are common to Baja California and the Mexican state of Sonora, but are found in only a few scattered canyons and washes of Anza-Borrego—the northernmost extension of their range.

This is an easy, educational loop winding up and down a rock-lined wash with sixteen plant identification stops keyed to the brochure. Most of the plants are common desert perennial shrubs such as burroweed, desert lavender, and brittlebush. Certainly, the most fascinating plants are the trail's namesake elephant trees, *Bursera microphylla*. The species name means "small-leaved," a common adaptation by desert plants to conserve water. The common name reflects the folded "skin" of the main trunk, much like that of an elephant.

General description:	A half-mile loop, with a self-guiding brochure, that follows the edge of an alluvial fan.
Length:	0.5-mile loop.
General location:	19.5 miles south of the visitor center in Borrego Springs, central Anza-Borrego Desert State Park, south-central California.
Trail condition:	Clear nature trail.
Special attractions:	Chuparosa and pencil cholla, fault lines, erosion.
Difficulty:	Easy.
Best season:	October through May.
Starting elevation:	1,080 feet (Narrows Earth Parking Area).
Maximum elevation:	1,130 feet.
Elevation gain/loss:	50 feet/50 feet.
USGS topo map:	Borrego Sink-CA (1:24,000).
For more information:	Anza-Borrego Desert State Park (see Appendix D).

Finding the trailhead: From the park visitor center in Borrego Springs, go east on Palm Canyon Drive to Christmas Circle (1.9 miles); at the circle turn south onto Borrego Springs Road (S3) Drive south-southeast 5.6 miles to the Y; continue on S3 to the right. Go 7.4 miles to intersection with

NARROWS EARTH TRAIL

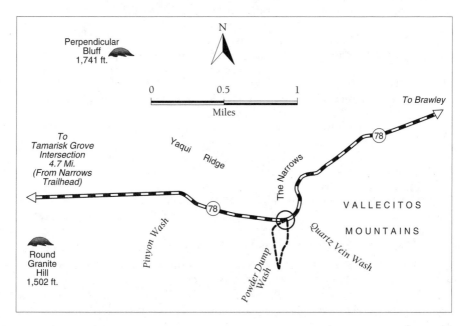

lifornia Highway 78 just beyond the Tamarisk Grove Campground. Turn left (east) on CA 78 and continue 4.7 miles to Narrows Earth Parking Area, on your right. There is no sign. The parking area is a wide spot on the right side of CA 78 immediately before the road takes a sharp right-angle turn (north) through The Narrows.

The hike: The trailhead for this short nature trail is on a busy state highway, a major through route for trucks. It is immediately west of a narrow gap (labeled "The Narrows" on the topographic map) where Pinyon Ridge almost meets the Vallecitos Mountains.

The signed, self-guided trail begins directly east of the parking area to your left. It's easy to miss spot #1, which is important since the brochures are located there. The points along the trail focus on the geologic history of the region, revealed in the naked rock walls of this canyon. Fault lines, rock formation, and erosion are some of the lessons of the Earth Narrows Trail. The seven stops on the loop provide an introduction to the forces that created Anza-Borrego topography.

From the top of the loop, Powder Dump Wash continues another 0.2 mile to a sharp rise. For a longer hike, and to apply your newly acquired knowledge, you can continue up the wash before returning to the parking area.

13 KENYON OVERLOOK TRAIL LOOP

General description:	A short point-to-point loop trail providing a panoramic vista from a rocky ridge in the central region of the park.
Length:	1-mile loop.
General location:	12.7 miles south of Borrego Springs, central Anza-Borrego Desert State Park, south-central California.
Trail condition:	Clear trail.
Special attraction:	An expansive view beyond the Vallecitos Mountains as far as the Salton Sea.
Difficulty:	Easy.
Best season:	October through April.
Starting elevation:	1,720 feet (Kenyon Overlook pullout).
Maximum elevation:	1,800 feet.
Elevation gain/loss:	80 feet/80 feet.
USGS topo map:	Borrego Sink-CA (1:24,000).
For more information:	Anza-Borrego Desert State Park (see Appendix D).

Finding the trailhead: From the visitor center in Borrego Springs, go east on Palm Canyon Drive 1.9 miles to Christmas Circle. At the circle, take Borrego Springs Road (S3) south for 5.6 miles to the Y. At the Y, turn right (south) staying on S3 (Yaqui Pass Road). Drive 5.8 miles and turn left into the Yaqui Pass Primitive Campground, the northern trailhead.

KENYON OVERLOOK TRAIL
• CACTUS LOOP TRAIL
• YAQUI WELL NATURE TRAIL

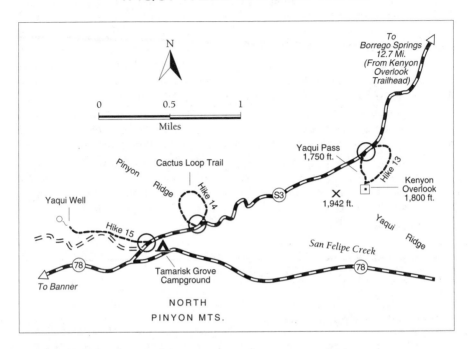

Ocotillo (left) on the Kenyon Overlook trail.

After hiking the point-to-point loop trail to the Kenyon Overlook Parking Pullout, walk back down the highway about 0.2 mile to the starting point at the Yaqui Pass Campground parking lot.

The hike: From the trailhead take the signed trail uphill. The trail maintains a gentle up-and-down grade through a series of parallel gullies lined with yucca, creosote bush, silver cholla, ocotillo, beavertail cactus, barrel cactus, and brittlebush. Soon the trail reaches the high point at a rocky ridge overlook. Turn left and walk about 30 yards to the overlook, which contains a monument in honor of William L. Kenyon, a noted desert conservationist and district park superintendent from 1947 to 1959. From here the desert spreads out like the pages of a book. Beyond is a seemingly endless series of arroyos (washes) that deposit gravel and silt in deltalike fans, two or more of which are called *bajadas*. These *bajadas* support a dense mantle of agave, called *mescal*. On a clear day the Salton Sea can be seen 30 miles to the east.

From the overlook return to the main trail, turn left, and drop gradually to the highway, which can be seen from this point. Upon reaching the highway make a right turn and walk 0.2 mile up the highway to the starting point at the Yaqui Pass primitive campground.

14   *CACTUS LOOP TRAIL*

General description:	A diverse array of cacti along a signed nature trail at a higher elevation (1,500 feet)—which means late season wildflowers—one or two weeks later than in Borrego Palm Canyon.

See Map on Page 51

Length:	1-mile loop.
General location:	14.6 miles south of Borrego Springs, central Anza-Borrego Desert State Park, south-central California.
Trail condition:	Clear trail.
Difficulty:	Easy.
Best season:	October to May.
Starting elevation:	1,500 feet (Tamarisk Grove Campground).
Maximum elevation:	1,730 feet.
Elevation gain/loss:	230 feet/230 feet.
USGS topo map:	Borrego Sink-CA (1:24,000).
For more information:	Anza-Borrego Desert State Park (see Appendix D).

Finding the trailhead: From the park visitor center in Borrego Springs, take Palm Canyon Drive east to Christmas Circle. At the circle, take Borrego Springs Road south (S3) and go 5.6 miles to a Y intersection. Bear right and continue on S3 for 7 miles to Tamarisk Grove Campground, on your left. The signed Cactus Trail Loop trailhead is across from the campground entrance. Park in the shade of the tamarisk trees along the south side of the highway.

Hiking the Cactus Loop Trail.

The hike: This short trail begins as a sandy winding path but becomes more rocky as it leads up the canyon. Signs identify jumping cholla, beavertail cactus, and saltbush. Walking up the canyon instead of driving the desert roads reveals the diversity of desert plant life and its adaptive strategies for desert survival. The nature trail route leads up the wash to the ridge's high point (1,520 feet), then winds gently down the ridge slope to the trailhead on S3. The exit sign is obscured by overgrown brittlebush but the trail itself is clear.

15   YAQUI WELL NATURE TRAIL

General description:	An easy trail to Yaqui Well and back with a plethora *See Map on Page 51* of cacti, identified by signs, and opportunities for birding at the watering hole.
Length:	2 miles round-trip.
General location:	Adjacent to Tamarisk Grove Campground, 14.4 miles from Borrego Springs, central Anza-Borrego Desert State Park, south-central California.
Trail condition:	Clear trail.
Difficulty:	Easy.
Best season:	October to April.
Starting elevation:	1,500 feet (Tamarisk Grove Campground).
Maximum elevation:	1,575 feet.
Elevation gain/loss:	75 feet/75 feet.
USGS topo maps:	Tubb Canyon-CA and Borrego Sink-CA (1:24,000).
For more information:	Anza-Borrego Desert State Park (see Appendix D).

Finding the trailhead: From the park visitor center in Borrego Springs, go east 1.9 miles to Christmas Circle. At the circle, turn south on Borrego Springs Road (S3) After 5.6 miles, bear right (south) on Yaqui Pass Road (also S3). Continue 7 miles to Tamarisk Grove Campground, which is across the road from Yaqui Well Nature Trail. Park along S3 outside the campground and cross the highway to the trailhead.

The hike: This is a well-signed varied nature trail, slightly longer than most of the others in the park. It begins at the highway but quickly angles up a rise on a gentle but rocky trail, and the hiker becomes enveloped in the desert. The nature trail signs are frequent and are clearly situated so the correct plant is labeled. Jumping cholla are the most numerous, but iron-wood and desert mistletoe also appear here.

Approaching the well from the east the trail becomes sandy and level for the last 0.6 mile. The foliage at the well provides a sharp contrast with the surrounding desert plants. A dense thicket of mesquite crowds around the watery seep. Hardy old mesquite and ironwood trees surround the area. The well is a popular watering spot for local animals, especially birds. Although you can drive to the well via the Yaqui Well Campground road, the walk through the desert makes the existence of this moisture more significant.

General description:	A long east-west trail that follows the old Pinyon Ridge jeep trail (closed to vehicular travel), passing by 4,573-foot Mount Wilson to a rocky overlook above Borrego Valley.
Length:	11 miles round-trip.
General location:	About 8 miles south of Borrego Springs in west-central Anza-Borrego Desert State Park, south-central California.
Trail condition:	Clear, mostly sandy trail that was once used by four-wheel-drive vehicles.
Special attractions:	One of the longer out-and-back hikes in the park with sweeping vistas of the central park region.
Difficulty:	Moderate.
Best season:	October through April.
Starting elevation:	3,960 feet.
Maximum elevation:	4,450 feet (below the north slopes of Mount Wilson).
Elevation gain/loss:	700 feet/700 feet.
USGS topo map:	Tubb Canyon-CA, 1:24,000.
For more information:	Anza-Borrego Desert State Park (see Appendix D).

Key points:

0.0   Trailhead.

5.0   Old jeep trail disappears; primitive trail continues.

5.5   Use trail disappears; hike north to overlook.

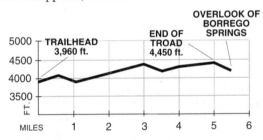

Finding the trailhead: Go 15 miles east of Warner Springs, on Park Route S22 (Montezuma Valley Road); 10.5 miles east of the intersection with S2 or 8 miles southwest of the park visitor center in Borrego Springs, take the Old Culp Valley Road south. Four-wheel-drive vehicles are recommended on this steep, sandy road. After 0.4 mile stay right at the first road junction. Continue on the main road, ignoring numerous turnouts. The Wilson trailhead is another 2.7 miles up the road, for a total of 3.1 miles from S22, and is marked by a small sign with a turnaround parking area just below a ridge dotted with sage, creosote, and granite boulders.

The hike: The trail climbs moderately the first 0.6 mile to the ridgetop, opening up panoramic vistas of the Vallecito Mountains to the southeast. It

WILSON TRAIL

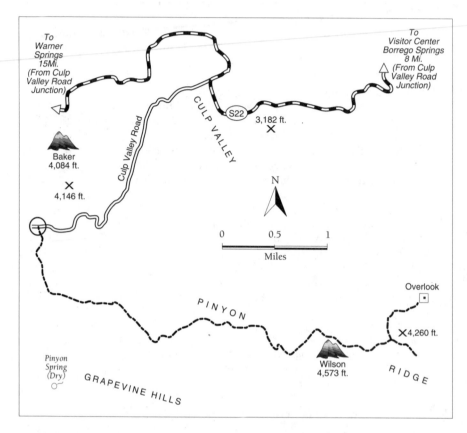

then gradually descends another 0.5 mile to a broad saddle adorned with a heavy mantle of juniper, cholla, and agave. After another 0.4 mile this former jeep trail tops out on a high ridge with an outcrop of sparkling light-colored granite boulders just to the right. This sandy track then levels, climbs, and levels again for another mile. In a few places the trail is somewhat overgrown by vegetation but all you have to do is look ahead 50 yards or so and you'll easily spot the remnants of the two-track jeep trail.

At this point the trail climbs steeply 0.2 mile, weaving between large boulders, then drops 0.1 mile, followed by a steep 0.2 mile climb to a high side ridge. It then drops slightly and levels out for 1 mile. Soon the ridge is sprinkled with a few pinyon pines and cedar adding variety to the mix of high desert flora.

The old jeep trail appears to end after 5 miles after climbing gradually to a downed post with a cement base. A more primitive path marked by rock cairns leads steeply up through thick brush for about 0.2 mile. The path tops out in a saddle between the rocky points, including 4,573-foot Mount Wilson, and continues across a broad, open plateau for another 0.3 mile. Here the sandy path disappears as the slope begins to drop eastward.

Wilson Trail leading to the northwest at mile 1.3.

Before heading back to the trailhead walk about 100 yards north to the rock-lined lip of the ridge for a stunning view of Borrego Springs, the Salton Sea, and surrounding desert basins and ranges fading far into the distance. This remote stretch of the Grapevine Hills is used extensively by mountain lions, bobcats, and coyotes as evidenced by abundant scat along the trail.

17   CALIFORNIA RIDING AND HIKING TRAIL
PEÑA SPRING AND CULP VALLEY OVERLOOK

General description:	This maintained section of the Riding and Hiking Trail is almost entirely downhill. It goes by Peña Spring, includes the Culp Valley Overlook, then descends to the valley floor and a cross-desert walk to the visitor center in Borrego Springs.
Length:	8.5 miles point-to-point (with car shuttle).
General location:	8 miles southwest of Borrego Springs on the Montezuma Valley Road, central Anza-Borrego Desert State Park, south-central California.
Trail condition:	Clear trail (except for some overgrown portions of the less-traveled section above Culp Valley Overlook).
Special attractions:	Views of Borrego Valley, Coyote Mountain, and the Santa Rosa Mountains.

CALIFORNIA RIDING AND HIKING TRAIL

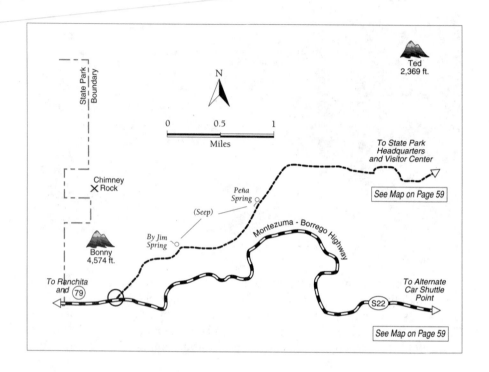

Difficulty:	Moderately strenuous.
Best season:	October to May.
Starting elevation:	4,000 feet.
Maximum elevation:	4,000 feet.
Elevation gain/loss:	40 feet/3,300 feet.
USGS topo map:	Tubb Canyon-CA (1:24,000).
For more information:	Anza-Borrego Desert State Park (see Appendix D).

Key points:

0.0-0.4	Overgrown section; watch for yellow-topped posts.
0.4	Trail stops heads for the saddle on a low ridge.
0.5	Stay left of the wash as the trail skirts the small valley.
0.7	Watch for a primitive stock tank on the hillside, left.
1.2-1.7	Culp Valley Overlook area, signs at trail intersections.
1.7-7.5	Trail descends to valley.
7.5-8.5	1-mile trailless hike to the visitor center. A marked wash (right) leads to the parking lot for horse parties.

CALIFORNIA RIDING AND HIKING TRAIL
• PANORAMA OVERLOOK/EXTENDED OVERLOOK
• BORREGO PALM CANYON NATURE TRAIL

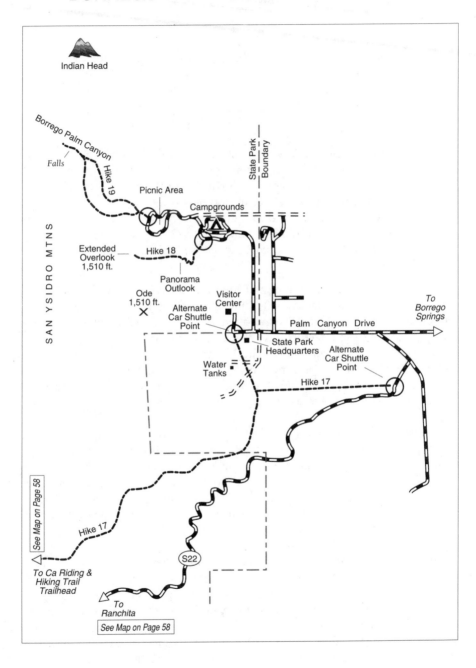

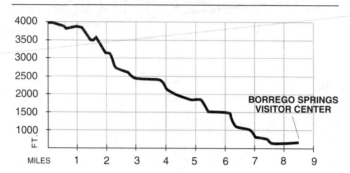

CALIFORNIA RIDING AND HIKING TRAIL
PEÑA SPRING AND CULP VALLEY OVERLOOK

Finding the trailhead: A small sign marks the trailhead 12 miles east of Warner Springs on Park Route S22 (Montezuma Valley Road), 6.8 miles east of Park Route S2. The trailhead is on the north side of the road. This point is 10 miles southwest of the visitor center in Borrego Springs.

The destination point for the car shuttle is the visitor center. Horse parties end their trip at a parking pullout at mile 16 on S22, 1 mile south. Hikers may also prefer this convenient destination since it eliminates a dry 1-mile walk across the valley floor.

The hike: The California Riding and Hiking Trail reaches the varied elevations of Anza-Borrego. Beginning at 4,000 feet in chaparral, it descends through mountain valleys to the desert floor. The transition of vegetative communities is as interesting as the view—and the trip down the ridge offers spectacular vistas.

As you drive to the trailhead, the length and the elevation gain of the Montezuma Road may be intimidating. The trail is nowhere near as arduous as the drive up! The trail avoids the rocky ridges you see from the road. Although there is little horse use on the trail due to steepness, neither is this a bighorn sheep trail.

The early section of trail is the most difficult to find since it is not used often and is overgrown with chaparral. Stay within 50 yards north of the road, and watch for yellow-topped posts hidden by aggressive shrubbery. You can see this peek-a-boo trail better by looking ahead about 50 yards. This section is not used frequently, compared with the last 5 miles of the hike, east of Culp Valley. Close to the Montezuma-Borrego Highway (S22), you may pick up traffic noise, but as you wind north of rock outcroppings and ridges that fades. Soon you are surrounded by wild country.

At the midsection of the hike the trail goes through Culp Valley, an area formerly used for grazing cattle. Traces of its ranching past are noticeable—such as the stock watering facilities you will spot to your left. Peña Spring, now barely a seep, creates a patch of greenery in the high valley before you climb to the Culp Valley Overlook. This section of the trail is easily accessible to the highway, with a parking area. Frequent visitors take the 0.5-mile hike to enjoy the view. Thus, more signs mark the trail. Apparently more hikers also start the journey here; the trail is more heavily used from this point to the valley below.

Although the Culp Valley Overlook itself is prominently marked with a sign, there are dozens of breathtaking overlooks on the descent to the valley. Don't use up your film on the first one you come to! This 5-mile section will provide many photo opportunities. The trail goes down a series of giant stair steps—sharp descents followed by small landings, each one hosting a cactus display and stunning diversity of plants. Between these sandy flat cactus gardens the trail drops sharply, often via rocky gullies. Even with the town of Borrego Springs spreading out below, you'll have a genuine sense of seclusion; the busy highway to Borrego Springs is beyond the ridge to the south.

Upon reaching the valley floor, you can follow the wide trail to your right to the parking area/trailhead created for horse-users. This is a convenient place for a car shuttle. To return to the visitor center complex, or the adjacent campground, go straight north from the end of the hillside trail. Trying to find a marked trail on the desert floor is time consuming and unnecessary, since you can see the rooftops of the park buildings immediately to the north. Use the highly visible tree-encircled water tanks as an intermediate guide. The visitor center is 0.3 mile beyond the tanks.

If your driver is late meeting you after your hike, waiting at the visitor center may be more a more attractive option than waiting at the parking lot on S22.

18 *PANORAMA OVERLOOK/EXTENDED OVERLOOK*

General description:	A short but steep climb via a switchback trail south up San Ysidro Mountain to a scenic overlook of Borrego Valley, continuing to a higher and even more expansive viewpoint.

See Map on Page 59

Length:	1.4 miles out-and-back; 2.6 miles round-trip to extended overlook.
General location:	Just west of campground near the Borrego Springs Visitor Center, northwestern Anza-Borrego Desert State Park, south-central California.
Trail condition:	Clear rocky trail to overlook; steep rocky use trail to extended overlook.
Special attractions:	The best all-around viewpoint of Borrego Springs Canyon and the adjacent valley, with the added lure of an extended ridgeline climb to as high and far as one has time and energy for.
Difficulty:	Moderate.
Best season:	October through April.
Starting elevation:	780 feet.
Maximum elevation:	1,020 feet (panorama overlook); 1,510 feet (extended overlook).
Elevation gain/loss:	240 feet/240 feet (panorama overlook); 730 feet/730 feet (extended overlook).
USGS topo map:	Borrego Palms Canyon-CA (1:24,000).
For more information:	Anza-Borrego Desert State Park (see Appendix D).

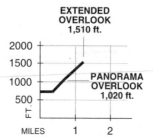

EXTENDED OVERLOOK 1,510 ft.

PANORAMA OVERLOOK 1,020 ft.

2000
1500
1000
500
FT.

MILES   1   2

Key Points:

- 0.0   Trailhead at campground.
- 0.4   Beginning of switchback trail.
- 0.7   Panorama Overlook (1,020 feet).
- 1.3   Extended overlook (1,510 feet).

Finding the trailhead: From the visitor center at the intersection of Park Route S22 and Palm Canyon Drive in Borrego Springs follow signs north 0.8 mile to the Borrego Springs Campground. The trail starts near campsite 71. A level 1-mile trail from the visitor center northwest to the campground also intersects the Panorama Overlook Trail.

The hike: From the signed trailhead next to the palm tree at campsite 71, take the trail across a flat alluvial fan along the base of the rocky hillside for 0.4 mile to the "Overlook Trail" sign where the trail begins to switchback up the slope. The clear but steep and rocky trail climbs 240 feet over a distance of 0.3 mile to an open knoll ringed by creosote bushes, offering a wide vista from the eastern foot of San Ysidro Mountain to Borrego Palm Canyon and Borrego Valley.

For an even more expansive view continue west up the ridge on a use trail, well-defined for the first 0.2 mile as it follows the initial level portion of the ridge. The use trail then winds upward through rocks and brush and

Indian Head Mountain as seen from the extended Panorama Overlook.

62

sometimes all but disappears. Simply follow the main crest of the ridge leading toward the distant summit of San Ysidro Mountain. At times the best footing is found along either side of the actual ridgeline.

After another 0.4 mile and 300-foot gain you'll reach a somewhat level rocky ledge with several flat spots. These make for a wonderful extended overlook—a good place to sit and soak up the majestic desert scenery of canyons, alluvial fans, mountains, valleys, and jagged, exposed ridges. The palm groves of Borrego Palm Canyon are hidden from view, but take time here to scan the slopes for desert bighorn sheep. As with most mountainous use trails, this one is easier to find going down than up.

This extended overlook is a logical turnaround point for a vigorous but moderate half-day hike, although it is possible to scramble up the ridge another 4 or 5 miles to the lofty summit of 6,147-foot San Ysidro Peak on the park's western boundary. This would be a very strenuous full day cross-country climb with more than a vertical mile of gain and loss. Many overly optimistic day hikers have mistakenly spent a cold night on this mountain, usually giving rise to search and rescue operations. Know your limits.

19   *BORREGO PALM CANYON NATURE TRAIL*

General description:	A self-guided nature hike to a palm grove, beginning and ending at Borrego Palm Canyon Picnic Area.
Length:	3.5-mile loop.
General location:	0.6 mile north of the Visitor Center in Borrego Springs, central Anza-Borrego Desert State Park, south-central California.
Trail condition:	Clear trail.
Special attractions:	Seasonal creek and waterfall at upper end of the palm grove; pupfish pond beside the parking lot at the trailhead. The sheep for whom the park is named are sometimes spotted on canyon slopes above the oasis.
Difficulty:	Easy to the oasis; moderate for the last 0.2 mile to the canyon overlook.
Best season:	October through April.
Starting elevation:	800 feet.
Maximum elevation:	1,300 feet.
Elevation gain/loss:	500 feet/500 feet.
USGS topo map:	Borrego Palm Canyon-CA (1:24,000).
For more information:	Anza-Borrego Desert State Park (see Appendix D).

See Map on Page 59

Key points:

0.0   Trailhead and pupfish pond.

0.3   Bridge across stream.

1.1   Second bridge. Sign on south side of bridge indicates loop trail for return trip.

1.5   Palm oasis.

1.75 Overlook above oasis.

2.4   Bridge; take loop trail.

3.5   Return to trailhead.

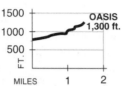

Native California fan palm grove at the Borrego Palm Oasis.

Finding the trailhead: From the park visitor center in Borrego Springs, go north 1 mile on an access road to Borrego Palm Canyon Campground and Picnic Area. The trail leaves from the northwest end of the picnic area. There is a day use fee to enter with a motor vehicle.

The hike: This trail provides a spectacular introduction to the beauties of the desert. The self-guiding brochure and the clear signs will help you become familiar with the plants and animals, geology, history, and ecology here. Ocotillo abound, as do honey mesquite, cheesebush, and chuparosa—the "hummingbird plant." Hummingbirds are plentiful, especially in spring. In winter and spring, water flows in the adjacent stream, with small waterfalls. Sharp-eyed hikers can often spot bighorn sheep on the mountain slopes of the canyon, especially in early morning or evening.

At 1.3 miles, the walk up the trail into the canyon changes radically. Before you is the view of a dense palm grove in the narrow canyon ahead. The trail winds through large boulders the last 0.2 mile to a small waterfall and one of the largest groves of California fan palms in the country. Be careful not to encroach on the palm grove—the fifty thousand visitors a year have caused some damage, especially to younger trees. Please remain behind the signed barricades, which are there to protect the fledgling palms. A short but steeper climb above the oasis leads to an overlook 30 feet above the streambed.

On the way out, an alternate route goes along the higher canyon slope to the west, amid a slope of ocotillo. This route also leads back to the parking lot; it is slightly longer (0.5 mile more) and more strenuous (100 feet elevation gain) than the path along the stream. But you also enjoy a loftier view of the canyon mouth below.

20 ALCOHOLIC PASS

General description:	An out-and-back hike to a sweeping vista of the northeastern section of Anza-Borrego.
Length:	3.4 miles round-trip.
General location:	8 miles north of Borrego Springs, north-central Anza-Borrego Desert State Park, south-central California.
Trail condition:	Clear trail, clear wash.
Difficulty:	Moderate.
Best season:	October through April.
Starting elevation:	800 feet.
Maximum elevation:	1,540 feet.
Elevation gain/loss:	740 feet/120 feet.
USGS topo maps:	Borrego Palm Canyon-CA and Clark Lake-CA (1:24,000).
For more information:	Anza-Borrego Desert State Park (see Appendix D).

Ocotillo and cholla cacti line the trail to Alcoholic Pass.

Key points:

 0.0   Trailhead. Well-traveled trail heads northeast.
 0.2   Trail climbs ridge.
 0.3   Trail steepens sharply.
 1.0   Register located west of the pass itself.
 1.1   The pass.
 1.7   Turnaround point.

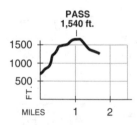

Finding the trailhead: From the park visitor center in Borrego Springs, go east on Palm Canyon Drive 1.9 miles to Christmas Circle; continue 0.6 mile past the circle and turn north (left) on DiGiorgio Drive. At 5 miles the pavement ends; continue north on Coyote Canyon Road, a rolling, soft dirt road, for 2.6 miles to the trailhead on your right.

The hike: For centuries, Alcoholic Pass has been used by the region's inhabitants to travel from Clark Valley (on the northeast) to Borrego Valley. These use trails were created by countless moccasins before our hiking boots arrived. As you climb to the pass with its sweeping view, you can develop many theories about the origin of the pass's name.

The hike takes off for the first 0.2 mile up a sandy slope to a trail marker indicating a right turn up a sidehill; the trail follows this ridge up a moderate incline. It becomes progressively rockier as it climbs to the trip register at 1 mile. At that point you have reached a sandy plateau with sweeping

ALCOHOLIC PASS

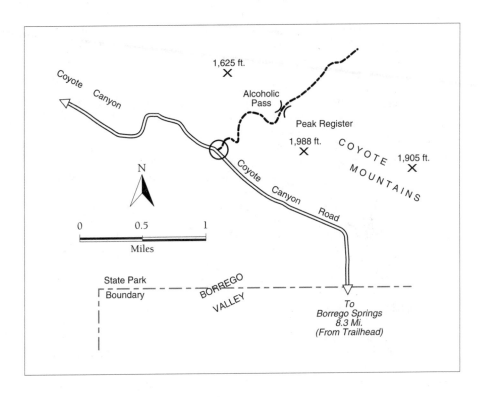

views of the San Ysidro Mountains to the west and the Santa Rosa Mountains through the pass to the east.

The winding flat trail continues beyond the register, soon turning upward and becoming more boulder-strewn. At the summit of the pass, it opens into a wide sandy wash sloping northeast down to the plateau above Clark Valley. About 0.6 mile beyond the pass, the wash opens into a high fan, spreading northeastward. This is a good spot to find a shady rock for lunch and/or contemplation before heading back to the trailhead.

General description:	A soggy, nearly flat hike out and back along Coyote Canyon Creek, following the historic Anza expedition route.
Length:	4 miles round-trip; 3 miles for optional side trip to Box Canyon.
General location:	9 miles north of Borrego Springs, Coyote Canyon region of Anza-Borrego Desert State Park, south-central California.
Trail condition:	Clear but very wet; bring your old sneakers.
Special attractions:	Extraordinary birding opportunity in lush near-jungle setting of water and willow thickets (bring binoculars).
Difficulty:	Moderate (due to constant slogging through muck and water).
Best season:	October through May. The Coyote Canyon area is closed to visitors from June 1 to September 30 to protect bighorn sheep access to water sources. The summer closure gate is at the Lower Willows trailhead.
Starting elevation:	1,140 feet.
Maximum elevation:	1,350 feet.
Elevation gain/loss:	210 feet/none.
USGS topo maps:	Collins Valley-CA and Borrego Palm Canyon-CA (1:24,000).
For more information:	Anza-Borrego Desert State Park (see Appendix D).

Key points:

0.0   Trail begins before Third Crossing.
0.15   "Rice Krispies Treat" bank on the right; wash sharply cuts the bank; for the Box Canyon side trip follow this wash up to the canyon then return.
0.2   First of many stream crossings.
2.0   Emerge from streambed to wide wash.
2.1   Trail goes west.
2.9   Collins Valley Road (dirt road). Turn left for road route back to trailhead.
4.0   Return to trailhead at Third Crossing.

Finding the trailhead: From the park visitor center in Borrego Springs, go east 1.9 miles on Palm Canyon Drive through Christmas Circle; continue east 0.6 mile and turn north (left) onto DiGiorgio Road. Drive north 5 miles, until the pavement ends. Continue north on unpaved Coyote Canyon Road 5.6 miles northwest to Lower Willows trail, which begins on the right side of the road immediately before the Third Crossing (signed). If you park at the Second Crossing (signed) due to high water and/or low clearance, walk up Coyote Canyon Road 0.7 mile to the trailhead.

LOWER WILLOWS/BOX CANYON • INDIAN CANYON
• COUGAR CANYON • SHEEP CANYON

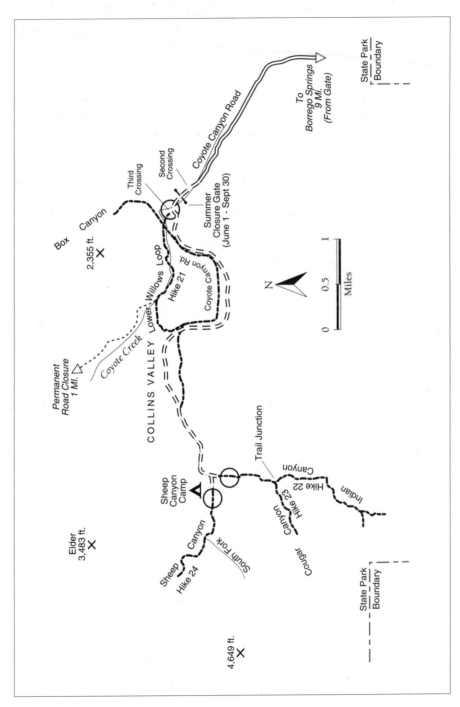

The hike: The hike up Lower Willows is certain to be a memorable one. In the middle of this arid landscape the trail follows the stream—along it, across it, in it. The well-signed trail is also used by equestrians since it provides access to Collins Valley and upper Coyote Canyon. The use by horses contributes to the muddy quality of the trail. Posted signs remind hikers that this is a fragile area and it is necessary to stay on the trail, which is often the streambed itself.

An optional side trip up Box Canyon at mile 0.15 provides an interesting contrast with the soggy world of Lower Willows. The gravelly Box Canyon wash leads to a bouldered canyon entrance. Smoke trees are plentiful. This dry canyon can be explored for 4 miles, where it opens to a wider valley.

For years the Lower Willows streambed was also a roadbed. The Anza expeditions came along this route. The second one, in 1775, came through with a group of 240 settlers and 800 livestock. The water was a welcome relief for the party, but the impact on the riparian zone must have been enormous.

The trail zigzags upstream through dense willow saplings. After several miles of this muddy experience, the trail emerges in a wide, dry, sandy wash and the beginning of Middle Willows. At this point, follow the yellow-topped white posts up the bank to the west. On the horizon across Collins Valley a prominent flat-topped mountain is an ideal beacon, helping you maintain your westward bearings to the Coyote Canyon Road.

Turn left and follow this very rough four-wheel-drive road back to the Lower Willows trailhead. On weekends especially, this section of road is a favorite of the four-wheel-drive crowd. A couple of dicey spots in the canyons challenge even high-clearance vehicles. Be cautious in these spots and give drivers a wide berth.

NOTE: This section of the park is closed to all visitors from June 1 through September 30 so the bighorn sheep and other species can enjoy the scarce water of Coyote Creek during the hot summer. The gated closure is located right before the Third Crossing.

General description:	An out-and-back hike to a hidden canyon with palm ⟨See Map on Page 69⟩ groves and lush vegetation, length depending on your means of transportation.
Length:	4.5 miles round-trip if you can drive to the trailhead; 11.5 miles if you hike from Third Crossing; 12.5 miles if you hike from Second Crossing.
General location:	Coyote Canyon, 15 miles north of Borrego Springs, in the north central portion of Anza-Borrego Desert State Park, south-central California.
Trail condition:	Good trail becoming more primitive as you climb.
Special attractions:	A delightful out-of-the-way canyon with a seasonal stream that is a refreshing break from the surrounding desert.
Difficulty:	Moderately strenuous.
Best season:	October through April. Coyote Canyon is closed to human visitors from June 1 through September 30 in order to protect bighorn sheep access to water sources.
Starting elevation:	1,600 feet.
Maximum elevation:	2,400 feet.
Elevation gain/loss:	800 feet/none.
USGS topo map:	Borrego Palm Canyon-CA (1:24,000).
For more information:	Anza-Borrego Desert State Park (see Appendix D).

Key points:

0.0   Cougar Canyon/Indian Canyon trailhead.
0.5   Faded trail signpost where Cougar Canyon goes right; continue south.
0.9   Trail hugs hillside to the right, and enters canyon.
1.8   Lone palm at canyon junction; Deering Canyon on the west, Indian Canyon continues south.

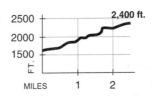

Finding the trailhead: From the visitor center in Borrego Springs, go east 1.9 miles on Palm Canyon Drive to Christmas Circle; continue 0.6 mile beyond the circle to a left turn on DiGiorgio Road. Drive 5 miles to the end of the pavement, then continue north on unpaved Coyote Canyon Road. The first crossing of the stream is not difficult under normal conditions. The Second Crossing may pose a problem for vehicles with low clearance; if so, park there and hike the rest of the way. The distance from the Second Crossing

This lone palm tree stands in the Valley of the Thousand Springs in Indian Canyon.

to the Indian Canyon trailhead is approximately 4 miles. After the Third Crossing, even high-clearance vehicles may have difficulty. Park near the stream, and hike from there.

The hike follows the road, so be careful about traffic, especially on weekends. After you climb the rise to the floor of Collins Valley you'll see a well-marked section of a horse trail (left) that shortens the trip and avoids road traffic. The actual trailhead is at a parking area 0.1 mile south of the Sheep Canyon road junction where a sign indicates Indian and Cougar canyons to the south and Sheep Canyon to the west.

The hike: This hike in Indian Canyon has no convenient road access if your vehicle is not suitable for rough terrain. But this verdant canyon hike is well worth the walk to the trailhead. The stream flow will be reduced in the fall, but the greenery will still be striking.

From the trailhead, the wide trail goes south up the sloping valley floor, surrounded by creosote. When the trail enters the canyon it follows the right bank of the stream into a lush riparian zone, with a small palm grove peeking above the bank 0.2 mile ahead. The trail weaves back and forth across the stream as it goes up the valley. Decades of hiking explorers have created a maze of pathways, making route-finding challenging. The trail becomes faint in places, but persistent hikers can pick a route by focusing on a distant goal, such as a grove of palm trees.

Heading up the valley through the cobweb of trails, you eventually arrive at a lone palm (0.3 mile from the canyon mouth) at the foot of a slender ridge that marks the confluence of two drainages: Deering Canyon on the west and Indian Canyon on the south. A trail leads to the top of the ridge, from which you gain a panoramic view of this inner valley. Up Deering Canyon, a stair-step palm grove leads up its steep drainage. Sycamores line the more gentle Indian Canyon to the left. Both of these options are worthy of further exploration, although the trail becomes less defined in either direction. Enjoy this remote wilderness before retracing your steps to the trailhead.

NOTE: If you plan to spend the night in Indian Canyon, remember the park policy regarding camping near water sources. To assure the nocturnal animals' access to water, it is essential that you camp at least 200 yards from the stream. Remember, too, that all human travel in Coyote Canyon is forbidden from June 1 through September 30; the closure is at the Third Crossing on Coyote Creek.

23 COUGAR CANYON

General description:	A moderate round-trip hike (if you can drive to the trailhead) up a sloping canyon floor in bighorn sheep habitat.
Length:	3 miles round-trip. The trip is lengthened by 7 miles (to 10 total) if you drive to the Third Crossing of Coyote Creek, or by 8 miles (11 total) if you can drive only to the Second Crossing.
General location:	15 miles northwest of Borrego Springs, in Coyote Canyon, north-central Anza-Borrego Desert State Park, south-central California.
Trail condition:	Clear trail, fading to primitive as you climb.
Special attractions:	Stream, palm grove, shaded pool, and silvery waterfall make this canyon delightful.
Difficulty:	Moderate.
Best season:	October to May. Coyote Canyon is closed June 1 to September 30 to protect bighorn sheep access to water sources.
Starting elevation:	1,600 feet.
Maximum elevation:	2,300 feet (the pool and waterfall).
Elevation gain/loss:	700 feet/none.
USGS topo map:	Borrego Palm Canyon-CA (1:24,000).
For more information:	Anza-Borrego Desert State Park (see Appendix D).

See Map on Page 69

Key points:

0.0 Cougar Canyon/Indian Canyon trailhead; trail goes south.

0.5 Trail junction. Faded sign indicates Cougar Canyon trail to right.

1.5 Trail fades as it climbs.

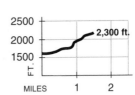

Finding the trailhead: From the Borrego Springs visitor center, go east on Palm Canyon Drive 1.9 miles to Christmas Circle; continue 0.6 mile beyond the circle to turn left on DiGiorgio Road. Drive north on DiGiorgio Rd. 5 miles until the pavement ends. Continue north 4.8 miles on Coyote Canyon Road, a primitive but passable route, to the parking area before the second crossing (marked with a sign, and also the site of a gauging station). Depending on the water level and clearance of your vehicle, you can also drive to park after the Third Crossing. The road beyond that point requires very high clearance, four-wheel-drive, and enormous courage.

The hike from the second crossing is about 4.6 miles to the Cougar Canyon/Sheep Canyon junction sign; from the third, it is about 4 miles to the junction sign. Follow the jeep road from the crossing, but take the equestrian trail to your left when you reach Collins Valley for a more direct route and to avoid motorized traffic on the road, especially on weekends. From the junction sign, follow the road another 0.3 mile to the Indian Canyon/Cougar Canyon trailhead.

The hike: This canyon journey is a delightful surprise, not only because of the lengthy hike just to get here, but also because the area's wonders are hidden from view even when you finally arrive at the canyon mouth. Have faith, and keep on hiking.

After Collins Valley and the dry lower reaches of Indian Canyon, the turnoff to Cougar Canyon seems like just another arid desert valley. Then, as you round the bend in the lower reaches of the canyon, your ears may detect the tinkling of a waterfall. Your eyes will be astounded with the lush riparian area. Sandy beaches and inviting pools dot the watercourse down the canyon, all reached by a labyrinth of trails that wind around boulders. Sycamores and palm trees are scattered along the stream bank above rock-lined grottos. Plan on taking time to explore and enjoy this rare water wonderland before your return trip.

The stream may be only a trickle in the fall, but the vegetation will still provide a colorful contrast with the rest of Collins Valley. If you plan to camp overnight, remember the park regulations about water sources. Since desert wildlife is largely nocturnal, considerate campers don't obstruct animals' access to water. Camp at least 200 yards away from the stream.

NOTE: The summer closure of Coyote Canyon, June 1 through September 30, makes this outing off-limits for that season.

General description:	A primitive hike through a lush canyon with year-round
	See Map on Page 69
	pools of water, and an optional tough side trip to an idyllic waterfall.
Length:	3 miles round-trip from Sheep Canyon primitive camp trailhead; 11 miles round-trip from the Second Crossing on Coyote Canyon Road.
General location:	7 miles northwest of Borrego Springs, in northwestern Anza-Borrego Desert State Park, south-central California.
Trail condition:	Good to primitive use trail with trailless sections on and above the canyon floor.
Special attractions:	Groves of sycamores and cottonwoods with scattered palm trees, waterfalls, pools, and shady grottos—a welcome contrast to surrounding desert.
Difficulty:	Moderately strenuous.
Best season:	November through April. The area above Lower Willows, which includes Collins Valley/Sheep Canyon, is closed to human visitors from June 1 through September 30 to protect bighorn sheep access to water sources.
Starting elevation:	1,600 feet.
Maximum elevation:	2,190 feet (end of primitive trail 1.5 miles up canyon).
Elevation gain/loss:	590 feet/none.
USGS topo map:	Borrego Palm Canyon-CA (1:24,000).
For more information:	Anza-Borrego Desert State Park (see Appendix D).

Key points:

0.0   Primitive camp trailhead near the mouth of Sheep Canyon (1,600 feet).

0.4   The South Fork enters from the left; continue right up the main North Fork (1,660 feet).

1.0   Trail reaches a deep pool just below a "weeping" rock wall.

1.5   The primitive trail disappears, making this a good turnaround point (2,190 feet).

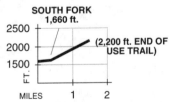

Finding the trailhead: From the park visitor center in Borrego Springs drive east 1.9 miles on Palm Canyon Drive to Christmas Circle; continue 0.6 mile beyond the circle and make a left turn on DiGiorgio Road. Drive 5.6 miles to the end of the pavement, then continue north on unpaved Coyote

Canyon Road. The first wash crossing is normally not difficult. The Second Crossing may stop low-clearance vehicles. If stopped, park and continue on foot up the Coyote Canyon Rd. The road distance from the Second Crossing to the Sheep Canyon trailhead is approximately 4 miles. After the Third Crossing even four-wheel-drive, high-clearance vehicles may be stopped at the foot of an extremely steep, rocky stretch of the road.

While hiking the road be on the lookout for four-wheel-drive vehicles, especially on weekends. After climbing to the floor of Collins Valley, veer left on a well-marked horse trail that shortens the distance and avoids vehicular traffic. Upon reaching the signed Cougar Canyon/Sheep Canyon Road junction, turn right (northwest) and proceed another 0.25 mile to the official trailhead at the primitive camp near the mouth of Sheep Canyon.

The hike: Water flows through the rugged confines of Sheep Canyon during most of the year, although the canyon is apt to be dry by the time autumn rolls around. Depending on the season, a bubbling stream flows down steep rocks into deep pools lined by shady grottos. A few palm trees scattered along the brushy cottonwood-sycamore bottom make this twisting gorge a true desert oasis. A primitive on-again/ off-again use trail winds up the lower reaches of Sheep Canyon into the North Fork.

From the primitive camp the rock-lined trail immediately crosses the wash. This primitive but well-defined trail (at this point) climbs a finger of sand between two branches of the braided wash before crossing to the right

Small waterfalls and deep pools are among the surprises in the remote North Fork of Sheep Canyon.

side of the canyon. The trail crosses the stream several times before working up a side ridge at 0.4 mile near the South Fork, which joins the main Sheep Canyon from the left. Several palms sit above in the lower South Fork, with a single palm positioned perfectly next to a waterfall in the main canyon. The South Fork is one of the steepest, roughest canyons in the park and should only be traversed by well-conditioned, experienced rock scramblers. It is possible to take a short but strenuous side trip by entering the South Fork at mile 0.4. The next 0.3 mile consists of gaining 350 feet through heavy brush and over rock slabs to the base of an idyllic 30-foot waterfall overseen by a small palm grove.

After enjoying this sublime setting, double back to the main canyon and continue up the left side of the North Fork. Shortly, the trail crosses the stream to the right side in a dense mixture of palm and sycamore trees. Within 0.2 mile a huge boulder blocks the trail close to a single large palm. Before climbing over the boulder, savor the music of rushing water and the stillness of the deep canyon.

At 0.7 mile the trail drops to several gigantic boulders that form a cavern. Backtrack about 30 yards to a faint path that climbs between the boulders. Maneuver under and around several rock overhangs to follow the most prominent path, which soon crosses over to the left side of the canyon. This is a scenic alcove, with palm trees wedged in a narrow rock chute surrounded by the geologic faulting of tilted rock beds. The trail pitches steeply upward before dropping to the palm grove.

At 1 mile the trail again descends, this time to a lovely pool. Climb the stair-step rock to the left of the pool, soon reaching an overlook above a "weeping" rock where running water fans out across the face of a wall. Continue up the rough, rocky slope to a level shelf where a noticeable trail is again picked up. At 1.2 miles the canyon narrows with bedded rock rising above two palm trees at 2,150 feet.

At 1.5 miles any resemblance to a trail vanishes near a lovely series of pools nestled beneath tall palms and sycamores. Extremely steep, loose, granitic side slopes demand slow and careful route-finding from this point on. This is a good turnaround point for a 3-mile round-trip sampler of the wild beauty of the North Fork of Sheep Canyon.

General description:	Two out-and-back day hikes through colorful canyons and chaparral/woodlands to prominent peaks by way of remote stretches of the Pacific Crest Trail (PCT).
Length:	Southern segment, 5 miles round-trip to Combs Peak; Northern segment, 5 miles round-trip to Table Mountain.
General location:	About 70 miles northwest of Borrego Springs, in northwestern Anza-Borrego Desert State Park, south-central California.
Trail condition:	Mostly clear with several good sections; short off-trail route-finding climbs to both summits.
Difficulty:	Moderately strenuous to Combs Peak; moderate to Table Mountain.
Best season:	October through May.
Starting elevation:	Southern segment, 5,050 feet; Northern segment, 3,500 feet.
Maximum elevation:	Southern segment, 6,193 feet (Combs Peak); Northern segment, 4,298 feet (Table Mountain).
Elevation gain/loss:	Southern segment, 1,143 feet/none; Northern segment, 950 feet/150 feet.
USGS topo map:	Bucksnort Mountain-CA (1:24,000).
For more information:	Anza-Borrego Desert State Park (see Appendix D).

Key points:

Southern segment:

0.0 Lost Valley Road (5,050 feet).

1.9 Saddle northeast of Combs Peak; beginning of off-trail climb to Combs Peak.

2.5 Combs Peak (6,193 feet).

Northern segment:

0.0 Upper Coyote Canyon Road.

0.3 Nance Canyon.

2.3 4,185-foot pass east of Table Mountain.

2.5 Table Mountain (4,298 feet).

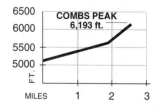

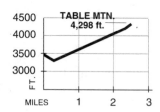

NORTH - PACIFIC CREST TRAIL:
COYOTE TO TABLE MOUNTAIN
• SOUTH - PACIFIC CREST TRAIL:
LOST VALLEY TO COMBS PEAK

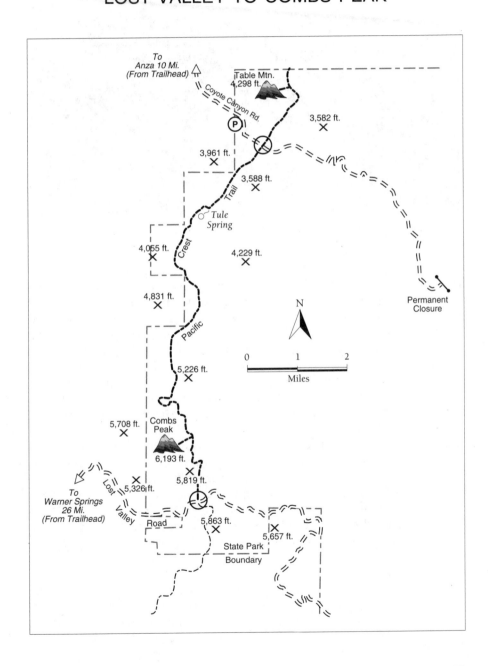

The Pacific Crest Trail emerges on Lost Valley Road, south of Combs Peak.

Finding the trailhead: To reach the Southern segment, take California Highway 79. About 3.3 miles south of Oak Grove and 10.8 miles north of Warner Springs, turn east on Chihuahua Road. After 6.5 miles the paved road curves right. Continue straight ahead to the end of the pavement and the beginning of the dirt Lost Valley Road. Continue past the biological station gate at 1.7 miles, reaching the park boundary at 3.1 miles. About 2 miles beyond this the Lost Valley Road intersects the PCT (5.2 miles beyond the pavement). The trail to Combs Peak takes off to the left, heading north.

To find the trailhead for the Northern segment, begin at the fire station in the town of Anza. Drive 1 mile east on California Highway 371, turn right (south) on Kirby Road, then drive 1.1 miles to Wellman Road. (The road names change, but simply follow the paved road). Turn left on Wellman Rd. and proceed 1 mile to Terwilliger Road. Go right (south) on Terwilliger Rd. for 3 miles to Coyote Canyon Road, turn left, and continue 1.9 miles to a T intersection. Turn right toward the signed Coyote Canyon dirt road (pavement ends here) and follow the main dirt road 2.1 miles to the Upper Coyote Canyon Road sign on a hill. Park here and walk about 0.1 mile down rough Coyote Canyon Rd. to the PCT road crossing. The trail to Table Mountain takes off to the left, heading north.

The hike: Anza-Borrego park contains six long segments of the Pacific Crest Trail (PCT), which are separated from one another by major road crossings or by stretches of the trail that extend outside the park boundary. It is the opinion of the authors that the four park segments of the PCT from

Pioneer Mail north to the Lost Valley Road either run too close to major roads for quality backcountry hiking, or are too long and dry for most destination-oriented day hikers. In contrast, the two remote northern segments presented here are split only by the rough Coyote Canyon Road, offering varied hiking opportunities in a scenic region of higher mountains and deep canyons.

The two PCT hikes described below are presented together because they are in close proximity along what is essentially the same stretch of the PCT. With a car shuttle it would be possible to take a 12-mile point-to-point day hike from Lost Valley Road north to Coyote Canyon Rd., which is the take-off for the out-and-back hike north to Table Mountain.

SOUTHERN SEGMENT

The PCT trailhead on the Lost Valley Road is 2 miles east of the park boundary sign. The PCT road crossing is faintly marked on a wooden post, along with a "Riverside County Line 6" sign. From the road hike left (north) on the PCT, which maintains a moderate grade along the eastern slopes of Bucksnort Mountain. After 1.9 miles of climbing along the steep side slopes, the trail comes to a small level saddle at 5,595 feet to the immediate northeast of Combs Peak—the apex of Bucksnort Mountain. Pause among the Coulter pines here for a 180-degree view from lofty San Gorgonio Mountain to the north to the stark crest of the Santa Rosa Mountains and Salton Sea eastward. Coulter pine is also called "big-cone pine," and no wonder. It displays the heaviest cones of all pine species on the planet—each cone weighing in at 4 to 5 pounds!

To expand the field of view from 180 to 360 degrees, climb southeasterly to the summit of Combs Peak, gaining 600 feet in 0.6 mile. Route-finding through dense brush is required, but the view alone makes the effort worthwhile. Return the way you came to complete this 5-mile round-trip sampler of the PCT.

NORTHERN SEGMENT

From the crest of the hill at the Upper Coyote Canyon Road sign near the park boundary gate, walk down the rough four-wheel-drive Coyote Canyon Rd. about 0.1 mile to its intersection with the PCT. This stretch of the PCT is also part of the California Riding and Hiking Trail. Take the trail to the north (left) which is marked by a mountain lion warning sign. The trail descends a gully, switchbacks once, then drops to the grassy bottom of colorful Nance Canyon. A gradual grade wraps around a low knoll, then crosses a rugged slope that provides vistas to the east and south of Coyote and other secluded canyons in the wild northern reaches of the park.

The trail continues climbing to a 4,185-foot brush-covered notch on Table Mountain. The actual summit of the broad expanse of the mountain is only a 0.2-mile, 110-foot off-trail climb to the west, less than 0.5 mile south of the north boundary of the park. Most of this 5-mile round-trip route crosses alternate Bureau of Land Management sections of land included within the park's boundaries.

JOSHUA TREE NATIONAL PARK

Straddling the transition zone between the Mojave and the Colorado deserts, and containing vast regions of enchanting granite rock formations, Joshua Tree National Park is the smallest of the federal parks in Southern California, and also the closest to the Los Angeles metropolitan area—with the expanding cities of Palm Springs, Palm Desert, and Yucca Valley at its very doorstep. Intensifying pressures on this desert area's wildlands inspired the supporters of the California Desert Protection Act.

Joshua Tree was changed from a national monument to a national park by the 1994 act, and was enlarged from 559,995 to 794,000 acres. The act was but one chapter in the legislative history of the Joshua Tree park and its varying size and status. The area was originally set aside as a national monument by President Franklin D. Roosevelt in 1936. Early desert conservationists led by Minerva Hamilton Hoyt had pressed the White House for such protection due to the destructive impact of automobiles and visitors in the 1920s and 1930s, and the wholesale removal of Joshua trees and cacti to satisfy urban gardeners, as well as the ravages of mining.

By executive decree, FDR established Joshua Tree National Monument, protecting 825,000 acres from further mining development and placing it under National Park Service administration. In 1950, the pressures of the Cold War and the mining industry caused Congress to remove 289,000 acres from the monument. Again, in 1961, Congress reduced the boundary to permit mining in the monument's perimeter. The 1994 act expanded the new national park to 794,000 acres with additions in the Little San Bernadino Range on the southwest, the Pinto Mountains on the north, the Coxcombs on the east, the Eagle Mountains on the southeast, and the Cottonwoods on the south. Simultaneously the act enlarged the area designated as wilderness in 1976 by 35 percent, to 630,800 acres. Thus, 70 percent of the present national park is wilderness.

The new park is undertaking an ambitious management plan in order to both protect its desert lands and provide recreational opportunities for the millions of visitors who arrive annually. A key component of such overall management is a new wilderness management plan where trails, campsites, and area closures are studied and reviewed with the help of a citizen review committee. Currently there are only six official hiking trails and ten nature trails in the park. The multitude of hiking trails developed as use trails are being studied to determine which should become official trails. Concerns over preserving archaeological and historical sites, managing the recreation demands of bicyclists and rock climbers, protecting desert habitat—and the wildlife that lives here—are among the competing factors that need to be evaluated in the park's infancy. Since park rules may change quickly in such an atmosphere, check at the visitor center in Twentynine Palms or Cottonwood for current regulations and guidelines before embarking on a backcountry visit in Joshua Tree National Park.

A Joshua tree attains monumental proportions on the Pushwalla Plateau.

OVERVIEW MAP

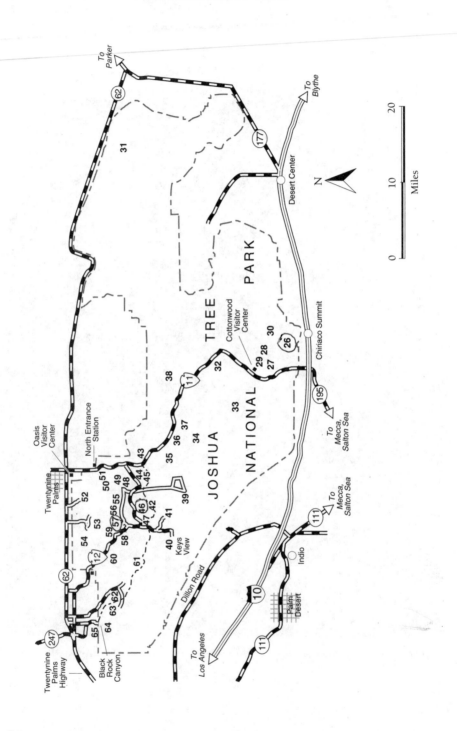

NATURAL HISTORY

Mountain ranges define the park's boundaries (the Little San Bernadinos, the Cottonwoods, the Eagles and Coxcombs, and the Pinto Mountains) and also dominate its center (the Hexies). The geologic feature that draws visitors, photographers, hikers, and climbers lies in the park's north-central section: the gargantuan monzogranite boulders, domes, and peaks. This ethereal landscape was formed over 180 million years, beginning with the earth's shifting plates and igneous intrusions from the earth's molten core. This activity took place beneath the earth's surface, which was covered by an immense inland sea. Eventually, rising mountain ranges altered climactic conditions, gradually reducing the sea. The former sea floor was forced upward. Lakes and rolling hills, grasslands and forests developed on the former ocean floor where mastodons, saber-toothed tigers, and other mammals roamed the land before their extinction. The pattern of lifting and eroding began creating Joshua Tree's canyons, rugged mountains, and exposed granite. Thousands of feet of layered sediment, volcanic ash, and metamorphic rock were eroded, producing Joshua Tree's well-known rounded granite topography. Geologic forces continue to modify Joshua Tree with weathering and the constant shifting of the earth's unstable crust.

PLANTS AND ANIMALS

Hiking in Joshua Tree National Park will quickly reveal the contrasts between Colorado and Mojave desert vegetation. Around the Cottonwood Ranger Station and in the Pinto Basin, creosote, ocotillo, sagebrush, and cholla are the dominant vegetative types in the lower, drier, and hotter Colorado Desert. In the Mojave desert, ranging from 3,000 to 6,000 feet in elevation and receiving 6 to 8 inches of rainfall per year, there is a virtual explosion of vegetation: pinyon-juniper forests on mountain slopes, smoke trees and mesquite with desert mistletoe in the washes, Joshua tree forests on the valley floors with manzanita, catclaw, and brittlebush, and the everpresent creosote bush.

Five desert oases are also found in Joshua Tree. These islands of native California fan palms have attracted animal and human visitors for centuries and remain magnets for wildlife and bird watchers today.

The preservation of the unique and fragile desert community of plants was one of the leading motivations in the establishment of Joshua Tree monument in the 1930s as well as the California Desert Protection Act of 1994. Joshua trees, the enchanting symbol of the park, are slow growers. This member of the agave family takes hundreds of years to reach its mature height of 30 feet. Joshua trees are shallow rooted, and thus susceptible to both wind and theft. They are now protected by federal law, as are all plants in the park.

The annual blooming of desert wildflowers occurs primarily from March through May depending on the weather and elevation. Several organizations provide flower information for the entire desert area on hotlines: Living

Desert, (619) 340-0435; the Mojave Native Plant Society, (702) 648-2177; and the Payne Foundation, (818) 768-3533. The Joshua Tree Natural History Association's pamphlet "Pollen on your Nose" ($0.25) is an illustrated guide to wildflowers, useful for changing the novice into a knowledgeable wildflower enthusiast.

Desert animal life here is predominantly nocturnal and usually invisible to the human eye. In Joshua Tree, coyotes are plentiful. Park officials are concerned with this omnivore's habituation to humans and their food, especially around the established campgrounds. Visitors are cautioned not to feed coyotes and to secure their food and garbage to prevent coyote theft. Jackrabbits, kangaroo rats, golden eagles, and yucca night lizards may be spotted going about their business of surviving in the desert. The widely acclaimed desert tortoise, listed as threatened under the Endangered Species Act, also lives here in the Mojave Desert. The tortoise's primary enemies (after vehicles) are ravens, whose population has skyrocketed. Hikers lucky enough to see one of these rare turtles can appreciate its presence from afar. All wildlife in the park is protected by federal law. No hunting or collecting is allowed.

The park has a diverse population of birds, many of whom are transients since the area is on a major migration route. For example, even here in the desert, herons and ducks can be seen on the Barker Dam Lake on their spring or fall trips. With more than 230 species on the checklist, birding in Joshua Tree National Park is exciting. The Natural History Association has published a birder's checklist with information on each species, available for $0.25.

HUMAN HISTORY

Ten thousand years ago, early humans found conditions in the Pinto Basin with its verdant meadows and slow river ideal for their hunting-and-gathering, semi-nomadic lifestyle. Little is known of post-glacial Pinto Man, however, since he traveled light and left no artifacts, only traces of habitation sites.

Serrano, Chemehuevi, and Cahuilla groups of Native Americans from the Great Basin and Colorado River to the east occupied the Joshua Tree area in small bands at the time of the European arrival in the 1700s. Their nomadic lives centered on the oases. They used a wide variety of desert plants as food and medicine. The Cottonwood Spring Nature Trail provides interesting information on these materials and Cahuilla use of desert products. These early groups hunted with bow and arrow and created pottery. They left behind petroglyphs, pictographs, and *morteros* at various sites in the park. All archaeological sites are protected by federal law; do not remove or deface any artifacts. Please leave them for future generations to enjoy.

American interest in this desert region began with miners in the 1860s. The intense search for and development of mineral resources was to continue for the following century. Due to abnormally wet winters in the 1880s, ranchers soon followed to build watering tanks and establish cattle herds on the sparse grasslands of Joshua Tree's higher valleys. Mining excitement continued, with numerous booms and consequent busts, but ranching faded as a profitable lifestyle when more normal precipitation returned in the early 1900s. Most of the barriers built to hold water, called tanks, have been erased as sand and sediment have filled in the reservoirs behind the crude dams. Barker Dam Lake is one exception; the others are vanishing into the desert. The Keys Ranch, a private inholding within the park, is a reminder of the ranching heyday in the desert. On the other hand, conspicuous mine sites, mills, mining equipment, and prospectors' dwellings are ubiquitous here. All mine shafts are considered dangerous and should be avoided by visitors. The vast majority have not been secured and are hazardous.

REGULATIONS

With the recent expansion and upgrade to national park status, coupled with federal budget reductions, the park administration is evaluating policies and programs to meet the dual goal of preservation and recreation. Check at the visitor center for updated regulations before embarking on your hike.

The entrance fee for Joshua Tree National Park is currently $5 for a seven-day pass. A $25 Golden Eagle Pass entitles you to unlimited park entrance at any national park for one year. Fee stations are located at all major park entrances.

There are nine campgrounds in the park. Elsewhere, camping is permitted at least 1 mile from a road, and 500 feet from any trail. Large sections of the park have been designated day-use only areas in order to protect access to water for desert wildlife, especially bighorn sheep. These Special Resource Protection Zones are currently in the Wonderland of Rocks/Queen Mountain/Fortynine Palms Canyon region in the north; northwest of Keys View in the central region; around the Pushwalla Plateau in the south; in a portion of the Coxcomb Mountains on the eastern end; and near Lost Palm Oasis in the southeast. If your plans include backcountry camping, be sure to check at a ranger station for the current day-use only boundaries, some of which may be changed as a result of backcountry plan revisions and wildlife requirements.

Gathering of firewood, or of any vegetation, is forbidden throughout the park. Ground fires are allowed only in established fire-rings in the campgrounds.

Backcountry campers must begin their trips at backcountry trail boards. Overnight parking is allowed only at these locations, since cars may not be left overnight elsewhere on the park roads. Campers must register at these boards before their trips. It is also suggested that day hikers register, for safety as well as for the park's statistical use.

Bicycles, like all vehicles, must remain on designated roads. To accommodate greater bike use, the park contemplates providing additional biking opportunities in the expansion areas of former BLM lands on the southern side of the Little San Bernadino and Cottonwood mountains.

Dogs and other pets must remain within 100 yards of roads and campgrounds, and must be leashed at all times. As in the case of all the desert parks, it is strongly recommended that all pets, especially dogs, be left at home. They are not adapted for the desert; the indigenous animal population does not appreciate them either.

The presence of private inholdings is a challenge for park administration. Boundaries are generally posted. Hikers must respect private property in their travels by closing gates and staying off private land when posted.

With the management of Joshua Tree in transition, it is wise to stop at the visitor station or a ranger station to get updated regulations and information on park policies. The visitor centers in Twentynine Palms and at the Cottonwood entrance have excellent maps, brochures, and books, as well as knowledgeable staff. Information on weather and road conditions is also essential for successful hiking in Joshua Tree National Park.

HOW AND WHEN TO GET THERE

Joshua Tree National Park is bounded on the south by Interstate 10. The Cottonwood entrance to the park is 65 miles west of Blythe and 52 miles east of Palm Springs. California Highway 62 (Twentynine Palms Highway) curves along the park's northern boundary. There are two entrances on the north: the West Entrance south of the town of Joshua Tree and the North Entrance south of Twentynine Palms. The latter is the location of the park's visitor center.

For air travel, the closest airport is at Palm Springs. Other commercial air facilities are in Riverside and Los Angeles, 100 and 150 miles west of the park respectively.

Daytime temperatures at Joshua Tree average around 100 degrees during June, July, August, and September. Comfortable hiking weather predominates during the rest of the year, although it can get toasty as early as May. July and August frequently bring brief thunderstorms; rain also occurs in December and January. Weather charts are not reliable, however. In February we experienced rain, snow, AND hot weather, so desert hikers need to be prepared for a variety of climatic conditions.

JOSHUA TREE NATIONAL PARK HIKES AT A GLANCE

Hike (Number)	Distance		Difficulty	Feature	Page
Arch Rock Nature Trail (43)	0.3	mile	E	Geology	143
Barker Dam (57)	1.1	miles	E	Hist. Site, Archeology	173
Black Rock Loop (63)	10.5	miles	S	Vista	193
Boy Scout Trail (59)	12.0	miles	M	Wash, Boulders	177
California R & H Trail:					
Covington to Keys View (61)	15.0	miles	S	Highest Peak	185
Keys View to Park Rte. 11 (42)	11.0	miles	M	Vista	138
Cap Rock Nature Trail (47)	0.4	mile	E	Nature Trail	151
Cholla Cactus Garden Nat. Tr. (37)	0.25	mile	E	Nature Trail	124
Contact Mine (51)	3.4	miles	MS	Mine Site	160
Cottonwood Spring/					
Morten's Mill (27)	1.0	mile	E	Oasis, Mill Site	94
Cottonwood Spring					
Nature Trail (29)	2.0	miles	E	Nature Trail	98
Covington Loop (62)	7.4	miles	M	Mine Site, Canyon	189
Coxcomb Mountains (31)	7.0	miles	M	Vista	103
Crown Prince Lookout (45)	3.0	miles	E	Vista	147
Desert Queen Mine–Wash (49)	4.0	miles	M	Mine Sites	154
Fortynine Palms Oasis (52)	3.0	miles	M	Oasis	162
Golden Bee Mine (34)	4.0	miles	MS	Mine Site	115
Hexahedron Mine (35)	8.4	miles	M	Mine Site	118
Hidden Valley Nature Trail (58)	1.0	mile	E	Nature Trail	175
High View Nature Trail (64)	1.3	miles	E	Nature Trail	196
Indian Cove Nature Trail (54)	0.6	mile	E	Nature Trail	167
Keys View/Inspiration Peak (40)	1.5	miles	M	Vista	131
Lost Horse Mine Loop (41)	7.0	miles	MS	Mine Site, Vista	134
Lost Palms Oasis (26)	8.8	miles	M	Oasis	91
Lucky Boy Vista (48)	2.5	miles	E	Vista	152
Mastodon Peak Loop (28)	3.0	miles	M	Mine, Mill Sites	96
Pine City (50)	3.4	miles	E	Mine Site	157
Pine City Canyon (50)	6.5	miles	MS	Canyon	157
Pleasant Valley/					
El Dorado Mine (36)	7.7	miles	M	Mine Site	121
Porcupine Wash/					
Ruby Lee Mill Site (32)	8.5	miles	M	Wash, Mill Site	107
Monument Mountain (33)	13.0	miles	S	Wash, Peak	110
Pushwalla Plateau/Canyon (39)	7.6	miles	MS	Vista, Canyon	127
Quail Wash (60)	8.2	miles	M	Vista	181
J. Lang Canyon (60)	14.2	miles	MS	Hist. Sites	181
Ryan Mountain (46)	3.0	miles	MS	Vista	149
Sand Dunes (38)	2.5	miles	E	Sand Dunes	125
Skull Rock Nature Trail (44)	1.7	miles	E	Nature Trail	145
Sneakeye Spring (53)	1.0	mile	MS	Canyon	164
South Park Peak Loop (65)	0.8	mile	M	Vista	198
Wall St. Mill (55)	1.5	miles	E	Mill Site	168
Wonderland Wash (56)	2.0	miles	E	Boulders	171

JOSHUA TREE NATIONAL PARK
TOPO MAP INDEX

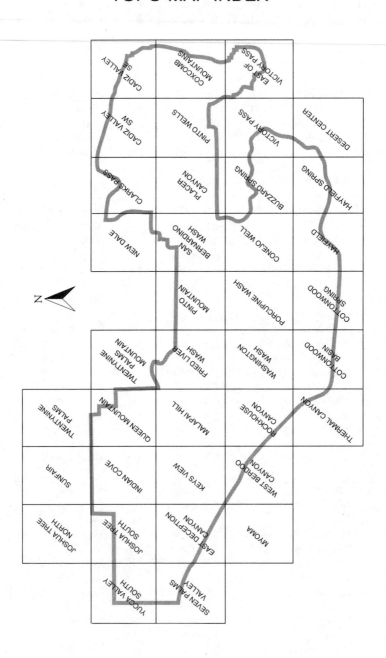

General description:	A moderate out-and-back day hike to an oasis, or an extended trip to Victory Palms.
Length:	8.4 miles out-and-back (overlook); 8.8 miles to oasis floor; additional 1 mile in to Victory Palms.
General location:	42 miles southeast of Twentynine Palms, and 30 miles northeast of Indio, southern Joshua Tree National Park, southeastern California.
Trail condition:	Clear trail.
Special attractions:	Oasis with largest group of California fan palms in Joshua Tree National Park.
Difficulty:	Moderate.
Best season:	October through April.
Starting elevation:	3,000 feet.
Maximum elevation:	3,440 feet.
Elevation gain/loss:	590 feet/690 feet.
USGS topo map:	Cottonwood Spring-CA (1:24,000).
For more information:	Joshua Tree National Park (see Appendix D).

Key points:

0.0   Trail begins above the oasis at Cottonwood Spring. Well-marked trail goes up wash and over ridge.

0.9   Signed junction with Mastodon Peak Trail on the right. Continue straight to oasis.

2.1   Trail descends to wash, then rises to another ridge.

3.0   Another descent down narrow crumbly ridge to wash before rising to the final ridge.

4.2   Overlook of palm oasis in canyon.

4.4   Floor of oasis.

5.4   Victory Palms

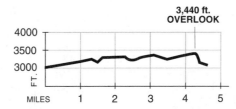

Finding the trailhead: From California Highway 62 in Twentynine Palms, take Utah Trail south 4 miles to the north entrance of the park; continue south on Park Route 12 4.8 miles to the Pinto Y intersection. Turn left onto Park Route 11, and go 32 miles to Cottonwood Visitor Center. Turn left 1.5 miles to Cottonwood Spring parking area.

From the south, take Cottonwood Canyon exit from I-10, 24 miles east of Indio. Go north 8 miles to Cottonwood Visitor Center. Turn right, and go 1.5 miles to Cottonwood Spring parking area.

LOST PALMS OASIS

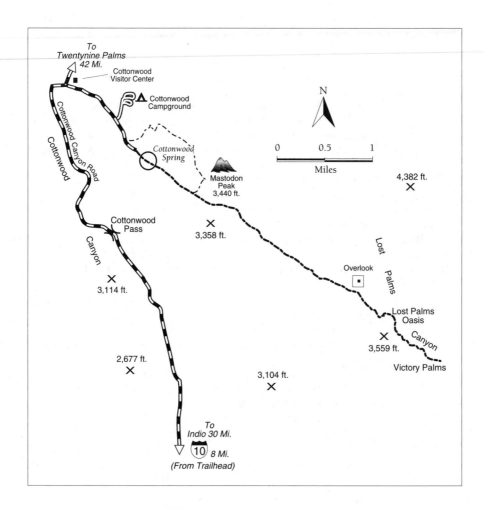

The hike: This is a dry, high hike with no protection from sun and wind. It is a heavily signed route, with arrows at every bend and every wash-crossing, and even mileage posts.

The trail follows the up-and-down topography of the ridge-and-wash terrain. At each ridge, one hopes to spot the oasis ahead, particularly if it is a hot and sunny day. Not until the final overlook will such hopes be realized. And after crossing numerous ridges, descending rocky paths to narrow canyons, and winding up to more ridges, it is a welcome sight!

This is the largest group of California fan palms in Joshua Tree National Park, and they are majestic. The oasis is a day-use only area to protect big-horn sheep access to water; you may be lucky enough to spot one of the elusive animals on the rocky slopes above the oasis.

The grove at Lost Palm Oasis extends for 0.5 mile down the valley.

A rocky path leads 0.2 mile from the overlook to the oasis. Large boulders, pools of water, intermittent streams, willow thickets, and sandy beaches make this a delightful spot in which to pause. The more energetic hiker may like to continue down the canyon through the willows and around the pools, along an intermittent rusty pipe that was used to channel water to a mining site far to the south. The trail becomes more challenging, with larger boulders to contend with. When your rock-scrambling is satisfied, it is time to return to the oasis, and retrace your steps to the spring.

General description:	A short hike in Cottonwood wash to visit a 1930s mill site.
Length:	1 mile round-trip.
General location:	About 42 miles southeast of Twentynine Palms and 30 miles northeast of Indio, in the southern section of Joshua Tree National Park, southeastern California.
Trail condition:	Clear wash.
Special attractions:	Cottonwood Spring, old mining road, mine site.
Difficulty:	Easy.
Best season:	October through April.
Starting elevation:	3,000 feet.
Maximum elevation:	3,000 feet.
Elevation gain/loss:	None/200 feet.
USGS topo map:	Cottonwood Spring-CA (1:24,000).
For more information:	Joshua Tree National Park (see Appendix D).

Key points:

0.0	Parking lot; take ramp down to oasis.
0.1	After enjoying the spring area, continue south in the wash.
0.25	Boulders block the easy wash; to the right is a section of road constructed by miners in the 1880s. This is Little Chilcoot Pass.
0.5	Morten's Mill site, with trailpost in the center of the wash. Turnaround point.

Finding the trailhead: From Twentynine Palms, take Utah Trail south 4 miles from California Highway 62 to the North Entrance of the Park. Continue south on Park Route 12 for 4.8 miles to left turn on Park Route 11 at the Pinto Y intersection (signed for Cottonwood Spring). Drive south 32 miles to Cottonwood Spring campground and visitor center. Turn left and drive 1.2 miles to the parking area. The oasis is down the ramp to the southeast; you can see the palm trees from the parking lot.

From the south, take I-10 24 miles east of Indio to the Cottonwood Canyon exit; turn north and continue 8 miles to the Cottonwood campground and visitor center. Turn right and drive 1.2 miles to the parking area.

The hike: Cottonwood Spring is a lovely patch of greenery in an otherwise arid landscape. The cottonwoods and fan palms were planted by the miners around the turn of the last century to make the spring conform to their concept of an oasis. In spite of this unnatural beginning, the sight is satisfying, and obviously the birds enjoy the location.

The hike down the wash provides a display of a wash plant community in the Colorado Desert. Mesquite and smoke trees are dominant.

COTTONWOOD SPRING/MORTEN'S MILL SITE
• MASTODON PEAK LOOP
• COTTONWOOD SPRING NATURE TRAIL

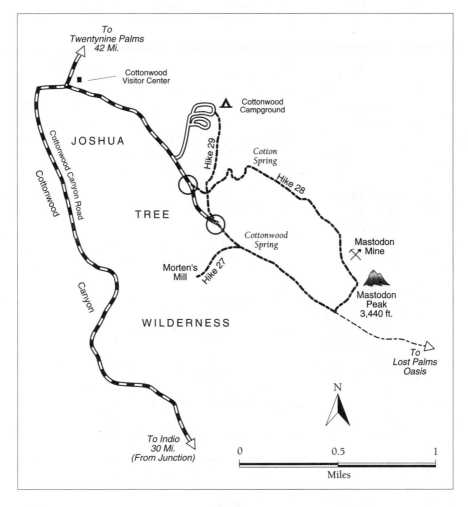

The ramp around the boulders in the wash will be quite a surprise. The determination of the miners of the last century to use this route for their vehicles is noteworthy. The ramp is massive, yet even with it in place, the trek up or down the wash must have been arduous with a loaded wagon.

Seeing the mill site will cure any thoughts of romanticizing the life of the prospector in these parts. Although the wash is lovely for its solitude and silence, living here must have been grim. "Cactus" Slim Morten (or Moorten) was here for fewer than ten years. All that remains of his mill are pieces of rusty equipment and rusting car parts.

The hike back up the wash brings you back to the oasis, which looks greener than ever after a sojourn into drier country.

General description:	A loop hike from the Cottonwood Spring Oasis to nearby Mastodon Mine, Winona Mill, and Mastodon Peak.
Length:	3-mile loop.
General location:	42 miles southeast of Twentynine Palms, or 30 miles northeast of Indio, southern Joshua Tree National Park, southeastern California.
Trail condition:	Clear trail.
Special attraction:	Spring, historic mine and mill site, monzogranite mound.
Difficulty:	Easy; moderate if the peak is included. The peak requires some scrambling, but provides excellent views.
Starting point:	3,000 feet.
Maximum elevation:	3,440 feet (Mastodon Peak).
Elevation gain/loss:	440 feet/440 feet.
USGS topo map:	Cottonwood Spring-CA (1:24,000).
For more information:	Joshua Tree National Park (see Appendix D).

See Map on Page 95

Key points:
0.0-0.2 Parking area. Take nature trail.
   0.2 Junction with Mastodon Peak Trail; turn right and immediately encounter the Winona mill ruins and Cotton Spring.
   0.3 Uphill to mine site.
   1.0 Mastodon Mine. Trail continues above the mine.
   1.1 Junction. Left to peak (0.1 round-trip).
   1.6 Junction with Lost Palm Oasis Trail. Turn right to return to parking area.
   2.6 Cottonwood Spring. Continue up ramp to parking area.

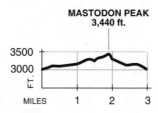

Finding the trailhead: From California Highway 62 in Twentynine Palms, take Utah Trail south 4 miles to the North Entrance of park; continue on Park Route 12 4.8 miles to Pinto Y. Turn left onto Park Route 11 and go south 32 miles to Cottonwood Visitor Center. Turn left and go 1.5 miles to the oasis.

From the south, take the Cottonwood Canyon exit from I-10 24 miles east of Indio; go north 8 miles to Cottonwood Visitor Center, then right (east)

Granite boulders, common throughout Joshua Tree National Park, lie in enormous piles on the Mastodon Peak trail on the southern edge of the park.

1.5 miles to Cottonwood Spring parking lot. Walk west from the parking lot, back up the road, 0.1 mile to beginning of nature trail on your right. Walk up the nature trail 0.3 mile to junction with Mastodon Peak route. From the Cottonwood Campground, the trail begins 0.2 mile from campsite 13A on loop A, via the nature trail segment which begins at the campground and meets at the same junction.

The hike: This trail takes you by two historical sites and a lofty overlook of the southern region of the park. Either approach to the trail includes the nature trail. The view of the old gold mill and the mine is in direct contrast with the Indians' use of the riches of the desert; the latter left no ruins or scars on the environment.

The trail is clearly marked with signposts and a rock-lined path. The lower section of the hike (0.0 to 0.2 mile) is up a sandy wash to the Winona mill site. Building foundations and other remnants are all that remain of the mill that refined the gold from the Mastodon mine in the 1920s. The exotic plant specimens at adjacent Cotton Spring were planted by the Hulsey family, who owned the mill and mine.

The trail winds up the hill above the mill to the mine, which was operated by George Hulsey between 1919 and 1932, when it was abandoned. Carefully thread your way up by the sign above the mine, and through the mine ruins (in direct contradiction of park warnings to stay clear of old mines) to a trailpost and arrow pointing east. A major freeway-style sign indicates your options and the various distances to the spring, the oasis, and the peak from this point.

The climb to the peak (0.1 mile) is on an unsigned trail, although the well-used path is easy to discern, and cairns appear at critical spots. The use trail goes to the right of a boulder pile, across a slab of granite, and winds around to the northeast side of the peak to the summit, on the opposite side from the mine site. Minor boulder scrambling is necessary. The view is well worth the effort.

After the peak, the trail resumes its zigzag rocky path through the canyon, well-signed with arrows. It is on this portion of the trail that you can see clearly the elephant likeness in the peak behind you. About 0.5 mile after the peak is the intersection with the Lost Palms Oasis Trail (Hike 26). Turn right for the 1.1 mile walk down the winding trail to Cottonwood Spring and the parking lot. Turn left for the longer hike to Lost Palms Oasis (6.3 miles round-trip from this junction and back to the parking lot).

29 COTTONWOOD SPRING NATURE TRAIL

General description:	An easy out-and-back nature trail from a desert spring.
Length:	2 miles out-and-back.
General location:	42 miles southeast of Twentynine Palms and 30 miles northeast of Indio, southern portion of Joshua Tree National Park, southeastern California.
Trail condition:	Clear nature trail.
Special attraction:	Identification of desert plants and their use by Native Americans.
Difficulty:	Easy.
Best season:	October through April.
Starting elevation:	2,900 feet.
Maximum elevation:	3,000 feet.
Elevation gain/loss:	100 feet/none.
USGS topo map:	Cottonwood Spring-CA (1:24,000).
For more information:	Joshua Tree National Park (see Appendix D).

See Map on Page 95

Finding the trailhead: From California Highway 62 in Twentynine Palms, take Utah Trail south 4 miles to North Entrance; continue south on Park Route 12 4.8 miles to Pinto Y. Turn left onto Park Route 11 and go 32 miles to Cottonwood Spring Visitor Center. Turn left and go 1.2 mile to Cottonwood Spring parking area. Walk 0.1 mile west along the road to the nature trail on your right. The trail also begins at the eastern ends of loops A and B in the campground and goes to Cottonwood Spring. If you're not camping there, however, it is not possible to park at the campground. From the south, take Cottonwood Canyon exit from Interstate 10, 24 miles east of Indio, and drive north 8 miles to Cottonwood Spring Visitor Center. Turn right and go 1.2 mile to the parking area.

The hike: The broad clear trail leads up a wash from the road near the spring, eventually winding up to a low ridge leading to the campground. This is one of the most informative nature trails in the park. The signs are legible and placed with the appropriate plant, and highly educational.

The information on this nature trail identifies the plants common to this region of the Colorado (Sonoran) Desert. The unique focus of the signs is on the Cahuilla Indians' use of the plants for food, medicine, and household goods. A Cahuilla elder provided the information. The detailed explanations of the processes used by the original inhabitants create genuine admiration for their sophistication. Several of the plants originally developed by the Indians are now grown and marketed commercially, such as creosote tea and jojoba.

If you choose to continue on to the Mastodon Peak trail (Hike 27), that intersection is halfway down the nature trail (at 0.5 mile) from its northern end. Or you can walk back down to the parking lot, reviewing the new information you have learned.

30 *CONEJO WELL/EAGLE MOUNTAINS*

General description:	A long but gently graded walk across open Colorado Desert, through a gap in the remote Eagle Mountains, to the remains of a historic well site.
Length:	12 miles round-trip.
General location:	About 42 miles southeast of Twentynine Palms and 30 miles northeast of Indio, in south-central Joshua Tree National Park, southeastern California.
Trail condition:	Clear troad/wash.
Special attractions:	Canyon, well site.
Difficulty:	Moderate.
Best season:	October through April.
Starting elevation:	3,000 feet.
Maximum elevation:	3,440 feet.
Elevation gain/loss:	700 feet/340 feet.
USGS topo maps:	Porcupine Wash-CA; Conejo Well-CA; and Cottonwood Spring-CA (1:24,000).
For more information:	Joshua Tree National Park (see Appendix D).

Key points:

- 0.0   Troad gradually climbs from the trailhead
- 3.0   Trail begins gentle ascent to the high point of 3,440 feet; possible cross-country route to Eagle Peak
- 4.5   Troad crosses a prominent northeast-southwest trending wash
- 5.3   Trail junction with troad to Conejo Well taking off to the right (south)
- 6.0   Conejo Well site

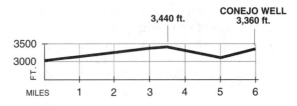

Finding the trailhead: From California Highway 62 in Twentynine Palms, take Utah Trail south 4 miles to the park's North Entrance; continue south on Park Route 12 4.6 miles to Pinto Y. Bear left onto Park Route 11 and drive 32 miles south to Cottonwood Spring Visitor Center. Turn left and go 1 mile to the campground. The trail begins at site 17 on the B loop. From the south, take Cottonwood Canyon exit north from Interstate 10, 24 miles east of Indio; go north 8 miles to Cottonwood Spring Visitor Center. Turn right, and go 1 mile to the campground/trailhead.

Eagle Peak as seen from the cutoff trail to Conejo Well site.

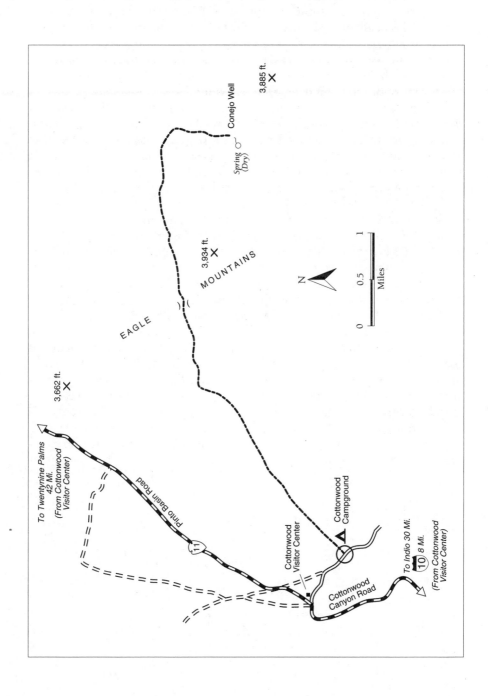

The hike: This clear, well-defined trail is actually a closed four-wheel-drive mining road managed as a hiking trail (a troad). It takes off in a north-easterly direction from the Cottonwood Campground. The first 100 yards pass a series of planted shrubs. The Eagle Mountains rise to the southeast above an alluvial fan coated with cholla, creosote, and yucca. The troad continues up a sandy wash marked every so often by rock cairns. At 0.5 mile the wash splits; stay left. The old two-track is plainly visible for the most part continuing in a nearly straight line.

At 2 miles the troad cuts north and crosses a large rock-walled wash. For the next 0.5 mile it crosses several side washes and small ridges. At this point it is heading northeast toward a broad sloping pass through the north end of the Eagle Mountains. For a strenuous side climb to 5,350-foot Eagle Peak, leave the troad at around mile 3 for a good approach. Look for a broad ridge leading to the south for a route to this apex of the Eagle Mountain Range.

At mile 3 (3,380 feet) California juniper become more prevalent along with denser clumps of yucca. The troad tops the broad pass at 3,440 feet then follows a wide wash through a gap in the Eagle Mountains, with Eagle Peak rising ruggedly to the south. The junction to the Conejo Well site takes off to the right (south) at 5.3 miles in a garden of cholla. This junction is easy to miss but it is marked by a rock cairn.

The Conejo Well trail takes off at a 45-degree angle to the right up the left side of a swale in a patch of brittlebush heading south toward a rugged canyon on the north side of Eagle Mountain. After another 0.5 mile it enters the mouth of a narrow rocky canyon distinguished by columns of red rock jutting upward to the slopes of Eagle Mountain. The old mining road climbs another 0.2 mile to the well site, where only a few rusted pipes and cans are found. Depending on the light a shallow cave appears to overlook the well site 0.3 mile upslope. In fact, the dark opening is merely a shallow rock overhang. Retrace your route to complete this 12-mile round-trip exploration of remote Colorado Desert country.

31 COXCOMB MOUNTAINS

General description:	An out-and-back day hike or overnight trip into the wildest and most remote corner of the park with hidden basins, expansive vistas, and jagged jumbles of granite in every direction.
Length:	7 miles round-trip.
General location:	About 45 miles east of Twentynine Palms, in northeastern Joshua Tree National Park, southeastern California.
Trail condition:	Clear washes with moderate bouldering at the mouth of the canyon.
Special attractions:	A profound feeling of solitude combined with the spirit of exploration in a remote, scenic canyon bounded by rugged peaks and rock formations.
Difficulty:	Moderate for the suggested route; peak climbing in this region is strenuous.
Best season:	October through May.
Starting elevation:	2,640 feet.
Maximum elevation:	3,090 feet (overlook of Pinto Basin).
Elevation gain/loss:	810 feet/360 feet.
USGS topo maps:	Cadiz Valley SW-CA and Cadiz Valley SE-CA (1:24,000).
For more information:	Joshua Tree National Park (see Appendix D).

Key points:
- 0.0   Mouth of canyon (2,640 feet).
- 0.0-0.3   Boulder scrambling.
- 0.8   Pass (2,970 feet).
- 1.7   Side wash enters from the southeast; continue up this wash.
- 2.5   Inner valley.
- 3.5   Overlook of the Pinto Basin (3,090 feet).

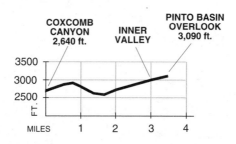

Finding the trailhead: From Twentynine Palms, at the traffic light junction of Twentynine Palms Highway and Adobe Road, drive east on California Highway 62 (Twentynine Palms Highway) 41.9 miles to an unsigned sandy dirt road, which is also 1.9 miles east of a parking turnout. This is a difficult road to find, so watch carefully. Turn right (south) and drive 4.5 miles

COXCOMB MOUNTAINS

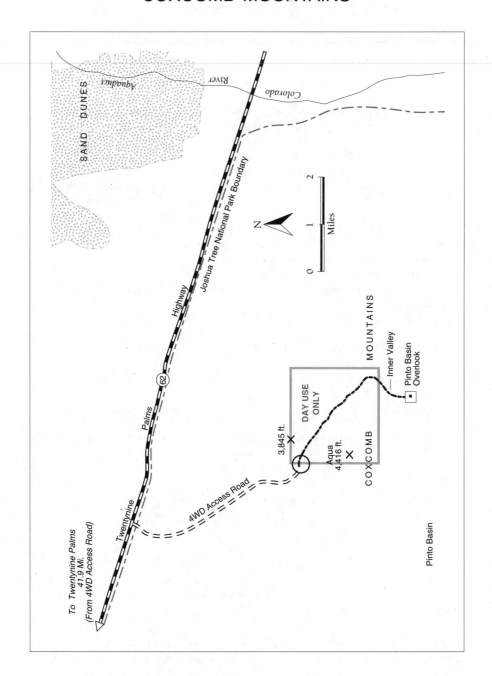

Looking southeast toward the Inner Valley.

southeasterly to the end of the road at the canyon mouth. Four-wheel drive is recommended due to the soft sand road surface. It is advisable to stop 0.5 mile before the end of the road and park to the right on firm ground above the wash. The final 0.5 mile is in a deep sandy wash and there is no place to park outside of the wash at the canyon entrance.

The hike: The Coxcombs are likely the most rugged and perpendicular mountains in Joshua Tree National Park, in its wildest and least-visited northeast corner. Their relative isolation alone, far from any services, makes their exploration a true wilderness experience. The recommended starting point for this hike provides the easiest access into the Coxcombs. It is also the only road access from the north, the other being from the south at Pinto Wells.

The mouth of the canyon is blocked by huge boulders, a somewhat formidable beginning to this otherwise moderate hike. Begin by taking a use trail to the right up and around the first set of boulders. The remaining boulders are easy to scramble over and around for the next 0.25 mile to where the sandy wash opens up and provides easy walking. The open wash also provides magnificent views of the rugged Coxcombs, especially to the right (south-southwest) with their great slanting blocks and vertical columns of reddish rock.

At 0.5 mile (2,840 feet) the wash splits; stay to the left and continue southeast up the smaller of the two washes. At 0.8 mile (2,970 feet) the first low pass is reached. Continue to the southeast on a faint use trail which drops down a series of small ridges and gullies toward the large wash seen far in the distance. Cathedral-like rock spires tower overhead. At 1 mile (2,840 feet) the rocky confines of a rocky wash is reached. At 1.4 miles (2,650 feet) the wash widens, joined by another wash from the right, with spectacular vistas back to the northwest. Continue down another 0.3 mile (2,610 feet) to where the main wash turns sharply to the left (north). This canyon wash is worth exploring as a side trip if time permits. It leads north to northwest another 1.5 miles to a canyon entrance that opens to a broad alluvial fan on the north side of the mountains.

Return to the junction at mile 1.7. The side wash entering from the right (southeast) is the route to the Inner Valley. Hike southeasterly up this winding but widening wash. At 2.1 miles (2,720 feet) a wash enters from the right; continue to the left up the main wash. Soon the country opens up into the lower end of the Inner Valley—a vast plateaulike expanse of open desert ringed by jagged spires, mounds, and formations of white to red rocks in every conceivable shape. The wash bends around to the left and heads southwest up the broad alluvial fan of the upper reaches of the valley. The fan/wash rises gradually for another mile to a prominent pass at mile 3.5 (3,090 feet), which serves as a panoramic overlook of the vast desert of Pinto Basin to the south. Hold onto your hat; this is also a natural wind tunnel.

Retrace your route to complete this 7-mile round-trip. If you're planning to stay overnight, find a sheltered campsite in the upper valley near the overlook or in the lower east end of the valley outside the day use area that includes much of this route—the limit is meant to protect wildlife, including rare desert bighorns. There are many tantalizing opportunities for boulder scrambling and canyoneering on all sides of the Inner Valley, particularly into some of the larger side canyons bordering the east side of the valley near the overlook. Overnight backpackers would need to carry at least 2 gallons of water per person per day.

General description:	A moderate hike at the eastern edge of the Hexie Mountains in the south-central area of the park.
Length:	8.5-mile loop.
General location:	About 30 miles southeast of Twentynine Palms and 40 miles northeast of Indio, south-central Joshua Tree National Park, southeastern California.
Trail condition:	Good troad; clear wash.
Special attractions:	Mill site, wash.
Difficulty:	Moderate.
Best season:	October through April.
Starting elevation:	2,400 feet.
Maximum elevation:	3,160 feet.
Elevation gain/loss:	760 feet/760 feet.
USGS topo map:	Porcupine Wash-CA (1:24,000).
For more information:	Joshua Tree National Park (see Appendix D).

Key points:
0.0-0.2 Backcountry board; follow jeep troad to borrow pit southwest of parking area.

0.2 Angle northwest across alluvial fan. Troad heads toward low notch at far end of ridge to west.

1.5 Broad high point (2,750 feet) marked with cairn. Troad winds between granite boulders with periodic cairns.

2.8 Wash narrows and troad cuts between two boulder piles. Look for the small Ruby Lee Mill site, marked only with tailings, stone foundation, the usual debris, and a small sign etched on a boulder.

3.0 Troad bears south. Cairns mark the route.

3.4 Troad drops to Porcupine Wash. Follow wash left (east).

7.8 Beyond canyon, bear left; look for petroglyphs.

8.5 Parking area.

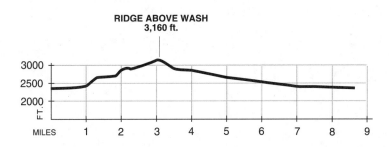

Finding the trailhead: From California Highway 62 in Twentynine Palms, take Utah Trail south 4 miles to North Entrance; continue on Park Route 12 4.6 miles to Pinto Y. Bear left onto Park Route 11, and go 21.3 miles south to Porcupine Wash Backcountry Board, on your right.

PORCUPINE WASH/RUBY LEE MILL SITE

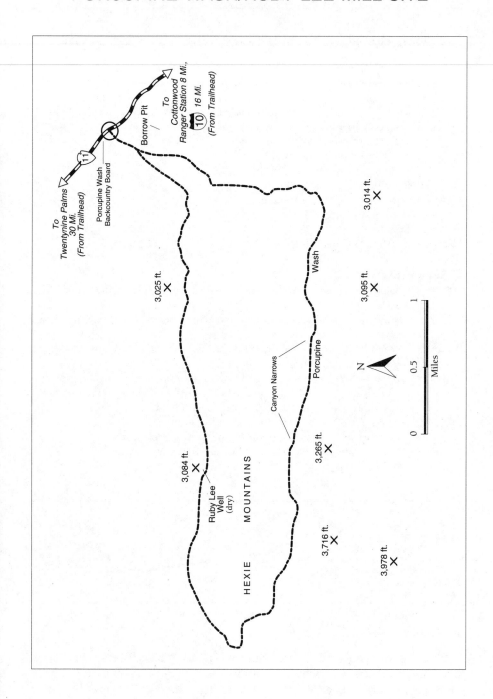

From the south, take Cottonwood Canyon exit from Interstate 10, 24 miles east of Indio. Go north 8 miles to Cottonwood Entrance. Continue north 8.9 miles to Porcupine Wash Backcountry Board, on your left.

The hike: With topo map in hand, you will enjoy this moderate hike. Although the directions make it sound extremely complex, this is a very straightforward hike. The troad is fairly visible; moreover, the ridge to the east and the Hexie Mountains to the south are permanent markers, so you won't lose your bearings. The granite formations here are imaginative. Porcupine Wash is especially artistic with its smoke trees and water-sculpted boulders. The small S-curve canyon midway down the wash displays the power of water in this arid environment.

The variety of desert topography and vegetation is especially striking. The boulder-strewn sloping alluvial fan of the first half of the hike displays the vegetation typical of the Colorado Desert. Cholla cactus and creosote dominate the landscape. Curving through the foothills of the Hexie Range and dropping to the wash you enter a new habitat, an active wash. The scouring action of flash flooding promotes the growth of smoke trees. The seeds require the grinding sands of floods to remove their protective covering in order to germinate, so instead of finding a water-swept wasteland you find a smoke tree paradise in the wash.

Porcupine Wash demonstrates a variety of wash architecture. Broad and narrow areas both exist, depending on the resistance of rock walls along the sides. The wash is wide at the junction with the Ruby Lee troad, but 2 miles farther east it becomes a slot canyon with narrow S-curves between the 200-foot-high walls. This narrow section lasts almost half a mile before the wash opens again.

The mill site dates from the mid-1930s. The mill's career must have been quite brief, judging from its size. Not much is left. This area of Joshua Tree was not productive for mining.

A petroglyph site is located near the mouth of the wash. The rock face upon which the signs are engraved is turned to the east. Clearly these messages are intended for travelers approaching the entrance of the wash, en route towards Monument Mountain, visible directly to the west. Their meaning, however, remains a mystery. As is the case with all archaeological and historic artifacts, these are protected by federal law. Leave them untouched for others to enjoy.

Emerging from the wash, bear left along the foot of the ridge. By heading north you will shortly see the parking area and backcountry board to the northeast, guiding you back to your car.

General description:	A long, strenuous point-to-point day hike or overnighter to the highest peak in the Hexie Range.
Length:	13 miles point-to-point (with car shuttle) or 6-mile round-trip to peak from the southern trailhead.
General location:	About 30 miles southeast of Twentynine Palms; 15.5 miles north of Interstate 10, in south-central Joshua Tree National Park, southeastern California.
Trail condition:	Clear wash use trail for 7.5 miles followed by 6.5 miles cross-country.
Special attractions:	Highest peak in Hexie Mountains, sweeping views.
Difficulty:	Strenuous, with some moderately difficult boulder scrambling.
Best season:	October through April.
Starting elevation:	2,390 feet.
Maximum elevation:	4,834 feet (Monument Mountain).
Elevation gain/loss:	2,550 feet/1,700 feet (point-to-point); 1,700 feet/1,700 feet (out-and-back).
Maps:	USGS Porcupine Wash-CA and Washington Wash-CA (1:24,000).
For more information:	Joshua Tree National Park (see Appendix D).

Key points:

0.0-0.2	Porcupine Wash Backcountry Board; head south past the borrow pit.
0.2-1.5	Continue south up Porcupine Wash.
1.5-2.5	Wash trail winds up a series of S-curves in a canyon.
2.5-4.5	Continue up wash.
4.5	Ruby Lee jeep trail enters wash from the right (north).
4.5-7.5	Continue up the wash into a broad basin.
7.5	Leave wash for cross-country route to Monument Peak.
10.0	Summit of Monument Peak.
13.0	Pinkham Road (point-to-point hike).

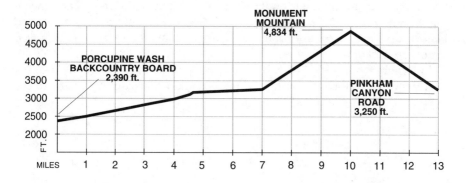

Finding the trailhead: From California Highway 62 in Twentynine Palms, take Utah Trail south 4 miles to North Entrance; continue on Park Route 12 4.6 miles to Pinto Y. Bear left onto Park Route 11 and drive 21.3 miles south to Porcupine Wash Backcountry Board, on your right. From the south, take Cottonwood Canyon exit north from I-10, 24 miles east of Indio. Go north 8 miles to Cottonwood Visitor Center; then continue north 8.9 miles to Porcupine Wash Backcountry Board, on your left.

For car shuttle: On Park Route 11, drive 8.9 miles south of the Porcupine Wash Backcountry Board to the Cottonwood Visitor Center. Turn right (north) on the four-wheel-drive Pinkham Road directly across the highway from the visitor center, and drive 5.2 miles to the dirt road turnout on your right. Park here for the point-to-point pickup or the round-trip climb to Monument Mountain.

The hike: From the backcountry board head almost due south past the borrow pit, staying close to a line of boulders to your right. Within 0.5 mile Porcupine Wash becomes well defined. After about 1.5 miles the wash bends gradually to the right in a westerly direction. Another mile will bring you into a canyon with a series of S-curves. The grade is gentle, and the open wash allows for easy going.

At 4.5 miles the remains of the old Ruby Lee Mill Road come into view as it meets Porcupine Wash from the north (right). Continue up the wash through a low canyon and into a broad basin, distinguished by increasingly dense yucca. The wash itself is lined with creosote bush and smoke trees. As the

Jackrabbit on the Ruby Lee trail.

PORCUPINE WASH TO MONUMENT MOUNTAIN

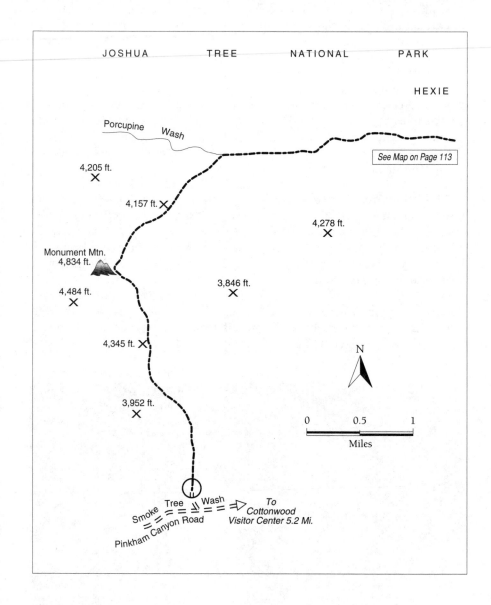

basin opens up the distinctive cone summit of Monument Peak can be seen on the skyline to the southwest.

Continue hiking up Porcupine Wash, passing a series of striking white rock columns at 5.2 miles. After another 0.1 mile the first large gully enters the main wash from the left. At 5.5 miles the remnants of the old overgrown four-wheel-drive road are visible on the right side of the canyon, but the

PORCUPINE WASH TO MONUMENT MOUNTAIN

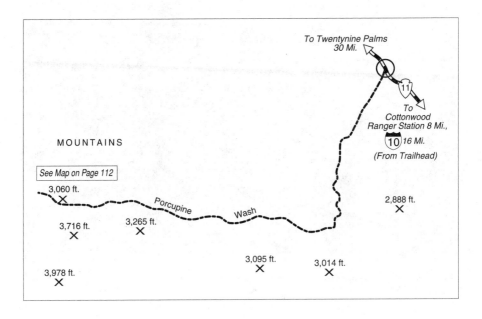

wash offers easier walking. At 5.6 miles Monument Mountain can be seen to the southwest.

At 5.9 miles a second major side canyon enters from the left. Stay to the right on a bearing toward Monument Mountain. The valley widens here with an increasing density of yucca.

At 7 miles the peak drops below the ridge to the south. Continue up the wash another 0.5 mile before cutting cross-country southward toward the first line of high ridges. The country is open with scattered catclaw, creosote, and yucca. Up on the ridge at about 3,950 feet, the summit will present itself—as well as a suitable route around a series of deep canyons leading to the north ridge. This ridge requires more rock scrambling than other possible routes to the east, but the approach is more direct with fewer ups and downs. Upon reaching the summit look for the peak register to learn of the experiences of previous climbers. More important, enjoy the spellbinding view with desert basins and ranges stretching as far as the eye can see.

For an out-and-back trip the route up can be retraced back to the Porcupine Wash Backcountry Board making for a long 20-mile day trip or a more reasonable overnight backpack with a night spent near Porcupine Wash if sufficient water is carried. To continue on a point-to-point route to Smoke Tree Wash on the Pinkham Road, take the southeast ridge for the shortest and easiest way down. The ridges and swales on the south side of the mountain are strewn with rugged outcrops of volcanic rock ribs that resemble

113

Looking down Porcupine Wash from where the troad crosses over from the Ruby Lee Mill site.

backbones of dinosaurs. There is some up-and-down and a bit of route-finding on this serpentine ridge, but avoid the temptation to drop off of it for a "shortcut." This prominent southeast ridge offers the best and most enjoyable means of covering 3 miles and losing 1,600 feet to Smoke Tree Wash. After descending the foot of the ridge, hike about 1 mile across the flat to the road and your waiting shuttle vehicle. This point can also be the start and end of a cross-country climb (6.5-mile out and back) to Monument Mountain.

General description:	A moderately strenuous hike to a historic mine site high in the Hexie Mountains.
Length:	4 miles round-trip.
General location:	18.6 miles south of Twentynine Palms, central Joshua Tree National Park, southeastern California.
Trail condition:	Clear troad/wash.
Special attraction:	High scenic overlook from a historic mine site.
Difficulty:	Moderately strenuous.
Best season:	October through April.
Starting elevation:	2,230 feet.
Maximum elevation:	2,900 feet.
Elevation gain/loss:	670 feet/670 feet.
USGS topo map:	Fried Liver Wash-CA (1:24,000).
For more information:	Joshua Tree National Park (see Appendix D).

Key points:

0.0   Unsigned trailhead on PR 11.

1.3   Troad crosses a wash and begins steep climb to mine.

2.0   Golden Bee Mine (2,900 feet).

The lofty vantage point of the Golden Bee Mine provides a stunning vista of Pinto Basin.

GOLDEN BEE MINE
• CHOLLA CACTUS GARDEN NATURE TRAIL

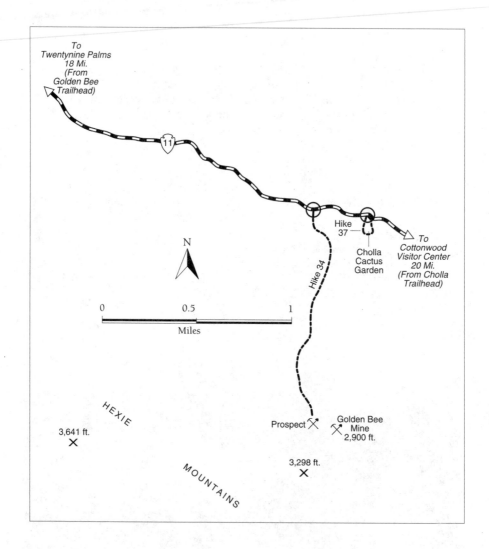

To
Twentynine Palms
18 Mi.
(From
Golden Bee
Trailhead)

11

Hike
37

Cholla
Cactus
Garden

To
Cottonwood
Visitor Center
20 Mi.
(From Cholla
Trailhead)

Hike 34

N

0   0.5   1

Miles

HEXIE

3,641 ft.
X

Prospect X

Golden Bee
Mine
2,900 ft.

3,298 ft.
X

MOUNTAINS

Finding the trailhead: From the park visitor center in Twentynine Palms go south on Utah Trail 8.2 miles to the Pinto Y. Bear left onto Park Route 11 and drive to milepost 10 just before the Cholla Cactus Garden Nature Trail. The trailhead is on the southeast side of PR 11, 0.25 mile northwest of the Cholla trail, where the troad is blocked off. This trailhead is 20 miles north of the Cottonwood Visitor Center and 18 miles south of the Oasis Visitor Center in Twentynine Palms.

The hike: The troad starts out on the south side of Park Route 11 next to a 25 mph speed limit sign and heads south between two small volcanic cones. For the first 1.3 miles the troad remains fairly level and is generally easy to follow. It crosses several washes marked by rock cairns. If you become temporarily lost, head toward the highest point on the southern horizon. In so doing, you'll eventually cross the troad when it becomes more distinct on the alluvial fan.

At 1.3 miles the troad crosses a wash and begins a steep 0.7-mile ascent to the mine. This extremely steep, rocky troad is washed out in a couple of places but well defined as a hiking route. From below, the uppermost mine site is hidden from view, but it sits in a notch in the left-hand (south) canyon. This 1930s mine contains a considerable amount of debris: metal, timbers, rusted pipe, rock walls, mine adits, tanks, and cable. Please do not disturb or remove any of these historic artifacts.

The mine is located near the top of a pass that drops southward into Fried Liver Wash. It provides a spectacular view to the north, particularly in the evening as the setting sun lights up Pinto Basin beneath the imposing mass of the Pinto Range.

General description:	A walk across an ancient dry lakebed, then a steep climb into the Hexie Mountains to sample the flavor of the historic mining era.
Length:	8.4 miles round-trip.
General location:	20 miles south of Twentynine Palms, in central Joshua Tree National Park, southeastern California.
Trail condition:	Clear troad/wash.
Special attractions:	Mine site, sweeping views of central park.
Difficulty:	Moderately strenuous.
Best season:	October through May.
Starting elevation:	3,250 feet.
Maximum elevation:	3,890 feet.
Elevation gain/loss:	770 feet/150 feet.
USGS topo map:	Malapai Hill-CA (1:24,000).
For more information:	Joshua Tree National Park (see Appendix D).

Key points:

0.0   Pleasant Valley Backcountry Board (3,250 feet).
0.3   Troad splits; stay to the right (east).
2.5   Fried Liver Wash fence crossing; go north.
2.8   Trail junction; take left-hand troad.
3.8   High point of the trail (3,890 feet).
4.2   Hexahedron Mine (3,870 feet).

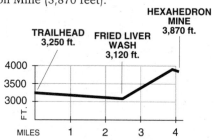

Finding the trailhead: From the park visitor center in Twentynine Palms go south on Utah Trail 8.2 miles to the Pinto Y. Stay to the right on Park Route 12 for 5.1 miles to the Geology Tour Road, which begins 15.1 miles southeast of the town of Joshua Tree. Turn left (south) on the Geology Tour Rd., which is signed "Squaw Tank" at the turnoff. The Pleasant Valley Backcountry Board/trailhead is on the left after 7.1 miles.

The hike: From the Pleasant Valley Backcountry Board this troad heads east in Pleasant Valley, along the foot of the Hexie Mountains across a dry lakebed. The rough-hewn Hexie Mountains rise to the immediate north. At 0.3 mile the trail splits; keep to the right. Old mine diggings can be seen on the hillside to the north. Soon the stark openness of the dry lakebed is moderated by a few Joshua trees near the trail.

HEXAHEDRON MINE

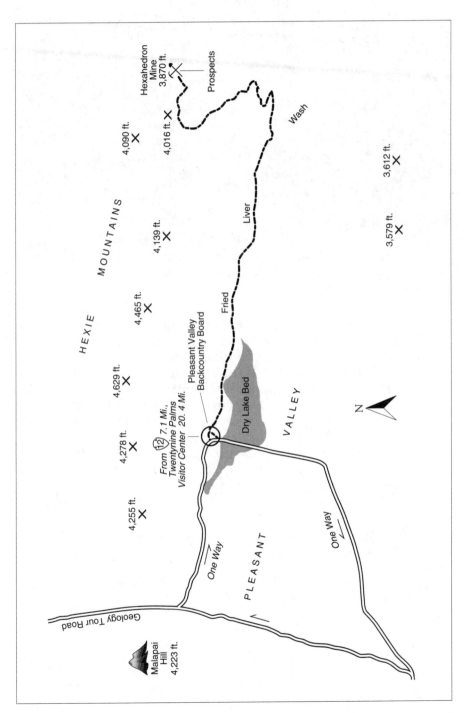

Hexahedron Mine
3,870 ft.

Prospects

4,090 ft.

4,016 ft.

Wash

3,612 ft.

M O U N T A I N S

4,139 ft.

Liver

3,579 ft.

H E X I E

4,465 ft.

Fried

4,629 ft.

Pleasant Valley
Backcountry Board

Dry Lake Bed

4,278 ft.

From (12) 7.1 Mi.,
Twentynine Palms
Visitor Center 20. 4 Mi.

V A L L E Y

4,255 ft.

N

One Way

One Way

Geology Tour Road

P L E A S A N T

Malapai
Hill
4,223 ft.

A roofless stone house stands guard near the Hexahedron Mine.

At 1.5 miles the trail passes a wooden post with no sign. The troad then enters the head of Fried Liver Wash, dropping very gradually to the southeast. A fence crosses the wash at 2.5 miles. Take a left here and follow the fence north for about 0.2 mile to an old iron gatepost where a troad continues uphill to the right. Follow the troad another 0.1 mile onto a flat containing a trail junction. At this point the troad leading up to the mine can be clearly seen on the hillside to the north. Turn left and climb the rough, rocky troad another 1.4 miles to the Hexahedron Mine.

A roofless stone house stands guard near the mine adit, offering magnificent vistas of monzogranite quartz mounds northward. The main adit lies a short distance beyond at the end of the troad. Retrace your route to complete this 8.4-mile round-trip. On the way back down you'll be able to clearly see the outline of the dry lakebed.

For those staying overnight, there are good campsites near the upper reaches of Fried Liver Wash.

36 PLEASANT VALLEY TO EL DORADO MINE/ PINTO BASIN

General description:	A varied point-to-point day trip from Pleasant Valley across the Hexie Mountains to an interesting historic mine, ending up along the northwestern edge of the Pinto Basin.
Length:	7.7 miles point-to-point.
General location:	About 25 miles south of Twentynine Palms, in central Joshua Tree National Park, southeastern California.
Trail condition:	Clear troad, wash routes.
Special attractions:	Eldorado Mine, distant views of the Pinto Basin and the Pinto Mountains.
Difficulty:	Moderate.
Best season:	October through May.
Starting elevation:	3,250 feet.
Maximum elevation:	3,250 feet.
Elevation gain/loss:	80 feet/770 feet.
USGS topo maps:	Malapai Hills-CA and Fried Liver Wash-CA (1:24,000).
For more information:	Joshua Tree National Park (see Appendix D).

Key points:
0.0   Pleasant Valley Backcountry Board.
0.3   Troad splits; stay right.
2.5   Fence crosses the wash; turn left (north).
2.8   Trail junction with the Hexahedron Mine troad; stay right.
4.1   Troad tops a pass at 3,170 feet.
5.7   Eldorado Mine (2,650 feet).
7.7   End point of hike at Park Route 11 (2,560 feet).

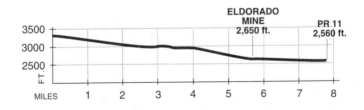

Finding the trailhead: From the park visitor center in Twentynine Palms go south on Utah Trail 8.2 miles to Pinto Y. Stay to the right on Park Route 12 and drive another 5.1 miles to the Geology Tour Road (signed "Squaw Tank" at the junction). From the other direction this turnoff is 15.1 miles southeast of the town of Joshua Tree. Turn left (south) on the Geology Tour

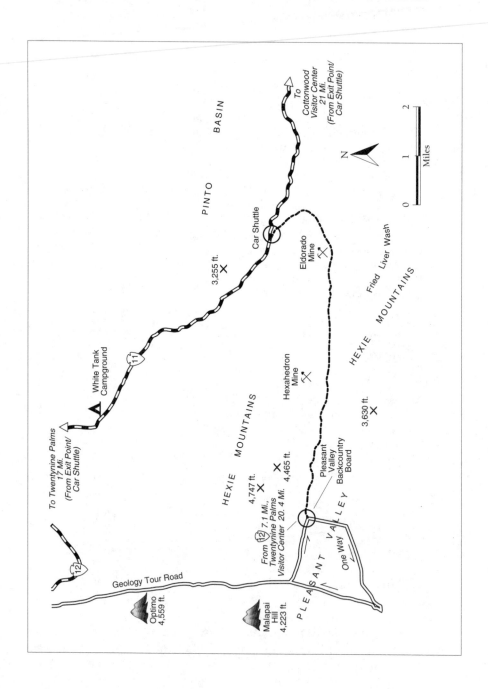

Rd. (washboard dirt) and drive 7.1 miles to the Pleasant Valley Backcountry Board, on the left side of Geology Tour Rd. in the one-way loop section in Pleasant Valley.

For a car shuttle: At Pinto Y bear left on Park Route 11. Drive south to pullout on the right just northwest of milepost 8.

The hike: This interesting point-to-point excursion of nearly 8 miles starts in Pleasant Valley along the upper Fried Liver Wash and the southern base of the Hexie Mountains, ending up in the northwestern edge of the vast Pinto Basin. The trip presents an opportunity to explore the sizable Eldorado Mine site.

The hike begins in a dry lakebed, which can be clearly delineated by walking up the sidehill to the north a 100 feet or so before returning to the troad. At 0.3 mile a left-hand turn heads toward the hills. Stay to the right on the main traveled troad heading east.

Within another 0.2 mile Joshua trees are first seen along the trail. At 1.5 miles the troad passes by an old wooden post with no sign. Soon the troad and Fried Liver Wash become one and the same. At 2.5 miles a fence crosses the wash next to a hillside to the left. Turn left (north) and follow the fenceline for about 0.2 mile to an old iron gatepost. Follow the troad leading uphill to the right. After another 0.1 mile you'll come to a trail junction in a flat; take the right-hand fork, which continues east in a small valley lined with Joshua trees. For a side trip take the left-hand fork to the Hexahedron Mine (see Hike 35).

At 3.8 miles the troad drops into a rough, rocky ravine, climbing out of it after another 0.1 mile. The gradual ascent continues for another 0.2 mile to a 3,170-foot pass overlooking the Pinto Basin to the east. After another 0.1 mile the troad all but disappears in the rock-strewn gully. Follow the wash down.

After 0.2 mile a small mine adit appears on the left, one of countless such holes in these hills. At this point the wash becomes sandier and easier to negotiate. Here and there a rusty water pipe sticks out. As the wash drops, the canyon opens up to ever-expanding views of Pinto Basin. After another 0.6 mile the wash widens, becoming more braided and difficult to walk down. At 5.7 miles the wash trail passes the Eldorado Mine. A single leaning building on the right looks as though a good puff of wind would blow it down. The huge piles of tailings give moot evidence that this mine produced the largest number of different minerals of any in the park.

If the Eldorado Mine is your destination and you've not arranged for a car shuttle, return the way you came for an 11.4 mile round-trip—a full day indeed. To continue the point-to-point hike, walk down the wash another 0.5 mile, gradually curving left (northward) around the base of the hill. Keep going another 1.5 miles north to northwest to an old mining road below the Tripples (Silver Bell) Mine which leads to the parking area immediately northwest of milepost 8 on Park Route 11 at an elevation of 2,560 feet.

General description:	A short, easy nature trail on the lower edge of the transition from Mojave to Colorado desert.
Length:	0.25-mile loop.
General location:	19 miles south of Twentynine Palms, south-central Joshua Tree National Park, southeastern California.
Trail condition:	Clear nature trail.
Special attraction:	Unusually dense stand of cholla cactus.
Difficulty:	Easy.
Best season:	October through April.
Starting elevation:	2,230 feet.
Maximum elevation:	2,230 feet.
Elevation gain/loss:	None.
USGS topo map:	Fried Liver Wash-CA (1:24,000).
For more information:	Joshua Tree National Park (see Appendix D).

See Map on Page 116

Finding the trailhead: From California Highway 62 in Twentynine Palms, take Utah Trail south 4 miles to North Entrance of park; continue on Park Route 12 south 4.8 miles to Pinto Y. Turn left onto Park Route 11. The Garden parking area is on the right near mile 10, 6.3 miles south of the intersection.

A dense stand of cholla cactus on the nature trail above Pinto Valley marks the northern end of the Colorado (Sonoran) Desert.

The hike: This massive array of cholla, a common species of the Colorado (Sonoran) Desert, is impressive even when it is not in bloom. From mid- to late February to mid-March, there is intense bee activity at the garden. Those with sensitivity or phobias about bees should avoid visiting at the pollination season.

This is a self-guided trail but there are no brochures available, so the numbers posted on the trail only tantalize the visitor. But even without a pamphlet for interpretation, the density of the cholla, which extend well beyond the fenced edge of the garden, is impressive.

The views of the Hexie Mountains, the Pinto Range, and the Pinto Basin contribute to making the Cholla Cactus Garden a spectacular spot on the edge of this southern desert region.

38   SAND DUNES

General description:	Easy out-and-back hike across the flat Pinto Basin to wind-shaped sand dunes that can be seen from the highway.
Length:	2.5 miles round-trip.
General location:	27 miles north of Cottonwood Visitor Center, in east-central Joshua Tree National Park, southeastern California.
Trail condition:	Open cross-country.
Special attraction:	Sand dunes.
Difficulty:	Easy.
Best season:	January through April.
Starting elevation:	1,790 feet.
Maximum elevation:	1,822 feet.
Elevation gain/loss:	32 feet/none.
USGS topo map:	Pinto Mountain-CA (1:24,000).
For more information:	Joshua Tree National Park (see Appendix D).

Finding the trailhead: The route takes off from the Turkey Flats Backcountry Board, which is on the east side of Park Route 11, 16.2 miles south of the Pinto Y and 27.5 miles north of the Cottonwood Visitor Center.

The hike: From the Turkey Flats Backcountry Board head northeast on a line toward the high point on the distant horizon, 3,983-foot Pinto Mountain. The sand dunes can be seen about a mile away as a low-lying dark ridge or mound.

Begin by heading 0.2 mile up a large wash, which leads to sand bowl. Continue northeasterly for another mile across a creosote-brittlebush flat to the sand dunes. This is a delightful place to visit during winter and, especially, spring, when primrose and other wildflowers are in bloom. Spend some quiet time here, wandering along this windswept uplift of sand, reflecting

SAND DUNES

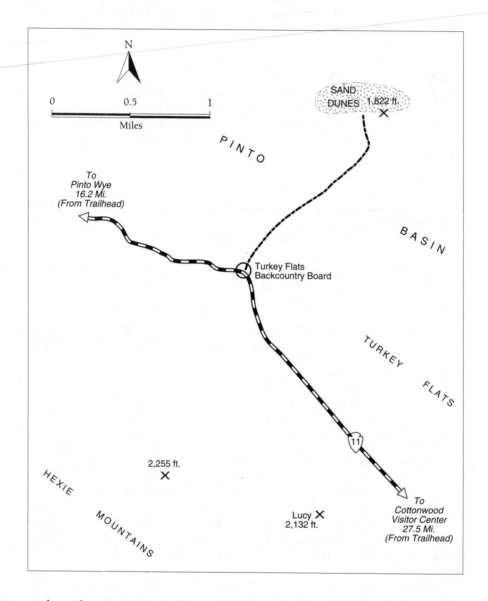

on how the ever-present desert winds have both created and kept in place these dunes over thousands of years.

To return, simply walk toward the highest point to the southwest, which is the crest of the Hexie Mountains, and you'll soon end up at the backcountry board on Park Road 11.

General description:	A moderately strenuous day trip to Pushwalla Plateau in the Little San Bernardino Mountains, with an optional canyon hike and side trips to historic mining sites.
Length:	5.6 miles round-trip to Pushwalla Pass, or 9.4 miles out-and-back to Pushwalla Plateau and Canyon with side trips.
General location:	About 27.5 miles south of Twentynine Palms, south-central Joshua Tree National Park, southeastern California.
Trail condition:	Clear wash, troad.
Special attractions:	Interesting stone wall mining structures, remoteness in a secluded corner of the park, expansive vistas from a high plateau to the Salton Sea and beyond.
Difficulty:	Moderately strenuous.
Best season:	October through May.
Starting elevation:	3,600 feet.
Maximum elevation:	5,260 feet (plateau summit).
Elevation gain/loss:	1,060 feet/1,060 feet (pass); 1,660 feet/1,660 feet (plateau).
USGS topo map:	Malapai Hill-CA (1:24,000).
For more information:	Joshua Tree National Park (see Appendix D).

Key points:

0.0	Pinyon Well trailhead.
0.8	Pinyon Well site.
1.2	Canyon forks; stay left up the main wash.
2.4-3.2	Side trip up the left-hand fork to the Henson Well Mill site.
3.6	Pushwalla Pass.
4.6	Pushwalla Plateau.
5.6-6.6	Side trip down Pushwalla Canyon.
9.4	Return to Pinyon Well trailhead.

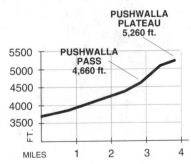

Finding the trailhead: From the park visitor center in Twentynine Palms go south on Utah Trail 8.2 miles to Pinto Y. Stay to the right on Park Route

Henson Well Mill site/mine ruins southeast of Pushwalla Pass.

PUSHWALLA PLATEAU/CANYON

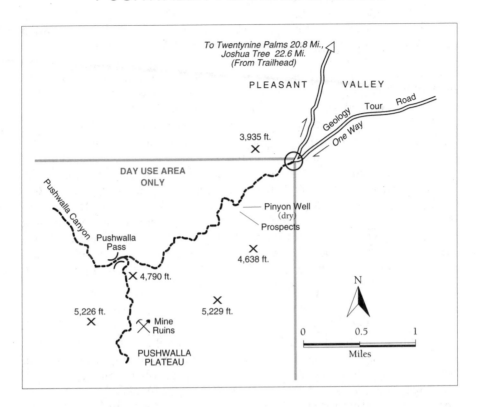

To Twentynine Palms 20.8 Mi.,
Joshua Tree 22.6 Mi.
(From Trailhead)

PLEASANT   VALLEY

Geology Tour Road
One Way

3,935 ft.
X

DAY USE AREA
ONLY

Pushwalla Canyon

Pinyon Well
(dry)
Prospects

Pushwalla
Pass

X
4,638 ft.

X 4,790 ft.

N

5,226 ft.
X

X
5,229 ft.

X Mine
Ruins

PUSHWALLA
PLATEAU

0   0.5   1

Miles

12 and drive another 5.1 miles to the Geology Tour Road, which is signed
"Squaw Tank" at the turnoff. From the other direction the turnoff is 15.1
miles southeast of the town of Joshua Tree. Turn left (south) on the Geology
Tour Rd., which is rough but usually passable for standard vehicles. The
unsigned trailhead is 10.2 miles south next to the 15 km post. Park at the
Pinyon Well parking area and begin the hike up the wash.

The hike: This is an interesting hike with several side options into a
remote and lightly used region of the park. All of the variations are out-and-
back. They include going up "Pinyon Well" canyon to Pushwalla Pass with
several side trip possibilities, continuing up to Pushwalla Plateau and dropping into the upper stretches of Pushwalla Canyon.

The trail starts up a wash near the mouth of the "Pinyon Well" canyon,
which drains east from Pushwalla Pass. The country is characterized by
scattered juniper and Joshua trees, punctuated with spires of columnar rocks
overlooking the canyon. The wash forks at 0.3 mile; stay to the right.

At 0.8 mile the canyon narrows just below the remains of a water trough
and concrete foundations at Pinyon Well. A mine shaft is fenced off for public
safety. At 1 mile (3,880 feet) a rock slide blocks the canyon; cut left on a use

trail that quickly leads back to the wash. Look here for the remnants of the original asphalt roadway built by the miners.

At 1.2 miles the canyon again forks; stay left up the main wash. At 1.6 miles a pinyon-juniper wash dotted with Joshua trees enters from the left (south) at 4,140 feet. For an expansive view of the canyon take a 0.2-mile walk up the open wash to where heavy brush makes further hiking difficult.

At 1.9 miles the wash forks with the trail to Pushwalla Pass continuing to the left. At 2.2 miles the wash is again blocked by a rockslide, which can be avoided by taking the use trail to the left. At 2.4 miles (4,400 feet) the wash again forks; the smaller wash to the right is the route to Pushwalla Pass.

For a 0.8-mile side trip to some historic mining ruins (shown on the topo map) head up the left-hand wash at mile 2.4. After about 0.1 mile, climb toward the right-hand canyon on the right side of the draw. Soon you'll see the largely overgrown mining road up ahead. Follow it another 0.2 mile to the two roofless rock houses sitting just above a wet spring. Retrace your steps back to the right-hand fork, which climbs up the wash another 0.4 mile to 4,660-foot Pushwalla Pass at the head of Pushwalla Canyon. The pass is marked by an iron post gate. Hold onto your hat for the pass is truly a classic high desert wind funnel, decorated by pinyon-juniper and live oak. If the pass is your goal, backtrack to complete your 5.6 mile round-trip.

PUSHWALLA PLATEAU

An old mining troad takes off to the south uphill about 50 yards east of Pushwalla Pass; several rock cairns mark the spot. The troad is quite steep in places but easy to follow. At 0.8 mile the troad passes by mining remains, including a rock foundation (5,120 feet). This is potentially a hazardous area because of unsecured vertical mine shafts nearby. The troad begins to fade here but simply continue straight, angling upward to the left another 0.2 mile to the 5,200-foot crest of the Pushwalla Plateau ridge. Joshua trees and rock mounds characterize the landscape. Savor the spectacular views southward to the Salton Sea and in every direction in these remote Little San Bernardino Mountains. Seldom visited ridges and canyons radiate below, and always there is the wind to keep you company.

PUSHWALLA CANYON

If time and energy permit, drop into the head of Pushwalla Canyon where Joshua trees grow out of the wide, sandy bottom. To get there from the pass walk around the right side of the iron gate and descend the troad on the left side of the gully to the broad wash. The canyon deepens as it drops, thereby enriching its sense of solitude. You'll lose 400 feet in the first 0.5 mile, so gauge your time accordingly for the return leg of this out-and-back adventure.

NOTE: An overnight trip is not recommended here because the day-use area extends several more miles down Pushwalla Canyon—and because a point-to-point hike all the way down Pushwalla Canyon to the Dillon Road would require an inordinately long car shuttle. However, if distance and shuttle time are not obstacles, this long point-to-point route is an adventurous option. At this writing there is no end-of-the-road parking area at the Pushwalla Canyon Road, which ends at the park boundary. However, the National Park Service does have plans to put in a backcountry board and parking area at this location in the near future.

Also for the adventurous hiker, the Pushwalla Canyon-Blue Cut loop provides a long 15-mile day trip or more moderate overnighter with a backpack camp in lower Pushwalla or upper Blue Cut Canyon outside of the day use area. The basic route involves descending Pushwalla Canyon about 3.5 miles below the pass; turning right up Blue Cut Canyon for about 2 miles to the pass; then dropping eastward into Pleasant Valley for the return trip to the Pinyon Well trailhead on the Geology Tour Rd.

40   KEYS VIEW LOOP/INSPIRATION PEAK

General description:	Road and loop trail on a peak in Little San Bernardino Mountains provides easy access to panoramic view, with additional side trip to Inspiration Peak.
Length:	0.25-mile loop plus 1.5 miles round-trip for peak hike.
General location:	20 miles south of the town of Joshua Tree, in south-central Joshua Tree National Park, southeastern California.
Trail condition:	Clear (loop); good (Peak).
Special attractions:	Spectacular view, air visibility conditions permitting, and information on air pollution in Joshua Tree National Park.
Difficulty:	Easy; moderate for peak hike.
Best season:	October through June.
Starting elevation:	5,150 feet.
Maximum elevation:	5,193 feet (Keys View), or 5,575 feet (Inspiration Peak).
Elevation gain/loss:	43 feet (Keys View Loop); 525 feet/100 feet (Inspiration Peak).
USGS topo map	Keys View-CA (1:24,000).
For more information:	Joshua Tree National Park (see Appendix D).

Key points:

0.0   Keys View Parking Area; trailhead on north end (5,150 feet).

0.5   First summit (5,558 feet).

0.6   Saddle (5,460 feet).

0.75 Inspiration Peak (5,575 feet).

Finding the trailhead: From California Highway 62 in the town of Joshua Tree, take Park Boulevard south 1 mile to where it becomes Quail Springs

Looking northeast from Inspiration Peak (5,575 feet) to the Wonderland of Rocks; visibility is reduced by air pollution from the west.

Road; continue 4.3 miles to the West Entrance of the park. Follow Park Route 12 for 11.2 miles to the Keys View Road (Park Route 13), which continues to the right (south). Turn south on Keys View; go 5.8 miles to end of the road.

The hikes: This clear, paved, barrier-free path to Keys View Loop is the highest trail in the park accessible by a paved road. You can count on a brisk breeze, so bring your windbreaker. The viewpoint is on the crest of the Little San Bernardino Mountains. As such, it provides an expansive view of the Coachella Valley and the San Bernardino Range to the west. Unfortunately, the view is all too often obscured by pollution from the Los Angeles Basin. Information boards contrasting smog levels give the viewer a good idea of how air pollution affects visibility at differing distances. The smog also endangers the biological integrity of the park itself.

At the lookout there is no diagrammatic map of the park or explanation of the area's geology, a situation often creating questions from visitors to Keys View. Either schedule this trip for late in your stay at Joshua Tree so you will be familiar with the park's landmarks, or bring your park map with you.

A short side trip to Inspiration Peak makes a nice addition for those who like to get even higher. A hiker symbol marks the trailhead on the north (right) side of the parking area at Keys View. The somewhat steep, rocky trail is well worn and in good condition. Nearly 400 feet are gained to a false summit in the first 0.5 mile.

KEYS VIEW LOOP AND INSPIRATION PEAK

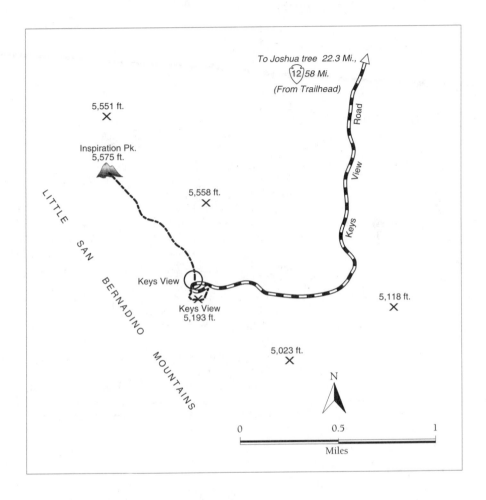

Look carefully for the trail continuing to the right. It drops 100 feet into a saddle and then climbs around the left side, gaining 120 feet in the next 0.25 mile. Keys View sits far below to the south, as do the Coachella Valley and prominent peaks of the higher San Bernardino Range. The added perspective gained on the steep canyons and high ridges makes this steep, short climb more than worthwhile.

An easily followed use trail continues another 0.1 mile northwest along the main crest until it reaches a mound of large boulders. The Inspiration Peak hike can be extended by scrambling over the rocks and dropping into another saddle containing a small storage shed. Climbing cross-country up the ridgeline to the next high point offers even broader views of the park stretching west and north to the Wonderland of Rocks.

From Inspiration Peak double back 0.75 mile on the trail leading back down to the Keys View parking area.

41 LOST HORSE MINE LOOP
LOST HORSE MOUNTAIN

General description:	A moderate round-trip in a historic mining district that can be extended for a longer loop trip with optional side trips to a peak and cabin ruins.
Length:	4 miles out-and-back; 6.4 miles for the loop; 7.8 miles for loop with side trips.
General location:	19 miles southeast of the town of Joshua Tree, in west-central Joshua Tree National Park, southeastern California.
Trail condition:	Clear troad to the mine and for most of the loop except for 0.2 mile cross-country to Optimist Mine, 0.6-mile round-trip to Lost Horse Peak, and 0.8-mile round-trip to Joshua tree cabin ruins.
Special attractions:	A large historic mine; unusual Joshua tree cabin ruins; superb views of the Wonderland of Rocks, Malapai Hill, and the vast expanse of Pleasant Valley; the challenge of cross-country route-finding for those hiking the loop.
Difficulty:	Moderate (out-and-back to the mine); moderately strenuous (loop hike with peak climb).
Best season:	October through May.
Starting elevation:	4,600 feet.
Maximum elevation:	5,120 feet (pass above Lost Horse Mine); 5,313 feet (Lost Horse Mountain).
Elevation gain/loss:	588 feet/588 feet (point above Lost Horse Mine); 638 feet/638 feet (Lost Horse Loop); 880 feet/880 feet (Lost Horse Loop with side trips to peak and cabin).
USGS topo map:	Keys View-CA (1:24,000).
For more information:	Joshua Tree National Park (see Appendix D).

Key points:

0.0	Lost Horse parking area/trailhead (4,600 feet).
2.0	Lost Horse Mine.
2.2	Lost Horse Point (5,188 feet).
2.4	Pass southeast of mine (5,120 feet).
2.7	Lost Horse Peak (5,313 feet).
3.4	Lang Mine.
3.6	End of trail/beginning of cross-country leg.
3.8	Optimist Mine.
4.5	Troad enters and follows wash.
4.9	Joshua tree log cabin ruins.
7.8	End of loop.

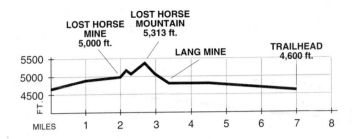

Finding the trailhead: Drive south on the Keys View Road, which begins 18 miles southeast of the town of Joshua Tree via Park Boulevard and Quail Springs Road, or 20 miles southwest of the Oasis Visitor Center at Twentynine Palms by way of Park Route 12. Continue south on the Keys View Road for 2.6 miles to the signed Lost Horse Mine Road. Turn left (southeast) and drive to the Lost Horse Mine parking area/trailhead which is at the end of this 1.1-mile dirt road.

The hike: This multifaceted hike offers something for every hiking enthusiast—a moderate out-and-back to a large mining complex, side trips to several high panoramic points, and a longer more strenuous loop for those wishing to add a bit of adventurous route-finding into the trip. The recommended direction for the loop trip is clockwise.

The clear and wide but somewhat rocky troad climbs moderately to 4,900 feet at 1 mile across high desert swales of juniper, yucca, a few stunted Joshua trees, and nolina (commonly called bear grass), a member of the agave family often mistaken for yucca because of its long spearlike leaves. At 2 miles the troad reaches the lower end of the Lost Horse Mine at 4,970 feet. This is the largest, essentially intact, historic mining site in the park, and one could easily spend several hours here observing rock buildings, mine shafts, a large wooden stamp mill, and a winch above the mill that was used to lower miners and equipment into the mine. The largest mine shaft, some 500 feet deep, is covered. However, other smaller ones remain unsecured on the hillsides, so exercise caution when wandering around this site.

This was one of the most profitable mines in the park. A German miner named Frank Diebold made the first strike. He was later bought out by prospector Johnny Lang who happened onto the strike in 1893 while searching for a lost horse. He and his partners began developing the mine two years later. Their process involved crushing ore at the mill then mixing it with quicksilver (mercury), which bonded with the gold so that it could be separated from the ore rock. After visiting the mine, you can double back the way you came for a moderate 4- to 4.5-mile round-trip.

For a bird's-eye view of the mine and its surroundings hike north 0.2 mile on the troad that climbs above the fenced-off stamp mill. A 0.1-mile use trail continues up to Lost Horse Point (5,188 feet) which affords a magnificent panorama of surrounding basins and peaks, including the Wonderland

LOST HORSE MINE LOOP

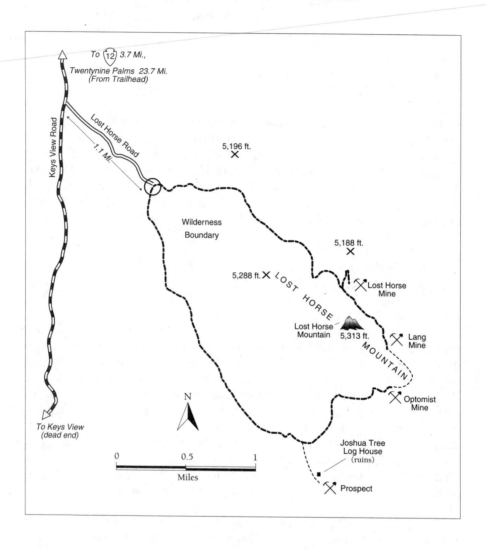

To (12) 3.7 Mi.,
Twentynine Palms 23.7 Mi.
(From Trailhead)

Keys View Road

Lost Horse Road

1.1 Mi.

5,196 ft.
×

Wilderness
Boundary

5,188 ft.
×

5,288 ft. × LOST HORSE

Lost Horse
Mine

Lost Horse
Mountain 5,313 ft.

Lang
Mine

MOUNTAIN

N

Optomist
Mine

To Keys View
(dead end)

0   0.5   1
Miles

Joshua Tree
Log House
(ruins)

Prospect

of Rocks to the north. From here you can see a troad running southeast to a pass. Using care on the loose rocks, drop down this troad and walk 0.2 mile to the pass if you want to climb 5,313-foot Lost Horse Mountain. From the pass climb southwest 0.3 mile up the ridge, gaining 200 feet, to the long ridgetop that forms the summit of the mountain. There is a faint use trail that is easier seen coming down than going up, but climbing is easy on or off the use trail.

To continue the 6.4-mile Lost Horse loop (not counting the additional distance of side trips) drop back to the pass and continue dropping steeply to the southeast on a rough and rocky troad 0.4 mile to the unsecured Lang

Lost Horse Mountain to the south as seen from point 5,188.

Mine (4,800 feet). The troad ends here; continue on a well-defined trail that contours another 0.2 mile on the hillside to a small flat spot marked by a large cairn. This is the end of the trail and the start of the short cross-country segment. Instead of dropping any farther, angle sharply upward and to the right (southwest) to the closest ridge, wrapping around the small hill to the right for about 0.1 mile. From here the stone chimney, tailings, and troad of the Optimist Mine can be seen downhill and across the gully to the south.

Drop down to the chimney in 0.1 mile and pick up the easy-to-follow troad, which winds uphill and to the right. The troad travels westward in and around several small hills and gullies 0.4 mile to a wooden post with the number 8. After another 0.4 mile the troad drops into a wide wash, which coincides with mile 4 in the 6.4-mile loop trip.

For an interesting short side trip to a Joshua tree log house, hike up the wash to the first fork at 0.2 mile. Continue southeast on the left-hand fork another 0.2 mile to the cabin ruins, which are on the left side of the wash along with the faint remnants of an old mining road. This structure stands as a rustic reminder of why Joshua trees are so scarce in this heavily prospected mining district.

Return to the junction and continue northwest down either the troad or the wash, both of which end up on the Lost Horse Mine Road about 100 yards below the parking area. The troad provides firmer walking but at times disappears in the wash. When in doubt simply follow the wash—eventually you'll pick up the troad on one of its several crossings. The wash is bounded by low-lying ridges with the valley opening up to vistas of distant mountains to the northwest. Joshua trees become larger and more abundant on this return leg of the loop as the distance increases from the mining sites. Upon reaching the Lost Horse Road, turn right and walk the remaining short distance to the parking area/trailhead.

NOTE: Those wishing to backpack and camp overnight on the loop route must start at the Juniper Flats Backcountry Board, 1.5 miles north of the turnoff to Lost Horse Mine on the Keys View Road. This fairly flat 2-mile trail intersects the Lost Horse Mine troad 0.25 mile east of the parking area, thereby adding 3.5 miles to the loop. There are several good campsites near the junction of the troad and wash near mile 4 of the loop.

42 CALIFORNIA RIDING AND HIKING TRAIL
KEYS VIEW ROAD TO PARK ROUTE 11

General description:	Two sections of the California Riding and Hiking Trail hiked as a single unit (11 miles) for a point-to-point day hike or broken into 6.5- and 4.4-mile one-way units, largely downhill over a broad trail.
Length:	11 miles one-way, with car shuttle.
General location:	15 miles southwest of Twentynine Palms, central Joshua Tree National Park, southeastern California.
Trail condition:	Clear trail.
Special attractions:	Solitude in a busy region of the park; sweeping vistas of the central park and the Pinto Basin.
Difficulty:	Moderate.
Best season:	October through April.
Starting elevation:	4,384 feet (Keys View Backcountry Board).
Maximum elevation:	4,540 feet.
Elevation gain/loss:	350 feet/793 feet.
USGS topo maps:	Keys View-CA and Malapai Hill-CA (1:24,000).
For more information:	Joshua Tree National Park (see Appendix D).

Key points:

0.0-0.7	Juniper Flats Backcountry board; trail leads northeast towards Ryan Campground, then turns east.
1.5	Saddle pass, high point of the hike (4,540 feet).
2.5	Mine site below trail to right; 50 yards later, trail goes right through prospectors' ruins.
6.5	Cross Geology Tour Road.
10.9	Arrive at Park Route 11; the board and parking area are 0.2 mile north.

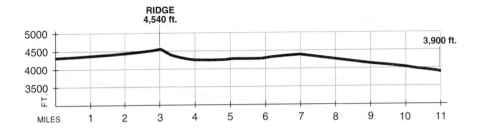

RIDGE
4,540 ft.

3,900 ft.

Finding the trailhead: From California Highway 62 in Twentynine Palms, take Utah Trail south 4 miles to North Entrance of park; continue on Park Route 12 for 15.8 miles to the Keys View Road left turn, which is at the Cap Rock Nature Trail. Turn left (south) on Keys View, and continue 1.1 mile to the Juniper Flats Backcountry Board on your right. The trail itself crosses Keys View Road just to the north of the board parking area. A spur trail leads you to the main trail.

For car shuttle: For a partial trip, your pick-up point is on Geology Tour Road, 10.2 miles down Park Route 12 from the North Entrance, on your left (sign at intersection is "Squaw Tank"); the backcountry board and parking area are south on Geology Tour Road, 1.4 miles, on your right. For the longer hike, the pick-up spot is on Park Route 11 near the Arch Rock Nature Trail and White Tank Campground. From the North Entrance go south on Park Route 12 for 4.8 miles to the Pinto Y junction; turn left on Park Route 11 and go south 2.3 miles to Twin Tank Backcountry Board, on your right.

The hike: Whether done as one long hike or two short hikes, these outings provide an excellent tour of the central area of Joshua Tree National Park. The California Riding and Hiking Trail is largely sandy. These sections feature a fairly broad pathway; the final 4.4 miles are on a trail as wide as a city sidewalk. In spite of its title, there is minimal horse usage. We never saw a hoofprint on our hike.

The trail is well-marked with arrowed signposts, and even features mile markers (mile 1 is on the slightly used portion starting near the North Entrance), so you always know where you are. Except for a gradual 250-foot rise in the first portion after Ryan Campground, the trail is nearly all downhill. This, combined with the easy footing, makes it possible to stroll along enjoying the scenery.

And the scenery is superb! From Keys View you cross the interior valley south of Ryan Mountain. Although you are not in a remote corner of the park, there is a definite sense of total solitude. Hiking through the valley and on down the ridge into Pleasant Valley you enjoy a wide field of vision, unlike the wash and canyon hikes elsewhere in the park. The Little San Bernardinos rise to the right, and the Pinto Mountains loom larger in the distance to the east. The distinctive peaks of Ryan Mountain, Malapai Hill, the Hexie Range, and Crown Prince Lookout punctuate your trip.

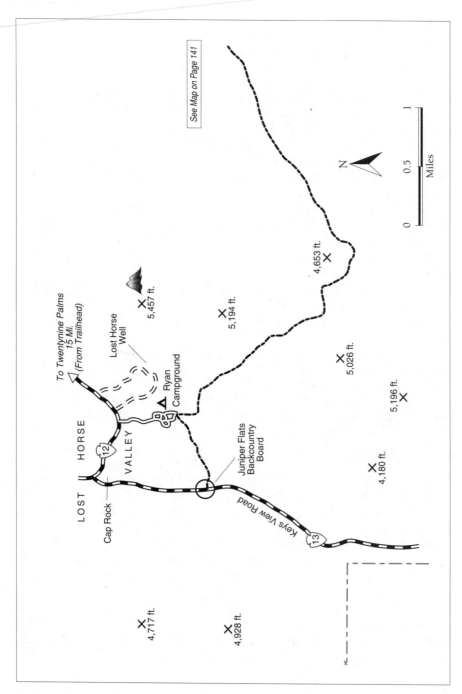

See Map on Page 141

N

Miles
0   0.5   1

4,653 ft.

5,457 ft.

5,194 ft.

5,026 ft.

5,196 ft.

Lost Horse Well

To Twentynine Palms
15 Mi.
(From Trailhead)

Ryan Campground

Juniper Flats Backcountry Board

4,180 ft.

LOST   HORSE   VALLEY

Cap Rock

Keys View Road

4,717 ft.

4,928 ft.

12

13

CALIFORNIA RIDING AND HIKING TRAIL
KEYS VIEW ROAD TO PARK ROUTE 11

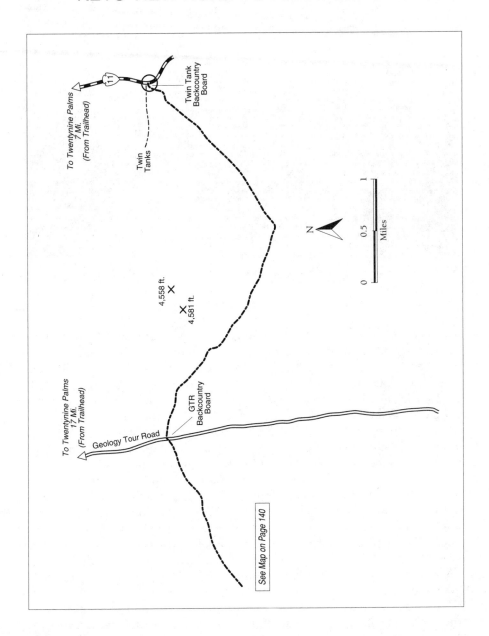

The final section of the hike is the easiest portion of the Riding and Hiking Trail in the park. Many hikers park at either end and do it as an easy out-and-back, avoiding the hassle of the car shuttle. West to east, of course, the downhill slope is advantageous. And what a vista it is as you descend gradu-

Hikers heading north on the California Riding and Hiking Trail toward the Geology Tour Road.

ally toward the Pinto Basin stretching before you into the hazy distance. With only a bit of imagination you can envision the early Pinto Basin inhabitants enjoying life around the lake that once lay in the grassy valley between the mountains. With a net loss of elevation of nearly 600 feet, the 4.4-mile section also gives you a relaxed opportunity to notice vegetation changes as you descend from the Mojave to the Colorado (Sonoran) desert. The Joshua trees are numerous and large at your 4,500-foot commencement at Geology Tour Rd. Gradually, they become more sparse, and quite small, until they are nearly nonexistent. Instead, creosote dominates, and cholla cactus increases. By the end of the hike you are in a new botanical environment.

If you have more time and energy, the Twin Tanks monzogranite region is immediately west of the backcountry board on Park Route 11. You can see the hulking granite formations to the north of the trail as you approach the board. These looming forms are quite a bit larger than they appear, for they are hiding in a ravine, crouching below the horizon. A 1-mile hike west of the board will take you to this fanciful granite playground with curiously eroded caves, tunnels, and sculptures.

NOTE: In Joshua Tree, the backcountry boards are not located exactly on the California Riding and Hiking Trail. In each case, the trail crosses the road slightly to the north or to the south of the board itself. The board structures are large enough for you to spot them above the desert vegetation, and feeder trails will lead you to or from the boards at the beginning and end of your hikes.

General description:	A short nature walk featuring geologic formations, and a side trip to an old cattlemen's tank that provides a patch of greenery for wildlife.
Distance:	0.3-mile loop (more for exploratory side trips in the rocks).
General location:	8.5 miles south of Twentynine Palms.
Trail condition:	Clear nature trail.
Special attractions:	White Tank granite formations, with geology lessons.
Difficulty:	Easy nature trail.
Best season:	October through April.
Starting elevation:	3,800 feet.
Maximum elevation:	3,900 feet.
Elevation gain/loss:	100 feet/100 feet.
USGS topo map:	Malapai Hill-CA (1:24,000).
For more information:	Joshua Tree National Park (see Appendix D).

Finding the trailhead: From California Highway 62 in Twentynine Palms, take Utah Trail south 4 miles to North Entrance of the park; continue south on Park Route 12 for 4.8 miles to Pinto Y. Turn left at the Y onto Park Route 11 and go 2.8 miles to the White Tank Campground, on your left. Turn into the campground and follow the inconspicuous nature trail sign to the trailhead, on the left immediately after the campground information board.

Obelisks of White Tank granite loom above the Arch Rock Nature Trail.

ARCH ROCK NATURE TRAIL

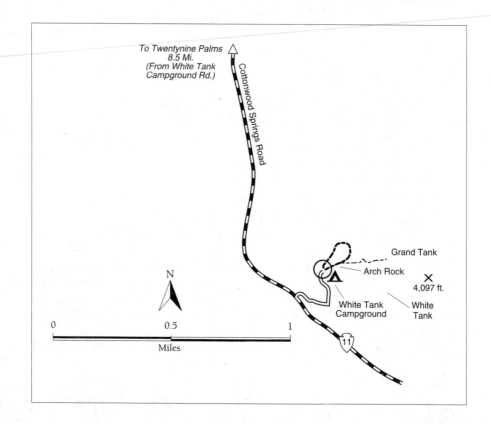

To Twentynine Palms
8.5 Mi.
(From White Tank
Campground Rd.)

Cottonwood Springs Road

N

Grand Tank

Arch Rock

✕
4,097 ft.

White Tank
Campground

White
Tank

11

0   0.5   1

Miles

The hike: The focus of this nature trail is on the unique geology of the fascinating rock formations that abound in this area of the park. Informational signs present a sophisticated series of geology lessons, far beyond the simplistic rock identification that usually occurs on such a trail. The trail itself is an adventure in geology as it winds through imaginative boulders to the famed Arch Rock.

A side trip from this rock through the slot to the northeast leads to the site of an old cattle tank, which is no longer holding water but has created a habitat for birds and other desert creatures.

The geology lesson covers the formation of igneous rock, the origins of White Tank granite, erosion, selective erosion, dikes, and faults. The remainder of your visit in the park will be greatly enhanced by this knowledge. For example, 1 mile directly east of White Tank Campground are the Twin Tanks. Like Arch Rock, these granite formations are gracefully sculpted by the forces of weather and are inviting to explore. Twin Tanks also has two partially buried old tank sites.

144

General description:	An easy nature loop through interesting rock formations, with periodic informational signs.
Length:	1.7-mile loop.
General location:	12 miles south of Twentynine Palms.
Trail condition:	Clear nature trail.
Difficulty:	Easy.
Best season:	October through April.
Starting elevation:	4,360 feet.
Maximum elevation:	4,425 feet.
Elevation gain/loss:	85 feet/85 feet.
USGS topo map:	Malapai Hill-CA (1:24,000).
For more information:	Joshua Tree National Park (see Appendix D).

Finding the trailhead: From California Highway 62 in Twentynine Palms, take Utah Trail south 4 miles to North Entrance of park; continue on Park Route 12 4.8 miles to Pinto Y. Bear right, still on PR 12, and continue 3.7 miles to the signed Skull Rock Nature Trail trailhead.

The hike: This loop trail is divided by Park Road 12. The northern half of the loop begins at the Skull Rock sign on the highway and goes northward; at 0.7 mile it ends at the Jumbo Rocks Campground entrance. To pick

This eroded monzogranite boulder gives Skull Rock Nature Trail its morbid name.

SKULL ROCK NATURE TRAIL
• CROWN PRINCE LOOKOUT

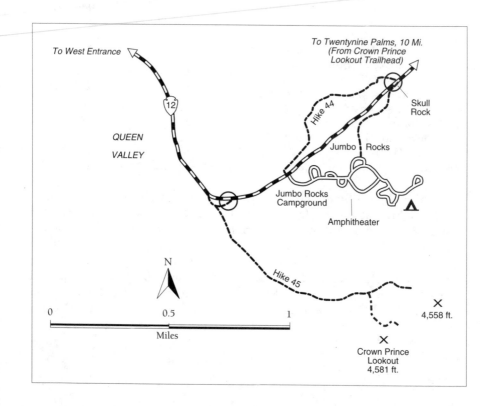

up the rest of the trail from there, it is necessary to walk down through the campground (0.5 mile) to the end of loop E to get to the other half. This northern half of the loop has not been renovated recently by the park. Several signs are so weathered they are illegible. The trail is haphazardly marked with rocks and not always clear. Although the eroded boulders are a spectacular sight, the information provided is not thematic. Basic geology, plant identification, and desert survival tips are intermixed.

Across the road, on the southern half of the loop, the signs are recent, more plentiful, and more instructive. They focus on desert diversity and the interconnectedness of the plants and animals that make this region their home. The famous, much-photographed Skull Rock sits at the entrance (or exit) of the southern loop, immediately adjacent to the road. From there, the trail winds southward 0.5 mile to the southern end of Jumbo Rocks Campground on the E loop. Hike up the campground road to pick up the northern loop opposite the campground entrance on Park Route 12.

45   CROWN PRINCE LOOKOUT

General description:	A hike to a high point above Jumbo Rocks Campground See Map on Page 146 with a wide view of Queen Valley from Pushwalla Plateau to Queen Mountain.
Length:	3 miles out-and-back.
General location:	12 miles south of Twentynine Palms, central Joshua Tree National Park, southeastern California.
Trail condition:	Clear troad.
Special attraction:	Overlook of Twin Tanks, Arch Rock, and Pinto Range.
Difficulty:	Easy.
Best season:	October through April.
Starting elevation:	4,400 feet.
Maximum elevation:	4,581 feet.
Elevation gain/loss:	181 feet/none.
USGS topo map:	Malapai Hill-CA (1:24,000).
For more information:	Joshua Tree National Park (see Appendix D).

The troad to Crown Prince Lookout leads clearly to the overlook jutting above the plateau in the distance.

Key points:

0.0-1.3   Gentle slope up sandy plateau to troad junction; go left or right.
1.5   Overlook

Finding the trailhead: From California Highway 62 in Twentynine Palms, take Utah Trail south 4 miles to North Entrance of park; continue south on Park Route 12 4.8 miles to Pinto Y. Bear right and continue on PR 12 another 3.7 miles to Jumbo Rocks Campground. Park in the visitor lot at the entrance, or along the north side of the road, and walk east along the road shoulder 0.25 mile to trailhead at the sharp curve in the road east of the campground. The troad is marked by six huge stones placed there to block vehicle access on this former jeep route. The trailhead is unsigned.

The hike: This easy hike follows a well-defined old jeep track up a broad sandy ridge. At 1.3 miles the troad splits at a Y. To the right the troad heads for a huge boulder pile; do not be intimidated, for the troad curves around to an adjacent promontory and does not climb the peak. From the vista point, you can see the valleys to the east and the vast White Tank granite formations that lie between here and the Pinto Mountains. This option is 0.2 mile from the Y.

Back at the Y, the left troad is also a gentle 0.2-mile track. It ends in a broad, sandy turnaround. A footpath continues to the right of a more modest boulder pile, and ends at the old mine site.

The walk back to Park Route 12 is entirely downhill.

General description:	This moderate out-and-back hike provides a central panorama of park from an easily accessible peak.
Length:	3 miles round-trip.
General location:	22 miles southeast of the town of Joshua Tree, central Joshua Tree National Park, southeastern California.
Trail condition:	Clear trail.
Special attraction:	Panoramic view from center of park.
Difficulty:	Moderately strenuous.
Best season:	October through May.
Starting elevation:	4,391 feet.
Maximum elevation:	5,461 feet (Ryan Mountain summit).
Elevation gain/loss:	1,070 feet/none.
USGS topo maps:	Indian Cove-CA and Keys View -CA (1:24,000).
For more information:	Joshua Tree National Park (see Appendix D).

Key points:
0.0   Trailhead.
0.1   Huge boulders frame trail.
0.4   Trail begins steep climb.
1.5   Summit of Ryan Mountain.

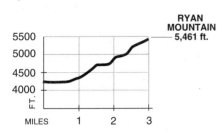

Finding the trailhead: From California Highway 62 in Joshua Tree, drive south on Park Boulevard for 1 mile. It changes to Quail Springs Road; continue 4 miles to North Entrance of the park. Follow Park Route 12 for 12.5 miles to Ryan Mountain Trailhead on your right (south). The signed parking area is 2.1 miles east of the junction with Keys View Road.

The hike: The trail leaves from the parking area through a massive boulder gate of White Tank granite sculpted by selective erosion. This well-signed official park trail is quite a display of rock workmanship. Steeper portions of the trail feature stair-steps artfully constructed from plentiful native rocks, so it's easy walking up and no skidding going down. The trail winds around the hill by the trailhead, and takes a relatively gentle slope to the peak.

If you have spent several days walking nature trails, visiting mine sites, and hiking canyon washes, this peak climb provides a welcome aerial view

149

RYAN MOUNTAIN
• CAP ROCK NATURE TRAIL

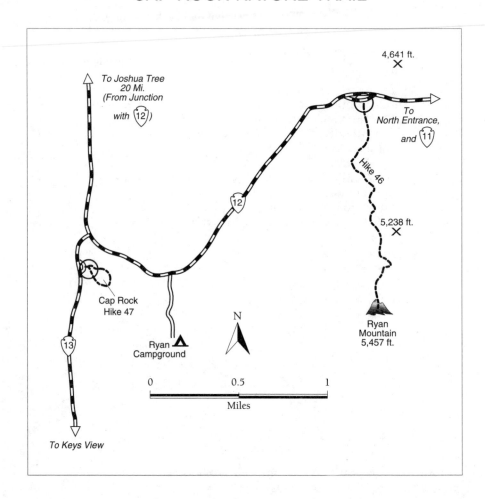

of where you've been in the central portion of the park. On your return, don't miss the Indian Cave sites at the western end of the parking area. A sign indicates their location. The fire-stained rock shelters provide a reminder of the centuries of use that this land has seen from human visitors.

General description:	An easy loop around rock formations adjacent to the picturesque Cap Rock.
Length:	0.4-mile loop.
General location:	20 miles southeast of the town of Joshua Tree, central Joshua Tree National Park, southeastern California.
Trail condition:	Clear nature trail, barrier-free.
Special attractions:	Interesting monzogranite rock formations.
Difficulty:	Easy.
Best season:	October through May.
Starting elevation:	4,240 feet.
Maximum elevation:	4,240 feet.
Elevation gain/loss:	None.
USGS topo map:	Keys View-CA (1:24,000).
For more information:	Joshua Tree National Park (see Appendix D).

See Map on Page 150

Finding the trailhead: From California Highway 62 in Joshua Tree, take the Park Boulevard exit south 1 mile where it turns into Quail Springs Road, and continue 4 miles to the West Entrance of the park. Continue on Park Route 12 for 15 miles to the right turn on Keys View Road. The Cap Rock Parking Area is on the east (left) side of road 0.1 mile from the intersection.

Cap Rock, with its sporty visor, is a popular spot for rock climbers.

The hike: This easy nature trail is paved and was designed to accomodate wheelchairs, although it has weathered considerably since it was built in 1982. The numerous signs have also weathered, some almost to illegibility. The focus of the information is on the desert plants that grow around these fascinating quartz monzonite boulder piles. Cap Rock itself is nearby; frequent use by rock climbers makes this an interesting scene.

48   LUCKY BOY VISTA

General description:	A short round-trip to a plateau vista and site of the old Elton Mine.
Length:	2.5 miles out-and-back.
General location:	16 miles southwest of Twentynine Palms, north-central Joshua Tree National Park, southeastern California.
Trail condition:	Clear troad.
Special attraction:	View of Split Rock region of north-central Joshua Tree.
Difficulty:	Easy.
Best season:	October through April.
Starting elevation:	4,430 feet.
Maximum elevation:	4,520 feet.
Elevation gain/loss:	90 feet/none.
USGS topo map:	Queen Mountain-CA (1:24,000).
For more information:	Joshua Tree National Park (see Appendix D).

This igneous dike intrusion in the monzogranite boulder on the trail to Lucky Boy Vista is a common sight in Joshua Tree.

Kev

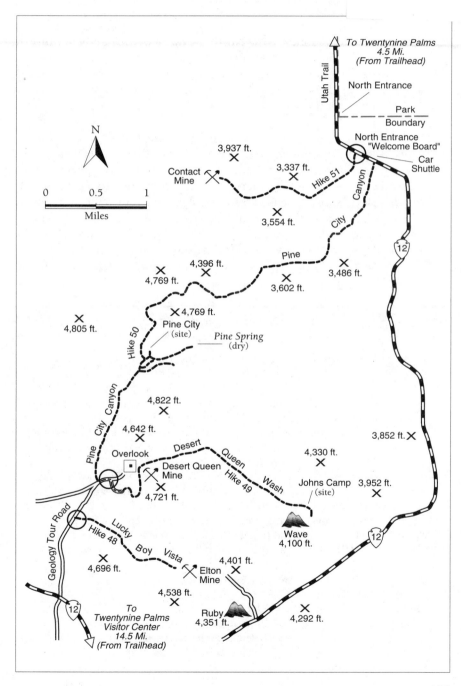

To Twentynine Palms
4.5 Mi.
(From Trailhead)

Utah Trail

North Entrance

Park
Boundary

North Entrance
"Welcome Board"

Car
Shuttle

N

0   0.5   1
Miles

3,937 ft.
✕

Contact
Mine

3,337 ft.
✕

Hike 51

Canyon

12

3,554 ft.
✕

City

Pine

4,396 ft.
✕

4,769 ft.
✕

3,602 ft.
✕

3,486 ft.
✕

4,805 ft.
✕

✕ 4,769 ft.
Pine City
(site)

Pine Spring
(dry)

Hike 50

Pine City Canyon

4,822 ft.
✕

4,642 ft.
✕

3,852 ft. ✕

Overlook
◼

Desert

Queen

4,330 ft.
✕

Desert Queen
Mine

Hike 49

Wash

Johns Camp
(site)

3,952 ft.
✕

✕
4,721 ft.

Geology Tour Road

Hike 48

Lucky

Boy

Vista

Wave
4,100 ft.

4,696 ft.
✕

4,401 ft.
✕

Elton
Mine

12

4,538 ft.
✕

12

To
Twentynine Palms
Visitor Center
14.5 Mi.
(From Trailhead)

Ruby
4,351 ft.

4,292 ft.
✕

points:

0.0 Trailhead; head east on wide, sandy troad.
1.0 Gate; continue around it on troad.
1.2 Mine site on right.
1.25 Overlook.

Finding the trailhead: From California Highway 62 in Twentynine Palms, take Utah Trail south 4 miles to the North Entrance of the park; continue on Park Route 12 4.8 miles to Pinto Y. Bear right and stay on PR 12 another 5.4 miles to the dirt road on your right (directly opposite Geology Tour Road, which goes south). Turn north on the dirt road and go 0.8 mile to a gated road going east. Park there.

The hike: This relatively flat hike to the Elton Mine site is on a broad sandy jeep track which is in better shape than the Geology Tour Road extension you take to get here. The trail climbs gradually above a yucca and pinyon boulder garden to the north. At 1 mile there is a gate; continue around it. Shortly afterwards you will see the fenced-off mine shafts on your right. Just beyond the mine on a lofty plateau is a magnificent overlook of the Split Rock region of the park. For a short hike, this outing provides you with an opportunity for desert solitude, a great view, and a historical site.

The reverse view on the trip back to the car is equally spacious.

49 DESERT QUEEN MINE AND WASH

General description:	An easy hike to an overlook of mine site above Queen Valley, with an optional moderate hike into the ravine for a closer look at the mine and extended hike down Desert Queen Wash.
Length:	1.2 miles out-and-back to overlook; 2.2 miles out-and-back to mine sites; 4 miles out-and-back for Desert Queen Wash.
General location:	15 miles south of Twentynine Palms, north-central Joshua Tree National Park, southeastern California.
Trail condition:	Clear troad; clear wash.
Special attractions:	Largest and longest running mine in the park; additional mines and miners' settlements.
Difficulty:	Easy (to overlook); moderate (to mine site and on down the wash).
Best season:	October through April.
Starting elevation:	4,436 feet.
Maximum elevation:	4,450 feet (overlook).
Elevation gain/loss:	14 feet/none to overlook; 60 feet/100 feet to mine sites; none/580 feet for wash hike.
USGS topo map:	Queen Mountain-CA (1:24,000).
For more information:	Joshua Tree National Park (see Appendix D).

See Map on Page 153

Key points:

- 0.0 Trailhead. Disregard cable barricade put there to deter vehicles, not hikers. Broad trail goes east.
- 0.3 Old stone ruins of miner's dwelling; rocky road winds down to wash below.
- 0.6 Climb to mines, then return to wash.
- 1.3 Huge boulders block the wash. Take crude trail on bank to right (west) to get around obstacle.
- 1.5 Where wash widens, old prospector site is on low shelf to your right.
- 1.8 Another boulder tumble blocks the narrow wash. Follow the cairns and the game trail to the left.
- 2.0 Silvery "anthill" above wash on left bank; bear right to John's Camp site on the low bank on the right. Return to trailhead by walking back to the wash.

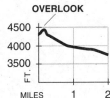

Finding the trailhead: From the visitor center in Twentynine Palms continue south on Utah Trail 8.2 miles to Pinto Y. Stay to the right on Park Route 12 and drive 5.1 miles to a right turn on a dirt road immediately opposite the signed Geology Tour Road, which heads south ("Squaw Tank" is the sign at the intersection). Turn north on the one-lane dirt road, and drive 1.4 miles to its end at the Pine City Backcountry Board and parking area.

The hike: This trip covers a variety of mine sites, from the most prosperous in the area (Desert Queen) to those that obviously were not successful. The Desert Queen was in operation from 1895 to 1961 and was one of the most productive gold mines in the Southern California desert. The magnitude of the Desert Queen operation is not evident from the gaping holes in the mountainside, but from the massive tailings that drip like blood down the mountain into the wash below. The debris left around the site—which continues to appear miles down the wash—is also evidence of the environmental repercussions of this industrial use of the desert.

The experience of hiking down the wash erases the sight of the damage to the mountainside. The huge boulders that rise above and periodically in front of you, blocking your way, are reminders of the forces of nature that are still in operation. The vegetation of the wash is profuse and diverse. Mesquite, creosote, and smoke trees line the wash, sometimes even blocking your passage. The intermittent power of rushing water scours the wash, but these durable plants enjoy this location.

Mining sites farther down the wash represent the other end of the economic spectrum from the Desert Queen. Unlike the Keys operation, the other sites are small. The artifacts found around the miners' dwellings indicate a grim existence for these workers. This was primitive living. The size of the tailings shows that the excavations were not extensive. These mining projects did not last long.

From the overlook, the remains of the Desert Queen Mine across the wash.

Walking back up the wash after visiting John's Camp, you can revel in the beauties of the canyon. Then, turning the last corner, you encounter the mining equipment left in the wash by the Desert Queen. Two distinct worlds are preserved by Joshua Tree National Park; we can learn much by being aware of both of them.

General description:	A hike to the picturesque former mining camp of Pine City, or a longer point-to-point hike past the site and down a colorful canyon with several steep rock pitches ending near the North Entrance.
Length:	3.4 miles round-trip (Pine City) or 6.5 miles point-to-point (Pine City Canyon).
General location:	15 miles south of Twentynine Palms, in north central Joshua Tree National Park, southeastern California.
Trail condition:	Clear troad to Pine City, cross-country on mostly clear washes down Pine City Canyon.
Special attractions:	Mining camp, dramatic canyon, boulder hopping.
Difficulty:	Easy (Pine City); Moderately strenuous (Pine City Canyon).
Best season:	October through May.
Starting elevation:	4,436 feet.
Maximum elevation:	4,560 feet (Pine City); 4,590 feet (Pine City Canyon).
Elevation gain/loss:	124 feet/none (Pine City); 124 feet/100 feet (Pine Spring); 156 feet/1,590 feet (Pine City Canyon).
USGS topo map:	Queen Mountain-CA (1:24,000).
For more information:	Joshua Tree National Park (see Appendix D).

See Map on Page 153

Key points:
0.0 Pine City Backcountry Board/trailhead.
1.1 Trail junction with right-hand trail leading to an old mine site; continue left.
1.6 Right-hand trail to Pine Spring; continue left.
1.7 Pine City site.
2.2 Troad ends on a ridge above Pine City Canyon.
2.3 Use trail drops to Pine City Canyon.
6.5 Pine City Canyon wash meets PR 12.

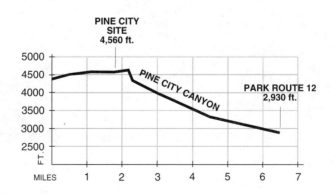

Boulder-hopping down through the narrows of Pine City Canyon.

Finding the trailhead: From the visitor center in Twentynine Palms continue south on Utah Trail 8.2 miles to Pinto Y. Stay to the right on Park Route 12 for 5.1 miles to the unsigned dirt road on your right (directly opposite Geology Tour Road, which goes south). Turn right (north) on the dirt road and drive north 1.4 miles to the end of the road at the Pine City Backcountry Board.

For car shuttle: Park at North Entrance introduction board, 0.5 mile south of the North Entrance on the west side of PR 12. The North Entrance is 4 miles south of Twentynine Palms.

The hike: Except for a few mine shafts grated over for public safety, all that remains of Pine City is the wind rustling through the pines. Still, the short and easy walk to the Pine City site provides ample opportunities for exploration and for savoring its bouldery beauty. The troad maintains an even grade across a high Mojave Desert plateau covered with Joshua trees.

At mile 1.1 (4,550 feet) an obscure trail leads to the right for 0.3 mile to a picture-perfect pocket of monzoquartz granite ringed with pinyon pines. The main trail to Pine City continues left. At 1.6 miles another trail takes off to the right, dropping 100 feet in 0.2 mile to the dry Pine City Spring. The spring lies just above the narrow notch of a steep, boulder-strewn canyon. This pleasant spot is well suited for a picnic or for just plain relaxing. Bighorn sheep rely on the cool shelter of this place when people aren't there.

NOTE: To avoid disturbance of sheep and other wildlife the Pine City/ Pine Spring/upper Pine Canyon area is within a much larger day use area. Camping is currently allowed south of Pine City in accordance with park regulations. Check at the visitor center in case these boundaries are altered.

From the Pine City turnoff continue left another 0.1 mile to the Pine City site which is immediately east of the troad in a wide, sandy flat next to a huge round boulder sitting atop a rock platform. One could easily spend several hours poking around the myriad side canyons and interesting rock formations that surround the Pine City site. The site contains at least one grated mine shaft and at least one more that is unsecured, so caution is called for. Return the way you came to complete this level 3.4 mile out-and-back hike.

To continue a point-to-point trip down Pine City Canyon, stay left on the troad for another 0.5 mile northeast of the Pine City site, to where it ends on a ridge next to a small hill. Drop into the broad saddle southwest of the 4,769-foot hill shown on the topographic map. If time and energy permit, this hill provides an easy walkup for a stunning view in all directions. From the saddle, drop down the steep gully to the main Pine City Canyon wash at 4,350 feet. A few rock cairns mark the way.

The upper reaches of Pine City Canyon are spectacular, lined with great columns of gray and red rock. The canyon drops steeply, requiring boulder hopping and, at times, the use of "all fours" to negotiate the steep but stable rocks. For out-and-back hikers wishing to sample a bit of this steep-walled canyon, hike a mile or so down to about the 4,000-foot level to a good turnaround point. This upper stretch harbors the deepest and most dramatic section of the canyon. Below 4,000 feet the canyon narrows and steepens with a several more difficult rock sections requiring skill and agility with both hands and feet. Here the canyon is trending east to northeast and is dropping about 500 feet per mile. Multicolored bands of rippled rock—purple, red, yellow—grace the floor of a canyon lined with barrel cacti.

At 3,350 feet the country begins to open up. Although high ridges are nearby, the wash leaves the deeper canyon. This is also where the transition from the high Mojave Desert to the lower Colorado Desert becomes apparent, where cholla cacti dot the open desert. The last two miles involve easy walking down a broad wash to Park Route 12, a mellow time to relax and reflect upon the rugged splendor of Pine City Canyon. The wash meets the highway about 0.2 mile south of the parking area/introduction board, which is 0.5 mile south of the North Entrance.

51   CONTACT MINE

General description:	A moderately strenuous round-trip to a historic gold and silver mining site.	See Map on Page 153
Length:	3.4 miles out-and-back.	
General location:	4.5 miles south of Twentynine Palms, northern Joshua Tree National Park, southeastern California.	
Trail condition:	Clear troad; clear wash.	
Special attraction:	Historic mine.	
Difficulty:	Moderately strenuous.	
Best season:	October through April.	
Starting elevation:	2,920 feet.	
Maximum elevation:	3,640 feet.	
Elevation gain/loss:	720 feet/none.	
USGS topo map:	Queen Mountain-CA (1:24,000).	
For more information:	Joshua Tree National Park (see Appendix D).	

Key points:

0.0-0.2   From board, follow old jeep trail southwest and left of huge boulders apart from the other disorganized piles of granite.

0.2   Wash; take the trail on top of the dike on the right.

0.4   Dike's end; bear right with the wash on faint trail around boulder pile.

0.45   Rising road ramp, dating from mining days, on left across the wash. Take this ramp up from the wash, and follow road to the mine. Cairns mark the trail.

1.6   Mine site visible on mountainside above.

1.7   Mine site; day-use only.

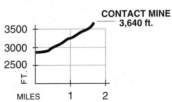

The view from Contact Mine looks out over the Pinto Range.

Finding the trailhead: From California Highway 62 in Twentynine Palms, take Utah Trail south 4 miles to North Entrance of park; continue on Park Route 12 for 0.25 mile to trailhead on right (west) at park entrance information board and parking area.

The hike: The old mining troad that takes you to the Contact Mine is as impressive in its engineering as the mine itself. The troad cuts through solid rock, avoids gullies with remarkable rock foundations, and cuts across the sides of steep hills. The hiking path has become very rocky due to erosion, but the workmanship of the original road builders is still evident.

The hiker is exposed to the elements along the entire trail. Pick a cool day to enjoy this one!

The rising troad provides stunning views into the Pinto Mountains to the east, as well as into the craggy chain of peaks running from Twentynine Palms southward. At each bend in the troad, as it winds around another rocky ridge, one expects to see the mine. Not until 1.6 miles are you rewarded with the sight of the mine above on the hillside. At this point are side-troads developed by the miners to handle two-way traffic. Count on spending additional time at the mine in order to prowl around the buildings and other artifacts, but beware of unsecured and hazardous mine shafts.

The hike back down reinforces one's awe with the work involved with developing the Contact Mine in the early 1900s.

General description:	Easily accessible from California Highway 62, this hike rewards the energetic hiker with a display of fan palms and a lush willow thicket.
Length:	3 miles round-trip.
General location:	6 miles west of Twentynine Palms and 11 miles east of Joshua Tree, northern edge of Joshua Tree National Park, southeastern California.
Trail condition:	Clear trail.
Difficulty:	Moderate.
Best season:	October through April.
Starting elevation:	2,720 feet.
Maximum elevation:	3,080 feet.
Elevation gain/loss:	360 feet/360 feet.
USGS topo map:	Queen Mountain-CA (1:24,000).
For more information:	Joshua Tree National Park (see Appendix D).

Key points:

0.0	Parking area; hike up trail on slope south of roadway.
0.3	Trail makes sharp turn to right; continue climbing.
0.5	Climb to top of ridge; first view of oasis.
1.0	Cross wash; continue downhill.
1.5	Oasis and valley beyond.

Towering California fan palms of Fortynine Palms Oasis.

FORTYNINE PALMS OASIS

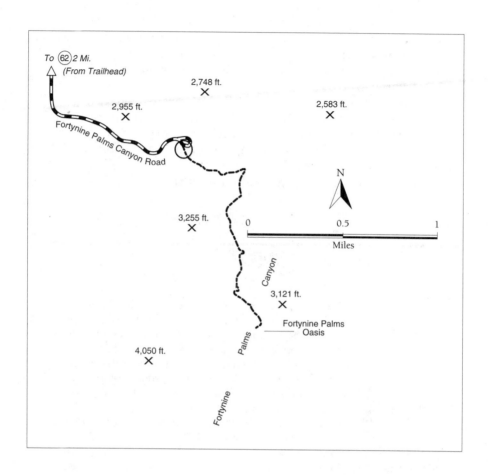

Finding the trailhead: From California Highway 62, 11.2 miles east of Park Boulevard in Joshua Tree, take Fortynine Palms Canyon Road south to the end (2 miles). From Twentynine Palms, take CA 62 for 5.5 miles west of Twentynine Palms to Fortynine Palms Canyon Road exit, then south 2 miles to the road's end at a parking area.

The hike: This is a clear but rocky trail to the Fortynine Palms Oasis. From the parking lot it climbs to its highest point in the first half of the trip; from this elevation you have a view of Twentynine Palms, and shortly later, as the trail curves to the right you have your first glimpse of the palms 0.75 mile ahead, down in a rocky gorge. The descent to the oasis traverses dry, rocky terrain; even the desert shrubs are dwarfed by the harsh conditions. Miniature barrel cactus dot the slopes. The windy, dry hills above make the oasis even more striking.

At Fortynine Palms, the huge old palms tower above a dense willow thicket that provides a congenial habitat for numerous desert birds. Hummingbirds are frequent visitors. The canyon is also a mecca for desert bighorn sheep. In this idyllic setting, the palm trees have a bizarre appearance. Their fire-scarred trunks bear tragic witness to the destructive urges of knife-wielding visitors who have tattooed the trunks with initials, signs, and names. The sight of these assaults on the palms is incongruous in such a setting, and highly disturbing.

For the adventuresome and energetic explorer, the canyon beyond the oasis (to the right) can be explored as far as time and interest permit. The use trail is intermittent, and boulders are challenging, but the curving canyon is inviting. After your exploration, the hike back to the parking lot provides sweeping views of the desert below.

NOTE: Day use only is permitted in this area to protect bighorn sheep access to water supply.

53 SNEAKEYE SPRING

General description:	A short but adventuresome trip involving some boulder scrambling to a defunct spring just south of the Indian Cove Entrance near Twentynine Palms.
Length:	1 mile out-and-back.
General location:	14 miles west of Twentynine Palms, north-central Joshua Tree National Park, southeastern California.
Trail condition:	Clear troad; cross-country boulder route in canyon.
Special attraction:	Hidden valley.
Difficulty:	Moderately strenuous, with boulder scrambling.
Best season:	October through April.
Starting elevation:	3,334 feet.
Maximum elevation:	3,500 feet.
Elevation gai/loss:	166 feet/166 feet.
USGS topo maps:	Indian Cove-CA (1:24,000).
For more information:	Joshua Tree National Park (see Appendix D).

Key points:

0.0 Parking area; follow troad southwest around large boulders.

0.2 Drop into wash; easiest ascent of canyon is via sandy hill to west (on left).

0.3 Top of sandy slope; begin climb over elephantine boulders into canyon.

0.5 Several branches of canyon to explore.

Finding the trailhead: From California Highway 62, 9.8 miles east of Park Boulevard in Joshua Tree, take Indian Cove south 3 miles to the campground. Bear right at the Y and follow signs for the hiking trail parking area.

SNEAKEYE SPRING
• INDIAN COVE NATURE TRAIL

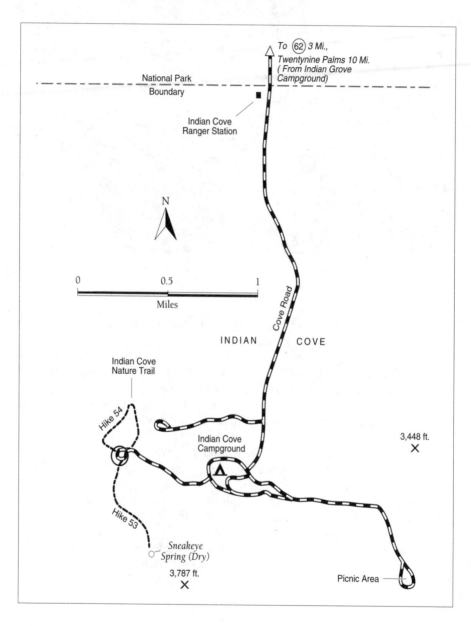

From Twentynine Palms, take CA 62 for 7 miles west of the Utah Trail junction to Indian Cove. Go south on Indian Cove 3 miles to the campground entrance. Bear right and follow signs to the hiking trail parking area.

View north to Twentynine Palms Valley from Sneakeye Spring.

The hike: This short but challenging hike takes you from a busy region of the park to an isolated high valley with pockets of greenery and oak trees, although the spring no longer is in evidence. This is a journey to an untrammeled wilderness. Due to its difficult entrance through the boulder-filled gorge, this hike appeals only to the adventuresome audience.

The first portion of the hike is deceptively easy. Curving around the monzogranite, the troad is clear and level. Only when you arrive at the wash will you perceive the difficulties that lie ahead. Careful climbing through the boulders is a pleasure due to their grainy surface. The greater hazard is the rapacious catclaw springing up wherever there is any earth available.

The high valley you reach on the northern edge of the Wonderland of Rocks has several side canyons to explore, and mature oak trees for shade and relaxation. There is no water, in spite of the name of the hike; be sure to bring plenty with you.

Descending through the boulders can be as tricky as climbing them. The 1-mile distance of the hike is misleading because such boulder travel is very time-consuming.

General description:	A short, signed nature trail on the northern edge of the Wonderland of Rocks.
Length:	0.6-mile loop.
General location:	12 miles east of Joshua Tree and 10 miles west of Twentynine Palms, northern edge of Joshua Tree National Park, southeastern California.
Trail condition:	Good wash.
Special attraction:	Nature trail featuring wash vegetation.
Difficulty:	Easy.
Best season:	October through April.
Starting elevation:	3,334 feet.
Maximum elevation:	3,334 feet.
Elevation gain/loss:	25 feet/25 feet.
USGS topo map:	Indian Cove-CA (1:24,000).
For more information:	Joshua Tree National Park (see Appendix D).

See Map on Page 165

Finding the trailhead: From California Highway 62, 9.8 miles east of Park Boulevard in Joshua Tree, take Indian Cove south 3 miles to the campground. Bear right at the Y, and follow the signs for the nature trail parking area. From the east, take CA 62 for 7 miles west of the Utah Trails intersection in Twentynine Palms; take Indian Cove south 3 miles to the campground and follow signs to the parking lot for the nature trail.

The hike: This self-guided nature trail is one of the more difficult such paths to follow due to scarcity of arrows, trail indicators, and informational signs. It begins just west of the parking area, travels across an alluvial fan, and down into a broad wash. A short 0.2 mile later, it exits the wash and returns to the parking area.

The information provided ranges from background on Paleo-Indians to desert plant and animal identification to physical geology. There is no thematic common denominator.

It's easy to miss the path's exit from the wash. Watch for the desert senna identification sign on your right immediately after the paperbag bush sign. That's your signal to bear right out of the wash to pick up the trail back to the parking area.

General description:	Well-preserved ore processing mill and other remnants of mining days provide historical interest to this easy, relatively level hike.
Length:	1.5 miles out-and-back.
General location:	20 miles southeast of the town of Joshua Tree, north central Joshua Tree National Park, southeastern California.
Trail condition:	Clear troad, clear wash.
Difficulty:	Easy.
Best season:	October through April.
Starting elevation:	4,280 feet.
Maximum elevation:	4,320 feet.
Elevation gain/loss:	40 feet/40 feet.
USGS topo map:	Indian Cove-CA (1:24,000).
For more information:	Joshua Tree National Park (see Appendix D).

Key points:

25 yards   Right at the fork; follow the troad. Ruins of pink adobe ranch house 200 yards to your left.

0.1   Two troads come together; rusty old truck 50 yards to your left. If you were tempted to investigate the ruins of the pink house to the left, this is where you will rejoin the Mill route.

0.2   Windmill and debris on your right; continue north, parallel to Wonderland.

0.4   Modern petroglyph commemorating death of Bagley, for which Keys served time in San Quentin.

0.6   Troad drops into wash and becomes more trail-like.

0.75   Park sign "Preserve America's Past" appears among the oak trees; mill site and various vehicles on your left.

Finding the trailhead: From California Highway 62 in Joshua Tree, take Park Boulevard exit and go 1 mile south where it becomes Quail Springs Road; continue on Quail Springs Rd. 4 miles to the park's West Entrance. Follow Park Route 12 for 8.7 miles to Hidden Valley Campground/Barker Dam Road. Turn left (east) into the campground. Bear right immediately after the entrance and follow the dirt road 1.6 miles to the Barker Dam Rd. Continue beyond the Barker Dam turnoff to the next dirt road to your left (0.15 mile). The sign at the turn reads "Day Use Only/Area Closed 6 P.M. to 6 A.M." The parking area is 0.25 mile from the sign. There is a Porta-Potty and a bike rack at the otherwise unmarked parking area.

The hike: This level hike displays the desert's power of preservation! Rusty old trucks still have their tires. Antique cars sit peacefully beneath oak trees. The mill, protected by the National Register of Historic Sites due to its local technological and mechanical uniqueness, still stands with its

WALL STREET MILL • WONDERLAND WASH
• BARKER DAM NATURE TRAIL/LOOP
• HIDDEN VALLEY NATURE TRAIL

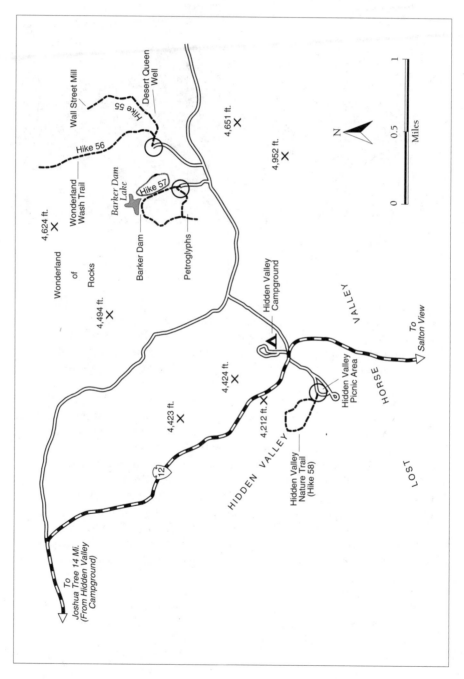

The rusty remains of the Wall Street Mill sit atop the hill adjacent to the majestic Wonderland of Rocks.

machinery intact, albeit a tad rusty. A barbed-wire fence also protects the mill from visitors. Nearby are hulks of vehicles and other artifacts of life in the desert 60 years ago. A park sign at the mill explains its workings, with an excellent drawing—actually a blueprint of its original design in the 1930s. This is a fun voyage of discovery, even for those who might not be machinery buffs.

The ranch house to the left of the trail and the windmill at mile 0.2 are remnants of the ranching era in the Queen Valley. The Keys family has been involved in both ranching and mining and still has a private inholding, the Desert Queen Ranch, to the west of this trail.

The Wall Street Mill was part of the Keyses' industrial complex. Built by Bill Keys to process the ore from the Desert Queen Mine, it was in operation for only a few years before falling into disuse. One reason for its short life span is that Bill Keys had a run-in with Worth Bagley, his neighbor, over the use of the road to the mill. The painted rock at 0.4 mile marks the spot of the final altercation and of Bagley's death. Convicted of murder, Keys spent 5 years in prison but was later exonerated. Apparently he had shot Bagley in self-defense.

The trail shares its trailhead with the Wonderland Wash hike (Hike 56). The proximity of the mill and the mounds of monzogranite provide appropriate contrast between the reign of man and of nature in this wild country.

Return to the parking area by the same wash/troad.

General description:	A flat, easy hike into a fantasyland of monzogranite sculptures and mounds.	See Map on Page 169

Length:	2.0 miles out-and-back (longer for exploration).
General location:	20 miles southeast of the town of Joshua Tree, north-central Joshua Tree National Park, southeastern California.
Trail condition:	Clear wash.
Special attractions:	Spectacular rock formations of all shapes and sizes, in every direction.
Difficulty:	Easy.
Best season:	September through May.
Starting elevation:	4,280 feet.
Maximum elevation:	4,350 feet (if you stay in the wash and resist the temptation to climb the rocks).
Elevation gain/loss:	70 feet/none.
USGS topo map:	Indian Cove-CA (1: 24,000).
For more information:	Joshua Tree National Park (see Appendix D).

Key points:

0.0 First fork immediately beyond trailhead; bear left to ruins of pink adobe ranch house.

0.3 Cut by house and enter wash to your left, following beaten use trail.

0.4 Continue winding north in the wash, between awesome rock formations.

1.0 Huge domes of monzogranite—the Astro Domes.

Finding the trailhead: From California Highway 62 in the town of Joshua Tree, take Park Boulevard south 1 mile to where it becomes Quail Springs Road. Continue on Quail Springs Rd. 4 miles to the West Entrance of the park. Continue southeast on Park Route 12 for 8.7 miles to the Hidden Valley Campground. Turn left into the campground, and take the immediate right turn (signed to Barker Dam). Follow this dirt road 1.7 miles to the first road on your left after the signed Barker Dam turnoff. The only sign on the Wonderland Wash road is "Day Use Only/Area Closed 6 p.m. to 6 a.m." Drive north 0.25 mile to a large unsigned parking area, which is also the trailhead for the Wall Street Mill hike (Hike 55). There is a Porta-Potty and a bike rack at the otherwise unmarked trailhead.

The hike: The use trail into Wonderland Wash is easy to follow due to the footsteps of the hundreds of rock climbers who enjoy these acres of White Tank granite. From the parking area, follow the trail to the first fork, and bear left towards the ruins of a pink house which you can see from the fork. Head for the house, then follow the beaten path to the left into the nearby shallow wash, only about 50 feet from the house site. The narrow

The trail up Wonderland Wash winds through a myriad of granite boulders of all sizes.

wash is easy to follow, with periodic pathways weaving from bank to bank as you follow it northward into the Wonderland.

Plentiful oak and prickly pear, as well as the remnants of a dam in the wash, are other attractions of this hike—but the primary focus is on the huge rock formations that stretch in all directions. This is an enchanted world of whimsically eroded granite mounds. Well into the wash (1 mile from the trailhead) are the formations known as the Astro Domes to rock climbers who enjoy scaling their massive surfaces. The voices of climbers usually can be heard echoing from various points among the boulders, and their silhouettes may startle you when they appear hundreds of feet above atop these obelisks.

The trip back down the wash to the trailhead will be equally interesting, since the rock formations look different from the new angle.

General description:	A 1-mile loop providing easy access to Wonderland of Rocks and the only lake in the park; this educational nature trail also passes through a rich array of petroglyphs.
Length:	1.1-mile loop.
General location:	20 miles southeast of the town of Joshua Tree, in the north-central region of Joshua Tree National Park, southeastern California.
Trail condition:	Clear.
Special attraction:	Nature trail, lake, archaeological site.
Difficulty:	Easy.
Best season:	October through May.
Starting elevation:	4,251 feet.
Maximum elevation:	4,320 feet.
Elevation gain/loss:	70 feet/70 feet.
USGS topo map:	Indian Cove-CA (1:24,000).
For more information:	Joshua Tree National Park (see Appendix D).

See Map on Page 169

Key points:
0.4   Barker Dam Lake.
0.8   Petroglyphs.
1.1   End of loop at the parking lot.

Finding the trailhead: From California Highway 62 in Joshua Tree, take Park Boulevard south 1 mile to where it turns into Quail Springs Road; continue on Quail Springs Rd. 4 miles to the West Entrance of park. Follow Park Route 12 for 8.5 miles to Hidden Valley Campground and Barker Dam turnoff to the east (left); bear right at the signed road immediately after entering the campground and drive 1.6 miles to the Barker Dam parking lot.

The hike: This highly informative nature trail is a step back in time, both in terms of prehistory and with respect to futile, short-lived attempts to raise cattle back in the early 1900s. Barker Dam was built by ranchers Barker and Shay in a natural rock catch basin to store water for cattle. In 1949-1950 the dam was raised by Bill Keys, owner of the Desert Queen Mine and the nearby Desert Queen Ranch, still a private inholding. When filled to capacity by seasonal rains, the lake behind the dam encompasses 20 acres. Because it is surrounded by a magnificent rock ring of monzonite granite, it looks almost as though it is nestled in a high Sierra cirque at 11,000 feet. Today, the lake is used by bighorn sheep and many other species of wildlife, including shorebirds and migratory waterfowl—some of the last creatures one would expect to find in the desert!

The trail is clear and sandy, winding through a couple of tight places in the rocks, reaching Barker Dam at 0.4 mile. Notable plant species enroute

The lake stretches toward the Wonderland of Rocks boulders behind Barker Dam.

include Turbinella oak, adapted to the high Mojave Desert above 4,000 feet, and nolina—a yucca look-alike that provided food for the Cahuilla Indians who baked it like molasses.

Bill Keys built innovative stone watering basins, designed to prevent spillage of the precious desert water, below the dam.

From Barker Dam lake the trail heads west and south through a series of intimate little alcove-like valleys containing rock-lined gardens of Joshua trees, cholla, and yucca. At 0.8 mile the trail comes to a signed path leading 100 feet right to a large panel of petroglyphs, which are etchings in stone made by early Native Americans. The petroglyphs are on the face of a large rock amphitheater/overhang. Sadly, a movie crew painted the carvings so that they would show up better on film. The rock faces just to the southeast of these vandalized petroglyphs contained undamaged petroglyphs, which are largely concealed by dense brush. This early encampment of immeasurable value includes rock mortars used for the grinding of nuts and seeds along with petroglyphs of a scorpion, a man with long fingers, women with dresses who were likely early settlers, and other figures better left to your imagination. Vegetation is being re-established along this cliff wall so please be careful to avoid trampling the new plantings and other vegetation.

The loop continues another 0.3 mile back to the parking area/trailhead.

General description:	This self-guided trail emphasizes the area's history as it travels the perimeter of Hidden Valley with very little change in elevation.
Length:	1-mile loop.
General location:	14 miles southeast of the town of Joshua Tree, north-central Joshua Tree National Park, southeastern California.
Trail condition:	Clear trail.
Special attraction:	Valley surrounded by mounds of monzogranite.
Difficulty:	Easy.
Best season:	October through April.
Starting elevation:	4,212 feet.
Maximum elevation:	4,212 feet.
Elevation gain/loss:	80 feet/80 feet.
USGS topo map:	Indian Cove-CA (1:24,000).
For more information:	Joshua Tree National Park (see Appendix D).

See Map on Page 169

Key points:
    0.0   Parking area; trail goes into narrow canyon leading to valley.
    0.1   Trail junction; follow trail left around the valley.
    1.0   End of loop.

Finding the trailhead: From California Highway 62 at Joshua Tree, take Park Boulevard south 1 mile to where it becomes Quail Springs Road. Continue on Quail Springs Rd. 4 miles to West Entrance of the park; stay on the same road (now Park Route 12) 8.7 miles to Hidden Valley Nature Trail and Picnic Area on your right. After your turn off the main road, follow the dirt road to the right less than 0.1 mile to the parking area.

The hike: The trail from the parking area winds upward through the boulders to Hidden Valley. This part of the trail consists of old asphalt, so following it is easy. The rest of the journey is unpaved but clearly marked with signs, arrows, or fallen logs. There is some low-intensity rock walking, but a bright new wooden bridge takes you over the most challenging part.

Many possible pathways diverge in all directions within the valley. Most are created by the numerous adventuresome rock climbers who are attracted to the massive blocks of granite that create the valley walls. It is likely that you will hear them and see them on your hike.

To follow the historical signs in chronological order, bear to the left when you enter the valley (0.1 mile from trailhead).

Indian life and settlers' activities are the emphasis in the early part of the trail. The abnormally high rainfall (10 inches/year) of the late nineteenth

Rock climbers are a common sight on the boulder piles in Hidden Valley.

century led to the development of cattle ranches here. The McHaney Gang allegedly used Hidden Valley as a base camp for their large rustling operation in the southwest, until they turned their energies to gold mining. They began developing the Desert Queen Mine in 1895. It was eventually taken over by Bill Keys, who became quite the desert magnate—successful rancher and miner until his death in 1969.

The advent of the automobile in the 1920s brought new visitors aplenty to the desert, seriously endangering the fragile environment. In the 1930s, Minerva Hamilton Hoyt led efforts to protect the region, resulting finally in Franklin D. Roosevelt's 1936 declaration of Joshua Tree National Monument. In 1950 the boundary of the monument was sizably reduced in order to permit extensive mining. The larger area was restored with the California Desert Protection Act of 1994. The nature trail provides a thorough overview of this history, as well as a parting reminder to the visitor to remain vigilant as a protector of our desert resources.

NOTE: This is a day-use area; no camping is permitted.

59   BOY SCOUT TRAIL/WILLOW HOLE

General description:	A largely downhill point-to-point hike along the west edge of the Wonderland of Rocks, requiring a car shuttle to the Indian Cove Entrance of the park.
Length:	8 miles one-way (car shuttle), with optional 4 mile round-trip to Willow Hole.
General location:	11.4 miles southeast of the town of Joshua Tree, in northwestern Joshua Tree National Park, southeastern California.
Trail condition:	Clear trail/wash with a steep but good trail segment between miles 4 and 5.
Special attraction:	Wonderland of Rocks.
Difficulty:	Moderate (from south to north downhill); moderately strenuous (from north to south uphill).
Best season:	October through April (Boy Scout Trail); October through May (Willow Hole).
Starting elevation:	4,040 feet.
Maximum elevation:	4,250 feet.
Elevation gain/loss:	290 feet/1,480 feet (Boy Scout Trail); 110 feet/110 feet (Willow Hole).
USGS topo map:	Indian Cove-CA (1:24,000).
For more information:	Joshua Tree National Park (see Appendix D).

Key points:

    0.0   Keys View Backcountry Board.
    1.3   Boy Scout Trail/Willow Hole Trail junction.

Side trip to Willow Hole:

0.0 Boy Scout Trail/Willow Hole Trail junction.
1.2 Trail enters and follows a wash.
2.0 Willow Hole.
4.0 Back to trail junction.
3.0 High point of the trail at 4,250 feet.
3.6 Trail drops into and follows wash.
4.0 Cement water trough and constructed rock wall across wash.
4.2 Trail makes a sharp left turn out of the wash.
4.6 Rocky trail climbs to 4,070 feet for a panoramic view.
4.9 Trail drops into wash and follows for 1 mile.
6.0 Trail crosses over into a side gully dropping to the main wash.
6.5 Trail leaves the canyon and cuts across open desert.
8.0 Indian Cove Backcountry Board.

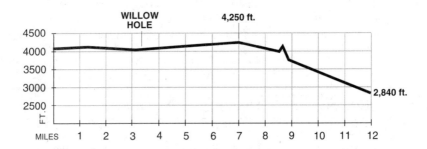

Finding the trailhead: From California Highway 62 in Joshua Tree, take Park Boulevard south 1 mile to where it becomes Quail Springs Road; follow it another 4 miles to the West Entrance of the park. Continue 6.9 miles to the Keys View Backcountry Board, which is the starting trailhead on the left (north) side of the highway.

Car shuttle: From CA 62, 9.8 miles east of Park Blvd., take Indian Cove Road south 1.6 miles to the Indian Cove Backcountry Board on your right (west side of the road).

The hike: The Boy Scout Trail provides access to several high-quality hikes within and adjacent to the Wonderland of Rocks. The most complete and enjoyable choice is to hike mostly downhill from Keys View Backcountry Board to the Indian Cove Backcountry Board, taking in an excursion deep into the fascinating Wonderland of Rocks at Willow Hole. This 12-mile journey on foot samples much of the diversity of this amazing landscape. If a car shuttle is out of the question, an excellent second choice is to hike 6.6 miles round-trip to Willow Hole. Both trips share the first 1.3 miles of the Boy Scout Trail from Keys View Backcountry Board. As such, they are included within this same hike description but presented separately.

The popular, well-signed Boy Scout Trail climbs gradually along the west side of the Wonderland of Rocks through a picturesque Joshua tree forest sprinkled with yucca and cholla cacti, gaining only 90 feet in the first 1.3 miles. The trail offers gorgeous views of the San Bernardino Mountains to

BOY SCOUT TRAIL/WILLOW HOLE

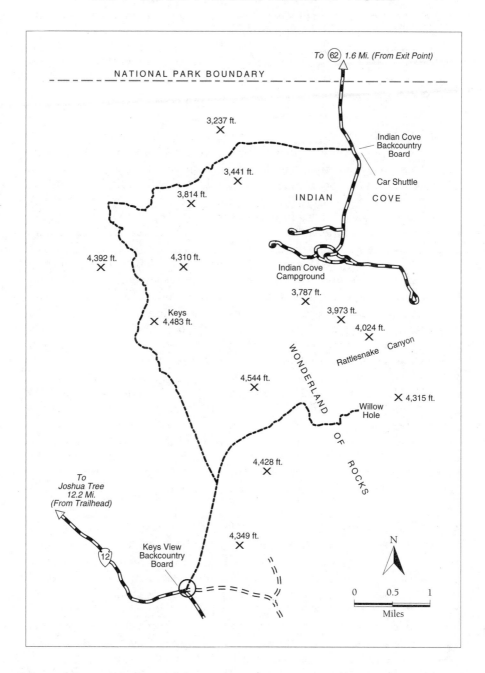

To (62) 1.6 Mi. (From Exit Point)

NATIONAL PARK BOUNDARY

3,237 ft.
X

3,441 ft.
X

3,814 ft.
X

INDIAN   COVE

Indian Cove
Backcountry
Board

Car Shuttle

4,392 ft.
X

4,310 ft.
X

Indian Cove
Campground

3,787 ft.
X

3,973 ft.
X

4,024 ft.
X

Rattlesnake   Canyon

Keys
X 4,483 ft.

4,544 ft.
X

WONDERLAND

X 4,315 ft.

Willow
Hole

OF

ROCKS

4,428 ft.
X

To
Joshua Tree
12.2 Mi.
(From Trailhead)

4,349 ft.
X

12

Keys View
Backcountry
Board

N

0   0.5   1

Miles

the southwest, and the nearby mounds of monzonite quartz add a real sense of majesty to this high Mojave Desert country. The right side (east) of the entire Boy Scout Trail is open to day use only so that desert wildlife can visit water sources undisturbed. Backpackers can camp on the west side so long as they are at least 500 feet from the trail. Also, be advised that there is no public access to the Desert Queen Ranch inholding which is just east of the Boy Scout Trail during the first half mile.

The following two hikes are described from the trail junction at 1.3 miles. The right-hand trail leads to Willow Hole and is signed "Day Use Only". The left fork is the Boy Scout Trail which is signed "Horse and Foot Trail" and "Indian Cove 7 miles".

WILLOW HOLE

The clear, sandy trail maintains a fairly constant but gradual downhill grade in a northeasterly direction, winding through impressive columns and pillars of white tank granite. At 1.2 miles the trail enters and follows a sandy wash. At 1.4 miles a wash enters from the right; continue left down the wider wash. At 1.7 miles another wash joins from the right, which makes for a tempting side trip into a secluded little valley. A large boulder blocks the wash 0.2 mile up, which is a good turnaround point or continue up a bit further by lifting yourself up and through the narrow rock notch to the clear wash beyond. Double back to the Willow Hole wash. At 1.8 miles the wash widens into a huge circular bowl surrounded by majestic cliffs. Willow Hole comes into view at 2 miles with its dense tangle of large willow trees creating a moist micro environment that holds seasonal pools of water. To get to the other side of the grove bend down and walk through the center of Willow Hole on an overgrown use trail or take a well-worn use trail around the right side. Either way the view from the east end of Willow Hole is very worthwhile, especially down the wash toward Rattlesnake Canyon. Retrace your route 2 miles back to the trail junction. About 0.6 mile on the way back it is possible to take the wrong wash in a narrow, rocky area. In general, stay right on the more traveled wash.

It is possible to continue another 3 miles on a strenuous cross-country route down the wash below Willow Hole to Rattlesnake Canyon, ending up at the picnic area southeast of Indian Cove Campground. This difficult, trailless route is known as the "Wonderland Connection" and would require a car shuttle.

BOY SCOUT TRAIL

From the trail junction at 1.3 miles take the left-hand fork. For the next 2 miles the trail stays fairly level in a high Joshua tree plateau with yucca/rock gardens galore. After climbing to 4,250 feet at mile 3 the trail gradually drops along rocky side gullies but remains clear and easy to follow. At about 3.5 miles to the end the trail is occasionally marked with steel pipe with two white stripes on top along with a few wooden posts. At 3.6 miles the trail drops into and follows a clear wash to mile 4 where a cement water trough and constructed rock wall are found in the wash.

At 4.2 miles the trail leaves the wash, making a sharp turn to the left (west). This turn is easy to miss, so watch for a steel pipe trail marker behind a pinyon pine to the left. This is also where the wash narrows and drops steeply into an extremely rugged canyon. This constructed portion of the trail is narrow and rocky but in good condition. It drops and then climbs to mile 4.6 where a good view opens up to the canyon far below. The trail then switchbacks steeply down to a wash at mile 5 (3,740 feet); following the wash for another mile. The wash is easy walking but is bound by extremely steep rocky slopes and cliff rock near mile 6.

At mile 6 a steel pipe on the right marks the departure of the trail from the wash where it then crosses over into the main wash, following it to mile 6.5. At mile 6.5 a well marked trail climbs out of the wash to the right and cuts across 1.5 miles of open desert-alluvial fan vegetated with creosote, yucca, cholla cacti and Mormon tea. Most impressive are the reoccurring mounds of granite sprinkled like great dollops of frozen yogurt across the desert. At mile 8 the trail ends at an elevation of 2,840 feet at the Indian Cove Backcountry Board.

60 QUAIL WASH TO WEST ENTRANCE WASH

General description:	A long but gentle point-to-point hike in open desert, washes, and canyons, with an optional side trip to the Lang Cabin and Mine up Johnny Lang Canyon.
Length:	8.2 miles one-way (with car shuttle), with optional 6-mile round-trip up Johnny Lang Canyon.
General location:	10 miles southeast of the town of Joshua Tree, western Joshua Tree National Park, southeastern California.
Trail condition:	Clear trail, troad, and washes, with primitive troad/trail leading to mine.
Special attractions:	A dense stand of Joshua trees, historic cabin ruins and mine, expansive views of Quail Mountain, and several scenic side canyons to explore.
Difficulty:	Moderate for point-to-point trip; moderately strenuous side trip to Johnny Lang Mine.
Best season:	October through May.
Starting elevation:	3,980 feet.
Maximum elevation:	3,980 feet (Quail Springs Picnic Area), or 4,800 feet at Lang Mine.
Elevation gain/loss:	420 feet/620 feet (point-to-point route only); 1,490 feet/1,690 feet (with side trip to Lang Mine).
USGS topo maps:	Joshua Tree South-CA and Indian Cove-CA (1:24,000).
For more information:	Joshua Tree National Park (see Appendix D).

Key points:
0.0   Quail Springs Picnic Area.
2.0   Junction with the troad heading south up Johnny Lang Canyon.

Side Trip to Johnny Lang Mine:

0.0 Junction with troad heading south up Johnny Lang Canyon.

1.3 Remains of Lang Cabin.

3.0 Johnny Lang Mine.

3.0 Second major valley to the south; leads toward Quail Mountain.

4.5 Mouth of Smith Water Canyon.

5.0 Trail enters recent fire area.

6.7 Trail reaches north boundary of park; turn right (west) up West Entrance Wash.

7.7 Leave West Entrance Wash and head northeast up a side wash.

8.2 Park Route 12, 1 mile south of West Entrance.

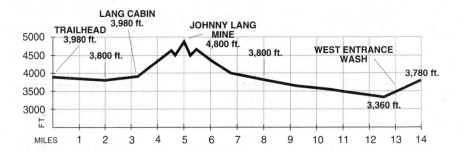

Finding the trailhead: From California Highway 62 in the town of Joshua Tree, take Park Boulevard south 1 mile to where it becomes Quail Springs Road; continue 4.3 miles to the West Entrance. Continue 6.1 miles on Park Route 12 to Quail Springs Picnic Area on your right.

For car shuttle: 1.2 miles inside of the West Entrance on Park Route 12 is a pullout on the north side of the road near the wash exit of the trail. The exit point of the hike is 1 mile south of the West Entrance on PR 12.

The hike: This troad starts out through an open Joshua tree desert ringed by a distant horizon of jagged peaks dotted with mounds of granite. The clear, sandy trail leads west-northwest and is easy to follow. At 0.6 mile it crosses the wash and continues on the left side, providing much firmer walking than the wash.

SIDE TRIP TO JOHNNY LANG MINE

The troad angles closer to the rocky hillside on the left (south) and intersects the Johnny Lang Canyon troad at mile 2.0. This is the first major canyon to the south. This troad is easy to miss but it takes off from the main trail at a 45-degree angle heading southwest from near the foot of the ridge. The Johnny Lang Canyon troad passes just to the left of a small hill 0.2 mile up. It then crosses a wash at 0.3 mile, angling southwest to the base of the hill. It turns south for another mile to the Lang cabin site, staying on the right side of this wide lower valley all the way to the cabin ruins. If in doubt follow the main Johnny Lang wash.

QUAIL WASH TO WEST ENTRANCE WASH

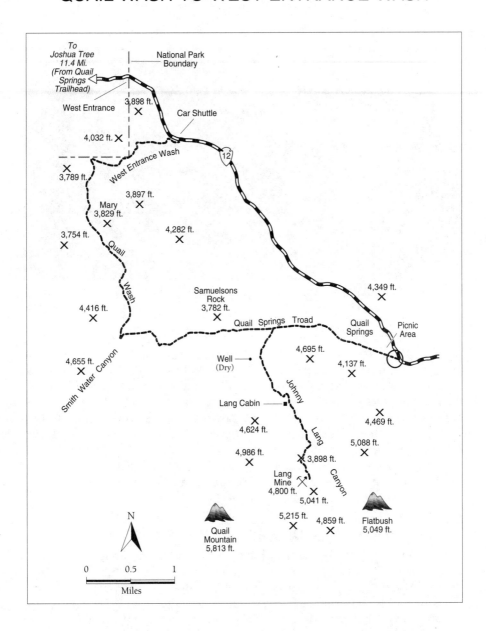

The remnants of the cabin, such as they are, are located on a bench about 50 feet to the right of the wash at 3,980 feet. All that remains are part of a rock foundation and piles of rusted cans and metal. A fairly well-defined use trail takes off from the cabin site. From here it is possible to see a large dark-topped hill (Point 4549 on the topo map) about 1 mile south; this is on the route leading up to the mine.

Fresh snow on Quail Mountain as seen from mile 3.0 onthe Quail Wash trail.

The use trail crosses the wash several times during the next 0.6 mile before coming to a manzanita flat just before a gully on the right. Cross the gully and head to the right up the ridge (south) toward the dark-topped hill (which has a knob and saddle to its left). On the backside of the hill you'll intersect the rocky remains of an overgrown troad which leads south into a gully below the mine. From this point you can see the mine tailings to the south high on the hillside just below a prominent rock outcropping. Drop into the gully then ascend the ridge southward, gaining 300 feet in the remaining 0.25 mile to the unsecured mine shaft. At 700 feet above the canyon the mine entrance and platform is certainly a room with a view. Retrace your route for the 3-mile descent back to Quail Wash.

CONTINUATION OF QUAIL WASH-WEST ENTRANCE WASH

Continue west on the main trail after passing Johnny Lang Canyon. At mile 3 the trail passes by the second major canyon to the south which leads up toward the highest point in the park—5,813-foot Quail Mountain. At 3.2 miles several steel posts mark a fenceline across the wash. The trail begins to leave the open desert, dropping into a wide gap through the mountains. At mile 4 the trail dips to the southwest and crosses the Smith Water Canyon Wash at 4.5 miles. Joshua trees are especially thick in this area. If time permits this is an interesting place to explore, both in lower Smith Water Canyon and south toward the Quail Spring site shown on the topo map.

At 5 miles the trail/wash enters a recent burned-over
ened Joshua trees dominating the landscape to the sout.
miles the trail weaves in and out of the wash. For the most
easier to find and follow than the trail. At 6.5 miles the trail,
at a National Park Service boundary fence in another recent b
6.7 miles the trail reaches a rock-cable boundary fence which is ag.
"NPS boundary US". Do not cross the fence onto the adjacent priva
erty. Instead, turn right and follow the fence on a well-defined use
eastward. Soon the trail disappears in West Entrance Wash. Continue up the
wide sandy wash for about a mile. Look for a side wash angling left (northeast) next to a distinctive rock mound on the left. Head up this wash where
you'll come to a rock ledge dropoff within 0.1 mile. Climb up the ledge and
continue up the wash another 0.4 mile to Park Route 12. At this point you've
walked a good distance so let's hope your shuttle will be waiting for you. If
not, at least you're only a mile south of the West Entrance.

61 CALIFORNIA RIDING AND HIKING TRAIL
COVINGTON FLATS TO KEYS VIEW, QUAIL MOUNTAIN

General description:	Point-to-point hike (with car shuttle) over varied terrain, with optional 5-mile side trip to Quail Mountain.
Length:	15 miles one-way (with car shuttle).
General location:	12 miles south of the town of Joshua Tree, central section of Joshua Tree National Park, southeastern California.
Trail condition:	Clear trail; good wash; short cross-country section to peak.
Special attractions:	Largest Joshua tree in the park; highest peak in the park (5,813 feet).
Difficulty:	Moderate (R & H Trail); strenuous (Quail Peak).
Best season:	October through May.
Starting elevation:	4,820 feet (Upper Covington Backcountry Board).
Maximum elevation:	5,000 feet (without Quail Mountain); 5,813 feet (with Quail Mountain).
Elevation gain/loss:	1,060 feet/1,560 feet for CA R & H Trail; plus 1,475/none feet for peak side trip.
USGS topo maps:	Joshua Tree South-CA; E. Deception Canyon-CA; and Keys View-CA (1:24,000).
For more information:	Joshua Tree National Park (see Appendix D).

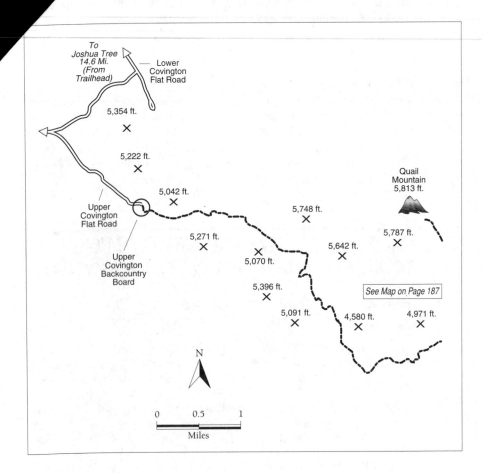

Key points:

0.0-1.5   Parking area; well-marked trail goes over a ridge and along hillside pinyon-juniper forest. The largest Joshua tree is in 0.1 mile.

1.7   Intersection with spur trail from Covington Picnic Area at milepost 28. Bear right.

2-3.5   Trail goes over a series of ridges.

5.0   Milepost 23, nearly hidden by large juniper on your right; side-trip to Quail Mountain. The road appears to be a flat wash lacking telltale wheel tracks. Turn left.

5.5   Road's end. Head northeast towards Quail Peak. Look behind and select distinctive features in the landscape to help you locate your return route. Cross through the prickly shrubbery towards a fire-break that cuts over the northeast ridge.

6.1   Two lower ridges and a wash; turn left and follow wash toward the mountain. Note your location so you can exit here on your return trip.

CALIFORNIA RIDING AND HIKING TRAIL
COVINGTON FLATS TO KEYS VIEW, QUAIL MTN.

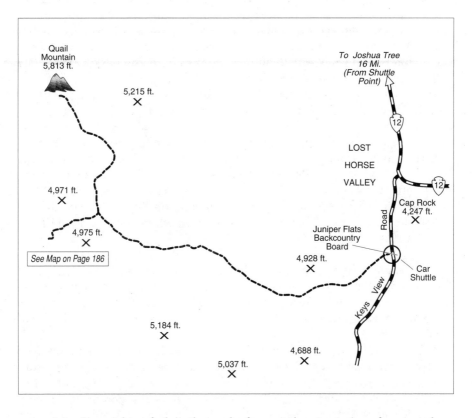

6.4   Bear right at fork in the wash after a rock outcropping of contorted striped strata on the left (west) side. (Cairns and footprints help).

6.8   Wash becomes narrow, rocky, and littered with downed trees, but stay in the ravine.

7.1   Emerge from the ravine, which has finally petered out; scramble up to the ridge to the right.

7.5   Huge cairn marks summit. Return the way you came.

10.0   Continuation of the trip to Keys View Road.

15.0   Backcountry board, to the right of the trail.

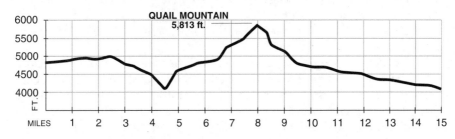

Finding the trailhead: From California Highway 62 and Park Boulevard in the town of Joshua Tree, go east on CA 62 for 3.4 miles to La Contenta. Turn right (south) on La Contenta and go 2.9 miles to Covington Flat Road. La Contenta is paved for only a mile; thereafter it is a washboardy narrow dirt road, but suitable for passenger vehicles. Turn right at the sign for "Backcountry Trailhead" and take a cut-over 1.9 miles to Upper Covington Road. Turn left, again following signs to the backcountry board, on Upper Covington Rd. and go 2 miles southeast to the board and parking area. The trail leaves from behind the board.

If covering the continuous length of the California Riding and Hiking Trail is not your goal, this segment of the trail can also be accessed by continuing on the Lower Covington Flat Road to the dead-end at the picnic area. The trail from the picnic area joins this trail after the first mile.

Car shuttle: From CA 62 in Joshua Tree, take Park Blvd. south 1 mile where it becomes Quail Springs Road, which you take for 4 miles to the West Entrance. Continue 10 miles on Park Route 12 to intersection of PR 12 and Keys View Road (Park Route 13). Bear right on Keys View and drive 1 mile to the Juniper Flats Backcountry Board, near where the California Riding and Hiking Trail crosses Keys View Rd.

The hike: Neither wide nor well-pruned, this section of the California Riding and Hiking Trail is evidently not heavily traveled, although it is frequently signed with arrows and mileposts. This is definitely a long-pants excursion or your legs will suffer on both the basic trail and the side trip to Quail Mountain.

Evidence of wildlife is considerably more plentiful on the first 5 miles of the trail from Covington Flat—deer, sheep, rabbits, rodents, coyotes—than elsewhere on the trail. Unlike the Riding and Hiking Trail segment out of the Black Rock Campground (Hike 63), this section shows no signs of use by horses. The first 5 miles are also highly enjoyable as you climb up and down over a series of descending ridges. The crest of each ridge provides a "Wow!" reaction as the panoramas of the park open before you. Even without climbing Quail Mountain this section of the Riding and Hiking Trail provides sweeping vistas of the Little San Bernardino Range to the south, the Pinto Range to the east, and the various pinnacles in the central section of the park.

The climb to Quail Mountain is easy to plan from this south approach since the peak is visible from your takeoff point at milepost 23 on the Riding and Hiking Trail, and most of the way after that as well. The approach up the wash is challenging, but it is better than trying the southeast ridge. The downfall of pinyon limbs that makes the wash/ravine so difficult is the result of a 1978 burn on the mountain.

As you climb to the naked summit you will be stunned by the dimensions of the cairn. It is a tower of well-placed rocks at least 5 feet high. From a distance the mountain looks exactly like the bird for which it was named. The views from Quail Peak are spectacular. The entire park spreads out in every direction. After enjoying the windy view, return via your route to the spur road and the Riding and Hiking Trail. The points you picked on your way up should help you locate the trail.

The last 5 miles down the Riding and Hiking Trail after the peak ascent are not anti-climactic. The overwhelming natural wonders of Joshua Tree are ever-present. The Wonderland of Rocks grows immense as you get farther into Juniper Flats. The White Tank formations of Ryan Mountain also become more massive as you approach Keys View Road. This hike represents the pinnacle of a Joshua Tree experience for both the ascent to the highest peak in the park and the journey through its wild heartland.

62 COVINGTON LOOP

General description:	A triangular loop over varied terrain in the high desert, with optional side trips to a historic mine and rugged canyon.
Length:	4.1-mile loop plus two side trips totaling 3.3 miles.
General location:	About 15 miles southeast of the town of Yucca Valley, in west-central Joshua Tree National Park, southeastern California.
Trail condition:	Clear trail on the two legs of the California Riding and Hiking Trail; clear wash on cross-country segment of loop.
Special attractions:	Largest known Joshua tree in the park; recent fire area; diverse topography, historic mine side trip; scenic canyon side trip.
Difficulty:	Moderate.
Best season:	October through May.
Starting elevation:	4,820 feet.
Maximum elevation:	4,970 feet.
Elevation gain/loss:	560 feet/560 feet (basic loop).
USGS topo map:	Joshua Tree South-CA (1:24,000).
For more information:	Joshua Tree National Park (see Appendix D).

Key points:
- 0.0 Covington Flat Backcountry Board (4,820 feet).
- 0.2 Upper end of a northeast-trending canyon.
- 1.3 Canyon wash crosses the north leg of the California Riding and Hiking Trail.
- 2.4 Riding and Hiking Trail junction.
- 3.6 Trail reaches high point on a ridge (4,970 feet).
- 4.0 Largest known Joshua tree in the park.
- 4.1 Covington Flat Backcountry Board (end of loop).

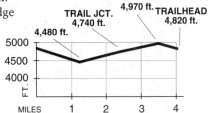

Finding the trailhead: From the intersection of Park Boulevard and California Highway 62 (Twentynine Palms Highway) in the town of Joshua Tree, drive west for 3.4 miles on CA 62 to La Contenta. Turn left (south) on La Contenta. The pavement ends after 1 mile. Continue straight ahead on an unsigned dirt road for 6.3 miles to Lower Covington Flat; turn right on the cutover road to Upper Covington Flat and drive 1.9 miles to a road junction signed "Backcountry Trailhead." Turn left on this road and drive 2 miles to the Covington Flat Backcountry Board and parking area at the end of the road.

The hike: This is a true loop with no route duplication unless the suggested side trips are taken. The recommended direction of travel is "clockwise." From the Covington Flat Backcountry Board begin the hike on the California Riding and Hiking Trail (CRHT). After less than 0.1 mile turn left on a well-traveled sandy wash leading to the upper end of a canyon entrance graced by pinyon pines, juniper, and Joshua trees. Large boulders block the entrance but it is fairly easy to lower yourself around, then down the rocks to the sandy wash below. At 0.9 mile the wash descends a great slab of rock that is easy to walk down. Bound by low ridges this northeast-trending wash joins the northern leg of the Riding and Hiking Trail at 1.3 miles. The trail is well marked in the wash crossing with metal pipe markers.

For a short side trip to a historic mine turn left (northwest) on the Riding and Hiking Trail. From here it is about 0.6 mile to the Covington Flat Picnic Area, which is encompassed within a recent fire area. The burn is entered

Large boulders guard the upper end of the canyon.

190

COVINGTON LOOP

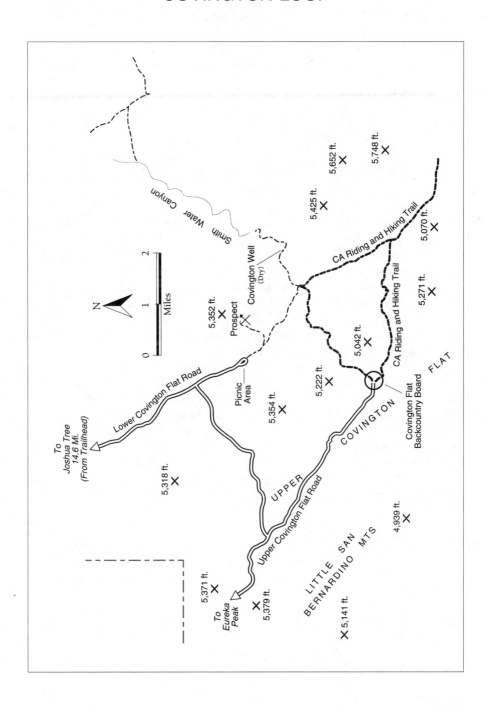

after about 0.3 mile. Look for a troad turning sharply right after another 0.1 mile next to a charred wooden trailpost. Follow the troad about 0.25 mile up to the mine site at the base of the steep, rocky hillside. Nearby is an ore cart, some tracks, tailings, and charred timbers. Double back to the wash/trail junction thereby completing this 1.3-mile side trip.

A second enjoyable side trip from this point is to hike into the upper reaches of Smith Water Canyon, which is directly northeast of the wash/trail junction. After about 0.4 mile the canyon begins to narrow somewhat. Look for the rock-lined dugout of the Covington Well (dry) which is hidden in brush on the right side of the upper canyon. After about 1 mile the canyon has dropped about 200 feet. It is lush enough for willow at this point but is also becoming rougher with large rocks in the wash bottom. It is possible to hike this scenic canyon north to Quail Wash but the lower end has some difficult boulders, including a 20-foot rock dropoff that may require ropes for safe descent.

To continue the loop, hike the mile back up to the trail/wash junction and begin the second leg by walking southeast on the Riding and Hiking Trail. This good trail, marked in places by steel posts, climbs an open alluvial fan of juniper and Joshua trees for 1.1 miles to the signed trail junction with the southern leg of the Riding and Hiking Trail. Milepost 28 sits just beyond the junction. Turn right on the Riding and Hiking Trail, which heads west back to the Covington Flat Backcountry Board. This final 1.7-mile leg of the loop is very scenic as it climbs some 250 feet across narrow gullies and up side ridges through dense pinyon-juniper cover.

About 3.6 miles from the starting point the trail tops out on a ridge at 4,970 feet. As the trail drops gradually into Upper Covington Flat the Joshua trees become noticeably larger until finally the largest known Joshua tree in the park is reached at 4 miles. The tree stands about 35 feet tall, but most impressive is its girth—at least 17 feet at the base. From a trail junction at this point take the left-hand trail 0.1 mile to the conclusion of the loop at the backcountry board.

NOTE: With a backcountry board as its starting point, this day hike can be expanded into an overnight backpack.

63 BLACK ROCK LOOP TRAIL
EUREKA PEAK AND BACK VIA CALIFORNIA RIDING AND HIKING TRAIL

General description:	A long hike to the highest summit in the northwestern section of the park and back to Black Rock Campground via the California Riding and Hiking Trail.
Length:	10.5-mile loop.
General location:	3 miles south of Yucca Valley, northwestern Joshua Tree National Park, southeastern California.
Trail condition:	Clear wash; clear trail; road.
Special attraction:	Highest peak in this area of the park.
Difficulty:	Strenuous.
Best season:	October through May.
Starting elevation:	3,980 feet.
Maximum elevation:	5,518 feet (Eureka Peak).
Elevation gain/loss	1,600 feet/1,600 feet.
USGS topo maps:	Yucca Valley South-CA and Joshua Tree South-CA (1:24,000).
For more information:	Joshua Tree National Park (see Appendix D).

Key points:

0.0 Trailhead. Go east towards nearby wash. First 2-mile section of Eureka Peak Trail coincides with CA R & H trail.

1.5 Junction with "FT." Ignore it. Stay left on R & H over saddle to upper valley.

2.0 Clearly marked junction with "EP" post marking your Eureka Peak trail. Turn up wash.

2.3 Junction with "SL." Disregard. Continue in well-traveled main wash as it climbs and narrows.

3.8 A comforting "EP" arrow post in the wash. Continue straight up the wash.

4.0 "BF/EP" signpost. Follow the "EP" arrow to the right.

4.3 "EP/BH" marker confirms you're on the correct trail as it becomes a twisting footpath up the ravine to the peak.

4.9 The mountain ridge. Turn left to the summit (0.1 mile), right to the parking area and Covington Road, which you'll take down to meet the CA R & H Trail for the hike back to Black Rock Campground.

5.2 At the parking area, turn left and take the road downhill to R & H Trail.

5.7 R & H Trail on your left in a valley before the Covington Road begins climbing. A large brown-and-white sign is 30 yards off the road; what you will probably notice first is the house-shaped backcountry regulations sign which is only 10 yards off the road under a huge Joshua tree. Head north down the sloping wash.

8.5 Back at original fork where you met the EP Trail. Continue on R & H Trail back to campground.

10.3 Watch for turn to left where the trail returns to the backcountry board and the wash (and the horse traffic); continue north. You can see the campground.

10.5 Back at the backcountry board.

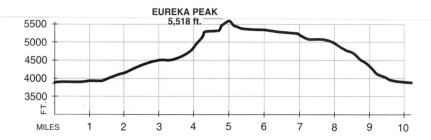

Finding the trailhead: From California Highway 62 in Yucca Valley, turn south on Avalon Avenue. Go 0.7 mile to where it becomes Palomar Drive. Continue south on Palomar Dr. for 2.3 miles to the left turn onto Joshua Tree Lane. Take Joshua Tree Ln. for 1 mile to dead-end at San Marino Avenue, where you turn right. Continue on San Marino Ave. for 0.3 mile to its dead-end at Black Rock Road. Turn left on Black Rock to the park entrance. The backcountry board, which looks unlike all other backcountry boards in Joshua Tree National Park (this one is simply a bulletin board) is on your left only 50 yards within the campground entrance. Park there. The trailhead is immediately east of the board area.

Descending the California Riding and Hiking Trail from Eureka Peak.

BLACK ROCK LOOP TRAIL TO EUREKA PEAK
AND BACK VIA CALIFORNIA
RIDING AND HIKING TRAIL

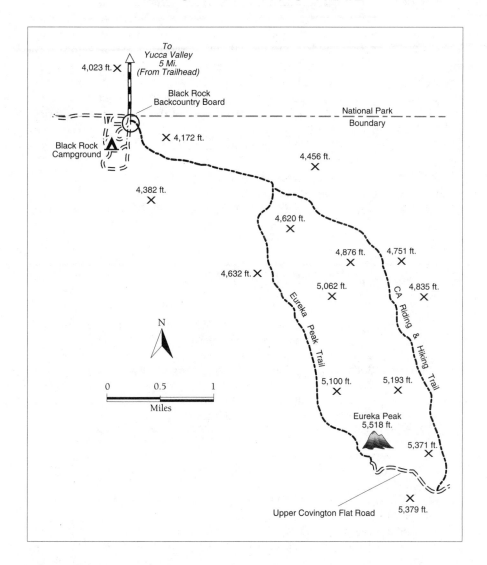

The hike: As the mileage log indicates, this is a very well-marked trail, both up Eureka Peak and down the California Riding & Hiking Trail return trip. In spite of that, there is a sense of wilderness excitement, since the hike to the peak gets out of the wash and into mountain canyons and ravines. Even with the intermittent signs you can feel like an explorer.

The view from the peak is magnificent. The San Bernardinos, with their mantle of snow in winter and early spring, rise in the western distance. The park's ranges stretch away to the south and east. Although there is a road and parking area immediately downhill from the peak, it does not appear to be heavily used due to its distance from California Highway 62.

The return journey down the R & H track is the most heavily horse-used portion of this trail through the park. Elsewhere there is no trace of horse traffic. Here, trail signposts are almost unnecessary—just follow the hoof-prints. Nevertheless, numerous arrow posts mark your way. There are, however, no mile markers as there are on the other sections. While signs on the higher section are nonexistent, the lower end of the trail sports freshly painted, stenciled, and planted signposts verifying your location.

For a day trip close to populated Yucca Valley this is the ideal outing. The exertion of the hike to the peak contrasts nicely with the relaxed stroll back down the wash via the Riding and Hiking Trail. The focus on wild mountains on the way up also contrasts with the views of the subdivisions of Yucca Valley on the way down.

NOTE: The Black Rock Canyon area has numerous hiking trails. A diagrammatic map is posted at the trailhead, or you can get one at the ranger station. These trails are signed. During the hike you will encounter numerous signposts.

64   *HIGH VIEW NATURE TRAIL*

General description:	Moderate loop to lofty viewpoint of surrounding peaks and town of Yucca Valley.
Length:	1.3-mile loop.
General location:	5 miles southeast of town of Yucca Valley, northwestern corner of Joshua Tree National Park, southeastern California.
Trail condition:	Clear nature trail.
Special attraction:	Hike to peak with view of western section of the park.
Difficulty:	Moderate.
Best season:	October through May.
Starting elevation:	4,120 feet.
Maximum elevation:	4,440 feet.
Elevation gain/loss:	320 feet/320 feet.
USGS topo map:	Yucca Valley South-CA (1:24,000).
For more information:	Joshua Tree National Park (see Appendix D).

Finding the trailhead: From California Highway 62 in Yucca Valley, turn south on Avalon and drive 0.7 mile when it becomes Palomar. Continue on Palomar 2.3 miles to turn left on Joshua Lane. Take Joshua Lane 1 mile to a T intersection at San Marino Drive. Turn right and go 0.3 mile to Black Rock Road. Turn left on Black Rock Rd. and drive south 0.5 mile to the entrance. Immediately before the entrance, turn right (west) onto a dirt road and go west 0.8 mile to the parking area.

HIGH VIEW NATURE TRAIL
• SOUTH PARK PEAK LOOP

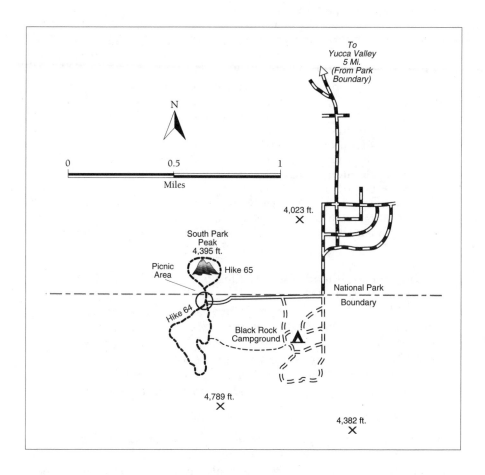

The hike: This nature trail travels to the top of a hill, providing a view over the Yucca Valley and the eastern end of the park. There is a register at the summit, as well as a bench. The trail follows a relatively gentle route as it climbs 320 feet. Numbered sites line the trail; the brochures are available at the Black Rock Ranger Station in the adjacent campground.

If you're staying at the campground, a hilly but far more scenic route exists that connects the campground with the nature trail. It leaves from the top of the loop above the ranger station, and enters the nature trail loop in its first section. Although it is clearly marked, this alternate route to the campground has an aura of wilderness. We spotted two coyotes hunting for rabbits in the middle of the afternoon on our loop hike from the campground.

65 SOUTH PARK PEAK LOOP

General description:	A short loop hike outside park boundaries, providing a sweeping view of the park's northwestern section and the town of Joshua Tree in the valley below.
Length:	0.8-mile loop.
General location:	4.6 miles south of the town of Yucca Valley, northwestern edge of Joshua Tree National Park, southeastern California.
Trail condition:	Clear trail.
Difficulty:	Moderate.
Best season:	October through April.
Starting elevation:	4,140 feet.
Maximum elevation:	4,395 feet (South Park Peak).
Elevation gain/loss:	250 feet/250 feet.
USGS topo map:	Yucca Valley South-CA (1:24:000).
For more information:	Yucca Valley Parks District; Joshua Tree National Park (see Appendix D).

See Map on Page 197

Finding the trailhead: From California Highway 62 in Yucca Valley, take Avalon Avenue south 0.7 mile to where it becomes Palomar Ave. Continue on Palomar Ave. 2.3 miles to Joshua Lane. Turn left on Joshua Lane and drive 1 mile to T intersection with San Marino Drive. Turn right on San Marino and go 0.3 mile to its end at Black Rock Road. Turn left on Black Rock, and go 0.5 mile toward park entrance. Immediately before the entrance, turn right (west) on the dirt road. Follow it 0.8 mile to parking area. The unsigned trail to the peak begins at the northwest corner of the parking area.

The hike: This gentle peak climb begins as an easy dirt trail. At 0.2 mile there is a comfortable new bench where the view first becomes excellent. Another bench is at the summit. The trail between the benches is steeper and rockier than the section from the parking area. The peak boasts quite a register. With a concrete pedestal and a Plexiglas box, it is an impressive item. The stack of registers within the box make great reading while you're resting on the bench. Lots of literary visitors climb South Peak.

The sprawl of the town of Yucca Valley and its subdivisions closing in on the park are swirling on the north—while to the south lies the vast open space of Joshua Tree National Park. As many who signed the register noted, this sight is confirmation that national park status is the best protection for desert areas, particularly near expanding centers of population.

Follow the trail past the register box for the descent to the wash on the back side of the peak, and the walk back to the parking area.

MOJAVE NATIONAL PRESERVE

"Big and empty" aptly describes Mojave National Preserve which, at 1.4 million acres, makes up 10 percent of the entire Mojave Desert region in its eastern end. The dry landscape we see now is the product of a wetter past, with ancient sedimentary rocks from what was once an ocean floor preserved by the stark aridity of today's climate. The preserve is a varied mix of jagged peaks, colorful serpentine canyons, booming sand dunes, volcanic cinder cones, dry lakebeds, historic mines, rock art by Paleo-Indians, and vast expanses framed by the largest Joshua tree forest in the California Desert.

In 1976 Congress established the California Desert Conservation Area, directing the Bureau of Land Management (BLM) to come up with a management plan for the half of this 25 million-acre region that is in the public domain. As a result, BLM set up the 1.5 million-acre East Mojave National Scenic Area in 1980. Unfortunately, the East Mojave continued to be impacted by indiscriminate off-road vehicle use, mining, overgrazing, and wanton vandalism. Greater protection was called for but the wheels of politics sometimes turn slowly. In 1986, U.S. Senator Alan Cranston of California first introduced the California Desert Protection Act, but passage took the same amount of time required for the 1964 Wilderness Act—eight long years! The act transferred the East Mojave from the BLM to the National Park Service and upgraded the designation from administrative "scenic area" to statutory "preserve."

"Preserve" rather than park status for Mojave means the continuation of pre-existing hunting in accordance with state regulations. Mojave National Preserve is the only National Park Service unit in the California Desert where hunting is permitted. As an added safety precaution hikers should wear hunter's orange or other bright colors when hiking in the preserve during the fall hunting season. Other "grandfathered" uses include mining pre-existing claims, and cattle grazing. Livestock grazing seems marginal at best in this sparsely vegetated land, but the OX Cattle Company (a major grazing permittee) is a colorful remnant of the Old West, with origins traceable to 1888.

GEOLOGIC SIGNATURES ON THE LANDSCAPE

When visiting the preserve one can look in any direction and be reminded of Mojave's geologic past—a land molded by earthquakes, fault lines, sinking valleys, and rising mountains formed by the tearing apart of the earth's crust. Domes, cinder cones, and lava beds tell the tale of volcanic eruptions of monumental proportions. The Mojave Desert was uplifted around 140 million years ago by pressure from plates of the earth's crust grinding against one another. Seventy million years of erosion reduced an astounding 20,000 to 25,000 feet of sedimentary rock to gently sloping terrain. The mountain ranges of Mojave were uplifted along rows of faults about 30 million years

OVERVIEW MAP

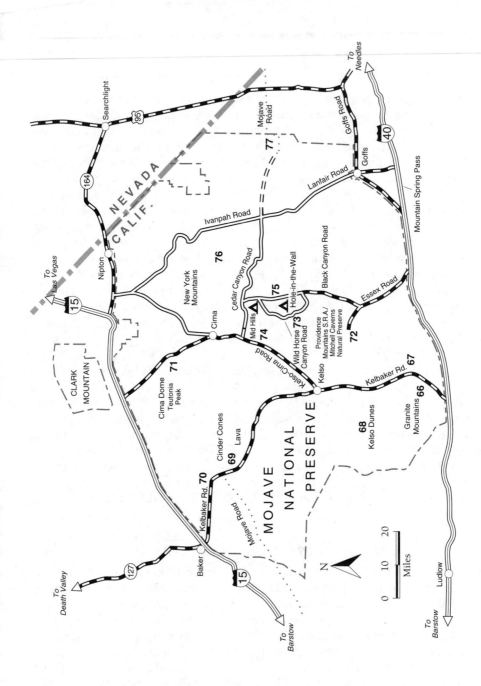

Hiker reaching the 3,000 foot summit of Kelso Dunes.

ago as continental plates collided. During a wetter time, 18 million years ago, Mojave resembled African savannahs with large herds of grazing animals.

As recently as 15,000 years ago the Mojave River flowed above ground into the now-gone Lake Manly in Death Valley. Then the climate became much drier after the last Ice Age, 10,000 years ago. This is partly because the Mojave Desert sits in the rain shadow of the lofty Sierra Nevada and other ranges to the south and west. Although many of the older cinder cones and lava flows date back at least 2 million years, some of the more recent activity took place only 800 to 1,000 years ago just west of Cima Dome—a huge 1,500-foot-high symmetrical mound of ancient granite exposed by erosion.

LIFE IN THE DESERT

Elevations in the preserve range from around 800 feet to the nearly 8,000-foot summit of Clark Mountain, supporting a corresponding diversity of plants and animals. The most common shrub at lower elevations—the creosote bush—is a perfectly adapted desert survivor with narrow, resinous leaves that prevent water loss. As the older stems in the plant's center die, a cloned ring of new stems is formed that can live for hundreds of years. Creosote bushes are able to completely tap surrounding soil moisture, which effectively keeps away competing vegetation. Above 3,000 feet the dark gray bark of the intricately branched blackbrush gives the land a dark, somber look. Joshua trees are prevalent here on well-drained gravel plains. These members of the agave family are usually the largest plants in their landscape. Their branches seem to lift upward like the arms of the biblical prophet Joshua; hence the name given by early Mormon settlers. Spanish bayonet and the larger Mojave yucca are also common in this midelevational range. Pinyon-juniper woodlands occur at still higher elevations, in such exposed places as the rocky slopes of the rugged New York and Providence mountains.

Mojave National Preserve is home to a seldom-seen but rich array of fauna—mammals, birds, insects, and reptiles, all of which are adapted to lack of water and intense heat. Coyotes are abundant, although you will not see and hear as many in the ranching country of East Mojave as you would in Death Valley or Joshua Tree. The abundance of rodents and rabbits can be determined as easily by looking up as down— raptors are commonly seen riding the air currents, seeking their prey. Several small bands of desert bighorn sheep keep a sharp eye out for the predatory mountain lion in secluded mountains and canyons. One of the more distinguished denizens is the threatened desert tortoise. Protection of tortoise habitat was one of the most compelling arguments for passage of the California Desert Protection Bill, so much so that someone placed a tortoise on President Clinton's desk when he signed the bill into law October 31, 1994.

HUMAN HISTORY

Paleo-Indians likely lived and hunted in the Mojave region around the end of the last Ice Age, 10,000 to 14,000 years ago. As the climate became more dry, these people made greater use of seeds, nuts, and roots for food. The more recent native people of the Mojave included the Chemehuevi, who were the southernmost band of Piutes. The harshness of the land kept their population small. In addition to being hunter-gatherers they were artists. However, the petroglyphs we see today throughout Mojave are largely the product of more ancient peoples who pre-dated the Chemehuevi. A good example of this artistry is found near Piute Creek along the Mojave Trail. Archeologists believe that some of the rock art are tribal clan markings of territory or trails.

The Mojave Trail was a route for both early Indian trading and European travel into the region. In 1776 a Spanish priest named Francisco Garces became the first European to visit what is now the Mojave National Preserve. Following the Mojave Trail, Garces and his Indian guides traveled past Piute Creek, the New York and Providence mountains, and Kelso Dunes. The first American to traverse the Mojave was the renowned trapper Jeddediah Smith. Smith made the difficult journey in 1826 and then again a year later in a much shorter time by traveling at night to escape the scorching 120-degree summer heat. The route was again followed in 1857 by Edward Beale, who laid out a wagon road along the Mojave Trail. Beale achieved notoriety by using camels as pack stock. After the road was completed the camels were turned loose in the desert and eventually died off. During the 1860s primitive army outposts were built along the road about a day apart. These outposts, such as the one at Piute Creek, were abandoned in 1868 when the overland mail route was rerouted away from the Mojave Road.

Miners swarmed into the region in the 1870s leaving countless prospect adits, tunnels and shafts. But the mines didn't boom until the railroad arrived in 1883. Ten years later a 30-mile shortline railroad from Goffs north to the New York Mountains replaced the Mojave Road as a freight route. The railroad served both mining and a developing cattle industry, which somehow survives to this day. Homesteaders came into the East Mojave around 1910 during a series of wet years, but most had left by 1925 after the normal dry weather resumed.

PARK REGULATIONS AND FACILITIES

The Mojave National Preserve is one of the newest, largest, least developed, and least regulated of all of the units in the National Park System. Sensitive and respectful visitor use will go a long way toward keeping regulations to a minimum. Unlike nearby Death Valley and Joshua Tree national parks, visitor entrance fees are not required at the preserve.

Nearly half of the preserve, some 700,000 acres, is designated Wilderness in twenty-two separate units. Some of the boundaries near roads and washes have been posted, but the job is far from being completed due to minimal staff and budget. Please respect the wilderness signs by doing everything possible to lessen the impact of your visit. The desert is at once both rugged and fragile. No off-road vehicular travel is allowed, so please keep vehicles on designated routes. As with the other parks, vehicles must be street legal.

At this time the National Park Service is continuing the long tradition of open desert camping in the preserve. Car camping is allowed at existing sites next to the road. If you're camping beyond the road backcountry permits are not required. The only requirements are to camp at least 0.25 mile from any water source to avoid disturbing wildlife, and to set up camp off the trail a minimum of 0.5 mile from any road or developed area.

There are only two developed trails in the preserve. A 2-mile (one-way) trail to Teutonia Peak on Cima Dome takes off from a signed trailhead on the Cima Road south of Interstate 15. An 8-mile (one-way) trail between Hole-in-the-Wall and Mid Hills campgrounds can be reached from either campground.

There are two developed fee campgrounds in the Preserve and one in the State Recreation Area. The Hole-in-the-Wall campground (35 sites) is 18 miles north of Interstate 40 on Black Canyon Road. The Mid Hills campground (26 sites) is 28 miles north of I-40 just off the Black Canyon Road. The Providence Mountains campground (6 sites) is 17 miles northwest of I-40 at the end of the Essex Road. All three are open year-round on a first-come, first-served basis. Fire-pits are provided at the campgrounds, but if you want a fire be sure to bring wood with you. Collecting or cutting wood in the desert is not allowed. With the exception of the Providence Mountains, water is scarce and unreliable at these campgrounds. As always, when traveling in the desert, bring more water than you think you'll need.

It may be tempting to feed wildlife but remember, "a fed animal is a dead animal." Wild creatures must remain wild if they are to survive. All elements of the environment—plants, cultural and historical artifacts, rocks—are protected so that they can be enjoyed by others. Pets must be confined or kept on a short leash. Better yet, leave them at home so that both they and you can have a better time. Although legal hunting is allowed in season, target shooting is not.

The exterior boundaries of the preserve contain a large amount of private inholdings. It is important to obey "No Trespassing" signs, close gates and, in general, respect private property.

PROVIDENCE MOUNTAINS STATE RECREATION AREA

In 1956 the State of California acquired the Mitchell Caverns from the Mitchell family. Subsequent land transfers from the BLM have increased the park to its present 5,900 acres along the rugged eastern slopes of the Providence Mountains, encompassed within the south-central portion of the preserve. To safeguard wildlife, only day use is allowed outside the campground. The extensive Mitchell Caverns are the only limestone caves in the California park system and can only be visited with a guided ranger tour.

The 1.5 mile hike/tour takes 1.5 to 2 hours and is offered one to three times a day depending on season and day of the week. There is one short nature trail near the visitor center/campground plus a longer trail to Crystal Spring which leads to the edge of the backcountry high in the Providence Mountains (see Hike 72).

HOW AND WHEN TO GET THERE

The "lonesome triangle" of the Mojave National Preserve is bounded on the north by I-15 and on the south by I-40. These two interstate highways join in Barstow, about 50 miles west of the preserve. The paved Kelbaker Road crosses the preserve from Baker south to I-40, halfway between Barstow and Needles. The paved Kelso-Cima Road takes off from Kelso Depot and heads north to I-15. Several shorter paved roads and good dirt roads access major mountain ranges and points of interest. The closest major commercial airport is 50 miles northeast of the preserve at Las Vegas. There are no motels or service stations in the preserve, and very few close by. Don't drive into the preserve without plenty of gas, food, and water. Services are available in surrounding communities, such as Needles on the east, Barstow on the west, and Baker to the north on I-15.

From the standpoint of hiking comfort, October through May is generally the best season to visit the preserve. Summer daytime temperatures typically exceed 100 degrees. Depending on winter and early spring rains, wildflowers burst forth in a splash of color during April or May.

MOJAVE NATIONAL PRESERVE HIKES AT A GLANCE

Hike (Number)	Distance		Difficulty	Feature	Page
Baker-Rhyolite Hills Loop (70)	2.0	miles	MS	Vista	216
Caruthers Canyon (76)	3.0	miles	M	Canyon, Mine Site	236
Crystal Spring (72)	2.0	miles	MS	Spring, Vista	221
Eagle Rocks (74)	2.0	miles	E	Boulders, Vista	229
Fort Piute (77)	7.0	miles	M	Hist. Site, Arch.	239
Piute Gorge	7.0	miles	S	Gorge	239
Hole-in-the-Wall to					
Mid-Hills (73)	8.4	miles	M/MS	Vistas	224
Kelso Dunes (68)	1.0	mile	E	Dunes	212
Dunes to peak	1.5	miles	MS	Vista	212
North Lava Bed Wash (69)	1.5	miles	E	Geology, Archeology	214
Quail Spring Basin (67)	6.9	miles	M	Boulders, Vistas	210
Silver Peak (66)	9.6	miles	S	Vista	207
Table Top Mountain (75)	7.0	miles	S	Vista	232
Teutonia Peak/					
Cima Dome (71)	4.0	miles	M	Vista	218

MOJAVE NATIONAL PRESERVE
TOPO MAP INDEX

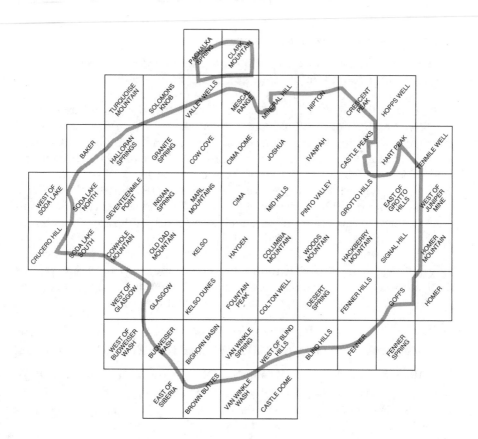

		PAHRUMP SPRING	CLARK MOUNTAIN					
TURQUOISE MOUNTAIN	SOLOMONS KNOB	VALLEY WELLS	MESCAL RANGE	MINERAL HILL	NIPTON	CRESCENT PEAK	HOPPS WELL
BAKER	HALLORAN SPRINGS	GRANITE SPRING	COW COVE	CIMA DOME	JOSHUA	IVANPAH	CASTLE PEAKS	HART PEAK	TENMILE WELL
WEST OF SODA LAKE	SODA LAKE NORTH	SEVENTEENMILE POINT	INDIAN SPRING	MARL MOUNTAINS	CIMA	MID HILLS	PINTO VALLEY	GROTTO HILLS	EAST OF GROTTO HILLS	WEST OF JUNIPER MINE
CRUCERO HILL	SODA LAKE SOUTH	COWHOLE MOUNTAIN	OLD DAD MOUNTAIN	KELSO	HAYDEN	COLUMBIA MOUNTAIN	WOODS MOUNTAIN	HACKBERRY MOUNTAIN	SIGNAL HILL	HOMER MOUNTAIN
	WEST OF GLASGOW	GLASGOW	KELSO DUNES	FOUNTAIN PEAK	COLTON WELL	DESERT SPRING	FENNER HILLS	GOFFS	HOMER
	WEST OF BUDWEISER WASH	BUDWEISER WASH	BIGHORN BASIN	VAN WINKLE SPRING	WEST OF BLIND HILLS	BLIND HILLS	FENNER	FENNER SPRING
	EAST OF SIBERIA	BROWN BUTTES	VAN WINKLE WASH	CASTLE DOME				

General description:	A troad hike to a spectacular view of south-central Mojave from a 6,365-foot peak in the Granite Mountains.
Length:	9.2 miles round-trip; an additional 0.4 mile for peak climb
General location:	90 miles east of Barstow in south-central Mojave National Preserve, southeastern California.
Trail condition:	Clear troad; use trail to summit.
Special attraction:	Eagle's view from mountaintop.
Difficulty:	Moderately strenuous to end of troad; strenuous for peak climb.
Best season:	October through June.
Starting elevation:	4,000 feet.
Maximum elevation:	6,365 feet.
Elevation gain/loss:	2,365 feet/none.
USGS topo map:	Bighorn Basin-CA (1:24,000).
For more information:	Mojave Desert Information Center (see Appendix D).

Key points:

0.0 Take any of the 3 troads (all banned to vehicles) off the plateau; they converge in the wash below. Head west toward the Granite Mountains up Cottonwood Wash.

0.2 Troad passes through 12-foot gate posts, and comes to a fork. Take the fainter (right) troad.

3.0 Troad enters the canyon, framed by huge boulders. Plow through the Mormon tea as you continue to follow the troad.

3.2 Slight shelf. Continue to hike straight up, looking at troad 50 yards ahead/above.

4.6 Troad ends. Use trail to Silver Peak marked by cairns.

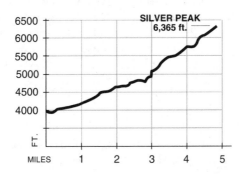

Finding the trailhead: From Interstate 40, 77.5 miles east of Barstow and 64 miles west of Needles, take the Kelbaker Road exit north into the preserve. 10.1 miles north of the freeway exit, take the unmarked dirt road on the left (west) of Kelbaker. There is another dirt road almost opposite this

SILVER PEAK

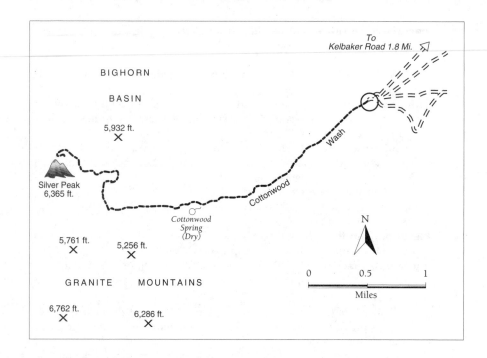

one going east on the other side of Kelbaker. Follow the dirt road west 1.8 miles to a small plateau, where a wilderness boundary post marks the end of motorized use. Park there. This spot is also an excellent car campsite.

The hike: From the parking area you can see the highest point on the western horizon, Silver Peak, your destination. The view from that point is magnificent, but the journey to get there is no less spectacular. This troad is deteriorating and provides challenging but enjoyable hiking. Turnout prom-ontories provide respite from the steep ascent, and panoramic views. The area is used by cattle, but there is also evidence of wild burros being in the valley. Don't be surprised to see either species.

The troad ends at 4.6 miles, at an elevation of 6,075 feet. Even if you do not go on to the summit, it's a great view from here. The troad winds around the mountain in its final 0.2-mile climb. The trail to Silver Peak climbs 300 feet in 0.2 mile, so it is quite strenuous. Your efforts are rewarded by being on the rocky summit, especially if it is a clear day.

The change in altitude on this hike results in a wide variety of desert plants, from the creosote-sage scrub at the parking area and throughout the lower valley to increasing cholla and eventually to pinyon-juniper wood-lands. Any hiker will also certainly notice the desert's ability to erase the evidence of past uses. The troad upon which you travel is a prime example.

A hiker enjoys the view eastward from the slopes of Silver Peak.

The remnants of cattle ranching are scattered around, deteriorating rapidly. This is a wilderness area that has earned that label.

The journey back the way you came is excellent for its scenery too, looking out at the southern extension of the Providence Mountain range (see Hike 67). In the valley below you will be able to see the entire troad as it goes nearly straight east to the parking area. Once you reach the alluvial fan and then the canyon floor, the troad surface becomes very gentle. We completed this leg of the hike in the dark (with the help of a half-moon), and, except for the catclaw, it was easy going.

description:	An easy loop with two side trips around granite formations and opportunities for climbing boulders and peaks.
Length:	5.8-mile partial loop; side trips of 0.5 mile and 0.6 mile; additional distance for investigating the granite mounds.
General location:	About 90 miles east of Barstow and 75 miles west of Needles, south-central Mojave National Preserve, southeastern California.
Trail condition:	Clear troad; short clear wash.
Special attraction:	Immense monzogranite boulder mounds, with views of Granite Mountains and the Kelso Dunes.
Difficulty:	Moderate.
Best season:	October through May.
Starting elevation:	3,560 feet.
Maximum elevation:	4,350 feet.
Elevation gain/loss:	840 feet/840 feet.
USGS topo map:	Van Winkle Spring-CA (1:24,000).
For more information:	Mojave Desert Information Center (see Appendix D).

Key points:

- 0.0 Trailhead; climb gentle alluvial fan.
- 1.5 Fork. Explore to left, then follow right troad.
- 1.9 Low pass over ridge.
- 2.0 Fork. Left troad is return loop. Take right troad.
- 2.5 At basalt outcropping go left up wash/troad.
- 3.4 High point of loop hike. Turn right for access to peak, left to meet main troad.
- 3.9 Intersect main troad. Turn right.
- 5.9 Return to trailhead.

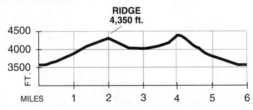

Finding the trailhead: From Interstate 40, 77.5 miles east of Barstow and 64 miles west of Needles, take the Kelbaker Road exit north into the preserve. About 10 miles from the freeway exit there is a dirt road on your right (east). There is another dirt road almost immediately across Kelbaker heading west at this spot. Take the dirt road to the east 0.9 mile to the wilderness boundary post on the right, marking the end of vehicular use. That marks the trailhead.

QUAIL SPRING BASIN

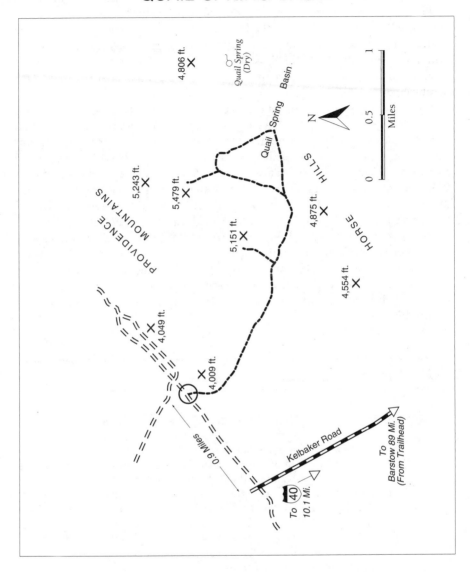

The hike: This hike in the south end of the Providence Mountains takes you on a gentle slope up from the valley floor, enabling you to see the panorama of this central Mojave region without climbing a mountain. The view of the Kelso Dunes, the Granite Range, and the Providence Mountains makes the first 2 miles of the hike (and the last two) most spectacular. Closer at hand, the first section of the hike travels through brittlebush and creosote bush, with mounds of monzogranite piled in fantastic shapes as a backdrop to the east. These are soaring boulders in a cathedral-like setting, and vertical columnar granite reaches hundreds of feet over you. In addition to their size, the boulders have been eroded into imaginative shapes, producing holes and caverns as well as cartoon representations of mice, skulls, and faces.

The peaks of these granite mountains look impressive as you hike up the rise from the parking area, but the loftiest one is in the back row, and can be viewed (and climbed, if you wish) from the eastern valley. Plenty of other bouldering activity exists for those who are not enticed by the peak. These large dollops of granite ice cream have a superb gritty yet firm surface for scrambling.

From the trailhead, the troad rises gently on the alluvial fan. A fork at 1.8 mile provides an opportunity to explore granite boulders by turning left on a short dead-end. Return to the main troad and continue over the high point on the ridge (4,350 feet) and drop to the fork at mile 2, where the return loop comes back on the left. Continue east into Quail Spring Basin. At mile 2.5, a basalt outcropping on your left marks the wash/troad where you turn and begin to climb northwest toward the notch in the Providence Range. As you continue to the junction at mile 3.4, the lofty granite spires become more awesome. At the junction, a side trip to the right takes you up a rocky gorge. For the very ambitious hiker, this would be the route to the loftiest peak (5,479 feet) above the basin. Your return to the trailhead follows the troad to the left back to the major intersection at mile 2. Magnificent vistas and fascinating rock formations are numerous throughout your trek with or without side trips.

68   KELSO DUNES

General description:	A short hike through a sand dunes ecosystem to a dune peak.
Length:	3 miles round-trip.
General location:	About 40 miles south of Baker, southwestern Mojave National Preserve, southeastern California.
Trail condition:	Line-of-sight cross-country sand dune route.
Special attractions:	Golden sand dunes in dramatic contrast with surrounding mountains and desert.
Difficulty:	Easy to base of large dune (1 mile); moderately strenuous to peak (add 0.5 mile).
Best season:	October through April.
Starting elevation:	2,520 feet.
Maximum elevation:	3,000 feet.
Elevation gain/loss:	480 feet/none.
USGS topo map:	Kelso-CA (1:24,000).
For more information:	Mojave Desert Information Center (see Appendix D).

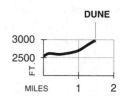

KELSO DUNES

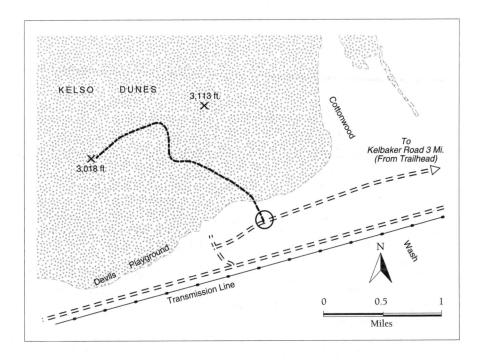

Finding the trailhead: From Interstate 40, 77.5 miles east of Barstow and 64 miles west of Needles, take Kelbaker Road north 15.3 miles to signed Kelso Dunes Road on your left. Drive west 3 miles on the wide but washboardy dirt road to the second parking area where there are two information boards on desert ecology and wildlife. The trail to the dunes is directly behind these boards.

The hike: The Kelso Dunes, "A Golden Desert Treasure Chest," were created by 10,000 to 20,000 years of unrelenting winds, sending the sand of the Mojave River delta into these ever-changing formations. This landform (created by wind) is actively moving, but only back and forth due to the contrary wind pattern.

The mountain ranges nearby represent violent volcanic activity. The dunes contrast sharply with the surrounding topography with their softly rounded shapes and their rosy glow. The fine sand consists of rose quartz, feldspar, and magnetite. The quartz gives it the rosy color. The magnetite produces a black stripe effect on the windswept ridges of the dunes.

Not an arid wasteland, the dunes are home to more than 100 species of plants, and many animals. The tracks of the latter—kangaroo rats, kit foxes, scorpions, among others—are visible along your hike. The dunes are also home to the Kelso Dune Jerusalem cricket, which exists nowhere else.

Follow the established foot trail as best way possible as you go northwest to the most westerly dune. The hike to the base of this hill is easy, rising only 250 feet in 1 mile. For an ascent of the dune, a moderately strenuous climb, hike to the saddle east of the tall dune, and hike westerly up the ridge to its apex (3,000 feet). From this lofty spot you can enjoy spectacular views of the Devil's Playground to the north and the Providence Range to the east. The dimensions of the Kelso Dunes are impressive, and are best seen in all their vastness from this high spot.

Hiking back, try to retrace your steps in order to minimize damage to the fragile dune environment.

69 NORTH LAVA BED WASH

General description:	A short loop or out-and-back hike in the Lava Beds, with interesting lava rock formations.
Distance:	1.5-mile loop or out-and-back.
General location:	About 14 miles southeast of Baker, in northwest Mojave National Preserve, southeastern California.
Trail condition:	Clear wash, primitive burro trail, cross-country segment (loop).
Special attractions:	Cutaway profile of lava beds next to a narrow turn of the historic Mojave Road.
Difficulty:	Easy.
Best season:	October through April.
Starting elevation:	2,290 feet.
Maximum elevation:	2,380 feet.
Elevation gain/loss:	90 feet/90 feet.
USGS topo map:	Indian Spring-CA (1:24,000).
For more information:	Mojave Desert Information Center (see Appendix D).

Key points:
    0.0   Trailhead.
    0.1   Climb up to the right to a primitive trail just below the lava rock cliff.
    0.5   End of cliff trail; climb (right) onto the adjacent plateau/ridge.
    0.9   Hike along the ridge cross-country; drop to the left (north) back to the wash and hike 0.6 mile back down the wash to complete the loop.
    1.5   Trailhead.

Finding the trailhead: From Baker on Interstate 15 drive south on the Kelbaker Road for 14.2 miles to the first major wash on the left (east) which is the trailhead. This point is also 22.4 miles northwest of Kelso on the Kelbaker Road and 0.4 mile north of the only gap in these lava hills. There is a place to park just off the highway adjacent to a prominent outcropping of lava rock.

NORTH LAVA BED WASH

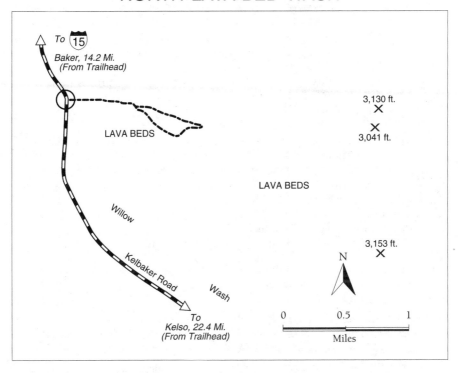

The hike: Begin the hike by climbing up toward the large outcrop of lava above and to the right of the trailhead. About 30 feet up and just below the cliff you'll pick up a faint trail, partly overgrown, that parallels the cliff face for about 0.5 mile. The slow but usable trail provides a good introduction to volcanic geology along this northern edge of the vast lava bed region of northwestern Mojave National Preserve. Especially interesting is the cut-away lava cliff face, which exposes the profile of the rock along with a colorful display of red, green, and gray lichens on the lava formations. The historic Mojave Road makes a sharp turn at this point. The Mojave Road was first used by Native Americans and later developed by the military to encourage settlement in the region.

At 0.5 mile the cliff trail ends at a jumbled lava talus slope. To add more variety to this overland route climb up to the plateau to the immediate right (south) and make a circle cross country for about 0.4 mile angling around to the left (north) into the main wash. Just above is a distinctive place in the wash that provides a good turnaround point for the hike. The wash opens up into a wide sandy oval encircled by smooth, gray stone and dark, deeply eroded lava. A side wash narrows up and to the right, but the main wash lies above a 20-foot dry gray stone/lava rock waterfall which can be easily climbed. From the dryfall the mostly clear wash can be easily followed for about 0.6 mile back down to the trailhead to complete this brief lava beds exploration.

General description:	A short, partly cross-country hike/climb with expansive views of cinder cones and lava beds.
Length:	2-mile loop.
General location:	About 12 miles east of Baker, in northwestern Mojave National Preserve, southeastern California.
Trail condition:	Clear troad, cross-country with short sections of burro trail.
Special attractions:	360-degree views of a vast lava-strewn landscape.
Difficulty:	Moderate overall but moderately strenuous on the descent because of loose rock.
Best season:	October through April.
Starting elevation:	2,030 feet.
Maximum elevation:	2,450 feet.
Elevation gain/loss:	420 feet/420 feet.
USGS topo maps:	Halloran Springs-CA; Granite Spring-CA; and Seventeenmile Point-CA (1:24,000).
For more information:	Mojave Desert Information Center (see Appendix D).

Key points:

0.0   Hike begins on a faint troad.
0.6   Troad/wash reaches mine diggings; begin cross-country climb.
1.0   Head south up a wild burro trail.
1.4   Rocky high point (2,450 feet).
1.7   Intersection of troad/wash.
2.0   Trailhead.

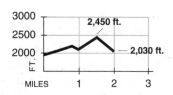

Finding the trailhead: From Baker on Interstate 15 head east on the paved Kelbaker Road for 11.1 miles to where the road bends to the right (south). If driving Kelbaker Rd. from the south this bend is 25.5 miles northwest of Kelso. Turn left (north) on a dirt road which parallels the wilderness boundary and drive 0.7 mile to a faint dirt road on the right (closed to vehicular use) which leads toward rugged rhyolite mountains to the immediate east. This is the trailhead. The most spacious parking is 0.1 mile north of a rock outcropping that has been used for open desert camping.

The hike: The troad immediately enters the wilderness in a northeasterly direction toward a gap in the hills to the left of the high point straight ahead, which is the high point of the loop. Although the hills lack an official name we are calling these jagged mounds of rhyolite the Baker–Rhyolite Hills because of their proximity to the town of Baker. After 0.3 mile the troad becomes difficult to find in this creosote alluvial fan. If you've lost the troad simply follow the wash to the northeast toward the gap in the hills.

BAKER-RHYOLITE HILLS LOOP

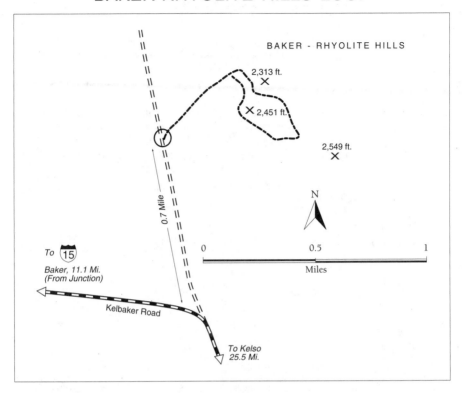

At this point the main wash hugs the higher hills to the right. At 0.6 mile some mine tailings are reached on the right at 2,160 feet which begins the cross country segment of the hike. Turn right (south) up the ravine for 0.1 mile to a low pass at 2,230 feet. For a quick overlook climb 100 vertical feet to the right. Continue into the next saddle to the west, then drop into the wash to the left. Turn right up the second side wash and pick up a well-defined wild burro trail. A steep-walled rock gully will be to your right.

Continue climbing southward toward a low point on the skyline to the left of the rocky pinnacle of the summit. The last 0.3 mile is without a trail; the route is easy to the 2,430-foot ridge. An occasional wooden post is reminiscent of the claim-staking days of early miners. Scramble the rocks to the northwest another 0.1 mile to the slightly higher rocky pinnacle of 2,450 feet. This is a good place from which to soak up the surrounding moonscape—from Club Peak to the northeast to the cinder cone-studded lava beds far to the southeast.

For the descent, work your way carefully down the loose rocks westward to a saddle at 2,370 feet. Continue the descent by turning right (northwest) and angling down the easier right side of the steep gully. After about 0.3 mile the bottom of the main wash is reached. Turn left (west) and follow the troad/wash another 0.3 mile back to the trailhead to complete this 2-mile hike/climb loop.

General description:	A short but steep round-trip on one of only two maintained trails in the Mojave National Preserve, within the Wilderness boundary, to a rocky point surrounded by an extensive Joshua tree forest.
Length:	4 miles round-trip.
General location:	About 35 miles southeast of Baker, north-central Mojave National Preserve, southeastern California.
Trail condition:	Clear troad first mile; good trail second mile.
Special attractions:	Volcanic geology interspersed with mounds of white monzonite, an extensive Joshua tree forest, and expansive scenic vistas.
Difficulty:	Moderate.
Best season:	October through June.
Starting elevation:	5,018 feet.
Maximum elevation:	5,640 feet (notch just below the summit of 5,767 foot Teutonia Peak).
Elevation gain/loss:	622 feet/none.
USGS map:	Cima Dome-CA (1:24,000).
For more information:	Mojave Desert Information Center (see Appendix D).

Key points:

0.0   Signed Teutonia Peak trailhead (5,018 feet).
0.5   First gate and a troad (5,100 feet).
0.9   Mine shafts and tailings.
1.0   Second gate and another troad.
1.1   Trail starts up northwest summit ridge (5,220 feet).
2.0   Notch in the rocks just below the summit (5,640 feet).

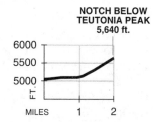

Finding the trailhead: From Interstate 15, 25 miles northeast of Baker, take the Cima exit to the paved Cima Road. Continue southeasterly on Cima Rd. for 11.2 miles, reaching the signed trailhead parking area on the west side of the road 0.1 mile north of Sunrise Rock (a pile of rocks adorned with a large white cross). Coming from the south on the Kelso-Cima Rd., the trailhead is 6.7 miles north of Cima Junction.

The hike: The Teutonia Peak Trail is one of only two maintained trails in the entire 1.4 million-acre Mojave National Preserve. It exists thanks to the volunteer efforts of the San Gorgonio Chapter of the Sierra Club, which has adopted the trail. The well-signed trailhead contains an informative wild-life/woodland vegetation exhibit board. Here you'll learn a bit about the ladder-backed woodpecker, Scott's oriole, desert night lizard, night snake,

TEUTONIA PEAK/CIMA DOME

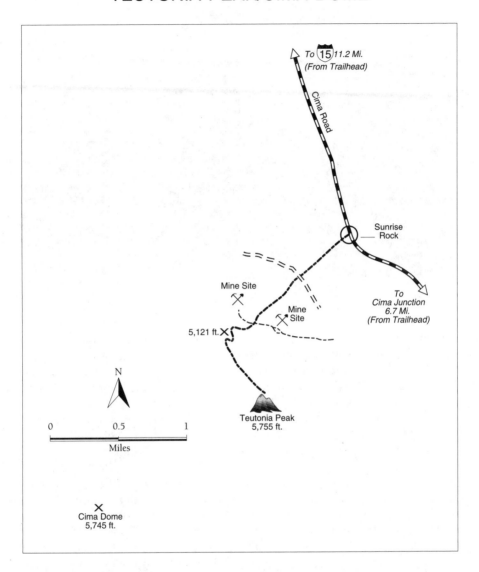

To (15) 11.2 Mi.
(From Trailhead)

Cima Road

Sunrise
Rock

Mine Site

Mine
Site

To
Cima Junction
6.7 Mi.
(From Trailhead)

5,121 ft.

N

0   0.5   1

Miles

Teutonia Peak
5,755 ft.

Cima Dome
5,745 ft.

and yucca moth, which pollinates the Joshua tree. The evergreen Joshua tree is not a tree at all but, rather, a striking member of the agave family.

For the first 0.5 mile the sandy, clear trail climbs gently through this vast Joshua tree forest to the first gate, crosses a troad, and continues southwest on a signed route. At 0.9 mile the trail reaches some old mine tailings and open shafts, the largest of which has been fenced off for public safety. Here the troad changes to a more narrow trail before coming to a gate and crossing another troad at 1 mile. Follow the sign straight. At 1.1 miles the base of the northwest summit ridge of Teutonia Peak is reached at 5,220 feet. The

Climbing the northwest ridge of Teutonia Peak.

trail is rocky but in good condition as it ascends a slope of prickly pear, yucca, juniper, and stunted Joshua trees. The final 0.5 mile is faint but easy to follow with occasional rock cairns to mark the way. At 2 miles the trail ends in a notch between two large mounds of monzonite granite just below the bouldery cliff summit of 5,767-foot Teutonia Peak.

Don't attempt the difficult summit unless you are an experienced rock climber. Instead, spend some time exploring the endless nooks and pockets surrounding the peak. Teutonia Peak is actually an extensive complex of granite outcroppings, boulders and huge mounds of monzonite. Walk out on the fairly level ridge to the east to gain an excellent overall perspective of the peak complex and much of the preserve to the north and east. Stunted Joshua trees mix with juniper all the way to this lofty 5,640-foot level.

The end-of-the-trail notch provides a magnificent view westward of Cima Dome, which gradually rises 1,500 feet above the surrounding desert to an elevation almost equal to that of Teutonia Peak. The dome is a huge 75-square-mile symmetrical hump of monzonite formed when a core of molten rock cooled and hardened deep beneath the surface of the earth. It has since been uncovered by millions of years of erosion resulting in the unusual landscape we see today. Cima Dome is adorned by one of the largest Joshua tree forests in the vast California desert. These trees are a different, more spindly variety than those found to the south in Joshua Tree National Park.

After you've soaked up the view and enjoyed a bit of exploration around the peak, double back on the trail to the trailhead to complete this diverse 4-mile round-trip hike/climb.

General description:	A short but steep canyon hike to a mountain spring high in the Providence Mountains, with towering columns of volcanic rock, sweeping vistas, and a chance to view birds, desert bighorn sheep, and other wildlife.
Length:	2 miles round-trip to Crystal Spring; 2.2 miles round-trip to overlook.
General location:	About 60 miles west of Needles, surrounded by the south-central region of the Mojave National Preserve, southeastern California.
Trail condition:	Clear steep rocky trail.
Special attractions:	Wildlife viewing potential; colorful rhyolite volcanic rock formations; sweeping desert vistas; and intimacy with a scenic mountain canyon.
Difficulty:	Moderately strenuous.
Best season:	October through May (November through March to avoid rattlesnakes).
Starting elevation:	4,300 feet.
Maximum elevation:	4,920 feet (end-of-trail/Crystal Spring); 4,960 feet (overlook).
Elevation gain/loss:	660 feet/660 feet (overlook).
USGS topo map:	Fountain Peak-CA (1:24,000).
For more information:	State of California Department of Parks & Recreation, Providence Mountains State Recreation Area/Mitchell Caverns Natural Preserve (see Appendix D).

Key points:

0.0   Crystal Spring trailhead (4,300 feet).
0.2   Trail steepens.
0.6   Trail levels out.
0.7   Trail crosses gully and climbs steeply to end.
1.0   End of trail at Crystal Spring (4,920 feet).
1.1   Overlook (4,960 feet).

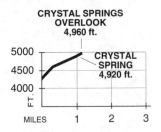

Finding the trailhead: From Interstate 40, take the Essex Road exit which is 43 miles west of Needles and 100 miles east of Barstow. Drive north on the well-signed paved Essex Rd. for 16 miles to the end-of-the road to the recreation area visitor center and campground. The signed trailhead to Crystal Spring is next to the picturesque stone visitor center, which was the residence of Jack and Ida Mitchell from the 1930s through the mid-1950s.

The hike: The short but steep Crystal Spring trail provides a wonderful introduction to the power and spellbinding beauty of a high desert canyon

Columns of rhyolite rise like great pillars above Crystal Spring.

CRYSTAL SPRING OVERLOOK

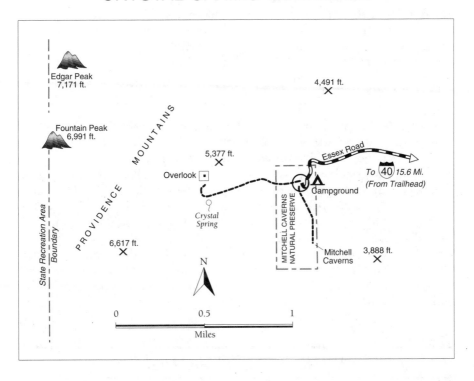

on the dramatic east slope of the perpendicular Providence peaks. Although steep and rocky in places, the trail is easy to follow to its end but be careful of catclaw and other spiny vegetation that can snag you along the way. As you climb you'll see the gently graded Mary Beal Nature Trail below and across the canyon.

Within only 0.2 mile the trappings of civilization seem far away with the continuing gain in distance and elevation. The rugged canyon contains an interesting mix of both limestone and volcanic rock, with the reddish volcanic extrusion known as rhyolite being most striking. The rock platform supporting the pipeline Mitchell built to water his resort in the 1930s is still visible across the canyon. The steep rocky hillsides and gullies are densely covered with prickly pear, barrel and cholla cacti as well as pinyon pine and Mojave sagebrush.

With the increase in elevation there is an increasing sense of entering a relatively lush microenvironment. For the first 0.7 mile the trail climbs on the left side of the ravine then crosses over to the right side at 4,680 feet. The trail continues steeply for the next 0.3 mile until coming to an "end of the trail" sign at 4,920 feet just below the spring. To reach the lower end of the spring continue hiking up a faint use trail on the left side which climbs and then quickly drops to the grottolike opening of the brush-lined spring. Cross over and climb the opposite slope to an overlook at 1.1 mile.

This 4,960-foot-high viewpoint, next to a jagged column of red rhyolite, is a great place to pause and soak up the view. On a clear day the Hualapai Mountains in Arizona are visible, 105 miles east. More than 300 square miles of the Clipper Valley can be seen, along with the low ridgeline of the ancient Colton Hills basalt, which at 1.8 billion years, are as old as the deepest layer of rock exposed in the Grand Canyon. Take time to feel the power of this secluded canyon but remember that the spring is used by bighorn sheep and other wildlife, so disturbance must be kept to a minimum.

The extremely thick growth of willow and other shrubbery at and above the spring inhibits farther travel directly up the canyon. To complete this 2.2-mile out-and-back hike retrace your route back to the visitor center.

From the overlook it is possible to continue climbing on a strenuous cross-country route to the top of 6,991-foot Fountain Peak or 7,171-foot Edgar Peak along the high crest of the Providence Range. Both summits are 6- to 10-hour round-trips and require an early start, good conditioning, and lots of experience in negotiating steep terrain with loose rock. From the overlook the recommended route heads toward a saddle to the immediate north, then southwest up a prominent ridge for 1.5 miles, and finally angles north another mile to Fountain Peak. Edgar Peak rises another extremely rugged mile to the north.

73 HOLE-IN-THE-WALL TO MID HILLS

General description:	A full-day point-to-point hike on one of only two maintained trails in the preserve, across rolling terrain with a deep volcanic canyon, and high desert vistas of volcanic plugs, granite mounds, and distant mountains.
Length:	8.4 miles one-way.
General location:	About 60 miles southeast of Baker, in central Mojave National Preserve, southeastern California.
Trail condition:	Clear trail/troad/wash.
Special attractions:	Deeply pocketed volcanic formations in Banshee Canyon and expansive views across much of the Preserve.
Difficulty:	Moderately strenuous if hiked uphill south to north; moderate if hiked downhill from north to south.
Best season:	October through May.
Starting elevation:	4,265 feet.
Maximum elevation:	5,600 feet (near north end of route).
Elevation gain/loss:	1,900 feet/715 feet.
USGS topo map:	Columbia Mtn-CA (1:24,000).
For more information:	Mojave Desert Information Center (see Appendix D).

Key points:

0.0 "Rings" trailhead at the Hole-In-The-Wall Picnic Area (4,265 feet).

0.2 End of steep descent to canyon floor (4,050 feet).

0.3 Mouth of Banshee Canyon (4,040 feet).

1.0 Signed trail junction with Wild Horse Canyon Trail; turn right toward the Mid Hills Campground.

1.7 Low pass (4,460 feet).

2.2 Troad junction; stay right.

2.4 Another troad junction; veer right.

2.5 Signed trail leaves troad and turns left (north).

4.3 Trail crosses Gold Valley Mine road; continue straight (north) and through a gate signed "3.8 miles to Mid Hills."

5.0 Trail crosses a fence signed "Mid Hills 3.1 miles."

5.7 Trail drops down a gully (5,090 feet).

5.9 "Follow wash" sign; turn left and proceed up the wash.

6.2 Signed trail leaves wash to the right; "Follow wash" sign points up the wash to the left to the Mid Hills Campground.

6.8 Fence/gate signed "1.2 miles to Mid Hills."

8.0 High point at 5,600 feet.

8.4 Signed endpoint at Mid Hills trailhead next to the windmill.

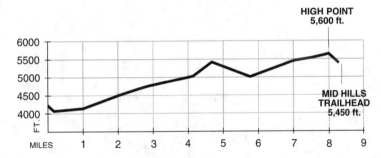

Finding the trailhead: From the north on Interstate 15 take the Cima exit 25 miles northeast of Baker. Drive southeast on the paved Cima Road for 28.5 miles to Cima Junction, turn right, and continue south on the Kelso-Cima Road for 4.9 miles to Cedar Canyon Road. Turn left (east) on Cedar Canyon Rd. and drive 6.4 miles to Black Canyon Road. Turn right (south) and drive 9.4 miles to the signed Hole-In-The-Wall Campground/Visitor Center. Turn right (west) and drive 0.2 mile to the Hole-In-The-Wall Picnic Area, where the trailhead is located.

The hike: Although more difficult, a south-to-north route on this trail, mostly uphill, is recommended for several reasons. First, if you leave during the morning—which you should certainly do given the length of the hike— you'll have the sun at your back rather than in your face, a definite plus during the warmer months. Second, by climbing up into the higher desert one can better appreciate subtle changes in vegetation and geology in this varied land. But perhaps the best reason is that you will better enjoy the

The aptly named Hole-In-The-Wall cliffs and narrows of Banshee Canyon.

HOLE-IN-THE-WALL TO MID HILLS

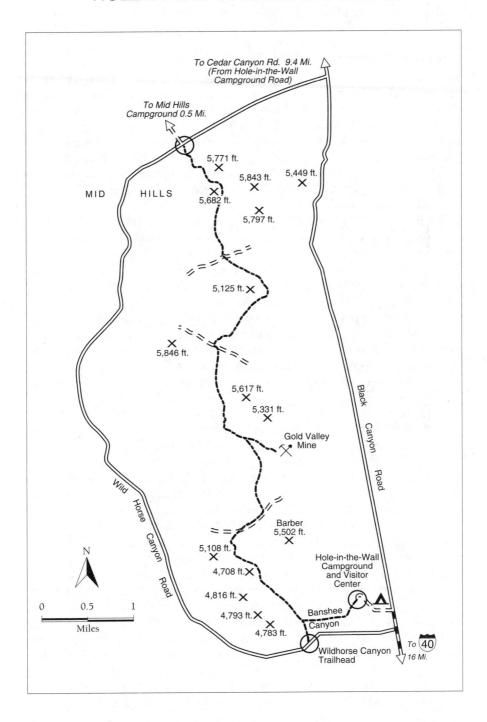

To Cedar Canyon Rd. 9.4 Mi.
(From Hole-in-the-Wall
Campground Road)

To Mid Hills
Campground 0.5 Mi.

MID   HILLS

5,771 ft. ✕

5,843 ft. ✕   5,449 ft. ✕

✕ 5,682 ft.

✕ 5,797 ft.

5,125 ft. ✕

✕ 5,846 ft.

5,617 ft. ✕

5,331 ft. ✕

Gold Valley
Mine ✕

Black Canyon Road

Barber
5,502 ft. ✕

Wild Horse Canyon Road

N

5,108 ft. ✕

4,708 ft. ✕

4,816 ft. ✕

4,793 ft. ✕

✕ 4,783 ft.

0   0.5   1

Miles

Hole-in-the-Wall
Campground
and Visitor
Center

Banshee
Canyon

Wildhorse Canyon
Trailhead

To 40
16 Mi.

fantastic volcanic geology of Banshee Canyon by dropping into it when fresh early in the day, rather than the other way around.

Significantly, this trail is one of only two official trails in the entire preserve. It is adopted and maintained by the Angeles Chapter of the Sierra Club.

When you get to the "Rings" trailhead at the picnic area be sure to walk left a short distance to the overlook, protected by a guardrail high above a narrow, pocketed canyon. One of many "holes" can be seen high in a volcanic wall to the south. Some 15 million years ago volcanic eruptions spilled layer upon layer of lava and ash here. The mesas seen in this area are isolated remnants of these lava flows. The many holes in the rock are the product of uneven cooling, made larger by erosion. It's a wonderland of caverns, ledges, and openings. The reddish color on the dark gray volcanic rock is caused by oxidation. Wind and moisture continue to mold this unusual landscape.

From the trailhead the descent into spectacular Banshee Canyon is extremely steep and potentially hazardous. Two sets of steel ring handholds are attached to pins in the rock. Although the rings add an element of safety, great care must be exercised when making the descent. The volcanic walls of the canyon are deeply pocked by erosion. Within 0.2 mile the 215-foot drop to the canyon floor has been achieved.

Numerous temptations for side climbing and exploration present themselves. When you're ready, continue down another 0.1 mile to the canyon mouth from where Barber Butte rises impressively to the north. Follow the signed hiking trail/troad across a wash. At 0.5 mile the trail intersects the wash. Bear right and follow a cholla-yucca lined wash surrounded by distant mesas. Look back to the sheer cliff walls of the canyon you've just descended.

At 1 mile the trail reaches a signed junction (4,150 feet). The Wild Horse Canyon trailhead is 0.25 mile south, and the trail to Mid Hills heads north. Turn right at this junction toward the Mid Hills Campground and continue up a ridge toward a gap in the mesas. Here the trail makes a gradual ascent of an alluvial fan. A wall of dark volcanic rock parallels the trail to the right.

At 1.7 miles a low pass is reached (4,460 feet). Dropping down another 0.1 mile, the trail crosses a gate signed "6.2 miles to Mid Hills." A deep lava canyon wash winds to the left. The steep, rocky trail drops to the wash where a trail sign points up the wash to the right. A troad junction appears at 2.2 miles; stay right. Striking white cliffs topped with a dark volcanic crown rise majestically to the left. Another troad junction is met at 2.4 miles; again follow the sign and veer to the right. At 2.5 miles the signed trail leaves the troad and turns left (north), leaving the sweeping mesas to the south. For the next mile the trail follows a wash and then climbs up a sandy ridge in high, open desert where white, granite boulders begin to dot the landscape.

At 4.3 miles the trail crosses a dirt road that leads to the tailings of the abandoned Gold Valley Mine, where a working windmill provides water for cattle. For a side trip to the mine/windmill site turn right at this junction and follow the road southeasterly for 0.5 mile.

Continuing north toward Mid Hills, the trail soon passes through a gate signed "3.8 miles to Mid Hills," intersecting a troad. For the next 0.5 mile the troad climbs a small pass from where, at 5,350 feet, a vast juniper-sage plateau opens up ahead with small, pointed peaks and mesas adorning the landscape. At 5 miles the troad crosses another fence signed "Mid Hills 3.1 miles". Take the signed trail to the right.

For the next 0.7 mile the trail descends a sandy gully to 5,090 feet then curves around to the left (north) and begins climbing. At 5.9 miles a "follow wash" sign points up the wash as it again turns left. The only confusing point in this otherwise well-signed hike is encountered at mile 6.2 where a "follow wash" sign points up the wash to the Mid Hills Campground and a signed trail leaves the gravelly wash to the right. Take the trail to the right.

At 6.8 miles the trail passes a gate signed "1.2 miles to Mid Hills". The steadily climbing trail reaches a spring/seep at 5,450 feet. It then drops into a narrow gully and climbs steeply to the high point of 5,600 feet at 8 miles. The end-of-the-trail windmill can be seen from here. A gradual drop over the final 0.4 mile to 5,450 feet concludes this point-to-point traverse from Banshee Canyon to the Mid Hills in the middle of Mojave.

74 EAGLE ROCKS

General description:	An easy hike to a unique formation of monzogranite boulders.
Length:	2 miles round-trip, with extra mileage for exploring the boulders and the valley between the piles.
General location:	About 55 miles east of Baker, south-central Mojave National Preserve, southeastern California.
Trail condition:	Clear troad.
Special attraction:	Granite formation is the highest point in this section of the Mid Hills.
Difficulty:	Easy to boulders; moderate for exploring boulder piles.
Best season:	October through May.
Starting elevation:	5,610 feet.
Maximum elevation:	5,610 feet.
Elevation gain/loss:	200 feet/100 feet.
USGS topo maps:	Columbia Mtn.-CA and Mid Hills-CA (1:24,000).
For more information:	Mojave Desert Information Center (see Appendix D).

Key points:
0.0   Trailhead, wilderness boundary marker at the dirt road.
0.5   Junction with another troad. Turn left uphill.
0.7   Y junction. Either way is 0.1 mile to granite fields; both are dead ends.
0.8   Boulder fields. Dead end of troad. Faint use trail down the valley between boulder piles.

Finding the trailhead: From the Desert Information Center in Baker, take Interstate 15 for 26 miles northeast to the Cima Road south exit. Drive southeast 17.8 miles to the junction with the Kelso-Cima Road in Cima. Turn right (south) on the Kelso-Cima Rd. and drive 4.9 miles to the Cedar Canyon turn, on your left (east). Turn left onto Cedar Canyon Road, which is paved only for the first 2 miles, and drive 6.4 miles east to Black Canyon Road, on your right. Turn right on Black Canyon Rd., and drive 2.1 miles to Wild Horse Canyon Road on your right (east). Turn right onto Wild Horse Canyon, and drive 2.8 miles to the first dirt road on your right after the Mid Hills Campground turnoff. Turn right on this unmarked dirt road, which occurs at the first sharp southward bend in Wild Horse Canyon. A limited use sign reminds drivers to stay on the road. Drive 0.2 mile on the dirt road to a junction. Bear right and drive 0.1 mile to the wilderness boundary post at the end of the troad on your right. Park at a wide spot on the road so as not to violate the limited use guidelines. The signed troad is your trail.

The hike: The Eagle Rocks tower above the Mid Hills and are prominent beacons along the entire Kelso-Cima Road. These lumpy granite formations stand out in sharp contrast with the angular mountains in this central Mojave region. They beckon the curious hiker from afar but, oddly enough, disappear from sight as you approach the trailhead, obscured by the surrounding hills.

The hike heads downhill on a gentle, sandy troad, gradually mixing with a small wash, until the junction at 0.5 mile. It is not until 0.6 mile that the Eagle Rocks gradually appear. And what a surprise they are!

Much like the monzogranite of Joshua Tree National Park, these hulking boulders have rounded contours, immense size, and fantastic shapes. The powerful boulders tower 350 feet above the base of the pile. There are even Joshua trees on the hillsides near the boulder piles. This form of igneous rock is, upon closer inspection, quite chunky, resembling conglomerate with rectangular pieces of quartz imbedded in the surface. It provides great traction for adventuresome rock scramblers. Advanced rock-climbing skills are mandatory for the larger boulders, but novices can enjoy exploring the perimeter of the mounds.

The small valley between the two dominant boulder piles is an enchanting nook of wilderness to explore. A use trail leads 0.7 mile down the narrow valley, following a small wash. The canyon protects large pinyon pine and live oak from the strong winds that dwarf these species in more exposed locations nearby.

EAGLE ROCKS

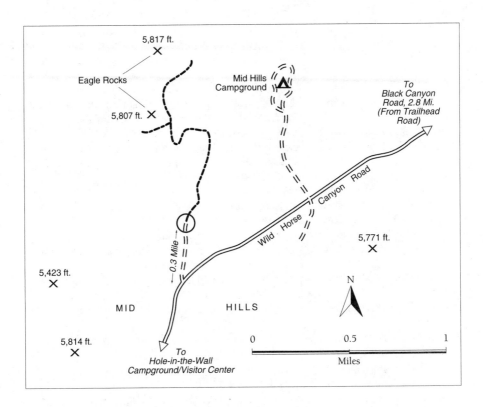

As you walk back along the troad to the parking area, you'll again be surprised at how quickly these granite obelisks disappear from view. Yet, as you travel around the preserve, you'll notice their prominence on the horizon.

General description:	A mostly cross-country climb of a distinctive, steep-sided butte in the heart of Mojave National Preserve, which can be done as either an out-and-back or loop hike.
Length:	7 miles (for both loop and out-and-back routes).
General location:	About 65 miles southeast of Baker, in central Mojave National Preserve, southeastern California.
Trail condition:	Clear troad/wash, with most of route cross-country.
Special attractions:	Ascent of an isolated flat-topped mesa, monzonite boulder formations, 360-degree view of almost all of the preserve.
Difficulty:	Strenuous.
Best season:	September through May.
Starting elevation:	5,180 feet.
Maximum elevation:	6,176 feet (Table Top Mountain).
Elevation gain/loss:	1,386 feet/1,386 feet (ridge route loop); 1,026 feet/30 feet (base of ridge route) out-and-back.
USGS topo maps:	Columbia Mountain-CA and Woods Mountains-CA (1:24,000)
For more information:	Mojave Desert Information Center (see Appendix D).

Key points:

0.0   Trailhead. Troad heads east up a draw (5,180 feet).
0.3   Gate/fence.
0.6   Junction; make a sharp left turn (north).
1.1   Windmill/water tank; beginning of cross-country route with two options: go west up ridge of Table Top Mountain or hike along base of the ridge.

Ridge Route:
1.4   Climb northeast to the summit ridge (5,430 feet).
1.7   Climb to a rocky ridge (5,700 feet).
2.3   Skirt to the right below cliff rocks.
3.2   Base of Table Top Mountain.
3.5   Summit (6,176 feet).

Base of Ridge Route:
1.9   Cross barbed-wire fence.
2.2   Look upslope and left for a large duckhead-shaped granite rock; this is a good place to begin climbing toward Table Top Mountain.
3.2   Southwest base of mountain.
3.5   Summit (6,176 feet).

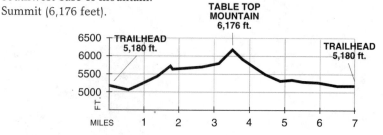

TABLE TOP MOUNTAIN LOOP

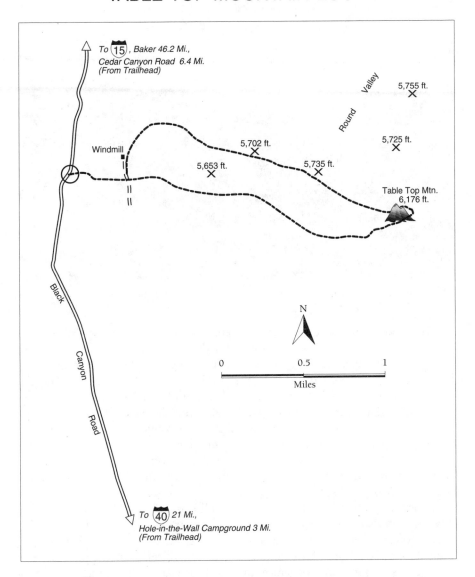

Finding the trailhead: From Baker drive east on Interstate 15; take the Cima Exit and head south on the Cima Road for 28.5 miles to Cima Junction. Turn right (south) on the Kelso-Cima Road and continue for 4.9 miles to the Cedar Canyon Road; turn left (east) on the Cedar Canyon Road and drive 6.4 miles to the Black Canyon Road; turn right (south) on the Black Canyon Rd. and drive 6.4 miles to the unsigned trailhead which is on the east side immediately north of a cattle guard. Pull off on the east side of the road and park in a large turnaround camping area. The trail begins on a troad on the northeast edge of the parking area.

Dropping down from the southwest face of Table Mountain.

The hike: There are a variety of approaches to Table Top Mountain, ranging from moderate to strenuous, but the final ascent to the summit is strenuous regardless of which route you choose. Table Top Mountain is bounded by a private subdivision in Round Valley to the immediate north, posted against trespass. There is also private land nearby to the south. One of the advantages of this suggested route is that it takes place entirely on public land. The somewhat long 3.5-mile (one-way) approach traverses a variety of terrain with constantly changing views.

Begin by heading east up a draw on a clear troad that provides an easy start to an otherwise strenuous hike. Continue walking slightly downhill on the troad as it passes through a gate/fence at 0.3 mile. At 0.6 mile make a sharp left turn at a junction. The troad climbs up a wash next to an old broken waterline for another 0.5 mile to a windmill/water tank used for watering cattle. An abandoned mine entrance and remnants of a mining road can be seen on the hillside to the left. A huge rock outcropping rises to the right, serving as a good landmark for the return trip along the base of the ridge. For point of reference, the windmill is the takeoff point for both the more difficult ridge route loop and the base of the ridge out-and-back trip.

For the ridge route, proceed to the right along a fence, cross it, and climb northeast to the summit ridge behind and to the left of the previously mentioned large rock outcropping. At 1.4 miles you'll likely end up close to a large rock cairn. From here climb straight up the ridge toward a prominent pinyon pine on the horizon. At 1.7 miles and 5,700 feet the ridge becomes very rocky but remains fairly level on a southeasterly line toward the flat-topped mountain. The ridge then drops to around 5,600 feet close to the wilderness boundary. For the next 0.4 mile the going is difficult, requiring boulder scrambling, bushwhacking and edging around sharp-spined yucca and other cacti. In general, skirt to the right of cliff faces and huge granite boulders.

At 2.8 miles the route becomes considerably easier with cow paths and side washes gradually climbing for 0.4 mile to the striking 5,810-foot western base of Table Top Mountain. The mountain is capped by sheer cliffs of dark lava atop a ring of white granite. The final 0.3-mile climb to the 6,176-foot summit is steep with loose rocks but the route is direct and straightforward. Once you arrive at the base of the cliffs the top is equally accessible by going either to the right or left and then up through a break in the cliffs. However, the route to the north (left) is somewhat faster.

On top, look for the peak register placed there in April 1983 by the Desert Peaks Chapter of the Sierra Club. The large plateau is well-vegetated with sage, Mormon tea, rabbitbrush, and juniper. By all means walk along the rim for a chance to see raptors in the cliffs as well as ever-changing vistas. Table Top Mountain is strategically located between the jagged peaks of the Providence Mountains to the southwest and the rugged New York Mountains and Castle Peaks to the north. Symmetrical Cima Dome fills the northwest horizon. Virtually all of the vast preserve can be seen from this central volcanic laccolith.

For the return journey, ease your way down a break in the cliffs just west of the summit, proceeding cautiously on the steep, loose rock. After losing about 250 feet in 0.3 mile at the base of the steepest slope of the mountain, angle to the right (west) along a juniper-clad ridge. Continue dropping for another 0.4 mile to 5,600 feet in a wide upper wash encircled by pinyon-juniper and boulders. At 0.9 mile the route crosses a bouldery draw; drop to the left for another 0.4 mile to a flat bench at 5,300 feet.

For those going up on this route, look for a distinctive duckhead-shaped rock upslope and to your left.

At 1.6 miles cross a barbed-wire fence and angle northwesterly near the hillside on the right. At 2 miles the route passes just below the high pillar of rocks seen earlier from the windmill site. The windmill is visible straight ahead to the northwest. Continuing westward you'll soon intersect the troad. Go left and walk down to the troad junction, then turn right for the final 0.6 mile to the trailhead, thereby completing this exhilarating loop in Mojave's heartland.

General description:	An out-and-back hike into a mountain canyon dominated by granite boulders and spires and an old mine site.
Length:	3 miles round-trip.
General location:	North-central Mojave National Preserve, 72 miles east of Baker, southeastern California.
Trail condition:	Clear troad.
Special attractions:	Granite formations, mine site.
Difficulty:	Moderate.
Best season:	October through May.
Starting elevation:	5,570 feet.
Maximum elevation:	6,150 feet.
Elevation gain/loss:	580 feet/30 feet.
USGS topo maps:	Ivanpah-CA and Pinto Valley-CA (1:24,000).
For more information:	Mojave Desert Information Center (see Appendix D).

Key points:

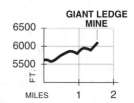

- 0.0   Trail begins at wide wash.
- 0.2   Left at fork. If you do explore to the right, you will find a well-appointed campsite.
- 0.8-0.9   Crossing the wash where there is often water in winter and spring.
- 1.5   Arrive at Giant Ledge Mine.

Finding the trailhead: From Baker, drive east on Interstate 15 for 25 miles to Cima exit. Go south on Cima Road for 28.5 miles to Cima junction. Turn right (south) on the Kelso-Cima Road for 4.9 miles. Turn left (east) on Cedar Canyon and drive 22.3 miles to its end at the Ivanpah/Lanfair intersection. Turn left (north) on Ivanpah Road and drive 5.7 miles to the New York Mountain Road (signed). The turn is in a cattle feedlot for the OX Ranch, and occurs right before a cattle guard. Drive 5.9 miles on New York Mountain Rd. and turn right onto an unmarked but well-traveled road into Caruthers Canyon. Continue north, disregarding a junction at 1.2 miles. At 1.8 miles, locate a suitable place to leave your vehicle in the wide area before descending to the wash. The road from the wash at that point becomes progressively more impassable. Instead the road becomes the hiking trail.

The hike: The lush canyon bottom here is framed by spires of golden granite. A diverse plant community flourishes in Caruthers Canyon due to high elevation and plentiful water. There is also evidence of animal life, although, as in most desert habitats, they remain invisible during the day. Animal footprints around standing pools of water indicate their presence. If water is in Caruthers during your visit, please be considerate of the canyon's permanent residents and don't use the stream as a thoroughfare or play area. Desert water is too precious for such disrespect.

CARUTHERS CANYON

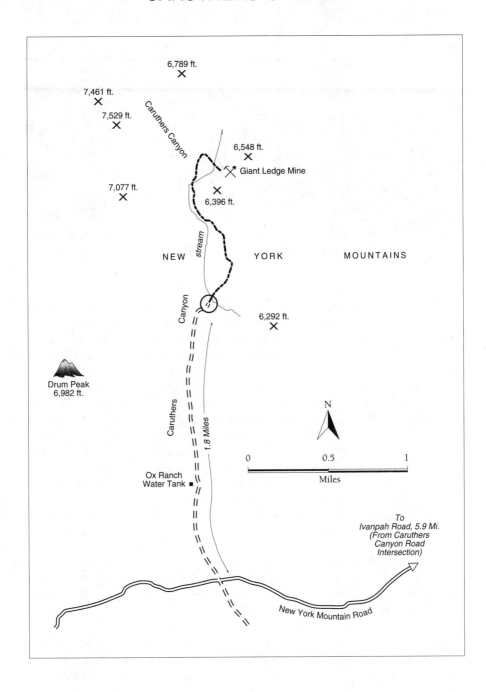

6,789 ft.
✗

7,461 ft.
✗

7,529 ft.
✗

Caruthers Canyon

6,548 ft.
✗

✗ Giant Ledge Mine

7,077 ft.
✗

6,396 ft.
✗

stream

NEW   YORK   MOUNTAINS

Canyon

6,292 ft.
✗

Drum Peak
6,982 ft.

Caruthers

1.8 Miles

N

0   0.5   1

Miles

Ox Ranch
Water Tank ■

To
Ivanpah Road, 5.9 Mi.
(From Caruthers
Canyon Road
Intersection)

New York Mountain Road

Granite mounds and spires rise with Caruthers Canyon in the New York Mountains.

Your troad route is the old mine road to the Giant Ledge Mine. Like most roads of this kind, it exhibits remarkable engineering, but it is very rough. One must be astonished that it could be used by mine vehicles, especially ones loaded with ore. In the past decades it has deteriorated. It becomes increasingly rocky as you climb at 0.7 mile. Although the road is legally open since it is not in wilderness, nature is taking care of things and reclaiming it from the four-wheel-drive crowd with well-placed rockslides and fallen boulders. For a hiker it also means slow going.

Numerous campsites dot the lower canyon. Some are tidy, but others are evidence of years of Bureau of Land Management's laissez-faire management, with scattered debris—broken glass, car parts, cans, bottles. The campsite on the spur at 0.2 mile is highly developed, with table, barbecue, and fire-ring. This is the work of an industrious camper!

The boulders of the canyon are certainly the most noteworthy focus of this trip. Fantastic balancing acts are everywhere. Twenty-ton boulders are frozen in a pirouette on 30-foot spires. Above the canyon on the eastern horizon is a hole-in-the-boulder that may grow to an arch eventually. The colors of the granite are as fascinating as the shapes. The central 300-foot granite mound has a golden tone, looking like a mound of petrified butterscotch. Your troad route curves around this formation, rising to the mine in the canyon above.

The mine site is a grotesque scar in this beautiful canyon. Massive tailing piles slump right into the creekbed below the mine. The hillside itself is pockmarked with gaping mouths of defunct mines. Be cautious near these, and do not go into them; often old mine shafts are unstable. The only equipment that remains is the chute used to deliver ore into the vehicles that carried it down the tricky mine road. The mine site provides a striking contrast with the natural beauty that surrounds it.

After carefully looking around the mine site, return down the canyon to your parking area at the mouth.

77   FORT PIUTE/PIUTE GORGE

General description:	A longer loop hike to the only year-round stream in the East Mojave Desert, retracing the route of early pioneers, visiting the ruins of an army fort, viewing petroglyphs, and returning via a gorge through the Piute hills.
Length:	7-mile loop.
General location:	About 85 miles west of Baker, eastern Mojave National Preserve, southeastern California.
Trail condition:	Clear troad; good trail; clear wash.
Special attractions:	Petroglyphs, the ruins of Fort Piute, water, and gorge that cuts through the Piute Mountains.
Difficulty:	Moderate to fort; strenuous return via gorge.
Best season:	October through May.
Starting elevation:	3,400 feet.
Maximum elevation:	3,600 feet (Piute Hill).
Elevation gain/loss:	1292 feet/1,292 feet.
USGS topo maps:	Signal Hill-CA and Homer Mountain-CA (1:24,000).
For more information:	Mojave Desert Information Center (see Appendix D).

Key points:

0.0   East on troad, winding north along fence.

0.2   Through the gate and up the rocky troad to the ridge.

0.5   Peak of saddle (Piute Hill).

0.5-1.1   Down the Mojave Road.

1.1   Erosion has taken out the roadbed; notice road drops into wash to your right.

2.0   After bend in wash, at reddish-orange rocks, road leads out of wash to left. This area has numerous petroglyphs. Be respectful.

2.1   Streambed. Cross and go upstream for 10 yards to cross in willows and pick up trail high on north bank heading east. Do not use streambed as trail.

2.6   Ruins of fort, turnaround. Return on north bank trail to intersection.

3.1   Continue west on high bank trail. Large cutaway mountain is your beacon.

3.8   Trail seems to end at a crumbling precipice where you see the wash below turning and disappearing into the gorge. On the hill above you to the right are numerous cairns marking the trail. Climb and continue northwestward.

Key points *(cont'd)*:

4.0   T intersection directly opposite the mouth of the gorge. Take the well-cairned trail to the left, zigzagging down to a feeder canyon from the north.

4.2   Down the canyon to the main gorge/wash. Several dryfalls require scrambling.

4.3-5.5   Up the gorge.

5.6   At gorge exit, notice cairn in wash and others on your left marking trail up from canyon to plateau above.

6.0   Trail comes over crest to parking area. Unless you have a driver to move your car for you, turn left and walk south on dirt road that parallels the hills, by a cattle stockade, to starting point.

7.0   Original parking area.

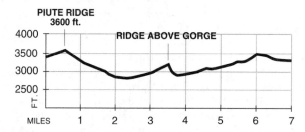

Finding the trailhead: From Baker, go east on Interstate 15 for 25 miles to Cima exit. Take Cima Road south 28.5 miles to Cima junction. Turn right (south) on the Kelso-Cima Road. Drive 4.9 miles to turn left (east) on Cedar Canyon Road. Drive on Cedar Canyon 22.3 miles to its end at the Ivanpah/Lanfair Road junction. Turn left (north), and make a right turn almost immediately onto a dirt road on your right with a small white "PT&T" sign. Head straight for a concrete building. Follow this road straight east for 3.9 miles, disregarding all other roads at intersections. At 3.9 miles, turn right on an AT&T cable route and continue east to the Piute Hills. At 10.3 miles from the Ivanpah turnoff, turn left onto a marginal dirt road just before reaching a cattle guard. Proceed north for 0.5 mile and park in a wide turnaround marked with several rock cairns. The trail is the road that leaves this parking area and goes east to the ridge of the Piutes.

The hike: The Fort Piute/Piute Gorge hike is the perfect journey for the hiking party or the individual with diverse interests. It has petroglyphs for the archaeologist, an original Mojave Road segment for the emigrant historian, an old army fort for the military specialist, and a spectacular mile-long gorge for the geology enthusiast. The combination of all these aspects also makes it exciting for the generic adventurer.

The distance from the main road intersection at Cedar Canyon and the Ivanpah/Lanfair Road to the trailhead should not intimidate you. The dirt road from this intersection is in better condition than many of the official roads in the Preserve. You cross no washes, nor are there any rocks or ruts to contend with. It's virtually a straight shot 10.3 miles east to the Piute Hills from the intersection on a road suitable for a passenger car.

FORT PIUTE/PIUTE GORGE

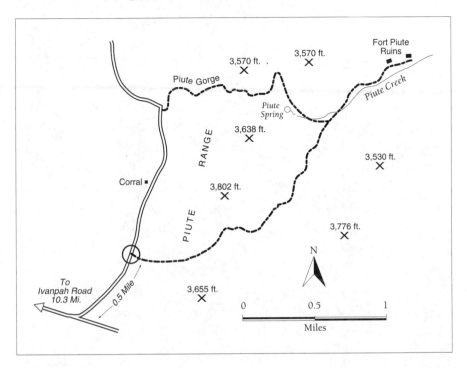

The counter-clockwise loop, as described here, begins at the south trailhead. In doing the hike in this direction, you are walking down the Mojave Road (labeled Old Government Road on the topo map) and not up, the way the emigrants did (unless you omit the gorge trip and return this way). While historically the eastward direction is incorrect, the Mojave Road would be an exercise in boredom after the magnificence of the Piute Gorge. This way the experiential height of the trip occurs on the trip out through the gorge—and the gorge is twice as impressive coming up from its lower eastern end.

The section of the hike (0.0 to 2.1 miles) on the Mojave Road is certain to create respect for the gutsy pioneers who used this thoroughfare. Built and guarded by the U.S. Army pursuant to our nineteenth-century policy to populate the West as quickly as possible, the Mojave Road followed an old Indian track. Be sure to pause at the saddle (0.2 mile from the trailhead), where the track is now closed to wheeled vehicles. Turn and look west. It is easy to relive the mixed feelings the emigrants must have had after struggling to reach this point, seeing the Mojave Desert stretching to the western horizon.

Hike on east down the Mojave Road. This segment rising from Fort Piute was known as one of the most arduous of the entire journey. As you will shortly discover, the volcanic rocks do not make a smooth road surface.

The Piute Gorge, cutting through the mountain range from the east.

Wagons without springs or shocks had a difficult time, as did the folks wh. had to walk along behind the Conestogas.

Where the road finally reaches the Piute stream are several petroglyph sites. Do not touch or deface them, but leave them for others to enjoy.

When you reach the stream (2.1 miles) you'll revel in the lush vegetation, the watercress, the sound of a gurgling brook. A considerate hiker does not use a riparian zone for a trail. Such use devastates vegetation and degrades the streambed. This resource is too precious for the desert residents to risk such destruction. Please use the trail high on the north bank instead. There's a more panoramic view from this high trail anyway.

Downstream 0.5 mile, the ruins of Fort Piute are impressive for their remoteness. All that remain are the stone foundation of the blockhouse and a stone corral. Duty here must have been grim. The vista out over the Great Basin is endless. The emigrants traveling by this point had survived an incredible journey.

Heading back westward from the fort along the same high north bank trail, the focus shifts to the mountain looming above. From this low point of the hike (2,700 feet) the Piute Hills look a lot more impressive than they do from the west where they're a low line of hills—nothing in comparison to the Providence and New York ranges. Your trip through the gorge will change this perception forever. Traveling above the canyon and above Piute Spring gives you an eagle's view of the depth of the gorge 300 feet below. The descent into the gorge is neither arduous nor dangerous if you take the prescribed route (see mileage log). Be sure to stay high until you nearly reach the mountainside and then travel down the side gorge, entering from the north just as the Piute wash disappears into the mountain.

The trip through the heart of the mountain range is a geologist's delight. The display of volcanic rock types, faulting and folding, and erosion is the most dynamic in the Mojave National Preserve. The peaks tower 600 feet above the sandy gorge floor. In places the gorge is no more than 10 feet wide. There are a few segments where stepping up a dry waterfall is necessary but there is no boulder scrambling.

Like Alice in Wonderland, you emerge from the west entrance into a totally alien landscape. "Where am I?" is one's first thought. The Mojave desert floor is 300 feet above the gorge exit, so the deeply eroded cliffs and mesas that greet you are unexpected. The well-cairned trail to the left, 0.1 mile from the gorge mouth, takes you back up to the familiar Mojave landscape, 1 mile north of where you started.

Whether your interests are Indians, emigrants, army recruits, or geology, this loop hike is sure to inspire you. It is definitely worth the long drive to the eastern edge of the preserve since it is unlike any other hike in the region.

Death Valley's intimidating name is said to have originated in 1849 when an anonymous member of a party seeking a shortcut to the newly discovered California gold fields turned around at the final view and exclaimed, "Good-bye, Death Valley!" Now it's our turn to say hello to one of the world's most imposing and contrasting landscapes. The extremes of Death Valley, from soaring snowcapped peaks to North America's hottest, driest, and lowest desert, command respect and entice discovery.

In 1933 President Herbert Hoover proclaimed Death Valley a National Monument, a status less protective than that of national park because of mining conflicts. The monument was expanded in 1937 when President Franklin Roosevelt added the 300,000-acre Nevada triangle. In 1952 President Truman added 40 acres of Devil's Hole in Nevada to protect a rare variety of desert pupfish. With mining a major issue in Death Valley, the 1976 Mining in Parks Act is of special significance. This law began phasing out mining in the monument by closing Death Valley to the filing of new claims. The number of old claims has since decreased from 50,000 to fewer than 150, with only one active mine remaining.

The status of the monument was further elevated in 1984 when the United Nations recognized Death Valley as part of the Mojave and Colorado International Biosphere Reserve. Finally, on October 31, 1994, Death Valley received long overdue national park classification when President Bill Clinton signed the California Desert Protection Act into law. The 2 million-acre national monument became a more than 3.3 million-acre national park, with 95 percent of the park designated Wilderness. In so doing, Death Valley became the nation's largest national park outside Alaska.

More than 200 miles of paved and dirt roads access the 1.3 million acres of additions, most of which are along the north-northwest boundary of the former monument. None of the additions contain developed trails but several superb cross-country and use trail hikes are described in this section. Examples of some of the park expansion areas include Eureka Valley (200,000 acres), which contains the highest dunes in California; Saline Valley and Range (400,000 acres) with warm springs, sand dunes, and mountain vistas; the Western Panamints (100,000 acres), which harbor bighorn sheep and the Panamint City ghost town; and the Northern Panamint Valley (100,000 acres) with stunning Darwin Falls and remote star dunes.

A LONG AND COMPLEX GEOLOGIC PAST

The land of extremes that is Death Valley is best dramatized when afternoon shadows from 11,049-foot Telescope Peak are cast across the 282 feet below sea level Badwater Basin. Combine this amazing vertical relief with recent volcanic craters, towering sand dunes, and flood-scoured canyons and you begin to appreciate a long and complicated geologic history.

OVERVIEW MAP

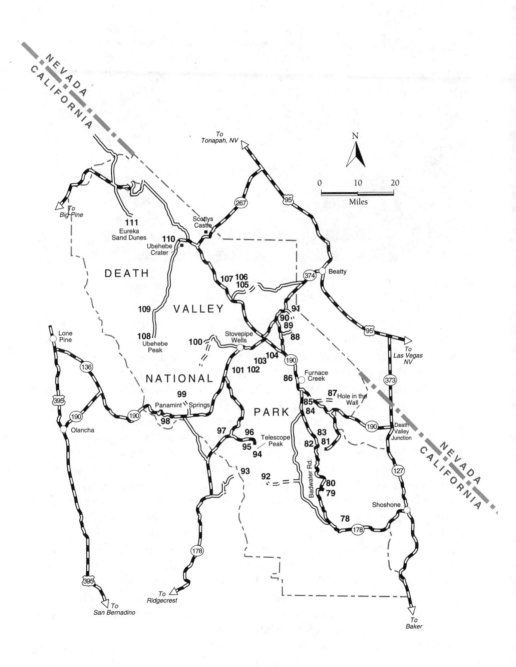

Dante's View provides a spectacular view of Badwater 5,600 feet below, with the snow-capped 11,148 foot Telescope Peak in the distance.

Death Valley is at the western and youngest edge of the Basin and Range Province (the Great Basin). As such, its relatively youthful topography is extreme, with mountains still growing and basins still sinking. The oldest rocks date back 1.8 billion years but have been too severely changed to be reliably interpreted for geologic history.

Rocks a mere half billion years old are more predictable. The Funeral and Panamint mountains are made up of these weathered limestones and sandstones. The rocks point to a warm, shallow sea from around 570 to 250 million years ago. The seas left layers of sediment and a myriad of marine fossils. Between 1933 and 1994 researchers discovered five hundred species of fossil plants and animals within the monument. Now that the boundaries have been expanded by 50 percent, the new park may prove to be the most fossil-rich national park in the United States and perhaps in the world.

Death Valley is next to the boundary of two inter-connected plates in the earth's crust. When the plates moved slowly in relation to each other, compression folded and fractured the brittle crust. This caused the land surface to push up and the sea to gradually recede west. Most of this faulting took place from 250 to 70 million years ago. Active mountain building then alternated with inactive periods of mountain-reducing erosion.

Volcanic activity prevailed from 70 to 3 million years ago. Mountain building stretched and weakened the earth's crust, forming weak spots through which molten material could erupt. This volcanic activity moved westward from Nevada, producing a chain of volcanoes east of the park from Furnace

Creek southeast to Shoshone. Eruptions of cinder and ash account for the flamboyant colors of borate mineral deposits at Artist's Palette.

Around 3 million years ago the floor of Death Valley began to form. Compression was replaced by a pulling apart of the earth's crust, causing large blocks of land to slowly slide past one another along faults. These extensional forces formed parallel north-south trending valleys and mountain ranges. The salt flats of Badwater Basin and the Panamint Range make up one block that is rotating to the east. The valley floor, known as a half-graben, continues to slip down along the fault at the foot of the Black Mountains. This dropping is evident in recently exposed fault scarps near Badwater. Meanwhile, erosion continues with flash floods carrying rocks, sand, and gravel from surrounding hillsides to alluvial fans that spread like gigantic funnels from every canyon mouth. More than 9,000 feet of sediments and salts lie beneath the half-graben floor at Badwater.

Climate has also been a major force in these ongoing changes. During the last major continental Ice Age, the bottom of Death Valley was covered by a system of huge lakes. As the climate warmed, the lakes disappeared—about 10,000 years ago. A much smaller lake system formed 2,000 years ago during a cold period. This water then evaporated, leaving behind today's salt deposits.

The Ubehebe Craters in the northern end of the park tell the tale of recent volcanic activity of several thousand years ago. The craters were formed by violent steam explosions caused when molten material mixed with groundwater. Erosion, earthquakes, and subsidence continue to reshape the surface of one of North America's most dramatic and ever-changing landscapes.

A TAPESTRY OF LIFE: DON'T LET THE NAME FOOL YOU

More than 970 plant species thrive in the incredibly wide range of elevations and habitats found within the park—from dry alkali flats below sea level to the subalpine crests of the highest Panamint summits. These species include nineteen endemics found *only* within the boundaries of the park, such as telescope bedstraw, Panamint monkey flower, and Eureka Dunes evening primrose. Another twenty-three species have the majority of their range within the park, such as magnificent lupine and Death Valley sage. No fewer than thirteen species of cactus grow within the park. Ironically, this driest of deserts is home to more species of marsh grass than cactus.

Spring wildflowers are a pageant worth waiting for. The white of desert-star, red of Indian paintbrush, pink of desert five-spot, yellow of desert trumpet, and blue of Arizona lupine are what dreams are made of. But as with everything, there are good years and bad years. A spectacular year for the showy plants of these desert annuals depends on well-spaced rainfall throughout winter and early spring, enough warming sun, and few drying winds. The premier blooming periods in the park are usually late February to mid-April in the lower elevations of valley floors and alluvial fans, early

April to early May for midslopes up to 4,000 feet, and late April to early June above 4,000 feet in the Panamints and other mountain ranges.

Death Valley is home to at least fifty-one species of mammals, thirty-six species of reptiles, five species of amphibians, and six species of fishes. Some of the animals, such as desert bighorn sheep, live near springs in inaccessible mountains and canyons. The nocturnal kit fox is common in most of Death Valley. Coyotes may be seen from the salt flats up to the highest mountain plateaus. Some species have been introduced, such as the burro was in the 1880s. The reptile list includes the threatened desert tortoise and the mostly nocturnal Mojave sidewinder rattlesnake. Five species of desert pupfish live in the park, four of which are endemic to Death Valley. These endemics are the Saratoga pupfish, Salt Creek pupfish, threatened Cottonball Marsh pupfish, and the endangered Devil's Hole pupfish. These tiny members of the killfish family vary from 1 to 2.5 inches long. They lived in ancient freshwater lakes during the last Ice Age. As the climate became drier the pupfish became isolated in widely separated warm springs and creeks, gradually adapting to higher temperatures and increased salinity.

HUMAN HISTORY

Death Valley has been the site of four Native American cultures, beginning about ten thousand years ago with a group of hunter-gatherers known as "the Nevares Spring people." Game was abundant during this wetter period. As the climate became drier they were replaced by the Mesquite Flat people about four thousand years later. Then the Saratoga Spring people arrived about two thousand years ago when the hot, dry desert was similar to today's conditions. These people were skilled hunters who created large, intricate stone patterns in the valley. Nomadic desert Shoshone moved into the valley about one thousand years ago. Like many people today, they camped near water sources in the valley during winter then headed up into the cooler mountains during summer to escape searing heat.

The first non-native people to enter the valley were two groups of emigrants on their way to the California gold fields in 1849. From the 1880s to early 1900s mining was sporadic in the region. Lack of suitable transportation limited mining to only the highest grade ore. Perhaps the best-known but short-lived mine was the Harmony Borax Works, active from 1883 to 1888. It was most famous for its twenty-mule wagons and the *Death Valley Days* radio and television programs. W. T. Coleman built the wagons that hauled the processed mineral 165 miles across the desert to the railroad at Mojave. Gold and silver mining picked up in the early 1900s with such large-scale ventures as the Keane Wonder Mine, but then came the Panic of 1907. Profitable large-scale hardrock mining in Death Valley ended around 1915. During World War II talc was mined here until markets made mining unprofitable. In 1989 these talc mining claims were bought by the Conservation Foundation and donated to the National Park Service in 1992.

WEATHER

This land of extremes doesn't end with topography, vertical relief, and a Noah's ark of wildlife. Recorded temperatures range from a sizzling 134 degrees to a freezing low of 15 degrees. An annual average of less than 2 inches of rain falls in the valley, which also experiences an average annual temperature of 76 pleasant degrees—somewhat deceiving given the summer averages at well above 100 degrees. Temperatures will be 3 to 5 degrees cooler along with increased precipitation for every 1,000-foot vertical increase in elevation. One balmy July day in 1972, with the air temperature at 128 degrees, a ground temperature of 201 degrees was measured at Furnace Creek. With no protective shade any attempt to hike the salt flats in these conditions could be a terminal experience. For hiking comfort, November to April is hard to beat. Average highs are in the 60- to 90-degree range on the valley floor, cooling considerably at higher elevations. The loftiest mountaintops are often snow-covered from November to May.

RULES TO BETTER ENJOY THE PARK

At this time backcountry hikers and campers are not required to obtain a special use permit, which is unusual for a "big name" national park. However, filling out a backcountry registration form is recommended, especially if hiking solo. These forms are available at the Furnace Creek Visitor Center or at any ranger station.

Limited open desert car camping is allowed at Death Valley, a sprawling park with more than 3 million acres of Wilderness and 350-plus miles of dirt roads. The basic rule is that backcountry camping is permitted 2 miles beyond any paved road, day-use only area, or developed area. Car campers must use pre-existing campsites and park next to the roadway to reduce impact and to avoid violating the wilderness boundary which, in most cases, closely parallels the road. A high-clearance vehicle is usually needed to travel 2 or more miles from pavement on a dirt road that is open for camping. Camping is not allowed on day-use only roads, including the Titus Canyon Road, West Side Road, Wildrose Road, and Racetrack Road from Teakettle Junction to Homestake Dry Camp. Camping is also prohibited at three historic mining areas, including the Ubehebe Lead Mine. Actually, the safe thing to do is to avoid camping at any mining area. Backcountry camping is not allowed on the valley floor from 2 miles north of Stovepipe Wells south to Ashford Mill.

Overnight group size is limited to fifteen people and no more than six vehicles. Larger groups must contact the Chief Ranger at (619) 786-2331 for a special use permit. Campsites in the backcountry must be at least 200 yards from any water source to avoid disturbing wildlife in these fragile and limited sites. Backcountry campers must also camp at least 2 miles from the closest maintained road. In view of the recent park and Wilderness designations at Death Valley it is important to obtain a copy of the latest backcountry regulations at the Furnace Creek Visitor Center or nearest ranger station.

Off-road vehicle use is prohibited, not only because the land away from roads is Wilderness, closed to motorized use, but also because the desert is fragile and painfully slow to recover from damage. Bicycles are permitted on all paved and open dirt roads, but are not allowed on trails, off roads, or in park Wilderness. Campfires are only allowed in fire-pits at developed campgrounds. If you want a fire, bring wood in from outside; gathering the scarce wood here is unlawful. Remember that the park is a museum of undisturbed nature, so removal of any rocks, wood, plants, animals, or historic artifacts is prohibited.

No matter how pitiful the begging coyote may appear, do not feed wildlife. To do so causes them to depend on unnatural food sources which is tantamount to a death sentence. Speaking of animals, leave your pets at home if at all possible. They must be restrained at all times and are not allowed off roads, on trails, or in park Wilderness. Of course, any type of weapon is strictly prohibited in the park.

CAMPGROUNDS AND SERVICES

Nine developed National Park Service campgrounds with more than fifteen hundred sites are well distributed in the central to north-central region of the park. Four of these are free, one of which, Wildrose, is open year-round, weather permitting. The Wildrose Campground is reached by way of the rough Wildrose Canyon Road. The other three higher elevation campgrounds, Emigrant, Thorndike, and Mahogany Flat, are open spring to fall depending on weather conditions. Of the five fee campgrounds, Furnace Creek and Mesquite Spring are open all year. Texas Spring, Sunset, and Stovepipe Wells are at or below sea level and are open October to April.

The main visitor center and Death Valley Natural History Association (DVNHA) is located at Furnace Creek with other visitor centers at Beatty, Nevada, and Scotty's Castle. The visitor centers are open everyday all year from 8 A.M. to 4 P.M. The main visitor center at Furnace Creek is open from 8 a.m. to 7 p.m. in the winter (November-April) and from 8 a.m. to 6 a.m. in the summer (May-November). These hours are subject to change, so check at the park upon your arrival. The National Park Service has prepared an excellent series of free handouts on such topics as geology, mining history, plants, wildflowers, wildlife, special points of interest, and more. During the high season of November through April rangers and naturalists present evening talks and guided nature walks.

The two park entrance stations are located at Furnace Creek and Grapevine, which is 3.5 miles from Scotty's Castle. The entrance fee is $5 per vehicle and is good for seven days. Annual passes to the park are $15. A $25 Golden Eagle Pass provides unlimited admission to the entire National Park System nationwide and is good for one year. U.S. citizens sixty-two and older can purchased a one-time Golden Age pass for $10 which allows unlimited entry to all National Park System areas. Golden Age pass holders also receive a 50 percent discount on campground fees.

Food, supplies, and gas can be purchased at Furnace Creek Ranch and Stovepipe Wells. Fuel can also be bought at Scotty's Castle. Distances in the sprawling park are vast so be sure to travel with plenty of gas, water, food, and other necessary supplies.

The few trails in the park that are formally maintained are described in some of the recommended hikes that follow. Use trails in drainages may largely disappear after a flash flood. Many of the trailless routes follow natural corridors, such as deep canyons. In the desert, hiking use is generally light with vast distances between trailheads which, in turn, lead to routes without directional signs. Lack of hiker conveniences found in other more heavily visited parks and Wilderness is more than made up for by solitude, and by the spirit of adventure that awaits those willing to explore this magnificent park on foot.

HOW TO GET THERE

Primary road access to the park from the south is via California Highway 127 from Interstate 15 at Baker. California Highway 178 leads west into the park from CA 127 near Shoshone. California Highway 190 heads west into the park from CA 127 at Death Valley Junction. On the west side, CA 178 takes off from U.S. Highway 395 and enters the park by way of Panamint Valley. CA 190 takes off to the east from US 395 at Olancha, entering the park just west of Panamint Springs. The network of roads within the park run the gamut, from all-weather pavement to a series of rocky washboard ruts that can loosen every bolt and try the patience of the most determined motorist. The closest large commercial airport is at Las Vegas, about 135 miles southeast of Furnace Creek.

DEATH VALLEY NATIONAL PARK HIKES AT A GLANCE

Hike (Number)	Distance	Difficulty	Feature	Page
Ashford Canyon (78)	3.2 miles	M	Mine Site	254
Badwater (82)	1.5 miles	E	Salt Flats	266
Dante's View (81)	1.0 mile	E	Vista	264
Darwin Falls (98)				319
Lower Falls	1.6 miles	E	Stream, Falls	319
Upper Falls	2.8 miles	MS	Vista	319
Desolation Canyon (84)	3.0 miles	M	Canyon	272
Overlook	3.2 miles	MS	Vista	272
Eureka Dunes (111)	3.0 miles	M	Sand Dunes	358
Fall Canyon (106)				344
Dryfall	6.0 miles	M	Canyon	344
Head of Canyon	16.0 miles	MS	Canyon	344
Golden/Gower Loop (85)	6.5 miles	M	Scenery, Geology	275
Grotto Canyon (102)	4.0 miles	M	Canyon	334
Harmony Borax (86)	2.0-5.0 miles	E	Hist. Site, Salt Flats	279
Hole-in-the-Wall North (87)	2.8 miles	M	Canyon	282
Hummingbird Spring (95)	3.0 miles	M	Hist. Site, Vista	310
Hungry Bill's Ranch (92)	3.6 miles	MS	Hist. Site, Vista	296
Keane Spring (91)	1.0 mile	E	Spring, Townsite	294
Keane Wonder Mine (88)	4.0 miles	MS	Mill & Mine Site	285
Keane Wonder Springs (89)	2.0 miles	E	Spring, Mine Site	288
Little Bridge Canyon (103)	7.0 miles	MS	Canyon	335
Marble Canyon (100)	1.05 miles	M	Canyon, Archeology	327
Monarch Canyon/Mine (90)	3.0 miles	E	Dryfall, Mill Site	290
Mosaic Canyon (101)				331
Lower Dryfall	2.8 miles	E	Canyon	331
Upper Dryfall	3.6 miles	M	Canyon	331
Natural Bridge (83)	2.0 miles	E	Geology, Canyon	268
Nemo Canyon (97)	3.6 miles	M	Canyon	316
Panamint Dunes (99)	9.0 miles	M	Sand Dunes	323
Red Wall Canyon (107)	7.0 miles	M	Canyon	347
Salt Creek Nature Trail (104)	0.5 mile	E	Nature Trail	337
Sidewinder Canyon (79)	4.5 miles	MS	Canyon	257
Surprise Canyon (93)	13.0 miles	S	Stream, Canyon, Mine/Townsite	300
Telescope Peak (94)	14.0 miles	S	Vista	306
Titus Canyon Narrows (105)	4.2 miles	E	Canyon	340
Klare Spring	12.0 miles	MS	Canyon, Spring	340
Ubehebe Craters (110)	1.5 miles	E	Volcanic Craters	356
Ubehebe Mine/ Corridor Canyon (109)	1.0-11.0 miles	M	Mine Site/Canyon	353
Ubehebe Peak (108)	6.2 miles	MS	Vista	349
Wildrose Peak (96)	8.4 miles	MS	Vista	313
Willow Canyon (80)	5.0 miles	M	Canyon	261

DEATH VALLEY NATIONAL PARK
TOPO MAP INDEX

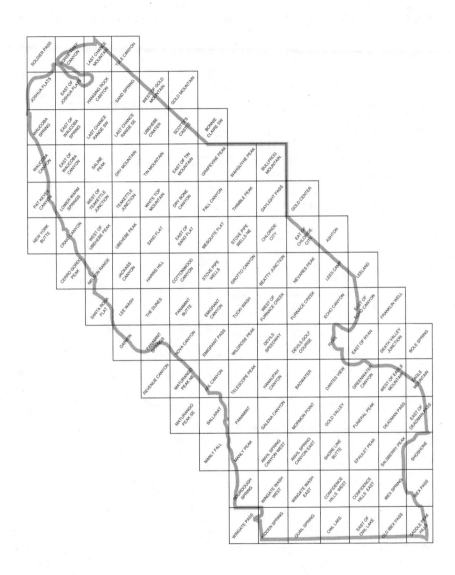

General description:	A steep, rocky hike up a remote and narrow canyon to an extensive mine site with several intact buildings.
Length:	3.2 miles round-trip.
General location:	About 90 miles northwest of Baker, in south-central Death Valley National Park, southeastern California.
Trail condition:	Good troad/wash.
Special attraction:	Historic early twentieth-century mine site.
Difficulty:	Moderate.
Best season:	October through April.
Starting elevation:	1,115 feet.
Maximum elevation:	2,205 feet.
Elevation gain/loss:	1,090 feet/40 feet.
USGS topo map:	Shore Line Butte-CA (1:24,000).
For more information:	Death Valley National Park (see Appendix D).

Key points:

0.0	Trailhead (1,115 feet).
0.2	Trail drops into the wash after climbing steeply for 250 feet.
0.3	Climb out of the wash (right), bypassing a dryfall/rockslide.
0.5	Troad follows wash up a rough, rocky surface.
0.8	Mine timbers/diggings (1,745 feet).
1.3	Troad crosses wash and climbs slope to the left (2,175 feet).
1.5	High point at 2,205 feet.
1.6	Ashford (Golden Treasure) Mine (2,165 feet).

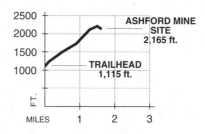

Finding the trailhead: From California Highway 127, 1.7 miles north of Shoshone, turn left (west) on California Highway 178 (East Side Road) which leads to the park boundary. After entering the park drive 25.1 miles to the signed Ashford Mill Road on the left, 1.9 miles north of Ashford Junction and 26.9 miles south of Badwater. Turn right (east) onto the unsigned Ashford Canyon Road leading northeast directly across from the Ashford Mill site. Follow this four-wheel-drive road for 3 miles to the mouth of Ashford Canyon. Park and hike from here. To avoid parking in the wash as well as the final rough 0.1 mile of road, park on the rise just before dropping to the canyon mouth.

ASHFORD CANYON/MINE

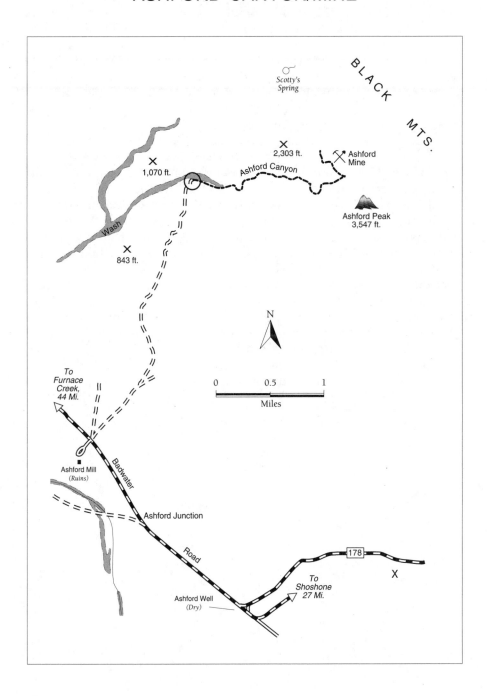

Scotty's Spring

BLACK MTS.

✕ 2,303 ft.

✕ 1,070 ft.

Ashford Canyon

Ashford Mine

Ashford Peak 3,547 ft.

Wash

✕ 843 ft.

N

0   0.5   1
Miles

To Furnace Creek, 44 Mi.

Badwater

Ashford Mill (Ruins)

Ashford Junction

Road

178

To Shoshone 27 Mi.

Ashford Well (Dry)

X

The hike: The Ashford (Golden Treasure) Mine was discovered in 1907 and was sold a few years later to supply gold ore to the Ashford Mill. The early years were probably its most productive, since the mine sold for more money than it ultimately yielded. The inefficiency of the mill was at least partly to blame.

From the mouth of the canyon the old mining troad climbs steeply up the left side of the deep, narrow Ashford Canyon. Rockslides and erosion are gradually erasing any sign of the troad as nature reclaims the land. But there is still enough evidence of rock construction and built-up roadbeds to make this route fairly easy to follow.

After dropping into the canyon bottom the road crosses the wash several times. Several steep sections of slanted rock are avoided as the troad pitches right or left. Huge round mine timbers and scattered diggings are found about halfway up. At 1.3 miles the road crosses the wash and contours to the left around the slope, climbs slightly, and then drops to the mining camp.

The buildings are still somewhat intact, containing some of the furniture and appliances used by the miners. Although they made no effort to clean up their trash, one has to marvel at the incredible determination and optimism the miners must have had to carve such an extensive operation out of such difficult terrain. The miners sure had a view in this southern stretch of the Black Mountains, with Ashford Peak soaring to the south and the rugged canyon below opening to the Owlshead and Panamint mountains westward. Retrace your route to complete this 3.2-mile round-trip exploration of some of Death Valley's mining history.

Other nearby mining sites include the Desert Hound Mine high on the mountaintop a mile to the northeast, and Scotty's Canyon a couple of miles north.

General description:	A canyon loop or out-and-back hike (with good highway access) through narrow tunnels and sheer rock slots requiring moderate scrambling to dramatic view of Death Valley.
Length:	4.5-mile loop or out-and-back.
General location:	About 100 miles northwest of Baker, in southeastern Death Valley National Park, southeastern California.
Trail condition:	Clear wash with short stretches of cross-country and moderate rock climbing.
Special attractions:	Steep, rugged canyon, opening to grand vistas of the floor of Death Valley; bighorn sheep habitat.
Difficulty:	Moderately strenuous.
Best season:	November through April.
Starting elevation:	200 feet below sea level.
Maximum elevation:	1,080 feet (Sidewinder Canyon).
Elevation gain/loss:	1,280 feet/none (out-and-back route); 1,390 feet/ 1,390 feet (loop route).
USGS topo map:	Gold Valley-CA (1:24,000).
For more information:	Death Valley National Park (see Appendix D).

Key points:

For the loop hike—

0.0 Trailhead just east of the Badwater Road; hike southeast to the most prominent canyon entrance in the low ridge straight ahead (200 feet below sea level).

0.2 Mouth of canyon ("North Sidewinder").

0.9 Canyon junction; stay left (southeast) (280 feet).

1.3 Open canyon wash becomes strewn with rocks (560 feet).

1.6 Canyon splits; stay to the right up the main branch (770 feet).

1.8 Reach head of "North Sidewinder" canyon, topping out on a high rounded ridge (1,010 feet).

1.9 Drop into the main Sidewinder Canyon (900 feet); turn left up canyon.

2.2 8-foot dryfall in Sidewinder Canyon (turnaround point).

2.2 Begin return leg of out-and-back or loop down Sidewinder Canyon.

2.3 "Slots" through the narrow canyon wall (980 feet).

2.5 Wash widens then narrows (900 feet).

2.7 More "slots" in the canyon with slant rock to descend (780 feet).

3.3 Narrow side canyon enters from the left; continue down main wash to right (480 feet).

3.5 Gravelley wash widens to a large.circular amphitheater.

3.6 Large side canyon enters from the left.

4.2 Sidewinder Canyon opens to a broad wash/fan at sea level with the trailhead in view to the right.

4.5 Completion of hike at trailhead.

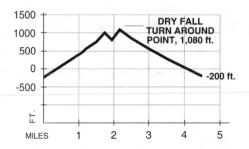

Finding the trailhead: From the Furnace Creek Visitor Center drive 1 mile south to the junction of California Highways 178 (Badwater Road) and 190; turn south on the Badwater Road and drive 33 miles to an unsigned dirt road that leads 0.2 mile left (southeast). This turn is easy to miss but it is just before the highway makes a half-circle to the west (toward the valley). Proceed on the dirt road for 0.2 mile to a T that contains a short stretch of pavement. Turn right on the T and drive to its end in less than 0.1 mile and park; this is the trailhead for both the Willow Canyon hike (Hike 80) and the Sidewinder Canyon hike/loop. The mouth of Sidewinder Canyon cannot be seen from the parking area but it is straight south about 0.3 mile up and across a rocky alluvial fan. To begin the suggested loop hike, head southeast into the most prominent canyon entrance to the right of the major notch in the main mountain front to the southeast.

The hike: Done as either a loop or out-and-back, this excursion into the lower end of rugged Sidewinder Canyon provides a solid introduction to the wild canyon country of the Black Mountains. The suggested loop route is no more strenuous than an out-and-back route up the main Sidewinder Canyon, but has the added advantage of a more diverse hiking experience.

Begin the loop by hiking 0.2 mile southeast to the above-described canyon entrance, which is an astounding 100 feet below sea level. The sides of this small canyon are made up of compacted conglomerate. At 0.9 mile and 280 feet the canyon splits; continue southeast up the left canyon. After another 0.2 mile the canyon narrows with low ridges on both sides. Soon the graveled bottom becomes a lot more rocky but the rocks can be easily negotiated.

At 1.6 miles and 770 feet the canyon again splits; stay right up the main branch. Here the canyon becomes increasingly shallow until its head is reached on a rounded ridge at 1.8 miles and an elevation of 1,010 feet. The larger Sidewinder Canyon sits below and to the right very close to where it exits the dramatically higher rhyolite walls along the face of the main uplift. Using great care in the loose rock, ease yourself down the slope to the wide, rocky 900-foot-high bottom of Sidewinder Canyon. Turn left (east) up the canyon, following it another 0.3 mile into the high, rugged mountains. At 2.2 miles (from the trailhead) an 8-foot dryfall is reached at an elevation of 1,080 feet. An experienced rock climber could climb the dry waterfall and

SIDEWINDER CANYON LOOP
• WILLOW CANYON

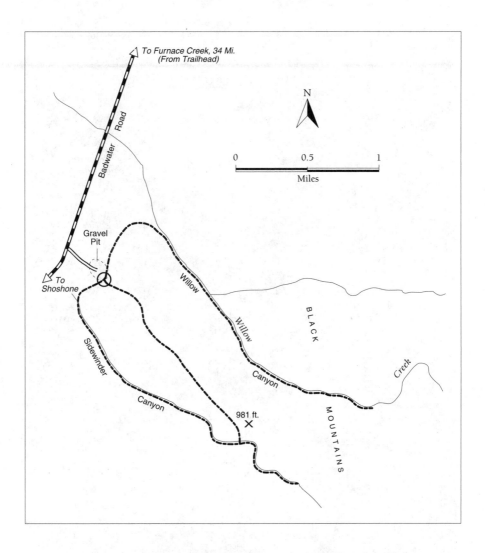

To Furnace Creek, 34 Mi.
(From Trailhead)

Badwater Road

N

0   0.5   1
Miles

Gravel Pit

To Shoshone

Willow

Willow

Canyon

Sidewinder

Canyon

981 ft.
X

B L A C K

M O U N T A I N S

Creek

continue up the canyon, but most people would have a difficult time pulling themselves over the exposed ledge. The base of this short waterfall is actually a good turnaround point for the 4.5-mile round-trip.

Just below the dry waterfall are a series of steep, slanted rocks that can be easily climbed and descended with moderate levels of skill and agility. This stretch of the canyon also contains impressive slots in the rock, with narrows intensifying the canyon experience. At 2.5 miles (on the return leg of the loop) the drop-in point is reached from the smaller canyon to the

The narrows of Sidewinder Canyon at 2.2 miles.

north. Continuing down Sidewinder, the wide wash soon funnels into a more narrow canyon. At 2.7 miles (780 feet) more "slots" appear in the rock with another slanted rock drop off. Here the conglomerate canyon walls are steep with deep overhangs and little alcoves along the narrow passageway.

At 3.3 miles (480 feet) a tight side canyon enters from the left that is worth a quick exploratory look. Continue right down the main wash. At 3.5 miles (380 feet) the graveled wash widens dramatically to a huge semi-circle presenting a grand view of Death Valley and the Panamints beyond. A narrow, dark, cavelike side canyon leads up to the left which can be explored for a short distance.

At 4.2 miles Sidewinder Canyon opens to a broad wash/alluvial fan exactly at sea level, but still high above the salt flats to the northwest. The trailhead can be seen to the right (north). Using line-of-sight, head northward across the rocky fan 0.3 mile to the trailhead, thereby completing this varied 4.5-mile canyon hike.

80 WILLOW CANYON

See Map on Page 259

General description:	A hike into a canyon with a seasonal waterfall.
Length:	5 miles round-trip.
General location:	About 100 miles northwest of Baker, southeastern section of Death Valley National Park, southeastern California.
Trail condition:	Good use trail in wash; clear canyon.
Special attractions:	Seasonal waterfalls, bighorn sheep habitat.
Difficulty:	Moderate.
Best season:	November through April.
Starting elevation:	-200 feet.
Maximum elevation:	1,400 feet.
Elevation gain/loss:	1,600 feet/none.
USGS topo map:	Gold Valley-CA (1:24,000).
For more information:	Death Valley National Park (see Appendix D).

Key points:
0.0-0.7   Use trail across alluvial fan to wash mouth.
0.7-2.1   Use-trail up wash to canyon mouth.
2.1-2.5   Canyon trail to dry/wet fall (depends upon season).

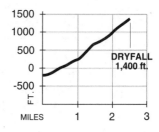

Finding the trailhead: From the California Highways 190 and 178 junction at the Furnace Creek Inn, go south on the Badwater Road (CA 178) for 30 miles to an unsigned dirt road on your left. Drive 0.2 mile to a T-shaped paved parking area adjacent to a gravel pit used during the construction of the East Road in Death Valley. The unmarked trail leaves from the northwest corner of the T lot. This parking area is also the trailhead for Sidewinder Canyon (Hike 79).

The hike: Although the ratio of hiking the alluvial fan to hiking in the canyon may seem lopsided, this hike features a gem of a canyon. Clearly a bighorn sheep playground, Willow Canyon cuts short your visit at a 70-foot wall with a spectacular ribbon waterfall in season. Prior to that obstacle, the canyon winds its narrow way like a street in a medieval city through sheer rhyolite walls, with a tinkling stream intermittently flowing down its center. Small falls, a shelf fall, and finally a long ribbon fall make the passage of the stream a delightful symphony of watery music.

The trip to this canyon follows a use trail that seeks the sandy sections of the fan and wash. Upon leaving the parking area, head northeast, staying below the eroding ash hillsides and their alluvial fans. The sloping forms of these latter features are the southern boundary of the Willow Canyon wash. Beyond their tilting faces, to the northeast, is a vertical wall of the same volcanic ash. This vertical wall is the northern boundary of Willow Canyon wash, and it is clearly seen as you wind your way up the fan following the sandy use trail, which takes you into the wash and on to the canyon itself.

Since you cannot see the canyon from the parking area— only the notch in the mountains beyond the volcanic ash hills suggests it—it is an exciting and abrupt change when the wash enters the canyon. Sheer rust-colored rhyolite walls tower above the gray gravel of the canyon floor. From the brightness of the open wash in the valley you are suddenly enshrouded in cool shadows. The warm wind of the valley becomes a cool breeze within the canyon walls. And, if the season is right, the sound of running water, cascading over the eroding canyon floor, breaks the silence.

Plentiful sheep sign confirms that this is bighorn sheep habitat, but it is unlikely that you will spot these elusive animals. If lucky enough to do so, please report sheep sightings to park personnel at the visitor center. The presence of water in Willow Canyon makes it a popular spot for the sheep.

Even in season, the stream in Willow Canyon is intermittent. At times it disappears underground, only to reappear again as another waterfall. Thus playing a hide-and-seek game, the stream brings visual and aural delight to the hiker. At 2.4 miles the stream drops over an extended shelf of rock in a 3-foot fall (easily climbed via a rock-step to the side). Immediately above the shelf, the stream vanishes again. The canyon narrows to less than 15 feet in width as the water-polished walls seem to close the canyon completely. Emerging from the narrows 0.1 mile later, you are confronted with the barricade that terminates the hike: a 70-foot sheer fall rising above you. The stream, when running, comes over this precipice in a silky ribbon. When dry, the fall is also striking for its marbleized water-smoothed surface.

Ribbon falls at end of Willow Canyon hike.

The return trip from the canyon involves retracing your steps. Leaving the canyon's watery world is done with reluctance; Willow Canyon resembles an oasis at the southern edge of Death Valley.

General description:	A short, easy hike offering magnificent panoramic views of the highest and lowest points in the continental United States, some of the most dramatic and colorful relief found anywhere.
Length:	1 mile round-trip.
General location:	About 115 miles north of Baker, in east-central Death Valley National Park, southeastern California.
Trail condition:	Clear trail; paved road access.
Special attractions:	Some of the best views to be found anywhere, with astounding vertical relief of nearly 6,000 feet directly above the lowest spot in the nation at Badwater.
Difficulty:	Easy.
Best season:	October through June.
Starting elevation:	5,475 feet.
Maximum elevation:	5,704 feet (Dante Point).
Elevation gain/loss:	229 feet/none.
USGS topo map:	Dantes View-CA (1:24,000).
For more information:	Death Valley National Park (see Appendix D).

Finding the trailhead: From California Highway 190, 11.9 miles southeast of the Furnace Creek Visitor Center and 18 miles west of Death Valley Junction, turn south on the signed Dante's View Road (paved, all-weather). Drive 13.2 miles on this steep, winding road to its end at the Dante's View parking area. The unsigned trail to Dante Point takes off to the north from the parking area and is clearly visible from the parking area as it climbs toward Dante Point.

The hike: If at all possible, take this hike in the early morning so that the sun is at your back for better photography and for enhanced enjoyment of the superlative vistas and astounding 5,755-foot drop to the salt flats of Badwater, which sit at 282 feet below sea level. The temperature at Dante's View averages 25 degrees cooler than that of Badwater. This exposed location is usually windy, necessitating a windbreak garment during the hike.

This lofty vantage point in the Black Mountains enables one to almost see, or at least visualize, how the mountains are both slowly moving to the left (south) and rising relative to the surrounding terrain. Looking across Death Valley to the highest point in the park, 11,049-foot Telescope Peak, it is easy to note the major vegetative life zones stretching westward like a giant map. Bristlecone and limber pines thrive high in the Panamint Range. Below is the pinyon-juniper zone. Dante's View is situated in a hotter, drier midslope of blackbush and sage. Floods from the mountains result in graveled fans with spreading root species such as creosote bush. Freshwater displaces salt from the edges of fans, allowing mesquite to grow. Pickleweed

DANTE'S VIEW

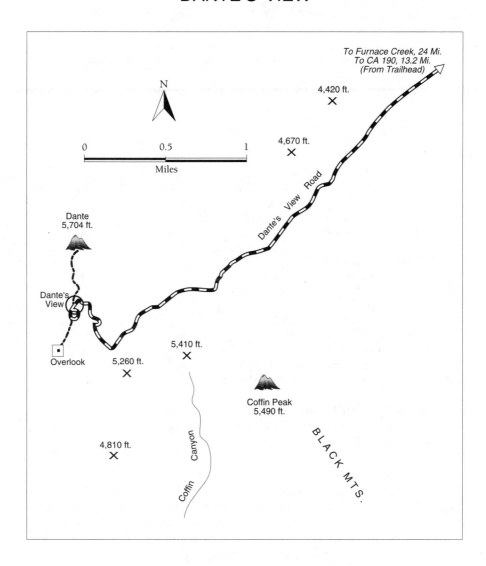

N

0   0.5   1
Miles

To Furnace Creek, 24 Mi.
To CA 190, 13.2 Mi.
(From Trailhead)

4,420 ft.
✕

4,670 ft.
✕

Dante's View Road

Dante
5,704 ft.

Dante's
View

Overlook   5,260 ft.
✕

5,410 ft.
✕

Coffin Peak
5,490 ft.

4,810 ft.
✕

Coffin Canyon

BLACK MTS.

gains a foothold in the brackish water below these edges. The muddy tans and grays of the valley floor grade into white beds of almost pure salt—a chemical desert.

From the parking lot hike north along the road for 0.1 mile to where the Dante Point trail begins a fairly steep climb up the hill. Soon it winds to the left (west) and contours gently along the west slope of the mountain. This contour route provides an even more impressive view down to Badwater, with an almost overwhelming sense of vertical relief—more than a mile straight down! At 0.3 mile the trail intersects the summit ridge then climbs the short distance to the 5,704-foot high point. Although unofficial, the trail is clear, well-defined, and easy to follow. Return the way you came to complete this 1-mile out-and-back ridge walk—and don't forget the film.

For a slightly different and well worthwhile perspective, hike a well-used path 0.25 mile southwest of the parking area. The rock outcropping at the point of the ridge is especially welcome as a windbreak for setting up a tripod for early morning photography.

82 BADWATER

General description:	A perfectly flat hike onto the salt flats at the lowest point in the United States.
Length:	1 to 1.5 miles round-trip.
General location:	About 85 miles northwest of Baker, southeastern Death Valley National Park, southeastern California.
Trail condition:	Clear salt flat.
Special attraction:	A vast bed of salt, 280 feet below sea level.
Difficulty:	Easy.
Best season:	Late October through March.
Starting elevation:	-280 feet.
Maximum elevation:	-280 feet.
Elevation gain/loss:	None.
USGS topo map:	Badwater-CA (1:24,000).
For more information:	Death Valley National Park (see Appendix D).

Finding the trailhead: On California Highway 178 (Badwater Road), 16.7 miles south of the California Highways 190/178 junction at the Furnace Creek Inn, the signed parking area for Badwater is on the west side of the road.

The hike: As bleak as it looks, a hike onto the salt flats at Badwater is arguably the ultimate Death Valley experience. If you have been to Dante's View or Telescope Peak, you probably saw the human "ants" on the white expanse of valley floor and wondered what could be so fascinating. Here you will find individuals, especially families, cavorting like they're at the beach or enjoying a spring snow. To gain a genuine sense of the enormity of the salt flats, hike beyond the heavily traveled section.

The hike begins at the parking area beneath the cliffs that soar up to Dante's View, 5,755 feet above. There's a "Sea Level" sign on the cliff face, high above Badwater, making very clear what minus 280 feet represent. Walk out to the salt flats on the causeway, but continue beyond the well-trod area, depending on the temperature and wind, to a clear area of the flats. Getting away from the highway is essential to get a sense of the magnitude of the salt flats.

BADWATER

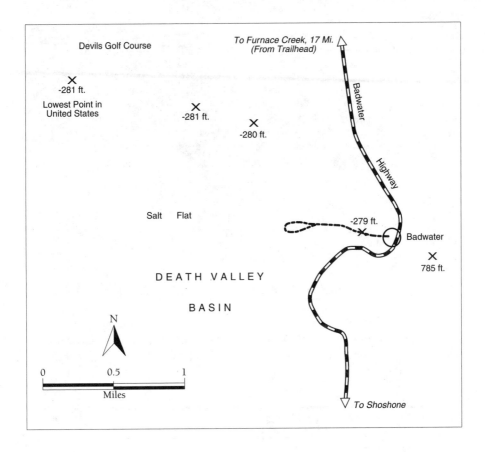

Devils Golf Course

To Furnace Creek, 17 Mi.
(From Trailhead)

✕
-281 ft.

Lowest Point in
United States

✕
-281 ft.

✕
-280 ft.

Badwater

Highway

Salt   Flat

-279 ft.
✕

Badwater

✕
785 ft.

DEATH VALLEY

BASIN

N

0   0.5   1

Miles

To Shoshone

Here fresh salt crystals are forming as groundwater percolates to the surface, bringing salt that crystallizes as the water hastily evaporates—chemistry in action. If you sit on the salt flats, you will find yourself among tiny salt pinnacles, a miniature mountainous world at the bottom of this mountainous basin. In close contact with the surface you will also discover that salt is a tough commodity. The white flooring of the flats is only inches thick, but very firm underfoot. Salt's power as an erosive force is noteworthy in this desert, where it functions much like frost heaves and ice do in a wet climate. Salt crystals grow and force apart boulders, breaking them down to be further eroded by wind and water.

Above the microworld of salt, the world of Death Valley soars. To the west is Telescope Peak (11,048 feet), the highest point in the park, less than 20 miles away. The difference in elevation between Badwater and Telescope Peak is one of the largest in the United States.

The view to the northeast on the salt flats of Badwater—282 feet below sea level.

A hike at Badwater is an essential introduction to the expanse of the valley floor. The emigrants and the miners who lived in this environment were a tough lot.

83 NATURAL BRIDGE

General description:	An easy, sloped, canyon hike to a natural bridge that arches over the trail and dryfall.
Length:	2 miles round-trip.
General location:	About 87 miles northwest of Baker, in east-central Death Valley National Park, southeastern California.
Trail condition:	Clear canyon.
Special attractions:	Geological phenomena: faults, slipfaulting, chutes and dryfalls, natural arch formation.
Difficulty:	Easy.
Best season:	October through April.
Starting elevation:	480 feet.
Maximum elevation:	1,000 feet.
Elevation gain/loss:	520 feet/none.
USGS topo map:	Devils Golf Course-CA (1:24,000).
For more information:	Death Valley National Park (see Appendix D).

NATURAL BRIDGE

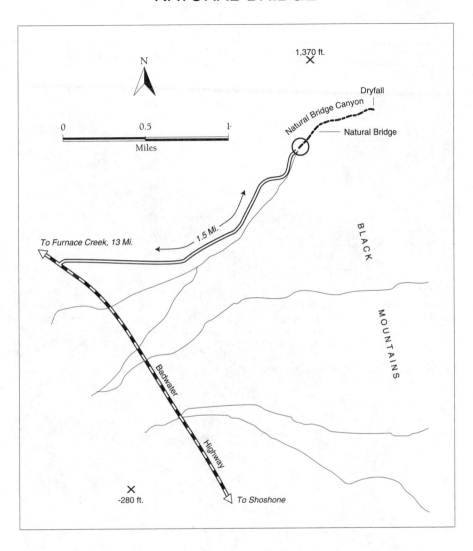

Key points:

- 0.0 Trail heads northwest from parking area.
- 0.4 Natural bridge over the trail.
- 0.8 Carefully climb smaller dryfall.
- 1.0 20-foot dryfall blocks the canyon.

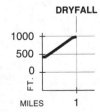

Finding the trailhead: From the intersection of California Highways 190 and 178 in Furnace Creek, drive south on the Badwater Road (CA 178) for 14.1 miles. Turn left (east) on the signed dirt road, and drive 1.5 miles to

The natural bridge.

the Natural Bridge parking area. The road is washboardy and rough, but is suitable for standard two-wheel-drive vehicles. The trail begins behind the information kiosk.

The hike: Death Valley's fascinating geologic history is featured on the kiosk at the trailhead of the Natural Bridge hike. Bedding and slipfaulting are explained on the board, so the canyon's display is even more impressive. Likewise, differential erosion is explained and illustrated, preparing you for the bridge. Fault caves, metamorphic layers of the Artist's Drive Formation, and mud drips are other topics covered in this condensed version of physical geology. The kiosk is worth a lengthy pause before embarking on the hike.

The canyon floor consists of loose gravel; that feature plus its sharp slope suggests this is a relatively young canyon. The Death Valley floor continues to subside while the Funeral Mountains rise. Geologic forces are still busy here.

The trail begins through deeply eroded volcanic ash and pumice canyon walls. The canyon gradually narrows. At 0.4 mile the bridge stretches over the canyon bottom. An ancient streambed is visible to the north of the bridge, where the floods swept around this more resistant section of strata before the pothole beneath it gave way to form the natural bridge.

Beyond the bridge mud drips, slip faults, and fault caves appear on your journey uphill, reinforcing the information you picked up at the kiosk. A dryfall at 0.8 mile can be climbed with moderate effort, but a 20-foot dryfall blocks travel at 1 mile.

Retracing your steps down the canyon reveals even more examples of geology in action. The shifting lighting creates iridescent colors. Traveling in the same direction as the powerful flash floods and their load of scouring debris emphasizes the impact of water in this arid environment.

General description:	A highly scenic but less crowded alternative to the nearby Golden Canyon hike with moderate canyoneering to a high pass overlooking the Artist's Drive Formation.
Length:	3 miles round-trip (head of Desolation Canyon); 3.2 miles round-trip to overlook.
General location:	About 125 miles northwest of Baker, in north-central Death Valley National Park, southeastern California.
Trail condition:	Clear wash with three short rock pitches.
Special attractions:	Deep, narrow, colorful canyon provides feeling of solitude, with broad vistas at the overlook.
Difficulty:	Moderate to the head of the canyon; moderately strenuous to the overlook.
Best season:	Early November to mid-April.
Starting elevation:	60 feet.
Maximum elevation:	620 feet (takeoff point to overlook); 740 feet to overlook.
Elevation gain/loss:	680 feet (to overlook)/none.
USGS topo map:	Furnace Creek-CA (1:24,000).
For more information:	Death Valley National Park (see Appendix D).

Key points:

0.0   Trailhead/parking area (60 feet).
0.1   Intersection with the Desolation Canyon wash; turn right up canyon.
0.3   Canyon splits; stay right (120 feet).
0.4   Canyon junction; stay right up the main wash (140 feet).
0.5   Canyon narrows.
0.6   Canyon steepens with moderate scrambling (240 feet).
0.7   Canyon widens to a junction; go right up the steeper, less colorful canyon with more stair-step rocks.
1.1   Canyon junction; stay right up a narrow gully (480 feet).
1.5   Canyon reaches a steep chute at 620 feet; end of the hike.
1.6   Scramble up a very steep, unstable slope (right) to the overlook (740 feet).

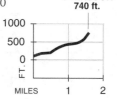

Finding the trailhead: From the park visitor center at Furnace Creek drive south 1 mile to the junction of California Highways 190 and 178 (location of the Furnace Creek Inn); turn right (south) onto CA 178 (Badwater Road) and drive 3.9 miles to the unsigned dirt road which takes off to the left (east) from the highway. Drive 1 mile to the end of this relatively smooth dirt road and find a place to park. Desolation Canyon is to the immediate left (northeast) of the road. Follow one of several well-worn paths that lead northeast over the low ridge to the broad lower end of Desolation Canyon.

DESOLATION CANYON

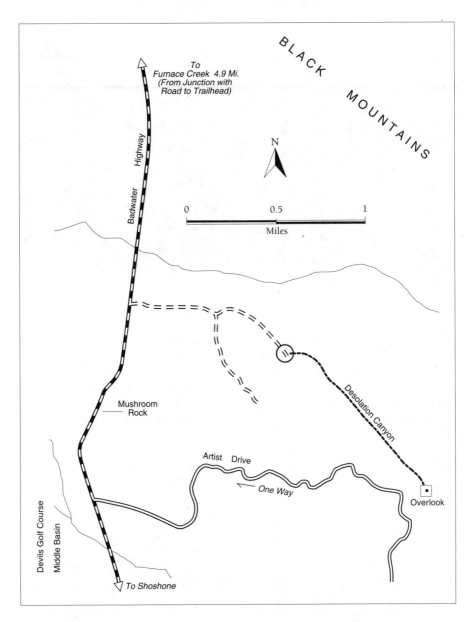

The hike: This is an enjoyable and highly scenic canyon hike for anyone, but it is especially appreciated by those without a four-wheel-drive vehicle in that access is just off the paved highway by way of a short, smooth dirt road. Despite its proximity to both the Badwater Road and Artist's Drive, the narrow canyon provides a deep feeling of intimacy and solitude. The entire out-and-back trip provides a superb opportunity to observe the

Hiking up the wash from the mouth of Desolation Canyon.

dynamics of badlands erosion which is everywhere, from mud-filled gullies to bizarre eroded shapes overlooking the canyon.

Because Desolation Canyon involves a short hike at low elevation, the recommended time of day for the hike is mid- to late afternoon when the cooler shadows fill the canyon. Upon return, late afternoon to early evening, brilliant light can be spectacular on the multicolored east-facing slopes above the canyon.

The main Desolation Canyon is just over the low ridge to the north from the end-of-the-road trailhead. Upon reaching the canyon in 0.1 mile, turn right and head up the wide wash that climbs gently to the first canyon junction at 0.3 mile, staying to the right. Continue right at the next junction at 0.4 mile. At 0.5 mile the canyon narrows with even narrower side draws. The next 0.1 mile brings a couple of stair-step rocks that are easy to climb, before the canyon again widens. At 1.1 miles (480 feet) what appears to be the main canyon to the left ends at a dry waterfall another 0.1 mile up. Continuing up the more narrow canyon to the right ends at a steep, unstable rock chute at 1.5 miles (620 feet). This is a good turnaround point.

If you've still got the urge and energy to explore, climb up to the right on loose, deep gravel to the 740-foot elevation overlook at 1.6 miles. This relatively lofty vantage point provides a spectacular view of the varied colors of the Artist's Drive Formation to the south. From this point the Artist's Drive road is only about 0.3 mile west. Return by way of Desolation Canyon to complete this colorful 3.2-mile round-trip badlands/canyon excursion.

General description:	A fascinating journey through geologic time, passing through rocks of different ages as the elevation increases then looping back down to the floor of Death Valley past borax mine tunnels.
Length:	6.5-mile loop (including two short side trips).
General location:	About 125 miles northwest of Baker, in north-central Death Valley National Park, southeastern California.
Trail condition:	Clear troad/trail/wash.
Special attractions:	Educational geology nature trail; colorful lakebed, exposed strata and alluvial fan formations; spectacular scenery.
Difficulty:	Moderate.
Best season:	November through April.
Starting elevation:	-160 feet.
Maximum elevation:	500 feet (overlook below Zabriskie Point).
Elevation gain/loss:	960 feet/960 feet (includes two short side trips).
USGS topo map:	Furnace Creek-CA (1:24,000).
For more information:	Death Valley National Park (see Appendix D).

Key points:

0.0 Golden Canyon nature trail trailhead at 160 feet below sea level.

1.0 End of nature trail at stop 10; 0.8-mile side trip to base of Red Cathedral.

1.8 Back to stop 10 and beginning of trail toward Manly Beacon.

2.3 High point of trail (440 feet) below Manly Beacon.

2.6 Trail/wash junction between Gower Gulch and Zabriskie Point.

3.6 Overlook below Zabriskie Point (500 feet).

3.8 Back to trail/wash junction; begin hike down Gower Gulch.

5.2 Gower Gulch reaches a 30-foot dryfall; take trail around to the right.

6.5 Complete loop back at the Golden Canyon trailhead.

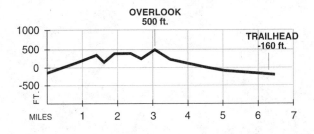

Finding the trailhead: From the north on California Highway 190, 1.2 miles south of the Furnace Creek Visitor Center, head south on the paved Badwater Road (California Highway 178). After 2 miles, turn left into the Golden Canyon parking area/trailhead on the east side of the road. From the south turn west on CA 178 2 miles north of the small town of Shoshone and continue into the park. From Ashford Junction continue north on the Badwater Rd. The signed Golden Canyon parking area is 14.4 miles north of Badwater and can be seen just off the highway to the right (east).

The hike: An excellent interpretive trail guide to this Golden Canyon nature trail is available for 50 cents at the Golden Canyon trailhead. Ten stops in this geology guide are keyed to numbered posts along the trail.

Golden Canyon was once accessed by paved road. Then in February, 1976, a four-day storm caused 2.3 inches of rain to fall on nearby Furnace Creek—one of the driest places on earth where no rain fell during all of 1929 and 1953. Runoff from the torrential cloudburst undermined and washed out the pavement so that today Golden Canyon is a wonderful place for hikers only. This pattern of drought and torrents follows countless periods of flash floods, shattering rockslides, and a wetter era when the alluvial fan was preceded by an ancient shallow sea—a land in constant flux.

At stop 2 it is easy to see how the canyon was carved out of an old alluvial fan made up of volcanic rock that pre-dates the origin of Death Valley some 3 million years ago. Layers in the rock tell the tale of periodic floods over the eons. Just above, the canyon displays tilted bands of rock caused by faulting where huge blocks of the earth's crust slid past one another. As you proceed up the canyon you are literally passing through geologic time. The Furnace Creek formation is the combination over time of sediments from a lakebed that dates back around 9 million years. Ripple marks of water lapping

A walk through geologic time in Golden Canyon is dramatized by the sheer amber face of the Red Cathedral in the background.

GOLDEN CANYON/GOWER GULCH LOOP

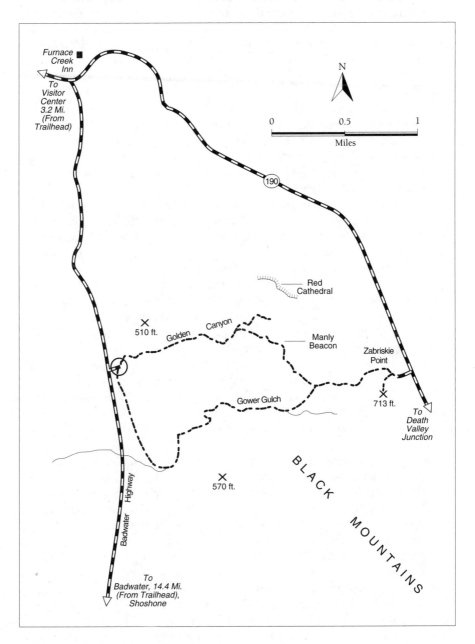

over the sandy lakebed hardened into stone as the climate warmed, and are evident on the tilted rock. Weathering and the effects of thermal water produced the splash of vivid colors seen today.

Mountain building to the west gradually produced a more arid climate causing the lake to dry up. At the same time the land tilted due to the widening and sinking of Death Valley and the uplift of the Black Mountains. Dark lava from eruptions of 3 to 5 million years ago slowed down erosion, explaining why Manly Beacon juts so far above the surrounding badlands. These stark badlands rising above the canyon at mile 0.5 are the result of rapid runoff from storms on erodable, almost impermeable rocks.

Several narrow side canyons invite short explorations on the way up Golden Canyon, particularly opposite stop 2, and to the left and just above stops 6 and 7.

The nature trail ends at stop 10, about 1 mile up the canyon at an elevation of 140 feet. For a 0.8-mile round-trip to the base of the Red Cathedral continue straight ahead up the broken pavement, past the old parking area, to a narrow notch at 320 feet, directly below the looming presence of the cathedral from where the highest point in the park—Telescope Peak—can be seen in the far distance.

Red Cathedral was once part of an active alluvial fan, outwashed from the Black Mountains to the south. The bright red results from the weathering of iron to produce the rust of iron oxide. The cliff faces are made up of the more resistant red rock crowning softer yellow lake deposits.

Upon returning to stop 10 (mile 1.8) follow the signed trail to the left (coming down) up a steep gully well marked with trailposts. The trail climbs across badlands beneath the imposing sandstone jaw of Manly Beacon. At 2.3 miles a high ridge saddle is reached below Manly Beacon at 440 feet. Follow the markers down a side gully to a wash/trail junction at 2.6 miles. The left-hand wash leads eastward up to Zabriskie Point. The right-hand wash/trail descends west to Gower Gulch. If you walk up the main wash, you will quickly come to the artificial cut made in the rock wall to divert Furnace Creek through Gower Gulch. This has resulted in a speeding up erosion in the gulch. Note the gray color of the rocks or bottom of the drainage washed in from Furnace Creek, contrasting with the red and yellow badlands.

Gower Gulch is largely the result of human construction to protect Furnace Creek from serious flooding. For a short side trip toward Zabriskie Point, turn left at the junction and follow the markers for about 0.5 mile from where you can select an excellent overlook of Zabriskie Point, the surrounding badlands, Death Valley, and the distant Panamint Range. Zabriskie Point is another 0.7 mile and 200 feet above and is accessible by road from the other side. It does indeed provide one of the most magnificent views in all of Death Valley but its proximity to a paved road may detract from the hiking experience on the Golden-Gower loop. Thus, the overlook below Zabriskie Point is recommended as the turnaround point for a scenic side trip. Zabriskie Point is a popular starting point for those hiking 3 miles downhill through Gower Gulch then across to the mouth of Golden Canyon.

Back at the trail junction (mile 3.6) there is no marker post leading the way toward Gower Gulch. Simply continue down the wash toward wide, gray Gower Gulch, which drops below mounds of golden badlands. At

3.9 miles a side wash intersects the main wash; continue downward to the right. Early day miners in search of borax have pocketed the walls of Gower Gulch with tunnels. These small openings are unsecured and potentially dangerous. A mile down, the wide gravel wash bends sharply to the left, narrowing dramatically with the bedding and faulting of red and green rock. The canyon floor then quickly drops 40 feet to below sea level.

At 5.2 miles the wash meets a 30-foot dryfall. A good use trail curves around the rock face to the right. From here the faint but easy to follow trail heads north 1.3 miles along the base of the mountains paralleling the highway back to the Golden Canyon parking area, thereby completing the basic 4.7-mile loop with an additional 1.8 miles of side trips.

86 HARMONY BORAX WORKS

General description:	A short hike on loop trail to a historical site on the valley floor.
Length:	1 mile round-trip, with 0.5-mile side trip to low overlook, and/or 5-mile round-trip (more or less) on to salt flats.
General location:	About 105 miles southeast of Lone Pine, in central Death Valley National Park, southeastern California.
Trail condition:	Asphalt walkway to Harmony Borax Works (wheelchair accessible); clear use-trail to overlook and to salt flats.
Special attractions:	Nineteenth-century industrial site; salt flats.
Difficulty:	Easy.
Best season:	October through March.
Starting elevation:	-40 feet.
Maximum elevation:	-20 feet (basic loop); sea level (overlook); -20 (salt flats).
Elevation gain/loss:	20 feet/none (loop and salt flats); 40 feet/none (overlook).
USGS topo maps:	West of Furnace Creek-CA and Furnace Creek-CA (1:24,000).
For more information:	Death Valley National Park (see Appendix D).

Key points:

0.0   Asphalt loop trail west of parking area.
0.2   Use trail leads south from asphalt path to hilltop (0.5 round-trip).
0.5   End of loop; use trail extends out into salt flats.

Finding the trailhead: The trailhead for the Harmony Borax Works Trail is 1.3 miles north of the park visitor center at Furnace Creek via California Highway 190. The 0.2-mile road on the left is signed. The asphalt walkway leads west of the parking area. For the 5-mile round-trip to the salt flats, the trailhead is located at the far side of Harmony Borax Works, heading west from the loop trail.

Harmony Borax Works, from overlook trail above the borax processing plant.

The hike: This desolate site was the scene of frenzied activity from 1883 to 1888, not in the pursuit of gold, like so much of the other mining activity, but of borax. Used in ceramics and glass as well as soap and detergent, borax was readily available here in Death Valley. Borax prices were highly mercurial due to soaring supply and moderate demand in the nineteenth century, so the industry was plagued by sharp boom and bust cycles. Here at the Harmony Works, the years of prosperity were typically brief.

Chinese laborers hauled the borate sludge in from the flats on sledges to the processing plant, remains of which are the focal point of this hike. There the borate was boiled down and hauled 165 miles across the desert to Mojave by the famed twenty-mule teams. One of the wagons that made this journey stands below the borax plant. Although the works were in operation only from October to June, working conditions for man and beast were harsh.

A side hike to the hilltop overlook gives you an excellent vista of the central valley floor. From here it is easy to imagine the usual workday in operation here at the Harmony Works. To the east of the hilltop is an area that appears to have been a dump for Furnace Creek. A rusty antique car rests on the hillside, surrounded by desert.

An optional hike to the salt flats likewise confirms the arduous conditions of life and work on the valley floor. An unsigned but well-trod path leads west from the end of the paved loop. It travels by a damp slough where groundwater is percolating to the surface, causing borate crystals to form. Farther out on the flats, mounds of borax mud remain where the

HARMONY BORAX WORKS

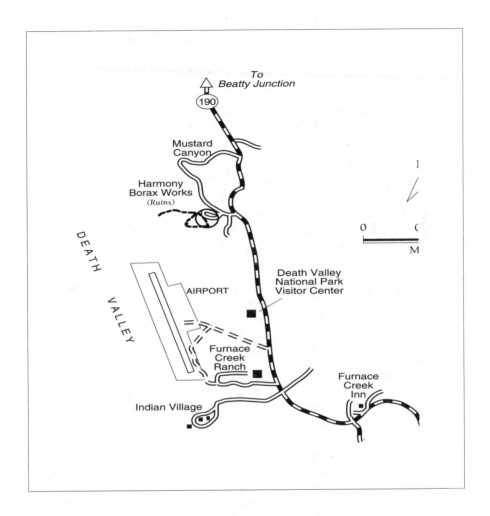

laborers made piles to validate the works' mining claim more than a hundred years ago.

Although this is a short hike, be sure to bring water. It's a dehydrating experience.

General description:	A round-trip hike up an alluvial fan and wash to striking canyon, ending at a dryfall.
Length:	2.8-mile loop.
General location:	About 135 miles northwest of Baker, southeastern area of Death Valley National Park, southeastern California.
Trail condition:	Good wash and alluvial fan; clear canyon.
Special attractions:	The pitted surface of volcanic ash cliffs; dryfall; bighorn sheep habitat.
Difficulty:	Easy.
Best season:	October through March.
Starting elevation:	2,000 feet.
Maximum elevation:	2,540 feet.
Elevation gain/loss:	540 feet/none.
USGS topo maps:	Furnace Creek-CA and Echo Canyon-CA (1:24,000).
For more information:	Death Valley National Park (see Appendix D).

Key points:

0.0 Head north from notch where road turns east, up wash and alluvial fan. The canyon mouth will become visible to the northwest on the mountain face as you approach it.

1.0 Canyon mouth.

1.3 Canyon narrows; dryfall blocks canyon.

1.6 Exit from the canyon; hike east along mountainside to the next canyon, blocked by boulders.

1.8 Hike south on fan/wash back to Hole-in-the-Wall notch.

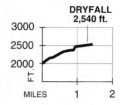

Finding the trailhead: From the junction of California Highways 190 and 178 in Furnace Creek, go southeast on CA 190 for 5.4 miles to the Hole-in-the-Wall dirt road on the left. The road is in the wash; a sign recommending four-wheel-drive vehicles stands 40 feet west of the road itself, on the bank of the wash. The first 4 miles of the road is rough and rocky, but is passable by passenger vehicle with careful driving. Drive 4 miles to the Hole-in-the-Wall narrows and park there. The hike goes directly north from the narrows. Four-wheel drive is needed beyond Hole-in-the-Wall.

The hike: Located less than 10 miles from busy Furnace Creek, this excursion to a lower canyon entrance provides desert panoramas, solitude, majestic rock formations, and varied terrain. A short side trip to the neighboring canyon demonstrates the powers of nature here in the Funeral Mountains.

The hike begins at the Hole-in-the-Wall cliffs of differentially eroded volcanic ash. The multitude of holes form enchanting shapes; some are

The Hole-in-the-Wall forms a perfect V-notch below the North Canyon.

HOLE-IN-THE-WALL NORTH

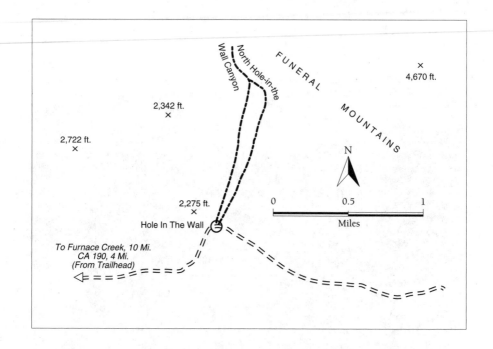

precise, while others droop. To the north, beyond the alluvial fan, lie the Funeral Mountains. Travel north-northwest using the varnished desert pavement where possible since the wash winds a bit and is loaded with boulders that make hiking difficult. You gain 420 feet in elevation by the time you reach the canyon mouth.

Here more towering limestone cliffs display the eyes and mouths of erosion holes. The canyon floor is a wide graveled wash. The canyon narrows and turns at 0.3 mile, only to be blocked by a 40-foot dryfall. The tempting side hill to the west is too unstable and dangerous for climbing, so this is the terminal point of the canyon hike. Instead, enjoy the vistas of the valley on your return trip.

At the canyon mouth, hike east 0.2 mile to the next canyon. This one is totally blocked by massive boulders, cutting all travel to its secret hinterland. The return descent to Hole-in-the-Wall features magnificent views of the Artist's Drive Formation at the northern end of the Black Mountains, with Death Valley stretching out beyond. Telescope Peak stands at 11,048 feet, on the far horizon. This is a spectacular array of Death Valley scenery.

General description:	A steep out-and-back hike on an old mining troad in the Funeral Mountains to the historic ruins of mines, a mill, and tramways.
Length:	4 miles round-trip.
General location:	100 miles east of Lone Pine, north-central Death Valley National Park, southeastern California.
Trail condition:	Clear, rocky troad.
Special attractions:	Historic ruins of a mill and an extensive mine tramway, scenic views down a rugged canyon to Death Valley.
Difficulty:	Moderately strenuous.
Best season:	October through April.
Starting elevation:	1,320 feet.
Maximum elevation:	2,880 feet (lower end of the Keane Wonder Mine).
Elevation gain/loss:	1,560 feet/none.
USGS topo map:	Chloride City-CA (1:24,000).
For more information:	Death Valley National Park (see Appendix D).

Key points:
0.0   Trailhead/parking area.
0.1   Kiosk below the Keane Wonder Mill ruins.
1.7   Aerial tramway terminal.
2.0   Stone building foundations and mine shafts below the main mine openings.

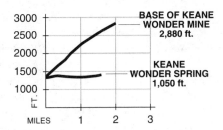

Finding the trailhead: From Nevada Highway 374 at Hell's Gate Junction head south on the Beatty Cutoff Road going toward Beatty Junction. After 4.3 miles turn left on the signed Keane Wonder Mine Road, a good gravel route, and drive 2.8 miles eastward to the end-of-the-road parking area below the Keane Wonder Mill.

From the visitor center at Furnace Creek drive north on California Highway 190 for 11.3 miles to the Beatty Cutoff Road, and continue right (north) on the Beatty-Daylight Pass Cutoff Road for another 6 miles to the Keane Wonder Mine Road. Turn right and drive the final 2.8 miles to the end-of-the-road parking area/trailhead.

The Keane Wonder Mine aerial tramway terminal overlooks a steep rugged canyon.

The hike: The Keane Wonder Mine was developed at a time and in a location of hundreds of gold, silver, and lead strikes. The relative success of this venture makes its history and today's ruins all the more intriguing. It all began in 1903 with an almost-unheard-of lucky strike by an unemployed Irish miner named Jack Keane and his partner. After months of futile searching for silver Keane accidentally stumbled across a huge ledge of gold, calling the find the "Keane Wonder Mine" out of his total astonishment at being so fortunate.

The news spread rapidly, and by 1904 the local gold rush was on. The mine changed hands several times, making a fortune for its original partners, and was capitalized with stocks sold to an eager public. In 1906 Homer Wilson bought the mine and started a consortium that operated the mine for a decade. Wilson ordered a twenty-stamp mill to crush the ore and a gravity-operated aerial tramway nearly 1-mile long. Loaded ore buckets coming down the canyon from the shaft pulled the empty buckets back up. The tram contained thirteen towers, with the longest span being 1,200 feet, and a vertical drop from top to bottom of 1,500 feet. Lack of water prevented the mill from operating at full capacity. Even so, total gold production from the mine was around $1,100,000, most of which was extracted between 1907 and 1911.

The Keane Wonder Mine was one of the two largest producing gold mines in the Death Valley region, the other being the Skidoo Mine. The artifacts and remnants of this mine have significant historical value and should not be removed or disturbed in any way.

KEANE WONDER MINE
• KEANE WONDER SPRING

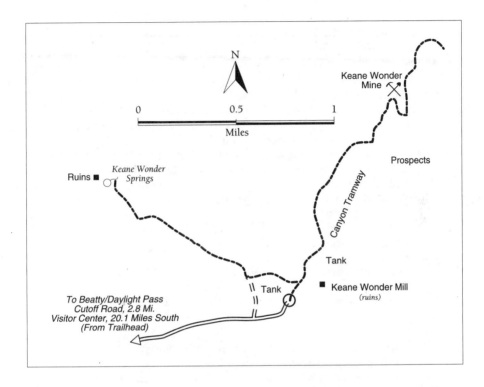

From the parking area climb 0.1 mile to the informative kiosk located just below the Keane Wonder Mill ruins. The sign contains a bit of the history of Jack Keane's amazing 1903 gold strike. From the trailhead extensive mining debris can be seen in the wash to the left. At 0.4 mile (1,700 feet) the troad crosses under the tramway and begins a very steep climb straight up the ridge. In just 0.7 mile another 650 feet elevation is gained, at which point the troad contours and climbs more moderately to the right above the tramway canyon leading to the mine. At 1.7 miles (2,720 feet) the troad reaches the large aerial tramway terminal structure along with several shallow mine shafts.

From here a level trail extends another 0.5 mile around the canyon to an upper mine area containing additional adits. The view down canyon makes this short extension of the hike more than worthwhile. Another narrow trail climbs steeply 0.2 mile to the base of the main mine, which peers from the steep mountainside at around 3,000 feet elevation. Several stone building foundations are passed along the way. Around the bend and at the base of the mine, the area beyond is closed to hiking for public safety. Unsecured mine shafts present hazards and should definitely be avoided. Enjoy them from a safe distance before retracing your route to the trailhead, as you complete this round-trip hiking climb to one of Death Valley's largest and most interesting early twentieth-century mining ventures.

89   KEANE WONDER SPRING

General description:	A nearly level trip to the spring that was essential to the Keane Wonder Mine and mill operations.
Length:	2 miles round-trip.
General location:	100 miles east of Lone Pine, north-central Death Valley, southeastern California.
Trail condition:	Clear trail; clear troad.
Special attractions:	Sulfurous spring, mine sites.
Difficulty:	Easy.
Best season:	Late October through March.
Starting elevation:	1,280 feet.
Maximum elevation:	1,320 feet.
Elevation gain/loss:	40 feet/none.
USGS topo map:	Chloride City-CA (1:24,000).
For more information:	Death Valley National Park (see Appendix D).

See Map on Page 287

Key points:
  0.0   Trail heads north above the pair of settling tanks.
  0.3   Trail crosses wash and continues following contour of hillside.
  0.6   Trail merges with troad from lower hillside; continue on troad to spring/mine site.
  0.8   First spring crosses troad. Aqueduct ditch parallels troad.
  1.0   Mine chute and cabin and another sulphur seep.

Finding the trailhead: From Nevada Highway 374, 19.3 miles southwest of Beatty, Nevada, turn left (south) on the Daylight Pass Cutoff and drive 4.3 miles to signed dirt road on your left. Take the gravel road 2.8 miles to Keane Wonder Mine parking area.

From Furnace Creek, go north on California Highway 190 11.3 miles north of the visitor center. Turn right (east) on Daylight Pass Cutoff, and drive 5.7 miles to the Keane Wonder gravel road on your right. Drive 2.8 miles to Keane Wonder Mine parking area. The trail to the spring begins at the northeastern corner of the parking area and heads north.

The hike: The Keane Wonder Mine complex was at its height in the gold boom from 1906 to 1912. It was resuscitated by optimistic prospectors and investors several times. The most recent renaissance was in 1935-1937 when cyanide leaching of the mine tailings took place on the site. The tanks used for that operation stand below the parking area.

Saltgrass marsh at Keane Wonder Spring.

Where the mine trail goes directly up the hillside, the use trail to Keane Wonder Spring goes left. The trail begins after you drop into the debris-strewn wash just north of the parking area. Emerging from the wash above the pair of settling tanks nestled together, you pick up the well-traveled trail. A broken pipeline lies 50 yards below on the hillside; it will lead you to the springs.

The trail travels by numerous mine openings and scenic travertine rock outcroppings. At 0.6 mile the trail merges with the troad coming up from lower on the hillside; you'll return to the parking area via the troad on the hike back. More mine openings and a stone foundation are nearby. The troad is meticulously bordered with rocks for most of the way.

Continuing northward, soon your nose will detect the scent of sulfur, even on a windy day. There, at 0.8 mile, the trickling stream from the spring crosses the road. Above the troad take a side trip to the spring. The salt grass marsh flourishes in the salt-encrusted soil 30 yards above the troad. A sign posted by the National Park Service warns of gas hazards in the mine shaft immediately above the spring. The area has many mine shafts, some flooded, all dangerous.

This mining wasteland is also full of wildlife. Heavy bighorn sheep use is evident from the droppings on the damp spring banks. Birds and crickets create a symphony of sound in the desert stillness.

Continuing northward, the troad follows a crude aqueduct and curves around, now totally out of sight of the parking area and industrial sprawl there. More of the ubiquitous mine sites and another sulfurous spring bracket the troad. At your destination, 1 mile, you'll find a mine chute and a miner's cabin. Rusty cans, pieces of pipe, and the usual pieces of nondescript rusty artifacts litter the ground. In the dry desert air, the cabin is so well-preserved it appears the miner left recently. Across the shallow gully to the west is a large rock outcropping atop a hill. Notice the stone walls built under the natural overhang. Did wind, or heat, or both drive the miner to take refuge in such a primitive rock shelter?

Return the way you came, continuing on the wide rock-lined troad at the junction you passed on the way in. In sight of the parking area, the troad dissipates in the mine debris in the gully near the largest of the remaining tanks. From there you have to pick your way back to your vehicle.

The amazing thing about the Keane Wonder Spring hike is its plethora of mine sites. The Keane Wonder Mine was heralded to be the richest gold strike in Death Valley, attracting a multitude of hopeful miners. At its height nearly five hundred prospectors were working in the area. Thus, everywhere you look, there's another mine mouth with its tailings dripping down the hillside. Mine tunnels like rabbit holes cut through the ridges and disappear into mountainside. Curious children and adults should avoid all mines.

90 *MONARCH CANYON/MINE*

General description:	An out-and-back hike down a rocky canyon in the Funeral Mountains to an 80-foot dryfall, well-preserved stamp mill, and desert spring.
Length:	3 miles round-trip (from Chloride City Road); 1.8 miles round-trip (from end of Monarch Mine Road).
General location:	About 95 miles east of Lone Pine, north-central Death Valley National Park, southeastern California.
Trail condition:	Four-wheel-drive road; mining troad; clear wash.
Special attractions:	Large, scenic dry waterfalls, birds, stamp mill.
Difficulty:	Easy.
Best season:	October through April.
Starting elevation:	3,520 feet (Chloride City Road) or 3,340 feet (end of four-wheel-drive road above dryfall).
Maximum elevation:	3,520 feet.
Elevation gain/loss:	None/570 feet (from Chloride City Road); 0/390 feet (from end of Monarch Mine Road).
USGS topo map:	Chloride City-CA (1:24,000).
For more information:	Death Valley National Park (see Appendix D).

Key points:
- 0.0 Trailhead at junction of Chloride City Road and Monarch Mine Road in upper Monarch Canyon.
- 0.6 End of Monarch Mine Road; 80-foot dryfall.
- 0.7 Mining troad drops to bottom of canyon wash.
- 0.8 Walk up the wash to the base of the dry falls.
- 1.2 Monarch Mine stamp mill ruins.
- 1.5 Monarch Spring.

MONARCH CANYON/MINE
• KEANE SPRING

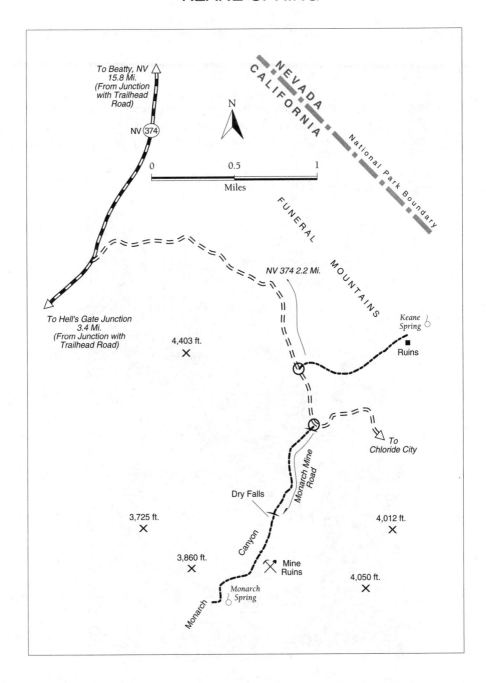

To Beatty, NV
15.8 Mi.
(From Junction
with Trailhead
Road)

NV (374)

N

NEVADA
CALIFORNIA

National Park Boundary

0   0.5   1
Miles

FUNERAL

MOUNTAINS

NV 374 2.2 Mi.

To Hell's Gate Junction
3.4 Mi.
(From Junction with
Trailhead Road)

4,403 ft.
✕

Keane
Spring

■
Ruins

To
Chloride City

Monarch Mine Road

Dry Falls

3,725 ft.
✕

Canyon

4,012 ft.
✕

3,860 ft.
✕

⚒ Mine
Ruins

4,050 ft.
✕

Monarch

Monarch
Spring

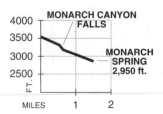

```
4000 ┬─ MONARCH CANYON
      │   FALLS
3500 ┼
3000 ┼       MONARCH
      │       SPRING
2500 ┼       2,950 ft.
   FT.│
      └──────────────
   MILES    1    2
```

Finding the trailhead: From Nevada Highway 374 (Daylight Pass Road) 3.4 miles east of Hell's Gate Junction in Boundary Canyon and 15.8 miles southwest of Beatty, Nevada, look for a road to the south that is marked only with a small sign recommending four-wheel drive. Carefully driven high clearance two-wheel-drive vehicles can negotiate this road for 2.2 miles

The base of the Monarch Mine stamp mill.

to the bottom of upper Monarch Canyon. High clearance four-wheel drive is required for vehicular travel beyond this point to Chloride City. The rough Monarch Mine Road takes off south from this point. This road junction can serve as the trailhead for the hike down Monarch Canyon. However, the hike can be shortened by 1.2 miles round-trip by driving down the Monarch Mine Road to a point just above the dryfall.

The hike: Hikers can start at the unsigned junction between the rough Chloride City Road and four-wheel-drive Monarch Mine Road (3 miles round-trip to Monarch Spring) or at the end of the Monarch Mine Road (1.8 miles round-trip). From the Chloride City Road junction the trip starts out in rounded, low-lying hills. The four-wheel-drive road descends southwesterly, entering a rocky canyon after 0.3 mile.

At 0.6 mile the road ends above a striking 80-foot dryfall. A major side canyon enters from the left, bounded by high cliffs marked by folded multicolored bands of rock. Continue left around the falls on the old mining troad. After another 0.1 mile the troad drops to the wash, which is covered with horsetails and Mormon tea. This is favored habitat for quail and other birds. The base of the dry falls is definitely worth visiting, so turn right and walk 0.1 mile up to the precipice. In addition to the main wide falls another smaller but equally high falls guards the canyon bowl to the left. The canyon walls are distinguished by shelf rock catch basins, overhangs, and contorted layers of colorful, twisted rock.

Proceeding back down the sandy canyon wash, an eroded-out mining troad crosses to the right and then drops back to the canyon floor at 1 mile. Rock cairns are in place for the return trip. At 1.2 miles the wood and cement ruins of the Monarch Mine stamp mill are reached on the left. The ore chute to the mill extends up an almost vertical rock face.

To further experience the rugged grandeur of Monarch Canyon continue down the wash another 0.3 mile to the brushy bottom just below Monarch Spring. Here the canyon bends sharply to the right and begins to narrow. Hiking below the spring would be difficult due to dense vegetation and loose, rocky sideslopes. Retrace your route.

General description:	A short out-and-back hike to a spring in the Funeral

See Map on Page 291

Mountains, a region with a colorful mining history.

Length:	1 mile round-trip.
General location:	100 miles east of Lone Pine, north-central Death Valley National Park, southeastern California.
Trail condition:	Clear troad.
Special attractions:	Ghost town site and spring.
Difficulty:	Easy.
Best season:	October through April.
Starting elevation:	3,470 feet.
Maximum elevation:	3,670 feet.
Elevation gain/loss:	200 feet/none.
USGS topo map:	Chloride City-CA (1:24,000).
For more information:	Death Valley National Park (see Appendix D).

Key points:

0.0   Trailhead on north side of the road. Bear right up to the low ridge at 20 yards.

0.3   Troad continues on rise above wash; continue northeast as other troad merges. Willows and cottonwoods in spring valley ahead.

0.4   Troad drops to wash and vanishes in eroded gullies; look for remnants of townsite.

0.5   Continue up wash/troad to spring.

Finding the trailhead: From Nevada Highway 374 (Daylight Pass Road) 3.4 miles east of Hell's Gate Junction in Boundary Canyon and 15.8 miles southwest of Beatty, Nevada, look for a road on the south side that is marked only with a small sign recommending four wheel drive. Turn south and drive 2 miles to a barricaded road taking off to the left to the Keane ghost town and spring. This troad serves as the trail.

The hike: The Keane Spring townsite attests to the value of desert water. Its short-lived existence (1906-1909) was based entirely on the availability of water here. When the Funeral Mountains were humming with mining activity during the rhyolite gold boom, Keane Spring promoters counted on providing the water necessary for both miners and ore processing. Ironically, the town was wiped out in a 1909 flash flood.

Why was the town nestled in the wash below the spring? In these rolling foothills of the Funeral Mountains, the open country features panoramic views of Death Valley and Tucki Mountain but also guarantees intense wind. The wash presumably offered protection from the latter. Apparently the dangers of flooding in the wash were ignored by the town's opportunistic promoters.

All that remains of the town of Keane Spring, nestled in the wash below the spring.

The only remains of the town are a few stone foundations left in tangled catclaw. Pieces of the old pipeline run from the spring to the southeast, in the direction of Chloride City, the primary water customer. Chloride City's brief period of prosperity was in 1906, until the San Francisco earthquake wiped out (economically) its investors. Keane Spring was thus declining long before the flood arrived.

The spring's output has diminished since the beginning of this century. Now there is no view or even gurgle of water from the dense thicket of rushes and willows that jam the narrow spring valley immediately above the town site. The presence of birds and vegetation demonstrate that enough moisture exists for them to flourish here. The coyote population is thriving also, judging from the droppings on the trail.

Keane Spring never was a very large town. With fewer than a dozen buildings and even fewer business establishments, its economic base was precariously thin. Nature has nearly erased its traces.

General description:	An out-and-back hike up a scenic stream canyon to the historic ruins of an 1870s ranch deep in the Panamint Mountains.
Length:	3.6 miles round-trip from Wilson Spring.
General location:	About 150 miles southeast of Lone Pine, in southwestern Death Valley National Park, southeastern California.
Trail condition:	Primitive use trail.
Special attractions:	Gushing springs, nearly a mile of live stream, deep canyon walls, and the historic ruins of an 1870s-vintage ranch.
Difficulty:	Moderately strenuous.
Best season:	October through May.
Starting elevation:	3,960 feet.
Maximum elevation:	4,850 feet (Hungry Bill's upper ranch).
Elevation gain/loss:	1,040 feet/150 feet.
USGS topo map:	Panamint-CA (1:24,000).
For more information:	Death Valley National Park (see Appendix D).

Key points:

0.0   Trailhead at Wilson Spring.
0.2   Use trail fades; cross canyon to right side.
0.5   Canyon narrows; cross and climb around rock spires to left.
1.5   Hungry Bill's lower ranch.
1.8   Hungry Bill's Ranch.

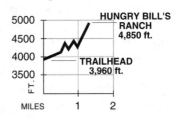

Finding the trailhead: From California Highway 190 at the Furnace Creek Inn, drive south on the Badwater Road for 7.1 miles; turn to the southwest on the washboard/gravel West Side Road (closed during summer) and continue south for another 21.7 miles to the Johnson Canyon Road; turn right (west) and drive 9.8 miles to the end of the road at Wilson Spring. The final 3.5 miles before the spring require a high-clearance four-wheel-drive vehicle. Those with standard two-wheel-drive vehicles should park at or near the burro pen before the rough road drops steeply into the canyon. This will add about 7 miles round-trip distance to the hike. The primitive use trail begins at Wilson Spring, following the stream drainage 1.8 miles to the upper ranch site.

The hike: The original Hungry Bill's Ranch in upper Johnson Canyon was first developed in the 1870s by Swiss farmers who sought to grow fruits

HUNGRY BILL'S RANCH/JOHNSON CANYON

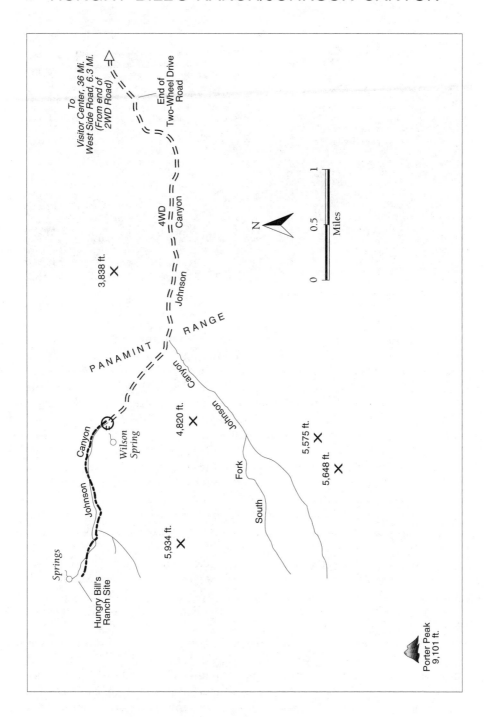

To
Visitor Center, 36 Mi.
West Side Road, 6.3 Mi.
(From end of
2WD Road)

End of
Two-Wheel Drive
Road

4WD

Johnson

Canyon

3,838 ft.
X

N

0   0.5   1
Miles

PANAMINT   RANGE

Johnson

Canyon

4,820 ft.
X

Wilson
Spring

5,575 ft.
X

5,648 ft.
X

Fork

South

Johnson

Canyon

5,934 ft.
X

Springs

Hungry Bill's
Ranch Site

Porter Peak
9,101 ft.

Johnson Canyon above Wilson Spring.

and vegetables for sale to the residents of Panamint City, over rugged Panamint Pass in Surprise Canyon. The mining camp had its brief heyday from 1874 to 1877. By the time the Swiss farmers were ready to sell their produce, bust had followed boom and the market had vanished! Later the ranch was occupied for many years by a Shoshone Indian named Hungry Bill, whose huge appetite matched his great girth. Today, all that remains are fruit trees and extensive stone walls.

The road up Johnson Canyon is very rough, requiring high-clearance four-wheel drive in order to reach the road-end trailhead at Wilson Spring. Wilson Spring is a lush and lovely spot with water pouring from a pipe, huge willow and cottonwood trees, and an informal campsite—a true desert oasis. In the absence of four-wheel drive plan on parking at the burro pen about 3.5 miles short of Wilson Spring, thereby adding 7 miles round-trip to the hike.

The South Fork of Johnson Canyon enters from the left 1 mile before reaching Wilson Spring. A four-wheel-drive road heads up the South Fork, ending after 0.3 mile at a dry campsite. This canyon is wide and graveled and can be hiked up toward the crest of the Panamint Mountains as a side trip.

To reach Hungry Bill's Ranch from Wilson Spring start out on the use trail that heads up the canyon on the left side from the road end. Within 0.1 mile the trail passes the circular stone remnants of an arrastra used by miners for crushing ore. At 0.2 mile the trail fades out. Cross the canyon wash to the right side and look carefully for the continuation of the trail.

At 0.3 mile the canyon narrows, bounded by high rugged cliffs of volcanic rhyolite rock. The primitive trail crosses back and forth through the wash. The canyon again narrows at 0.5 mile; cross and climb around rock spires to the left. At 0.6 the trail passes hand-built rock walls, climbing to 4,400 feet then losing 100 feet as its drops to the stream bottom. With a profusion of birds, frogs, lush vegetation, and water, this delightful stretch of Johnson Canyon is a refreshing celebration of life!

At 0.9 mile the trail reaches an overlook (4,450 feet) after contouring up and down along the steep rocky slopes. The trail then drops another 50 feet to the stream, crosses to the right, then the left, and continues up canyon to the lower ranch site on the right (north) side at 1.5 miles (4,600 feet). Each stream crossing features well-placed stepping stones, so you are guaranteed a dry journey. At the lower ranch, the rock walls, fruit trees, and gurgling rivulet are overseen by massive cliffs toward Panamint Pass.

Cross to the left side and follow the primitive trail another 0.1 mile where the stream has disappeared beneath the ground—a completely different and drier world. At 1.8 miles the stream resurfaces at the main Hungry Bill's Ranch—a huge open area on the left (south) side of the canyon. The site includes fruit trees surrounded by extensive rock walls. A rock-walled roofless house protected by a stone wall windbreak sits on a hill above the ranch. Hungry Bill certainly had a stunning view of an incredibly rugged cliff face, and down across Death Valley to the Black Mountains. It is interesting to reflect on the life he must have led.

You'll probably have an easier time following the use trail back down to Wilson Spring than you did on the way up. With the scenic canyon, rough trail, and ample exploration opportunities at the ranch there is no need to hurry.

General description:	A long out-and-back hike up and alongside a year-round canyon stream to the site of a Panamint Range mining town.
Length:	13 miles round-trip.
General location:	About 80 miles southeast of Lone Pine, west central Death Valley National Park, southeastern California.
Trail condition:	Clear canyon troad.
Special attractions:	Year-round stream, lengthy dramatic canyon with more than 3,000-foot elevation gain, blending of old and new at historic mining site, Panamint peaks above.
Difficulty:	Strenuous.
Best season:	September through May.
Starting elevation:	2,660 feet.
Maximum elevation:	6,100 feet.
Elevation gain/loss:	3,440 feet/none.
USGS topo maps:	Ballarat-CA and Panamint-CA (1:24,000).
For more information:	Death Valley National Park (see Appendix D).

Key points:

0.0   Hike up former road by Novak Mill. Do not linger near the millsite; the Novak family is wary of intruders.

0.1-0.5   Troad and river share the same bed, necessitating much stream-hopping.

1.0   Gorge shared by troad and river; agility required.

1.2   Another gorge, steeper than the previous one, leads to valley.

2.8   Junction with canyon from south; continue on troad (left) up main canyon.

3.5   Last willow grove; dry feet from here.

4.5   Entering pinyon-juniper vegetation. Panamints in view to east.

4.9   Mine opening on the right.

5.0   Canyon junction: Woodpecker from the north, Cannon from the south.

5.4   Marvel Canyon joins from the south; troad junction. Low rock wall on the left. The chimney of the Panamint City smelter is visible a mile ahead.

6.2   Junction with Sourdough Canyon from the north.

6.5   Smelter ruins. Roads branch off to various other mine sites in Magazine, Water, and Frenchmans canyons.

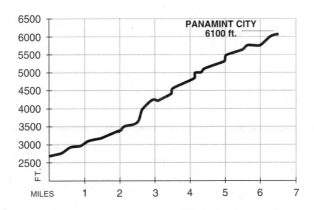

Finding the trailhead: From California Highway 190, 34.5 miles southwest of Stovepipe Wells and 2.6 miles east of Panamint Springs Resort, go south on Panamint Valley Road for 13.9 miles to junction with the Trona-Wildrose Road. Turn right (south) and drive 9.5 miles to Ballarat Road (signed) on your left. Turn left and go 3.6 miles to the tiny town of Ballarat. Turn left at the general store, which is a good stop for ice, cold sodas, and lively conversation with the proprietor. From the store, drive north on Indian Canyon Road 1.9 miles to Surprise Canyon Road on your right, which is marked by a signpost and by a large white boulder with a red S7 on it. Turn right and drive 4.1 miles to the road's end at the Novak Camp. Park on the side and speak to the owner if he is around. Do not block the road or the driveway. Be considerate of private property owners.

The hike: The Surprise Canyon hike is located on the very western edge of the expansion area of Death Valley National Park above the Panamint Valley. The BLM Surprise Canyon Wilderness Area lies on both sides of the Surprise Canyon Road off of Indian Canyon Road. Here the BLM's open desert camping regulations are in effect; there are plentiful campsites along the first 2 miles of Surprise Canyon Road before it climbs the alluvial fan.

The Novak property, labeled Chris Wicht Camp on the topo map, straddles the end of the driveable road. Mr. Novak permits hikers to park at the side of the road, but he does not tolerate visitors poking around the mill site upstream from his housing area. Restrain your curiosity; there will be plenty to explore in Panamint City, 6 miles and 3,000 feet higher ahead.

Schedule this hike for a weekday if possible. The Surprise Canyon Road to Panamint City, nearly totally washed out by the 1984 flash flood, is a favorite location for jeepsters who enjoy winching their vehicles up and down the slippery rock chutes in the river's two gorges. Especially in spring, weekend hikers could find their peaceful outing affected by this enthusiastic group.

Another practical piece of advice is to waterproof your boots before hiking here—especially if the springs are running at full capacity. The troad/river combination makes for very damp hiking in the lower 3.5 miles of the

SURPRISE CANYON TO PANAMINT CITY

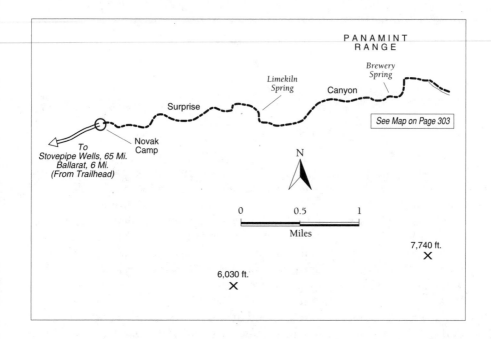

PANAMINT
RANGE

Brewery
Spring

Limekiln
Spring

Canyon

Surprise

See Map on Page 303

Novak
Camp

To
Stovepipe Wells, 65 Mi.
Ballarat, 6 Mi.
(From Trailhead)

N

0   0.5   1

Miles

7,740 ft.
X

6,030 ft.
X

canyon. This is a minor inconvenience in this adventuresome climb to Panamint City.

The vegetation and wildlife of Surprise Canyon is varied and plentiful, due to the presence of water and the elevation change. At the parking area you may spot the famed rare Panamint daisy growing in profusion along the top of the streambank. Birds and burros frequent the lower canyon. The hike will travel through several vegetative zones as it climbs, from the riparian willow groves to creosote scrub community to pinyon-juniper forest. From the destination in Panamint City the lofty cliffs of the mountain range soar above forested slopes.

Right from the start the hike up Surprise Canyon is a startling change from the drive through Panamint Valley. Even the bumpy ride up the road to the parking area does not hint at the water and greenery that greet you at Novak Camp. The first half mile from the camp involves repeated zigzags along the shallow stream to dry sections of the largely washed out troad. To enjoy the views of the rugged canyon walls it is necessary to pause between stream leaps.

At 1 mile, hand and foot scrambling is necessary to get up the sloping gorge, where wet rocks are quite slippery. Another more challenging gorge lies 0.2 mile beyond, leading up to a broader valley. An amusing sight above the gorge is the deserted mine vehicle perched in the eroded troad. More

SURPRISE CANYON TO PANAMINT CITY

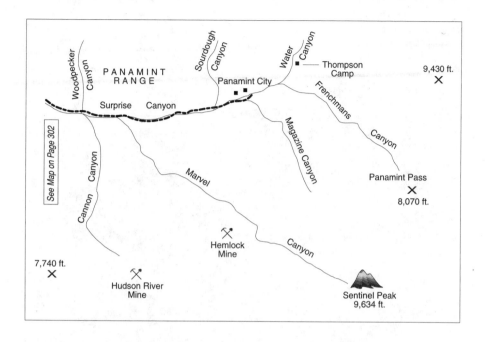

vehicles lie in the brush, probably brought down the valley by the 1984 flood. During this lower third of the hike to Panamint City the watery trail periodically becomes dry, but the flow from Limekiln and Brewery springs along the canyon revives the creek.

At 3.4 miles the damp trail bisects an arched willow grove and cuts by a rocky grotto. This is the last contact with the stream until the return trip. The next mile and a half of the hike climbs 1,000 feet, with rugged canyon walls of contrasting colors on both sides. Juniper, Mormon tea, and barrel cactus crowd the lower slopes with barren cliffs bursting above.

By 5 miles you'll begin to spot remains of Panamint City's vast mining activities. Up to two thousand people lived in the narrow city during its brief heyday in the mid-1870 silver boom. Even today validated mining claims exist here.

At 6.2 miles you'll arrive at the central city site, where it is evident that mining and residential activities have occurred recently. Several cabins are located in the valley above the smelter ruins. Respect private property during your visit. The interface of old and modern mining is also in evidence. Aluminum and plastic debris from the 1950s is mixed with the more traditional rusty tin cans and barrel hoops of ghost towns. Amazingly, much industrial equipment is located in this hard-to-reach spot—a 20-foot propane tank, two trailers, various trucks, and other heavy machinery. Some

Incredibly a few diehard four-wheelers still winch their vehicles straight up this cliffy section near the top of the rocky gorge in Surprise Canyon.

1950s-vintage buildings are interspersed with remains of the last century's occupation.

The narrow valley floor below the modern mining outpost is overgrown with creosote and catclaw. Amid the shrubbery are the stone walls and foundations of the nineteenth-century dwellers. Near one of the larger building sites a garden of iris continues to spring merrily into life, a living artifact of Panamint City's brief but optimistic history. A large stone-walled livestock paddock remains on the north side of the troad; it is apparent that the wild burros of the canyon still like to hang out here.

Binoculars will enable you to explore the canyon visually without plowing through the dense vicious shrubs. Several other canyons branch out at the eastern end of Surprise Canyon. With topo map in hand, you can explore Frenchmans Canyon to the southeast toward Panamint Pass, or Water Canyon to the northeast. Thompson Camp, in the latter, is 0.5 mile beyond the upper end of Panamint City by way of an aqueduct troad. A couple of wooden-shell buildings and a water tank mark its 6,500-foot location. There is also a lush spring (Thompson Spring), with a large wooden cask cistern that used to supply the mining community. It is an excellent source of water even today.

Above the industrial city rise the peaks of the Panamints. The towering wall of the divide rises sharply 3,000 feet above the town, dwarfing the 100-foot chimney of the deteriorating smelter. The miners have come and gone, but the majesty of this desert mountain range persists.

General description:	A strenuous 7- to 10-hour out-and-back trail to the highest point in the park, with spectacular vistas made even more impressive given the astounding elevation difference of 11,300 feet.
Length:	14 miles round-trip (out-and-back route).
General location:	About 85 miles southeast of Lone Pine, in west-central Death Valley National Park, southeastern California.
Trail condition:	Clear trail.
Special attractions:	Highest summit in the park, summer hiking, incredible vertical relief, expansive vistas, rare bristlecone pine forest.
Difficulty:	Strenuous.
Best season:	Mid-May to mid-November. Check at ranger station for weather information affecting the Wildrose Canyon Road.
Starting elevation:	8,133 feet.
Maximum elevation:	11,048 feet (Telescope Peak).
Elevation gain/loss:	3,075 feet/160 feet.
USGS topo map:	Telescope Peak-CA (1:24,000).
For more information:	Death Valley National Park (see Appendix D).

Key points:
   0.0   Trailhead at Mahogany Flat Campground (8,133 feet).
   2.6   Arcane Meadows (9,620 feet).
   4.3   Saddle before the summit ridge to the peak (9,500 feet).
   4.5   Unsigned trail junction with the side trail to the dry Eagle Spring (9,480 feet).
   7.0   Summit of Telescope Peak (11,048 feet).

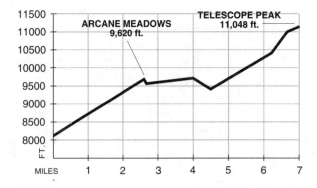

Finding the trailhead: The trail begins at the south end of the Mahogany Flat Campground, at the end of the upper Mahogany Flat Road 8.7 miles east of Wildrose Junction. To reach the trailhead take the Emigrant

TELESCOPE PEAK

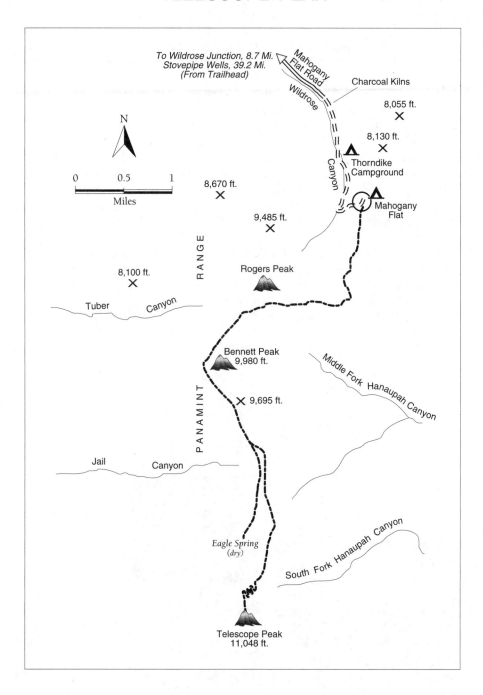

To Wildrose Junction, 8.7 Mi.
Stovepipe Wells, 39.2 Mi.
(From Trailhead)

Mahogany
Flat Road

Charcoal Kilns

Wildrose

8,055 ft.
×

8,130 ft.
×

Thorndike
Campground

Canyon

N

0   0.5   1
Miles

8,670 ft.
×

Mahogany
Flat

9,485 ft.
×

RANGE

Rogers Peak

8,100 ft.
×

Tuber   Canyon

Bennett Peak
9,980 ft.

Middle Fork Hanaupah Canyon

PANAMINT

× 9,695 ft.

Jail   Canyon

Eagle Spring
(dry)

South Fork Hanaupah Canyon

Telescope Peak
11,048 ft.

Canyon Road 20.9 miles south of California Highway 190 to Wildrose Junction. Continue on Mahogany Flat Road. The upper section of the road is rough and steep for the final 1.6 miles after the charcoal kilns.

During winter Mahogany Flat Road above the charcoal kilns is often blocked by snow, adding 3.2 miles to the already long round-trip distance to Telescope Peak. If you are unable to drive all the way to the campground start the hike from the Thorndike Campground (7.8 miles east of Wildrose Junction) or from the Charcoal Kilns parking area (7.1 miles east of Wildrose Junction). This will add 0.9 mile or 1.6 miles respectively to the hike each way, making an early start imperative.

The hike: The 7-mile trail to the top of Telescope Peak is one of only two constructed backcountry trails in all of Death Valley National Park. Although no rock cairns or tree blazes mark the way, the clear trail is easy to follow throughout its length. After the snow melts by mid- to late spring there is no water anywhere along the high, dry ridge route so be sure to carry an ample supply.

An average 8-percent grade is maintained, but there are long stretches where no significant elevation is gained or lost as well as several very steep switchback pitches to the summit. This high ridge trail hike is especially enjoyable during summer when temperatures are usually unbearable in the valleys on both sides of Telescope Peak—11,000 feet below. This lofty stretch of the Panamint Mountains catches and holds a lot of snow during winter,

11,048 foot Telescope Peak rises to the south.

but the peak can sometimes be climbed without difficulty as early as mid-March with only a mile or so of deep ridgeline snow to "posthole" up just before reaching the summit. During winter it may be easier and safer to avoid the first 2 miles of steep sidehill trail by proceeding straight up the ridge over Rogers Peak. Winter climbers should register at the Wildrose Ranger Station before and after the climb, and carry and know how to use ice axes, crampons, and winter clothing.

Backcountry camping is allowed 2 miles beyond the trailhead, but the first level and somewhat protected tent site is 2.6 miles in along the edge of Arcane Meadows.

From the signed trailhead the trail starts in a forest of large, old pinyon and limber pines, thinning gradually as the elevation increases. A trail register is positioned at 0.2 mile. The trail climbs moderately for 2 miles with spectacular views into the rugged North Fork Hanaupah Canyon which drains eastward to Death Valley. At 2.6 miles the broad plateau of Arcane Meadows is reached at an elevation of 9,620 feet. This high sagebrush saddle is on the north summit ridge of Telescope Peak directly below and southwest of the communications facility on Rogers Peak. Twisted tree trunks add a distinctive foreground to the sweep of the high Sierras far to the west, with the wide Tuber Canyon dropping steeply at first and then more gradually into a broad valley.

At 2.7 miles the trail leaves Arcane Meadows as it wraps around the west to northwest-facing slopes of 9,980-foot Bennett Peak. Expect that about 0.5 mile of this stretch of trail will be snow-covered into early May.

At 4.3 miles the trail reaches the 9,500-foot saddle south of Bennett Peak. In another 0.2 mile the nearly level trail intersects an unsigned side trail which takes off to the right, climbing first then dropping 1 mile to dry Eagle Spring. Talus rock mixed with matted low-lying vegetation and prickly pear cactus add an unusual alpine tundra/high desert flavor. At the junction follow the trail to the left around the east side of the mountain and then back up to the summit ridge at 5 miles (9,640 feet).

After another 0.5 mile the trail reaches the south upper end of the rugged cliffs of Jail Canyon at 9,970 feet. Huge bristlecone pine snags provide irresistible photo opportunities. The trail begins a series of steep switchbacks just east (right) of the sharp summit ridge, attaining an elevation of 10,400 feet at 6.2 miles. Gigantic gnarled bristlecone pines adorn these higher slopes. Some of these ancient trees have been bored and are around 3,000 years old. Members of the same species in the nearby White Mountains are among the oldest living creatures on earth at some 4,600 years!

The 11,000-foot mark is finally achieved at 6.8 miles. From here the trail climbs three mounds along the ridge before reaching the one farthest south at 7 miles—this is 11,048-foot Telescope Peak. The summit consists of a long rocky point, dropping off steeply to the south, west, and east. Mercifully, the actual peak is often less windy than the exposed ridge going up, so if conditions are tolerable spend some time reading and signing the peak register.

The vertical relief is amazing, almost impossible to comprehend unless you make it to the top and look down on the salt flats of Badwater—the lowest point in the Western Hemisphere—more than 11,300 feet directly below. This monumental elevation difference is exceeded in the United States by only three other mountains—Mount Rainier in Washington and Mounts McKinley and Fairweather in Alaska. Telescope also affords a grand distant view of the highest point in the continental United States—14,494-foot Mount Whitney.

The vast desert basins of Panamint and Death Valley surround jagged canyons that emanate from Telescope Peak like spokes on a wheel. The remarkable contrast of basins and ranges that seem to stretch to infinity on a 360-degree arc is made even more dramatic when snow mantles the summit and higher ridges. Retrace your route to conclude a long, invigorating day on Death Valley's rooftop.

95 *HUMMINGBIRD SPRING*

General description:	An exploratory hike into pinyon-juniper canyon below Panamint Mountain cliffs to a dry spring.
Length:	3 miles round-trip.
General location:	About 75 miles southeast of Lone Pine, in west-central Death Valley National Park, southeastern California.
Trail condition:	Good troad, wash.
Special attractions:	Remote canyon, bighorn sheep habitat, traces of miner use.
Difficulty:	Moderate.
Best season:	October to mid-November, March through June.
Starting elevation:	6,400 feet.
Maximum elevation:	7,320 feet (Hummingbird Spring).
Elevation gain/loss:	920 feet/none.
USGS topo map:	Jail Canyon-CA and Telescope Peak-CA (1:24,000).
For more information:	Death Valley National Park (see Appendix D).

Key points:
- 0.0   Head south up the eroded troad.
- 0.7   Troad and wash divide. Follow road to the right.
- 1.2   Troad ends at junction of three small gullies.

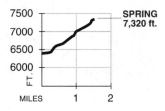

310

HUMMINGBIRD SPRING

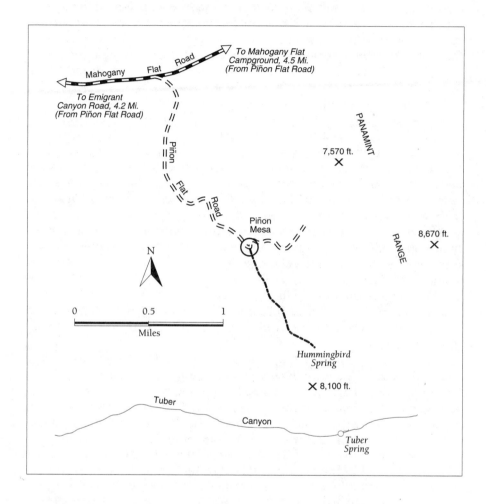

Finding the trailhead: From California Highway 190 take the Emigrant Canyon Road 21.3 miles southward to the junction with the Wildrose Canyon Road. Continue east on the Mahogany Flat Road, passing the ranger station and campground on the way up Wildrose Canyon. Four miles east of the campground turn right (south) on the Pinyon Flat Road; there are "jeep" (i.e., four-wheel-drive recommended) and "no fires" signs on a post. The gravel road becomes too rough for all but high-clearance four-wheel-drive vehicles at 1.5 miles. Park along the road, and hike up the road 0.2 mile to where it bends sharply northeast and rises to the Pinyon Mesa picnic area. To prevent vehicular use, stones block the old road that continues straight south. This is the trailhead.

The hike: This hike provides exploratory opportunities for history buffs or anyone who might enjoy a destinationless ramble in a lovely remote canyon high above Death Valley. Although the spring has ceased to flow, the area contains dense pinyon-juniper vegetation thanks to its mountainside setting. The elevation makes the hike suitable for a summertime outing in the Wildrose region of the park. Also, when the wind is intense on the ridges of the Panamints, the Hummingbird Spring valley offers some protection.

From the trailhead the troad quickly deteriorates to a rocky trail. The area is a favorite of the resident feral burro population. Their tracks and droppings are everywhere. Avoid confrontations with these wild animals. It is unlikely that your paths would cross, since they are not interested in human contact. Whatever trail maintenance has been done for 60 years has been done by the burro pack that uses these pathways. The burros compete with bighorn sheep. As such, the Park Service will try to remove many of the burros from wild sheep range.

As you climb the troad/wash/burro path you will spot remnants of prior human habitation: rusty cans, barrel hoops, lumber. Several pieces of galvanized pipe can be seen in the underbrush. Watch too for ax cuts on the pine stumps. This is a visual treasure hunt for the history detective. The actual site of the spring and the buildings have vanished, but enough clues remain to suggest their whereabouts. Following the troad/wash will bring you to a high junction of washes directly below a prominent 8,100-foot cliff face of the Panamints.

The immense value of water in the mining era in Death Valley is evident from the Skidoo Pipeline, which crosses the Mahogany Flat Road just before the Pinyon Flat turnoff. This 1907 pipeline carried water from Birch Spring in Jail Canyon to the south of Telescope Peak to the town of Skidoo, 23 miles north. This project cost $250,000 (in 1907 dollars). Even a small spring, like Hummingbird, was important to the residents of the valley.

Exploring the various small washes and ridges that extend down from the towering cliff of the Panamint Range behind Hummingbird Spring expands the hike and turns it into a rambling adventure. When you turn for the descent to your car, you will also enjoy vistas of Wildrose Peak and Canyon.

General description:	A day hike/climb to a high Panamint summit on one of the two constructed backcountry trails in the park, from which the highest and lowest land in the Lower 48 states can be seen.
Length:	8.4 miles round-trip.
General location:	About 80 miles southeast of Lone Pine, in west-central Death Valley National Park, southeastern California.
Trail condition:	Clear trail.
Special attractions:	Spectacular views from mountain peak.
Difficulty:	Moderately strenuous.
Best season:	September to mid-November, March through June (depending on snow level).
Starting elevation:	6,870 feet.
Maximum elevation:	9,064 feet.
Elevation gain/loss:	2,274 feet/80 feet.
USGS topo maps:	Wildrose Peak-CA and Telescope Peak-CA (1:24,000).
For more information:	Death Valley National Park (see Appendix D).

Key points:

0.0 Trail climbs then levels as it follows contour of hill.
0.9 Head of Wildrose Canyon.
1.2 Defunct water gaging station; trail bends and steepens.
1.8 Saddle; views of Death Valley and Badwater to the east. Trail turns north and climbs to second saddle.
2.9 Second saddle with more panoramas. Trail drops slightly, then switchbacks up the eastern side of Wildrose.
4.1 South peak, the false summit.
4.2 North peak, the genuine summit, with register in ammo box.

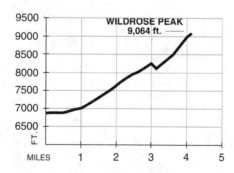

Finding the trailhead: From California Highway 190 at Emigrant Junction, drive south on the Emigrant Canyon Road 20.9 miles to Wildrose Junction; continue east on the Mahogany Flat Road (paved for 4.5 miles) and drive 7.1 miles to the Wildrose Charcoal Kilns parking area. In winter this road may be impassable; check with park authorities for weather and road conditions. The signed trail to Wildrose Peak begins at the west end of the kilns.

The hike: Wildrose Peak provides panoramic views of Death Valley and the surrounding mountain ranges. This official park trail to Wildrose travels through classic pinyon-juniper forest to a high saddle, then zigzags to the broad, open summit of this central peak in the Panamint Range. The meadowlike mountaintop is nearly always windy; appropriate clothing is a requirement, as are binoculars to enjoy the sweeping 360-degree view. Summer hikers will appreciate bug dope to combat flies and gnats.

In spite of its rather impressive elevation gain, the Wildrose trail begins modestly. From the kilns at the trailhead, the trail charges 50 yards uphill to the northwest, achieving a 60 foot gain, but then follows the contour of the hillside for nearly the next mile. This section is a gentle warm-up for the hike ahead. Along the route, rock outcroppings extend to the west, hovering over Wildrose Canyon below. This is classic mountain lion country.

Climbing only slightly, the trail joins a troad coming up from the canyon. Numerous pine stumps are a reminder of the logging done over a century ago to supply the charcoal kilns during their brief use in the 1870s. At the head of the canyon, the trail begins its climb. At 1.2 miles, the remains of a USGS water gaging station stand on the left of the trail. There is no longer any groundwater to measure. From here the trail bends north and steepens sharply, gaining over 600 feet in less than a mile. Rising to the first saddle,

From the top of Wildrose Peak a hiker looks northeasterly down the South Fork of Trail Canyon and onto Death Valley far to below. Telescope Peak rises to the south.

WILDROSE PEAK

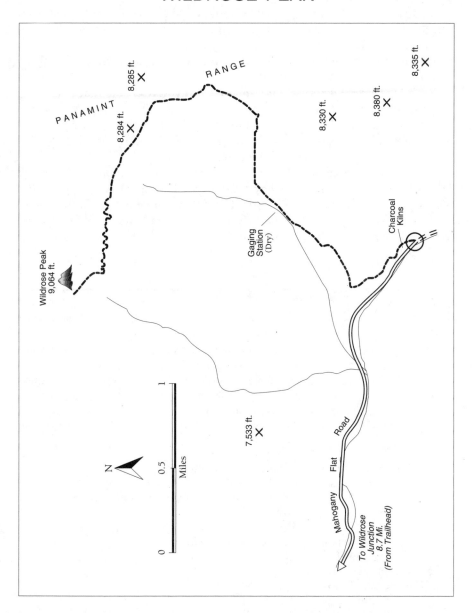

8,285 ft. ✕

8,284 ft. ✕

PANAMINT

RANGE

8,335 ft. ✕

8,380 ft. ✕

8,330 ft. ✕

Charcoal Kilns

Gaging Station (Dry)

Wildrose Peak 9,064 ft.

7,533 ft. ✕

Mahogany   Flat   Road

To Wildrose Junction 8.7 Mi. (From Trailhead)

N

0   0.5   1

Miles

you will enjoy a magnificent view of Death Valley below through the ever-greens.

The trail climbs around three small rises before emerging on a ridge above the saddle below the peak. Here, at 3.1 miles, and 8,230 feet, you can pause and view the length of Death Valley. From here, a mile of switchbacks lead to the summit. The trail snakes north than south then north, and so on, up the 800-foot climb. The changing direction enables you to enjoy a variety of vistas as you ascend the mountain, particularly as you near the wind-swept summit which is clear of major vegetation.

A small rock wall on the peak was designed to give some protection from the wind. Or you can drop just a couple of feet down on the leeward side of the mountain to enjoy your stay and write a note for the peak registry. From Wildrose you can see the vast area of mining activity in the north end of the Panamint Range. Just to the northeast in the canyon below there is a massive mining camp. Further along Emigrant Canyon Road the mountainsides are crisscrossed with mining roads. Rogers (with the microwave station) and Telescope Peaks loom above to the south. To the west is the mighty wall of the Sierras. To the east, across the valley, are the Funeral and Black Mountains. This is an eagle's view of the Death Valley world.

The hike back down the mountain allows you to relax and focus on a new view of the scenery. Death Valley Canyon, extending eastward below the high saddle, is just one of the dramatic sights you may notice on the downward trip. Although this is a heavily used trail, its bending pathway preserves the sense of solitude for the hiker.

97 NEMO CANYON

General description:	A point-to-point hike through open desert and down a wide graveled wash, bounded by low ridges and multicolored badlands, providing a pleasing contrast to nearby mountain climbs.
Length:	3.6 miles one-way.
General location:	About 85 miles southeast of Lone Pine, in west-central Death Valley National Park, southeastern California.
Trail condition:	Cross-country; open graveled wash.
Special attractions:	Gentle downhill traverse, colorful rock formations, several short, narrow side canyons for further exploration.
Difficulty:	Moderate.
Best season:	October through May.
Starting elevation:	4,583 feet.
Maximum elevation:	4,583 feet.
Elevation gain/loss:	None/1,383 feet.
USGS topo map:	Emigrant Pass-CA (1:24,000).
For more information:	Death Valley National Park (see Appendix D).

Key points:
0.0 Trailhead in Nemo Canyon wash.
1.8 Mud Springs.
3.6 Wildrose Canyon Road.

NEMO CANYON

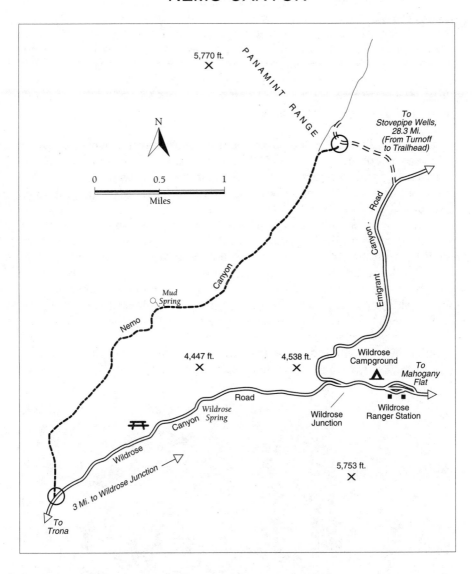

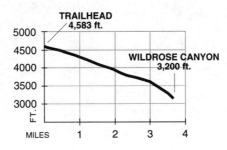

Finding the trailhead: From Wildrose Junction (0.2 mile west of Wildrose Campground and Ranger Station), drive 2.2 miles north on the paved Emigrant Canyon Road, turn left (northwest) onto an unsigned gravel road that takes off from the paved road as it veers right (northeast). Drive 0.7 mile to the end of the road at a paved T next to a gravel pit. A USGS benchmark is adjacent to this spot, which is the trailhead/jumping off point for the hike. The end point is the broad mouth of Nemo Canyon on the Wildrose Canyon Road, down the canyon 3 miles southwest of Wildrose Junction and one mile southwest of the picnic area.

The hike: This moderate point-to-point down-canyon traverse begins in open desert country dotted with creosote brush and Mormon tea. Nemo Canyon drops moderately to the southwest. To avoid walking toward the sun and into a stiff afternoon wind, make this a morning excursion if at all possible.

The canyon is wide open with low-lying hills and ridges. Soon, a few scattered yucca begin to appear. At first the wash is braided and graveled but it becomes better defined with a sandy bottom after about one mile. At 1.5 miles the valley narrows a bit. In another 0.2 mile red rhyolite bluffs rise on the left side. Around the corner the valley opens in a semi-circle with several side canyons entering from the right. The white saline seep of Mud Spring is also to the right at 4,020 feet. At 2 miles 100-foot-high cliffs rise on the left as the canyon narrows slightly. After another 0.2 mile the wash parallels brightly colored badlands—red, white, black, gray, pink, and tan—with steep bluffs rising several hundred feet on the left. At 2.4 miles a huge

Conglomerate mounds and spires in lower Nemo Canyon.

318

valley enters from the right. At 3.0 miles and 3,550 feet the canyon is marked by brown, deeply eroded conglomerate cliffs and spires. Soon large granite boulders appear, resting precariously atop spires of brown conglomerate. At times loose gravel impedes walking, but the steady downhill grade helps. At 3.5 miles the canyon opens to the wide Wildrose Valley . In just another 0.1 mile Nemo Canyon meets the rough Wildrose Canyon road at 3,200 feet, thereby completing this point-to-point downhill traverse.

98   DARWIN FALLS

General description:	A short hike to a delightful moist microclimate tucked in a scenic canyon.
Length:	1.6 miles round-trip to lower falls; 2.8 miles round-trip to middle valley and overlook.
General location:	About 35 miles southeast of Lone Pine, west central Death Valley National Park, southeastern California.
Trail condition:	Clear trail to lower falls; some boulders to middle valley; primitive burro trail to overlook.
Special attractions:	Year-round stream with waterfalls in densely vegetated canyon.
Difficulty:	Easy (to lower falls); moderately strenuous (to middle valley or overlook).
Best season:	October through June.
Starting elevation:	2,360 feet.
Maximum elevation:	2,500 feet (lower falls); 2,560 feet (middle valley); 2,640 feet (overlook).
Elevation gain/loss:	140 feet/none (lower falls); 200 feet/none (middle valley); 280 feet/none (overlook).
USGS topo map:	Darwin-CA (1:24,000).
For more information:	Death Valley National Park (see Appendix D).

Key points:

0.0-0.2   Trail follows stream up narrow valley floor.

0.4   Vehicle barricade at entrance to canyon.

0.7   USGS stream gauging station on right bank.

0.8   Lower falls. Drop back downstream 50 yards to pick up trail to middle valley and overlook.

0.9   Middle valley; thread way through willows to high basin and pools below falls (at 1 mile); return to same trail to ascend to overlook.

1.2   Burro use trail to view of highest falls.

1.4   Falls overlook.

Finding the trailhead: From Panamint Springs, 29.6 miles southwest of Stovepipe Wells on California Highway 190, drive west 1.1 miles to the signed Darwin Falls road on the left. Turn left (south) on the dirt road, and

A difficult rock scramble above Darwin Falls yields a grand view of the upper Darwin Falls—a narrow stream of water plummeting more than 80 feet.

DARWIN FALLS

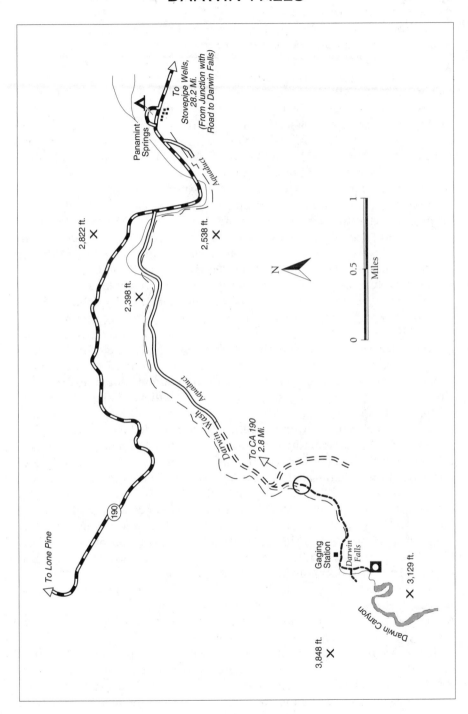

drive 2.6 miles to the signed side road on the right for Darwin Falls. You will notice a pipeline running along the road. The road is rough but passable for a standard passenger vehicle.

Continue another 0.2 mile, dropping into the Darwin Falls streambed/wash to the signed trailhead parking area.

The hike: Nestled at the western edge of the expansion area of Death Valley National Park, Darwin Falls was formerly a BLM Area of Critical Environmental Concern (ACEC). During its years of jurisdiction, the BLM took firm measures to protect the area against vehicular intrusion. Welded pipe barricades are still in place, along with stern warnings against such misuse. The BLM's 8,600-acre Darwin Falls Wilderness Area is immediately west of the park adjacent to the canyon.

Darwin Stream is the only permanent water in this area of the park. Flowing from the China Garden Spring, Darwin supplies the Panamint Springs Resort with water via a pipeline which is visible on both the drive and the hike to the falls. This year-round water source sustains dense willow and cottonwood thickets in the valley and canyon as well as a thriving population of birds. Cliff swallows and red-tailed hawks soar overhead. Brazen chuckwalla lizards stare at intruders from their rocky lairs.

This hike is a radical change from the usual Death Valley outing. Right from the parking area, a streak of greenery and a glistening brook lead up the gently sloping valley floor. Hopping from one side of the stream to the other begins here, and will continue throughout the hike. Steady footwork will prevent getting soaked, but care is especially required on the smooth slippery boulders farther up the canyon. The Darwin Mountains of black rhyolite tower above the bright green grass, the willow saplings, the horsetails and cattails.

At the notch of the canyon's mouth, another welded barricade remains, as does a BLM sign reminding visitors of Darwin Falls' value to vegetation and to wildlife. Bathing and wading are prohibited. The high dry trail is above the stream on the south side of the canyon. There are many bends in the narrow canyon. With the steep canyon walls, as well as the willow and cottonwood thickets, this is a shady hike, an excellent outing for a hot sunny day! A USGS gauging station is on the north side of the stream. With its aluminum phone booth architecture it looks decidedly out of place in this Garden of Eden. Beyond the station you need to watch your footing when clambering over the smooth water-eroded boulders.

At 0.8 mile, after hearing them in the distance, you reach the falls. Double falls cascade over a 25-foot dropoff, surrounded by large old cottonwoods. Sword ferns, watercress, and cattails flourish in the pool below the falls. This is the turnaround point for the shorter hike.

To explore farther, retreat 50 yards downstream and pick up the use trail up the south wall. The best option (there are several use trails) takes off on a solid outcropping of greenish granite, and traverses the canyon wall to the valley above the fall. Climbing the finely grained granite must be done with caution. It doesn't crumble, but it can be very slippery. From the trail, thread your way through the dense willows and cottonwoods to the upper end of the valley adjacent to a very loose talus slope. Here the three-tiered upper falls plummet 140 feet from the cliff above. This is not a heavily visited spot. In the narrow canyon your only company is probably the cliff swallows swooping overhead.

To continue to the overlook, return down the valley to the same trail and follow the burros' use trail on up the canyon's south wall. The trail emerges 140 feet above the valley. From the pinnacle at the point where the stream bends sharply from its easterly flow to a northern direction is the only view of the highest fall. Here the stream takes an 80-foot clear drop. This is the turnaround point for the longer hike.

Emerging from Darwin Canyon is an Alice-in-Wonderland experience. After being surrounded by humidity and greenery the beige world of the desert looks one-dimensional. The valley below the canyon is a striking transition zone, with the soft greenery of the stream ecosystem juxtaposed with the jagged dark rhyolite cliffs of the mountains to the south. The hike to Darwin Falls is a carnival of sensory perceptions. The smells, sounds, feel, and sight of this watery world makes this an exceptional experience.

99 PANAMINT DUNES

General description:	Cross-country open desert hiking to relatively inaccessible, high star sand dunes in the expanded western region of the park.
Length:	9 miles round-trip.
General location:	About 60 miles southeast of Lone Pine, in west-central Death Valley National Park, southeastern California.
Trail condition:	Cross-country on mostly firm, sandy, open desert.
Special attractions:	Remote, pristine star dunes with spectacular views of the Panamint Valley and surrounding mountain ranges.
Difficulty:	Moderate.
Best season:	Mid-October to mid-April.
Starting elevation:	1,585 feet.
Maximum elevation:	2,700 feet.
Elevation gain/loss:	1,115 feet/none.
USGS topo map:	The Dunes-CA (1:24,000).
For more information:	Death Valley National Park (see Appendix D).

Key points:
    0.0   Begin hike across open, sandy desert at 1,585 feet.
    2.5   Lower edge of dunes with creosote bush dominating (2,020 feet).
    3.5   Base of higher dunes (2,420 feet).
    4.5   High point of dunes (2,700 feet).

Looking southeast from the 2,700 foot crest of the Panamint Dunes to snow-capped Telescope Peak.

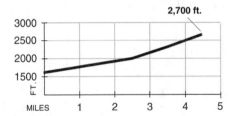

Finding the trailhead: From Panamint Springs drive east on California Highway 190 for 4.9 miles to the signed Big Four Mine Road. Turn left (north) on the Big Four Mine Road and drive 6.1 miles to where the road begins to deteriorate as it bends east. This is the north end of the North Panamint Dry Lake bed. Park on the left (west) side of the road at the bend and begin the hike from here. The access road is rough and graveled but can be negotiated by standard vehicles driven slowly and carefully.

The hike: The Panamint Dunes are clearly visible to the northwest from the trailhead/parking area. Because these extensive dunes rise several hundred feet they appear deceptively close. In fact, they are 4 miles away across open desert, requiring a steady 1.5 to 2 hours of walking just to reach the higher complex of dunes. This relative inaccessibility, as compared to most other dunes in the California desert region, accounts for their pristine quality.

These ever-changing mounds of sand are home to several endemic plants, dune grass, vetch, and more. The Panamint Valley is the site of mysterious

PANAMINT DUNES

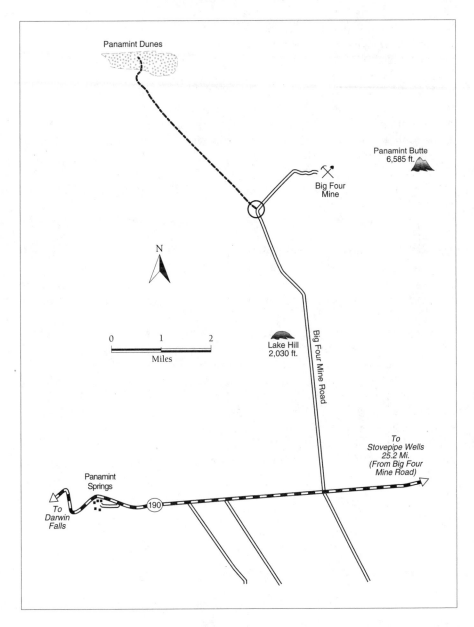

Panamint Dunes

Panamint Butte
6,585 ft.

Big Four
Mine

N

Big Four Mine Road

Lake Hill
2,030 ft.

0   1   2
Miles

To
Stovepipe Wells
25.2 Mi.
(From Big Four
Mine Road)

Panamint
Springs

190

To
Darwin
Falls

rock alignments, some of which may be called "intaglios." Intaglios are of prehistoric human origin and are huge animal shapes, perhaps hundreds of feet in size. These shapes, one of which is reported to be of a hummingbird, can be discerned from an airplane but not from the dunes. Fortunately, the park wilderness designation now protects these artifacts from the destructive impact of off-road vehicles.

At first the line-of-sight cross-country route to the dunes crosses a short section of rough, rocky alluvial fan. Don't be discouraged, for soon the open desert floor is made up mostly of well-compacted sand and desert pavement with more solid footing. The ascent is gradual, averaging only about 250 feet per mile. At 2.5 miles and 2,020 feet elevation you'll reach the lower edge of the dunes, with large creosote bushes dominating the landscape. The going becomes a bit slower in the softer sand.

After another mile and 400-foot ascent the base of the higher dunes is attained. Dune grass appears in sporadic patches with the indentations of animal and insect tracks seemingly everywhere. From here pick out a sandy ridge route to the apex of the dunes, attained after another mile, somewhere around 2,700 feet elevation. Depending on angle to the wind and relative moisture, climbing the nearly 300-foot-high dunes can be tiring, but the effort by way of a route of swirling, twisting ridges to the top will be well rewarded.

The star-shaped configuration of these dunes is especially apparent on the northern backside. Here swirls of sand wrap around small circular basins and bowls forming an intricate maze of shapes and patterns. Some of the sand basins resemble perfectly rounded craters. The view from the knife-ridge apex of the dunes is magnificent. Panamint Springs can be seen far to the southwest. The vast Panamint Valley stretches southward with the distinctive volcanic remnants of Lake Hill rising from the dry lake bed. Lofty Telescope Peak crowns the Panamint Mountains, with the multicolored bands of Panamint Butte dominating the immediate southeast horizon.

To return follow a line-of sight route toward Telescope Peak—by far the highest point to the south—and you'll end up at or very close to the trailhead, thereby completing this varied 9-mile trip to the Panamint Dunes. At first glance one might think that all dunes are somewhat similar, just another "pile of sand" as we heard one casual observer to say. Not so. Each of the four dune hikes suggested in this book, and their desert basin and range settings, is so different from the others that they can hardly be compared.

General description:	A long out-and-back day hike up a deep, narrow canyon in the Cottonwood Mountains, with colorful rock formations, petroglyphs, and expansive views of remote backcountry.
Length:	9.6 miles round-trip from the road closure 2.6 miles up Marble Canyon Road; if your vehicle is parked at the signed Cottonwood-Marble Canyon junction add 5.2 miles to the round-trip hiking distance.
General location:	About 135 miles southeast of Bishop, in west-central Death Valley National Park, southeastern California.
Trail condition:	Clear troad for 1.1 miles; clear wash thereafter.
Special attractions:	Deep canyon narrows; colorful rock bands; petroglyphs.
Difficulty:	Moderate.
Best season:	October through May.
Starting elevation:	1,790 feet (vehicle closure sign 2.6 miles up Marble Canyon Road).
Maximum elevation:	3,110 feet (junction of Marble and Deadhorse Canyons).
Elevation gain/loss:	1,320 feet/none.
USGS topo map:	Cottonwood Creek-CA (1:24,000).
For more information:	Death Valley National Park (see Appendix D).

Key points:

0.0 Trailhead at signed vehicle closure 2.6 miles up the Marble Canyon Road where canyon walls are only 6 or 7 feet apart.

0.3 Canyon (right) leads to a 15-foot dryfall; stay left.

1.1 Huge boulder blocks the canyon ending the previously open four-wheel-drive road; climb up stepping stones to the right.

1.4 Overhangs create a cavelike effect in the canyon.

2.3 Major junction; continue left (west) into a narrow, dark-walled canyon.

3.5 Canyon again narrows; semi-circular alcove on the right.

4.0 Another boulder blocks the canyon; climb a staircase of rocks on the left.

4.8 Deadhorse Canyon enters from the south.

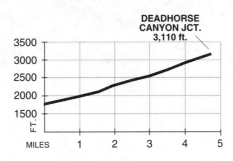

Slotted rock overhangs deepen the sense of isolation in the narrows of Marble Canyon.

MARBLE CANYON

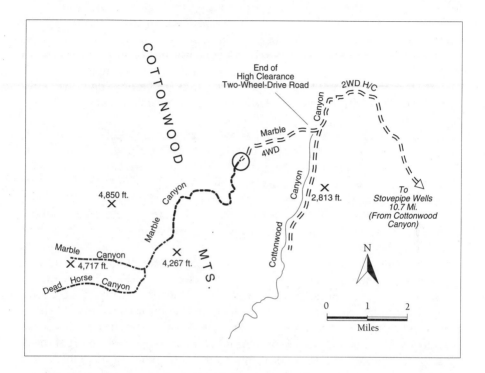

Finding the trailhead: From Stovepipe Wells Village on California Highway 190 head west on the Cottonwood Creek Road. The Cottonwood Creek Road begins by bearing left at the entrance to the Stovepipe Wells Campground. The two-wheel-drive portion of this slow, rocky road ends after 8.4 miles when the road drops steeply into Cottonwood Wash and turns left up canyon. High-clearance four-wheel drive is advised beyond this point due to soft gravel and high centers. The junction of the Cottonwood and Marble Canyon Roads is 10.7 miles from the Stovepipe Wells Campground. Cottonwood Canyon is to the left. The Marble Canyon Road continues to the right another 2.6 miles to the signed vehicle closure at the canyon narrows, but park at the junction if you have any doubts about whether your vehicle can negotiate these final very rough 2.6 miles.

The hike: The adjacent Cottonwood and Marble canyons are as different from each other as night and day. Cottonwood is wide and open whereas Marble is a wonderland of intimate narrows and dark alcoves.

The recommended trip described below is an out-and-back exploration of scenic Marble Canyon all the way up to its junction with Deadhorse Canyon. However, a much longer 23-mile backpacking loop through both canyons can be undertaken by those willing to cache water on this dry route and commit a minimum of three days. The loop can start from the Cotton-wood-Marble Canyon Road junction. Begin by hiking 8.5 miles up the Cottonwood Canyon Road, cross over into Marble Canyon by way of Deadhorse Canyon, and descend 7.4 miles down Marble Canyon from the mouth of Darkhorse Canyon to the point of origin at the road junction. About half of this loop is on open four-wheel-drive roads, with the remainder being canyon washes and an overland cross-country route. Marble Canyon is susceptible to flash flooding with a corresponding danger of being caught in one of its steep chutes with no escape. Do not attempt to hike the canyon if wet weather appears imminent.

For the Marble Canyon out-and-back day excursion, the hike might start out of vehicular necessity at the Cottonwood/Marble Canyons Road junction, but the real adventure begins 2.6 miles up at the canyon gap/road closure. On the way up at mile 2.3 petroglyphs can be seen at the mouth of the canyon. Sadly, some of these irreplaceable cultural links to the past have been senselessly defaced by vandals. There are more pristine petroglyphs farther up Marble Canyon, readily seen going up but more difficult to spot on the way down.

At the trailhead the canyon is only about 6 feet wide, coinciding with the wilderness boundary which is signed with a closure to vehicular travel. At 0.3 mile a canyon enters from the right which leads quickly to a 15-foot dryfall. Continue left up the creosote-Mormon tea bottom next to great stair-step beds of tilted gray and red rock. At 1.1 miles a huge boulder blocks the canyon which can be bypassed on the right by climbing up stepping stones. At 1.3 miles the canyon narrows to sheer, gray cliffs where graffiti mars still more petroglyphs. Here every turn in the twisting canyon brings new variety, with arches being formed from smooth, gently eroded gray cliffs. Overhangs create an almost cavelike effect.

At 1.6 miles the valley opens dramatically only to narrow again at 1.9 miles. Once more the valley widens with brilliant displays of reds, tans, and grays on both sides at 2.3 miles. Here a major canyon enters from the right; stay to the left (west) by entering dark-walled narrows which soon give way to a long, open stretch. The canyon closes in again at 3.5 miles, marked by a distinctive semi-circular alcove on the left. Soon white and gray bands of marble resembling zebra stripes border a wonderland of grottos in the narrow canyon. A second large boulder blocks the wash at 4 miles, but can be easily bypassed by climbing a "staircase" rock on the left. A small side canyon, overlooked by buttes and pinnacles, enters on the right at 4.2 miles.

Dead Horse Canyon joins Marble Canyon from the south (left) at 4.8 miles, at an elevation of 3,110 feet. The wide Dead Horse Valley looks deceptively like the main drainage, but Marble Canyon cuts sharply to the right (west). There are several spacious and excellent campsites at this junction, above the wash, for those willing to pack sufficient water for an overnight stay.

Many years ago someone etched "Gold Belt Spring 4 miles" into the desert varnish of a large rock with an arrow pointing up Marble Canyon. Another 0.2 mile above the junction a massive white cliff oversees the left side of Marble Canyon as it climbs steeply toward Goldbelt Spring.

As you return down canyon to the trailhead you'll appreciate hav
the sun at your back both for the morning ascent and the afternoon
This trip is well worth a full day of canyon exploration.

101 *MOSAIC CANYON*

General description:	An out-and-back hike in a picturesque canyon near Stovepipe Wells.
Length:	2.8 miles round-trip to lower dryfall; 3.6 miles round-trip to upper dryfall.
General location:	About 85 miles east of Lone Pine, in north-central Death Valley National Park, southeastern California.
Trail condition:	Clear wash trail; clear canyon floor trail.
Special attractions:	Patterned walls of multicolored rock, water-sculpted formations.
Difficulty:	Easy to lower dryfall; moderate to upper dryfall.
Best season:	October through April.
Starting elevation:	950 feet.
Maximum elevation:	1,480 feet to lower dryfall; 1,800 feet to upper dryfall.
Elevation gain/loss:	530 feet/none; 850 feet/none for upper fall.
USGS topo map:	Stovepipe Wells-CA (1:24,000).
For more information:	Death Valley National Park (see Appendix D).

Key points:

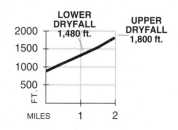

0.0-0.2	Trail in wash from parking area behind information sign.
0.2	Canyon.
1.4	40-foot dryfall blocks canyon; 50 yards back, cairns and arrows mark side trail detour.
1.8	50-foot marble chute blocks canyon.

Finding the trailhead: From California Highway 190, 0.1 mile southwest of Stovepipe Wells Village, head south on the rough but passable Mosaic Canyon Road (signed). After 2.1 miles the road ends at the Mosaic Canyon parking area and the trail takes off immediately (south).

The hike: The fault in the Tucki Mountains that produces Mosaic Canyon consists of mosaic breccia and smooth Noonday formation dolomite,
formed in a sea bed 750 to 900 million years ago. After being pressurized
and baked at more than 1000 degrees F, then eroded, the resulting rock has
startling contrasts of both texture and color.

Mosaic Canyon drains more than 4 square miles of the Tucki Range, so it
is to be avoided, like all canyons, in flash flood conditions. Rushing water,
carrying its load of scouring boulders, has created smooth marbleized

MOSAIC CANYON • GROTTO CANYON
• LITTLE BRIDGE CANYON

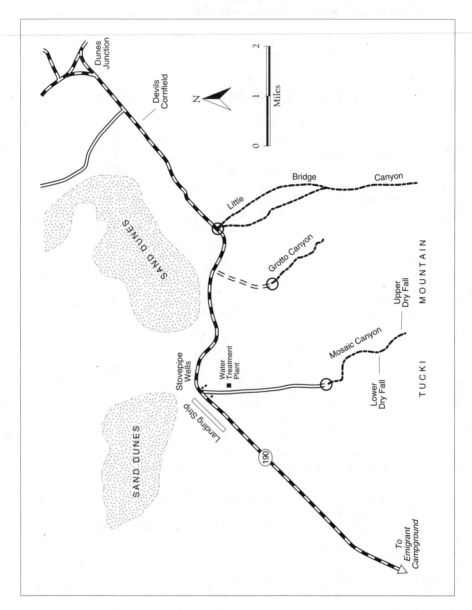

waterways out of the otherwise lumpy breccia. Silky surfaces gradually change to rugged lumps from the canyon floor up its walls, reflecting the varying depths of floodwaters.

Like other canyons in Tucki Mountain, Mosaic Canyon is alternatively wide and narrow. The wider spots are more numerous, and are broad enough almost to qualify as valleys. Often parties of hikers arrive at these open areas and turn back, figuring that the canyon excitement has ended. With plenty of water and a broad-brimmed hat, you can continue exploring the depths of Mosaic. If it's a hot day, be aware that this is not a deep shady canyon like the ones in the Grapevine and Funeral mountains.

The first 0.2 mile of canyon features the smooth marble surfaces that have made Mosaic a favorite destination of Death Valley visitors. After that, the canyon opens to a wide colorful amphitheater, swinging eastward to a broad valley with a 40-foot butte standing in the center. Use trails go in all directions, converging at the end of the valley where the canyon narrows again. To the right of this butte, a deep wash will eventually become a new branch of Mosaic Canyon.

At 1 mile, a small pile of boulders blocks a narrow spot. A well-traveled path to the left provides an easy detour. After another wide spot, the canyon narrows again, where an abrupt 40-foot dryfall blocks your passage. It is possible to get around this barrier by way of a well-traveled and cairned trail. Drop 50 yards back from the dryfall to the trail on the sloping canyon wall to the south. This trail takes you to the upper region of Mosaic Canyon where another 0.5 mile of marbleized chutes and narrows awaits you. A steep marble chute, 50 feet high, halts the hike at 1.8 miles. It's a striking spot, with eroding, fragmented Tucki Mountain rising above the silky smooth waterslide.

The hike back down the canyon provides new views of Death Valley and the Cottonwood Mountains in the distance. Sliding down the short water chutes on the return to the trailhead increases the marbleized beauty of these breccia formations; generations of hikers have added to water's erosive force in creating these smooth rocks.

General description:	An out-and-back canyon hike through water-carved grottos See Map on Page 332 and narrows of polished rock to a high, dry falls.
Length:	4 miles round-trip.
General location:	About 85 miles east of Lone Pine, in central Death Valley National Park, southeastern California.
Trail condition:	Clear wash, clear canyon floor.
Special attractions:	Water-carved grottos.
Difficulty:	Easy.
Best season:	October through April.
Starting elevation:	260 feet.
Maximum elevation:	800 feet.
Elevation gain/loss:	540 feet/none.
USGS topo map:	Grotto Canyon-CA (1:24,000).
For more information:	Death Valley National Park (see Appendix D).

Key points:

0.0-0.8 Up gravel jeep road in wash.
0.9 Canyon narrows.
1.8 First dryfall.
2.0 Second dryfall.

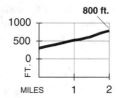

Finding the trailhead: The Grotto Canyon access road heads south from California Highway 190, 2.4 miles east of Stovepipe Wells Village and 3.9 miles west of Sand Dunes Junction. The road is signed for Grotto Canyon and four-wheel-drive vehicles. After 1.1 miles the road ends for most vehicles above the wash, which is soft gravel. The road/trail continues on up the wash to the canyon.

The hike: With careful driving, a passenger vehicle can negotiate the road to the wash on the Grotto Canyon hike. The soft gravel of the wash for the mile to the canyon entrance requires high clearance and four-wheel drive. No signs or markers punctuate the end of the road, but severe washouts end vehicle access just before the first dryfall. Conditions in this canyon change with each flood. At times the gravel is deep and the dryfalls are easy to scale, but often floods have scoured the gravel away making exploring more of a challenge.

Like the other Tucki Mountain canyons, Grotto is a very broad canyon, up to 200 yards wide in many areas. Deeply eroded canyon walls stand like medieval castle ramparts, with short serpentine pathways in their lower reaches. The narrows at 1.8 mile bring welcome shade after the journey up the graveled canyon bottom. A pair of ravens nesting in the aerie alcove above the grotto may provide suitable visual and sound effects for the hiker approaching the almost cavelike section of the canyon. About 0.1 mile back down the canyon, a cairned trail on the eastern side leads you around this barrier to the canyon above. Another dryfall will block your travels there.

Even with its proximity to Stovepipe Wells, Grotto Canyon is not heavily visited. Thus the adventuresome hiker can enjoy desert exploration and solitude without a lengthy drive. The high silence above Mesquite Flat rings in your ears—between cries of the ravens.

Hiking back to the road, the dunes stretch out below, framed by the Cottonwood and Grapevine Mountains. Grotto Canyon is a desert wonder of a smaller dimension.

103 *LITTLE BRIDGE CANYON*

General description:	A longer round-trip hike that can be done as either a loop See Map on Page 332 or out-and-back across a broad alluvial fan to a wide canyon with an arch and natural bridge.
Length:	7 miles (for both loop and out-and-back routes).
General location:	About 87 miles east of Lone Pine, in central Death Valley National Park, southeastern California.
Trail condition:	Cross-country alluvial fan and clear canyon wash.
Special attractions:	A small arch and free-standing natural bridge.
Difficulty:	Moderately strenuous.
Best season:	Mid-October through April.
Starting elevation:	20 feet below sea level.
Maximum elevation:	1,920 feet (above the natural bridge).
Elevation gain/loss:	1,960 feet/20 feet (loop route).
USGS topo map:	Grotto Canyon-CA (1:24,000).
For more information:	Death Valley National Park (see Appendix D).

Key points:

0.0	Head southeast up an alluvial fan toward Little Bridge Canyon.
0.5	Power line.
0.6	Deep graveled wash.
1.0	High-walled gravel wash; continue up the left-hand side.
1.5	Wash narrows; climb left past a 5-foot dryfall.
1.6	12-foot dryfall; climb a faint use trail to the right.
2.3	Head of the gully just south of the mouth of Little Bridge Canyon.
2.4	Mouth of Little Bridge Canyon.
3.0	Small arch on right (west) side of the wide wash/canyon.
3.4	Natural bridge on the right side of the canyon.
3.5	Canyon narrows above; can be hiked for several more miles.

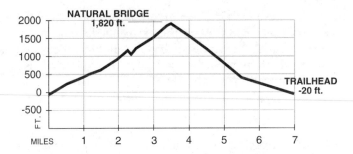

NATURAL BRIDGE
1,820 ft.

TRAILHEAD
-20 ft.

Finding the trailhead: The unsigned trailhead/route takes off to the south from California Highway 190 between Stovepipe Wells and Sand Dune Junction (junction of CA 190 and the Scotty's Castle Road). Little Bridge is the first major canyon east of the signed Grotto Canyon Road. The actual starting point/pullout on CA 190 is 4.4 miles west of Sand Dune Junction and 3 miles east of Stovepipe Wells.

The hike: Little Bridge Canyon isn't deep and narrow but it does contain several hidden points of wonder, making its exploration interesting and enjoyable. Unlike nearby Grotto and Mosaic canyons it is lightly visited, primarily because one must hike about 2.5 miles across a graveled alluvial fan just to reach the canyon entrance. One way to add a bit of spice to these first couple of open desert miles is to approach Little Bridge Canyon by way of a southeast-trending gully that parallels the steep mountain slopes on the right (west). By hiking up this gully, then up Little Bridge Canyon, and returning to the trailhead/parking area back down the alluvial fan, a loop of about 7 miles can be attained without increasing the round-trip distance of a less interesting out-and-back route.

Begin the hike by heading south to southeast across desert pavement then up the alluvial fan toward the power line and the Little Bridge Canyon entrance, which cannot be seen from the highway. Soon after passing under the power line at 0.5 mile you'll enter a deep, graveled wash. At 1 mile the route reaches a high-walled wash where the walking becomes more difficult in loose gravel. Soon a major canyon enters from the right; continue southward up the left-hand wash. At 1.5 miles the wash narrows; climb to the left over a 5-foot dry falls. A 12-foot falls appears around the bend. Backtrack a short distance and take a faint use trail on the right side (going up) which climbs and then drops above the dry falls. Soon the wash narrows to only 3 or 4 feet.

At 1.9 miles large boulders block a narrow gap; climb around to the left with rock walls rising on the right. At 2 miles the canyon opens up, with its head being reached at 2.3 miles just south of Little Bridge Canyon.

The sand dunes of Mesquite Flat can be seen back to the north, with Little Bridge straight ahead and to the right. Drop 20 feet into the wide wash, turn right, and enter the red-walled Little Bridge Canyon entrance at 2.4 miles (elevation 1,100 feet). At 2.5 miles the canyon narrows a bit, bounded by bright red walls. Compared to most Death Valley canyons, this one runs due north straight as an arrow. Striking clefts of white quartzite appear on the right at 2.7 miles, contrasting dramatically with adjacent dark rhyolite. Loose gravel makes for tiring walking, but the effort is soon rewarded with a small arch on the right (west) side at 3 miles (1,510 feet).

At 3.1 miles a sizable canyon suitable for a side trip enters from the right. At 3.4 miles the main canyon again narrows, with a large cave high on the right side and the namesake natural bridge of Little Bridge Canyon also on the right side (1,820 feet). This stunning sweep of white quartzite has a 20-foot-high opening bounded by a 40-foot-high arch. The notch above and to the right of the natural bridge ends quickly at a dry falls but provides a photographic angle for the bridge. With juniper clinging to the cliffs this is indeed a tranquil and picturesque spot.

Hike up canyon another 0.1 mile to a white quartzite gap for expansive views of the dunes northward and of great mounds of dark rhyolite rock overhead. The canyon narrows above but can be hiked for several more miles by those with sufficient time, energy, and water. To return, hike back down the canyon past the junction point with the side gully route. Continue to the right down the canyon and gradually angle left across the alluvial fan toward the sand dunes, aiming toward the highway/parking area starting point, to complete this adventurous 7 mile round-trip loop.

104 SALT CREEK INTERPRETIVE TRAIL

General description:	A fully accessible nature trail along Salt Creek, with pupfish, pickleweed, and salt grass, and an optional point-to-point extended hike north to Devil's Cornfield.
Length:	0.5 mile (loop); 5 miles one-way extended hike.
General location:	About 95 miles east of Lone Pine, north-central Death Valley National Park, southeastern California.
Trail condition:	Clear boardwalk; use trail to Devil's Cornfield.
Special attractions:	Salt Creek's vegetation and wildlife: pupfish, pickleweed, salt grass.
Difficulty:	Easy.
Best season:	February through April.
Starting elevation:	-150 feet.
Maximum elevation:	-140 (nature trail); -90 feet (hike to Devil's Cornfield).
Elevation gain/loss:	10 feet/none (nature trail); 60 feet/none (Devil's Cornfield).
USGS topo maps:	Beatty Junction-CA (Salt Creek Nature Trail); Stovepipe Wells NE-CA; and Grotto Canyon-CA (5-mile one-way hike), (1:24,000).
For more information:	Death Valley National Park (see Appendix D).

Key points:
0.0   Boardwalk begins west of parking area.
0.1   Go straight at the first bridge for proper number sequence.
0.25 Use trail at end of loop leads up Salt Creek towards Devil's Cornfield;
      continue boardwalk for return to parking area.
5.0   CA 190 at Sand Dunes Road.

Finding the trailhead: From California Highway 190, 2.4 miles north-west of Beatty Junction and 4 miles south of Sand Dune Junction, turn southwest on the Salt Creek Road and drive 1.2 miles to the Salt Creek Nature Trail. From the park visitor center in Furnace Creek, drive north on California Highway 190 for 13.8 miles and turn left on signed Salt Creek Nature Trail Road, 1.2 miles to end.

The end point on the one-way hike to Devil's Cornfield is where the Sand Dunes Road joins CA 190 from the north, 6.3 miles east of Stovepipe Wells Village and 1.1 miles west of Sand Dune Junction on the south side of the highway across from the Sand Dunes Rd.

The hike: Salt Creek Nature Trail is a full accessible lollipop-shaped boardwalk hike, with trailside signs providing interpretive information. The extended hike continues 4.5 miles up Salt Creek to the Devil's Cornfield on Highway 190. There is a beachlike quality to the short hike, not only due to the boardwalk designed to protect this delicate habitat, but also due to the aroma of salt water and the salt grass and pickleweed growing in dense clumps on the sandy stream banks.

The Salt Creek Pupfish, endemic to Death Valley, are the stars of this hike. In the spring there are hundreds of them in the riffles and pools of the creek. In other seasons they are dormant (winter) or the stream is reduced to isolated pools (summer and fall).

The boardwalk runs alongside the creek and then crosses it in several spots so it provides an excellent vantage point to watch the pupfish in the clear shallow water or the deep pools. Pupfish are small (not much longer than an inch) and fast, and enjoy zipping up and down the shallow riffles to bunch up in schools in the deeper terminal pools. As prehistoric Lake Manly dried up and grew saltier, these little fish were able to adapt to the new salty environment. Slimy green and brown algae, caddis flies, beetles, and water boatmen flourish here too, providing an adequate diet for the pupfish.

The walk out along Salt Creek is a startling change from the usual Death Valley desert floor hike. The sound of the merry running water in the winter and spring, with the flourishing growth of salt grasses, suggests a stroll on the beach. All that are missing are the seagulls. With the interpretive signs along the trail, you can enjoy the fish and birds as well as learn about the dynamic changes of the desert habitat and the ability of some species to adapt to its harsh conditions.

SALT CREEK INTERPRETIVE TRAIL

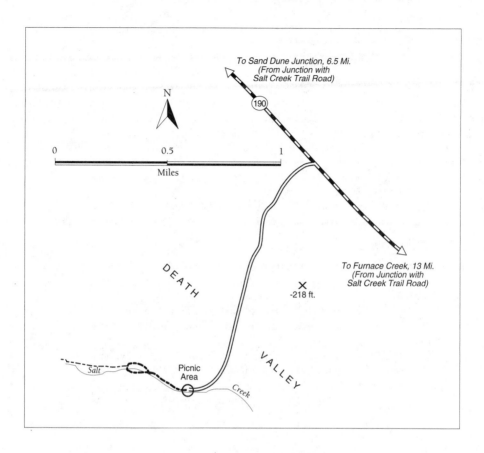

To undertake the point-to-point hike up Salt Creek (which disappears at 2 miles), take the use trail from the far and of the loop, heading north to CA 190 at the Sand Dune Road. Make sure your car shuttler is reliable, because you won't feel like reversing your route to Salt Creek.

General description:	A hike into a dramatic canyon in the Grapevine Mountains.
Length:	4.2 miles round-trip through Narrows, or possible 12 miles round-trip to Klare Spring.
General location:	About 120 miles southeast of Bishop, north central Death Valley National Park, southeastern California.
Trail condition:	Clear, four-wheel-drive road.
Special attractions:	Majestic cliffs, arched caverns, narrow canyon.
Difficulty:	Easy (Narrows), or moderately strenuous (Klare Spring).
Best season:	October through April.
Starting elevation:	950 feet.
Maximum elevation:	1200 feet (Narrows); 3,160 feet (Klare Spring).
Elevation gain/loss:	250 feet/none (Narrows); 2,210 feet/none (Klare Spring).
USGS topo map:	Fall Canyon-CA (1:24,000).
For more information:	Death Valley National Park (see Appendix D).

Key points:

0.0 Follow four-wheel-drive road east into Titus Canyon.

2.1 Narrow canyon opens into broader valley. Turnaround spot for shorter hike.

5.9 Klare Spring on north side of road. Look for petroglyphs east of the spring. Turnaround for long hike.

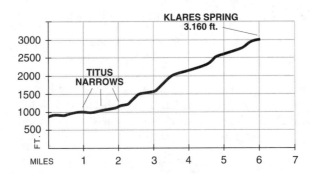

Finding the trailhead: The two-way road to the mouth of Titus Canyon is 11.9 miles north of Scotty's Castle Road (California Highway 374) and California 190 junction, and 17.9 miles south of the Grapevine Ranger Station on the Scotty's Castle Road. Take the signed dirt road east 2.7 miles up the alluvial fan to the Titus Canyon mouth, where there is a parking area. The Titus Road is one-way from the east, beginning at the canyon mouth. Embark on this hike early in the morning to reduce the chance of meeting vehicles; the 26-mile length of the Titus Canyon Road means it is unlikely that vehicles will arrive in the lower section of the canyon before 10 A.M.

TITUS CANYON NARROWS • FALL CANYON
• RED WALL CANYON

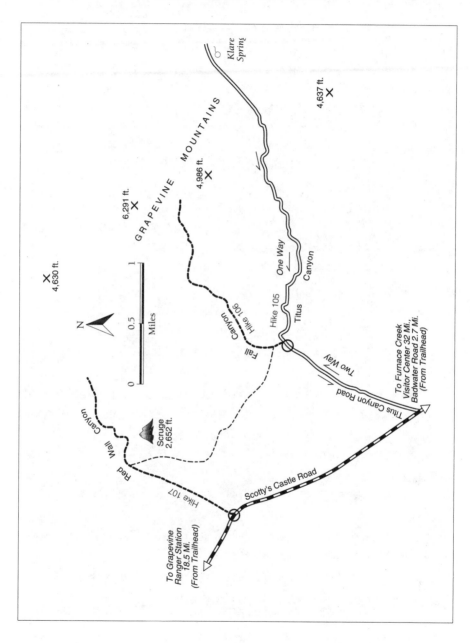

Monumental proportions of Titus Canyon.

The hike: Titus Canyon is the longest and one of the grandest canyons in Death Valley. The Titus Canyon Road was built in 1926 to serve the town of Leadville, an investor scam which became a ghost town the following year. This 26-mile one-way unpaved road is accessible only by high-clearance vehicles. Visiting majestic Titus Canyon by vehicle may not be the most satisfactory way to enjoy its scenery. By driving the two-mile two-way portion at the western end of the Titus Road, you can park and hike the dramatic narrows of the canyon. By getting an early start in the morning, you are less likely to encounter vehicles on the road. Driving to the canyon mouth also enables you to omit the alluvial fan hike, so common in canyon hiking in Death Valley.

Titus Canyon is a slot canyon, immediately narrow at its mouth. From the brightness of the desert floor you are plunged into the cool shadows of the canyon. Cliffs tower hundreds of feet above. Breezes rush down through the funnel of the canyon. The display of cliffs continues without intermission for two miles as you hike up the primitive canyon road. The variety of colors and textures on the canyon walls is immense and ever changing. The limestone layers are twisted and folded; fault lines run at all angles. In addition to the power of the earth's surface to rise and fall and shift, the power of water is visible throughout the slot canyon. The water-smoothed walls indicate the level of flooding. The curves of the canyon's path reveal the erosive power of the swift floods as they roar down the narrow opening with their load of scouring boulders. Flash floods are a real danger in Titus; often the road is closed for days after a storm in the area.

The 2-mile hike through the Narrows is overpowering. Like walking down the nave of a European cathedral, hiking up (and later down) Titus is both a soaring experience, but also an immensely humbling one. The Titus Canyon Fault, which created the canyon, slices through the heart of the Grapevine Mountains, laying their innards bare for the geologist and layman both to enjoy. With the road as a walking surface, your attention can be totally devoted to noticing the details of this mountain cross-section. This is a rare occasion in hiking in Death Valley.

For the longer hike, continue up the road another 4 miles. The canyon floor is considerably broader, although quite steep, after passing from the Narrows at 2.1 miles, but the towering peaks of the Grapevines still provide a spectacular backdrop for the canyon hike. The spring is on the north side of the road. The springs are critical habitat for bighorn sheep, which gather nearby in hot summer months. Some marred petroglyphs are above the spring, a reminder that it is both unlawful and boorish to harm such artifacts. Return the way you came, enjoying your downhill trip.

General description:	An out-and-back hike up a narrow, twisting, high-walled See Map on Page 341 canyon in the colorful Grapevine Mountains to a dry waterfall.
Length:	6 miles round-trip (to dry falls); 16 miles round-trip to the head of the canyon.
General location:	About 120 miles southeast of Bishop, northern Death Valley National Park, southeastern California.
Trail condition:	Clear use trail and cross-country on a clear wash.
Special attractions:	One of the deepest and most spectacular canyon narrows in the park.
Difficulty:	Moderate (to dryfall); moderately strenuous if continuing above.
Best season:	October through May.
Starting elevation:	950 feet.
Maximum elevation:	2,170 feet (to base of dry falls).
Elevation gain/loss:	1,240 feet/20 feet (to base of dry falls).
USGS topo map:	Fall Canyon-CA (1:24,000).
For more information:	Death Valley National Park (see Appendix D).

Key points:

0.0	Trailhead at the mouth of Titus Canyon.
0.7	Use trail meets the Fall Canyon wash.
0.8	Mouth of Fall Canyon.
1.3	Canyon narrows dramatically.
2.9	Rock cairns mark a faint scrambling use trail to the right which climbs above the dry falls.
3.0	20-foot dryfall.
3.1	Canyon narrows.
3.5	Canyon opens up to high peaks and ridges beyond.

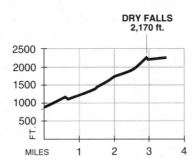

Finding the trailhead: The trailhead is at the Titus Canyon Mouth parking area 2.7 miles north of California Highway 267 (Scotty's Castle Road) on the Titus Canyon Road. The two-way road to the mouth of Titus Canyon takes off 11.9 miles north of the California Highways 374/190 junction, and

The mouth of Fall Canyon.

17.9 miles south of the Grapevine Ranger Station on the Scotty's Castle Road. Proceed northeast on the signed Titus Canyon dirt road 2.7 miles up the alluvial fan to the mouth of Titus Canyon, where there is a parking area. Follow the distinct but unsigned trail north of the parking area 0.7 mile to an extensive wash leading to the mouth of Fall Canyon.

The hike: Do not attempt this hike if wet weather appears likely. Fall Canyon is highly susceptible to flash flooding. You could easily be trapped in one of the narrow stretches of the canyon by a raging torrent if caught during a mountain storm.

From the parking area at the mouth of Titus Canyon hike north on an unsigned but easy to follow use trail, climbing gradually across several low ridges and gullies. At 0.5 mile the trail enters a side wash and then swings to the right (north) toward Fall Canyon. At 0.7 mile the use trail tops out above Fall Canyon wash at 1,170 feet, drops into the wide graveled wash, and vanishes after another 0.1 mile at the canyon mouth. At first the canyon is wide, up to 150 feet in places. At 1.3 miles the walls steepen and close in; dark shadows fill the bottom adding to a feeling of intimacy. The canyon quickly opens to a huge amphitheater-alcove, bounded by sheer cliffs on the left, bending tightly to the right. At 1.5 miles a large rock sits in a wide bottom which opens to colorful bands of red, white and gray on the cliff faces. Continue left up the main wash. The canyon narrows again at 1.8 miles, its sides pocketed with a myriad of ledges and small alcoves, only to open again with the west rim soaring 1,000 feet overhead. At 2 miles a narrow side canyon enters from the left just above a massive boulder that blocks much of the wash. Continue to the right up the main wash next to an isolated rock pinnacle.

Soon the canyon narrows once more with rock overhangs reaching out above. At 2.2 miles colorful folded rock dramatizes the powerful forces that continue to shape this rugged landscape. The canyon squeezes to a gap of only 8 feet at 2.6 miles, widens, and then narrows again at 2.9 miles. A sheer 20 foot high dry falls is reached at 3 miles at an elevation of 2,170 feet. The falls cannot be safely or easily climbed so this is a good turnaround point for an exhilarating 6-mile round-trip exploration of Fall Canyon.

If you want to continue up Fall Canyon drop back down the wash less than 0.1 mile and look for rock cairns on the left (south) side (right side of the canyon going up). This bypass route around the falls should only be attempted by those with at least moderate rock climbing skills and experience. Begin by climbing a steep but solid rock pitch to a well-defined use trail that angles above and around the right side of the falls. Exercise caution on the loose gravel directly above the canyon. Immediately above and beyond the falls the canyon becomes extremely narrow, bounded by sheer cliffs, folded layers of rock, overhangs, and semi-circular bends of smooth gray rock. There are a few short rock pitches that can be easily scrambled up.

At 3.2 miles the tight chasm opens to more distant cliffs but the actual wash remains narrow. At 3.4 miles a massive boulder blocks most of the wash, with the easiest way around being to the left. Here the hardest part about turning around is turning around; every steep-walled bend entices further exploration. The gray-walled canyon, polished smooth by the action of water, is left at 3.5 miles with the valley opening to reddish rhyolite cliffs and peaks.

At 4.1 miles and an elevation of 2,710 feet dramatic cliffs rise above steep slopes punctuated with jagged columns of dark rhyolite. Anywhere in this stretch provides a good turnaround point, but it is possible to continue climbing northward for another 4 miles to the head of the canyon, where the country opens up into low ridges, high plateaus, and open desert. Retrace your route to complete your exploration of this enchanting canyon.

107 *RED WALL CANYON*

General description:	An expansive desert/canyon hike into a rugged, brightly colored canyon in the Grapevine Mountains.
Length:	7 miles round-trip, or 8.5 miles for a point-to-point variation.
General location:	About 110 miles southeast of Bishop, in northeastern Death Valley National Park, southeastern California.
Trail condition:	Open wash; gravel canyon floor.
Special attraction:	Dramatic canyon with sharply contrasting colors.
Difficulty:	Moderate.
Best season:	October through April.
Starting elevation:	440 feet.
Maximum elevation:	2,200 feet.
Elevation gain/loss:	1,760 feet/none (round-trip); 2,100 feet/1,000 feet (point-to-point).
USGS topo map:	Fall Canyon-CA (1:24,000).
For more information:	Death Valley National Park (see Appendix D).

See Map on Page 341

Key points:

0.0 From whatever point on Scotty's Castle Road you select, aim for the Grapevine Mountains. The canyon mouth is where the red and black rock faces meet. The alluvial fan emerging from the canyon forms a distinct triangle. Head up this alluvial fan, cross-country or via one of the washes.

3.0 Enter canyon.

3.5 20-foot dryfall blocks canyon. Use of knotted rope of unknown age and origin is not recommended for scaling the fall.

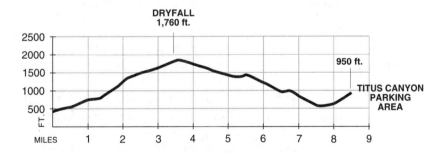

Finding the trailhead: The main wash of the alluvial fan is 18.6 miles north of Sand Dunes Junction on California Highway 190 (this junction is 16.9 miles north of Furnace Creek), 17.4 miles south of Scotty's Castle, and 14.1 mile south of the Grapevine Ranger Station. The hike takes off from Scotty's Castle Road, 3.8 miles north of the Titus Canyon Road exit, and heads northeast across 3 miles of sloping desert alluvial fan to the mouth of Red Wall Canyon.

The hike: Although rock-climbing skills are needed to proceed beyond a dry waterfall 0.5 mile up the canyon, this hike provides delightful vistas in the lower canyon region for the casual hiker. The trip can also be extended to a point-to-point excursion (with a car shuttle) by hiking from Red Wall to the Titus Canyon parking area, 3.5 miles to the south.

The approach to the canyon via the alluvial fan is not particularly challenging, but it is certainly not easy! The easiest hiking is on the dark desert pavement of the old alluvial fan. The wash route changes directions with its tributaries so it's necessary to cut from wash to wash to maintain the route to the canyon mouth. Above the wash, the sections of smoother varnished desert pavement provide some respite, but these sections are brief, interspersed with sections of cobbled and bouldered eroded washbeds.

The canyon mouth opens to the northwest; except for the red/black wall contrast it is nearly hidden in the cliff faces. The canyon, which looked so narrow or invisible during the approach, is surprisingly wide, at least 50 yards from wall to wall. At the entrance, the north wall is a sheer red cliff face, while the south side is a black slope. 0.2 mile further, the canyon takes a sharp turn to the north and suddenly the Red Wall towers 400 feet above you on the right. A narrow S-curve brings you to another red wall, now on your left. A short distance farther an even redder wall appears. The red walls, alternating with the black, provide a blast of sharp color on the beige desert palette.

At mile 0.4 in the canyon, water-sculpted narrows enclose an easily climbed low dryfall. Just beyond this obstacle is the 20-foot dryfall that blocks the canyon to all but seasoned rock climbers. Don't trust the knotted rope hanging at the dryfall. Using ropes of unknown origin, age, or strength is never recommended. So this is a good turnaround or lunch spot.

In Red Wall, the variety of canyon architecture lures you onward as the canyon is constantly bending out of sight. Only upon turning around for the hike back are you aware of the elevation gained (800 feet in 0.5 mile). The descent from the dryfall provides numerous vistas of Death Valley in the distance.

The sharp slope of the canyon floor and its heavy gravel surface both indicate that this is a relatively young canyon. There is still a lot of erosive energy in the uplifting Amargosa Range, of which these Grapevine Mountains are a part.

For the avid desert hiker, another approach (or exit) for the Red Wall hike is from the Titus Canyon/Fall Canyon trailhead. From the Red Wall Canyon mouth you can see the most efficient pathway across the fan and the ridges to the south. Since the finger ridges hide sharply eroded dropoffs, aim for their lower western edges in your southward hike. A faint use-trail is intermittent on this cross-country hike, visible only on the desert pavement ridges, and marked by a few cairns.

Like all rugged cross-country journeys, this hike does not allow a direct line. Detours are constantly required for steep ridges, deep washes, and high alluvial plateaus. Eroded cliffs of volcanic ash badlands obstruct the shortest distance from Red Wall to Titus. With neither shade nor cover, this trip should only be undertaken with plenty of water.

In the midst of a busy section of the park, this canyon-to-canyon hike, 2 miles from the road below, provides a taste of true desert travel. The silence of the desert surrounds you. The difficulties of desert hiking abound. From your 1,000-foot elevation you enjoy sweeping views of the valley below as well as the Grapevines above. Your destination dances in the distance as both Fall and Titus canyons at once appear close but don't get any closer! A cooperative partner can let you off at the alluvial fan on the Grapevine Road then meet you at the Titus parking area several hours later. The hike south to Titus takes twice as long as the direct hike up the fan, but it is worth the effort.

108 *UBEHEBE PEAK*

General description:	A steep out-and-back hike to a remote peak in the southern Last Chance Range with spectacular views of surrounding basin and range country.
Length:	6.2 miles round-trip.
General location:	About 115 miles southeast of Bishop, in northwestern Death Valley National Park, southeastern California.
Trail condition:	Clear, changing to good, then to primitive, and finally no trail for the final 0.4 mile to the summit.
Special attractions:	One of the few Death Valley peaks largely accessible by trail; "moving rocks" near the base of the peak; the feeling of isolation in a remote corner of the park; magnificent views.
Difficulty:	Moderately strenuous.
Best season:	October through June.
Starting elevation:	3,710 feet.
Maximum elevation:	5,678 feet (Ubehebe Peak).
Elevation gain/loss:	2,188 feet/220 feet.
USGS topo map:	Ubehebe Peak-CA (1:24,000).
For more information:	Death Valley National Park (see Appendix D).

Key points:

0.0   Trailhead at the Grandstand parking area on the Racetrack Road (3,710 feet).

1.8   Trail switchbacks to north ridge of peak (4,880 feet); trail splits—stay left.

2.4   Trail reaches ridge on west side of mountain becoming rougher and more faint (5,440 feet).

2.7   Trail drops to saddle between the two peaks (5,220 feet); begin route-finding segment to peak.

3.1   Ubehebe Peak (5,678 feet).

Finding the trailhead: From the junction of the Scotty's Castle Road and the Ubehebe Crater Road in the northeastern corner of the park head northwest on the paved Ubehebe Crater Road. The pavement ends after 5.3

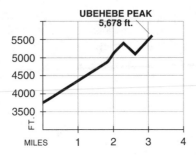

UBEHEBE PEAK
5,678 ft.

FT.

MILES   1   2   3   4

miles at the turnoff to Ubehebe Crater. Continue south on the washboard dirt Racetrack Valley Road 19.7 miles to Teakettle Junction. Take the right-hand turn for Racetrack Valley Road and drive another 5.7 miles to the Grandstand parking area which is opposite the "Grandstand" of gray rocks in the dry lakebed east of the road. The trail heads west from the parking area toward the prominent Ubehebe Peak.

The hike: Before climbing Ubehebe Peak, a short 1-mile round-trip hike east to the Grandstand is a worthwhile warm-up, and also provides a good perspective on your journey to the top of Ubehebe Peak. From the Grandstand a pre-climb visual orientation involves identifying Ubehebe Peak on the left with your route going up the east face of the north peak, then around the back side into the prominent notch, then left up the skyline to the peak.

The Grandstand is a large 70-foot high mound of gray rocks rising in stark contrast to the surrounding white flatness of the Racetrack playa, or dry lakebed. For added perspective, walk around the Grandstand then scramble up some of the large boulders. The Grandstand can be easily climbed 40 to 50 feet above the playa. Be on the lookout for the tracks of "moving rocks" streaked across the lakebed sediment. The mystery of these mobile rocks is heightened by the fact that no one has ever seen them move. Most likely the rocks are swept by powerful winds when the lakebed is slickened by heavy rain. If time allows upon completion of the peak climb, drive south from the Grandstand another 2 miles. Walk to the east toward the base of Peak 4,560. This is where you will find the best view of the mysterious trails of the moving rocks.

Be sure to carry sufficient water for this high, dry desert peak climb. The clear trail, originally an old mining path, begins by ascending gradually to the northwest up an alluvial fan clothed with desert trumpet and creosote bush. Within 0.5 mile the trail begins a long series of steep switchbacks up the east face of the 5,519-foot north peak. This imposing buttress is made even more impressive with broken cliffs of desert varnish. After climbing nearly 1,200 feet in 1.8 miles the trail reaches the north ridge of the peak, just after passing an outcropping of limestone where the blue-green copper of malachite rock lines a shallow mine digging. From this point a trail takes off to the right, ending after 0.1 mile at an overlook above an old mine

UBEHEBE PEAK

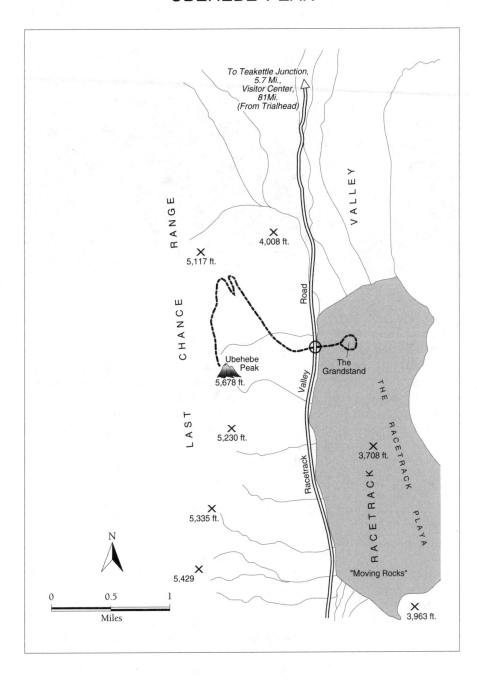

To Teakettle Junction,
5.7 Mi.,
Visitor Center,
81Mi.
(From Trialhead)

VALLEY

RANGE

CHANCE

LAST

Road

Valley

Racetrack

× 4,008 ft.

× 5,117 ft.

Ubehebe Peak
5,678 ft.

The Grandstand

× 5,230 ft.

× 5,335 ft.

× 5,429

THE

RACETRACK

RACETRACK

PLAYA

× 3,708 ft.

"Moving Rocks"

× 3,963 ft.

N

0   0.5   1
Miles

Ubehebe Peak (right) with the playa (dry lake bed) far below.

entrance. The summit of Ubehebe Peak can be seen in the distance beyond the north peak which rises directly above.

Continue up the left-hand trail, which climbs steeply up the ridge through the rocks to 5,160 feet at 2 miles. The trail then wraps around the west side of the mountain reaching an elevation of 5,440 feet at 2.4 miles. From here on the trail becomes rougher and more faint, compensated somewhat by stupendous views of the playa to the southeast. The trail then drops for another 0.2 mile to the 5,220-foot saddle between the two peaks. Any resemblance to a trail ends at the saddle, which is a good turnaround point for those not wishing to scramble the steep rocky ridge another 0.4 mile and 460 vertical feet to Ubehebe Peak.

To attain the summit climb southward straight up the rugged spine of the north ridge. Much of this route is marked by rock cairns. There are no technical sections but care must be exercised in negotiating narrow chutes around steep rock faces. The quartz granite top of 5,678-foot Ubehebe Peak contains a summit register and is marked by a wooden triangle. Although narrow there are lots of ideal sitting spots upon which to relax and soak up the incredible 360-degree vista.

The Saline Valley lies 4,500 feet below to the west. Beyond is the soaring 10,000-foot crest of the Inyo Mountains with the even higher Sierra Nevada looming further to the west. The crown of Death Valley—lofty Telescope Peak—can be seen to the southeast, along with the vast wooded plateau of Hunter Mountain. Perhaps most impressive is the eagle's-eye view of the gleaming white Racetrack playa encircling the tiny dark specks of the Grandstand far below.

General description:	A hike to a historic mine site and tram, and a longer round-trip in Corridor Canyon.
Length:	1 mile round-trip to mine; 2 to 10 miles round-trip for Corridor Canyon.
General location:	About 105 miles southeast of Bishop, north-central Death Valley National Park, southeastern California.
Trail condition:	Clear trail (mine); clear wash (canyon).
Special attractions:	Remains of early twentieth-century mine; colorful canyon with excellent vistas of cliffs and mountains.
Difficulty:	Moderate.
Best season:	October through March.
Starting elevation:	3,950 feet.
Maximum elevation:	4,240 feet (mine).
Elevation gain/loss:	290 feet/none (mine); none/840 feet (canyon).
USGS topo maps:	Ubehebe Peak-CA and Teakettle Junction-CA (1:24,000).
For more information:	Death Valley National Park (see Appendix D).

Key points:
Mine:
0.0-0.1 Back up road from the miner's shack, on north side by low stone wall, trail leads up hillside.
0.4 Tram cable tower at hilltop.
0.5 Overlook.
Canyon:
0.0 Mine chute; head west down wash.
0.3 Chute canyon enters from left.
1.0 Dramatic cliffs.

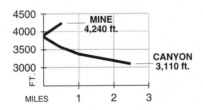

Finding the trailhead: From Grapevine Junction, take the Ubehebe Crater Road northwest 5.5 miles to the end of the pavement and sign for Racetrack Valley Road. Turn right onto Racetrack Valley Road. Four-wheel drive is recommended, but under normal weather conditions is unnecessary. The Racetrack Valley Road is severely washboarded, but contains no other obstacles as far as the Racetrack. Go south on Racetrack Valley Road 19.6 miles to Teakettle Junction. Bear right, and continue 2.2 miles to the right turn to Ubehebe Lead Mine road (signed). The dirt road leads 0.7 mile to parking area at the mine site.

UBEHEBE LEAD MINE/CORRIDOR CANYON

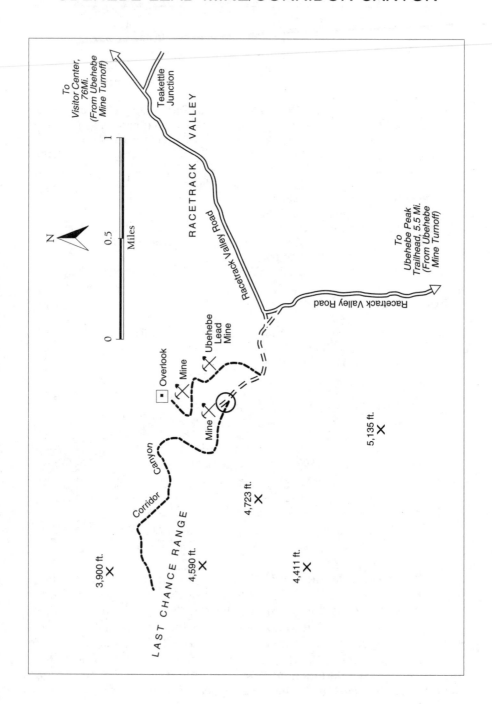

To
Visitor Center,
76Mi.
(From Ubehebe
Mine Turnoff)

Teakettle
Junction

RACETRACK VALLEY

Racetrack Valley Road

To
Ubehebe Peak
Trailhead, 5.5 Mi.
(From Ubehebe
Mine Turnoff)

Racetrack Valley Road

N

0   0.5   1

Miles

Overlook

Mine

Ubehebe
Lead
Mine

Mine

Corridor Canyon

3,900 ft.
X

4,590 ft.
X

4,723 ft.
X

4,411 ft.
X

5,135 ft.
X

LAST CHANCE RANGE

The hike: The Ubehebe Mine has a lengthy history, beginning in 1875 when copper ore was found here. The copper mine was not fully developed until early in the twentieth century, but the profitable ore was soon depleted. In 1908, lead mining began and continued until 1928. Ubehebe Mine had another renaissance in the 1940s as a zinc mine. Mining activity came to an end in 1951.

After all this mining it is not surprising to find a plethora of mining artifacts in the valley and in the hills above. A miner's house is still standing. Its door and windows ajar, stripped of its plumbing (the range lies outside), it is a well-preserved remnant of its midcentury inhabitants. Remember that it may be unwise to enter deserted buildings due to deer mice and hanta virus.

In the wash above there are other traces of rude dwellings of miners. Stacked stone walls are still in place. The men worked inside rock walls by day, and slept in them at night. Rusty debris and small, level tent sites are scattered about. The usual squeaky bedspring (burned and rusted) lies amid the creosote bushes. This is an appropriate place to pause and contemplate the bustle of activity and spirit of optimism that must have prevailed in this mining valley in its various heydays.

Below the housing area sits the ore chute, with rail tracks still leading from a mine opening. The area looks like it had been deserted only a year ago. The sagging old tram cable still hangs from the tower atop the hill to the valley floor. Unsecured mine openings dot the hillside. Although the National Park Service has not posted its usual warning sign, do not get close to mines; the tram should also be given a wide berth.

The hike up the trail to the overlook gives you a magnificent aerial view of the mine encampment and the rolling hills of the Last Chance Range. Mine openings proliferate like rodent burrows. The rust-colored rock and earth in piles at each opening gives the mining operations an eerie fresh appearance, as if the work here just stopped yesterday instead of 50 or 100 years ago. Numerous wooden posts mark the mountainside along the trail to designate claims of long-gone prospectors. Crossing carefully beneath the hilltop tram tower, you arrive at trail's end and a view westward of winding Corridor Canyon.

The Corridor Canyon hike ranges from 2 to 10 miles round-trip, depending on the turnaround point you select. From the mine chute, drop down the wide and graveled wash to the head of Corridor Canyon, generally westward. At 0.3 mile a tantalizing narrow stair-step chute of a canyon enters from the left, inviting exploration—although large boulders may prevent you from getting very far.

At about 1 mile impressive cliff walls soar high to the left whereas the right side is marked by folded rock layers altered by fault lines. Below, as the canyon turns left, are colorful bands of rock. The cliffs are pockmarked with caverns and other small openings, some of which serve as active dens for animals.

The canyon is unique in that it provides both a closed-in experience as well as far distant vistas of cliffs, overshadowed by even higher cliff layers beyond, opening to expansive views of adjacent and faraway mountains. The wide wash provides moderately easy walking with a day hike turn-around point extending up to 5 miles one-way.

110 UBEHEBE AND LITTLE HEBE CRATERS

General description:	A short loop hike around the large Ubehebe Crater and several smaller ones, as well as a down-and-back hike to the bottom of the crater.
Length:	1.5-mile loop around craters; 0.6 mile round-trip to bottom.
General location:	About 90 miles southeast of Bishop, in northern Death Valley National Park, southeastern California.
Trail condition:	Clear trails of volcanic cinder.
Special attractions:	Volcanic craters and complex erosion patterns.
Difficulty:	Easy; moderate to the bottom of the crater.
Best season:	Late October through April.
Starting elevation:	2,580 feet.
Maximum elevation:	2,900 feet.
Elevation gain/loss:	320 feet/320 feet; none/473 feet for crater hike.
USGS topo map:	Ubehebe Crater-CA (1:24,000).
For more information:	Death Valley National Park (see Appendix D).

Key points:
- 0.0 Trail goes south of information board at the parking area.
- 0.1-0.3 Trail climbs; bear left at Y. The trail to the right is eroding on both sides and becoming hazardous.
- 0.4 Maze of use trails on small plateau between craters; sign directs you to Little Hebe, directly south. Follow trail around Little Hebe.
- 0.7 Back at intersection, continue hike around the large Ubehebe Crater.
- 1.5 Return to trailhead or take optional trail to bottom of crater.

Finding the trailhead: From the Grapevine Junction of Scotty's Castle Road and Ubehebe Crater Road, 45 miles north of Furnace Creek, take Ubehebe Crater Road northwest. Drive 5.7 miles to the Ubehebe Crater parking area for the Ubehebe Crater/Little Hebe Crater trailhead. The parking area is eastern side on the one-way loop of paved road at the end of Ubehebe Crater Road.

The hike: The volcanic region at the north end of the Cottonwood Mountains, near Scotty's Castle, is evidence of recent cataclysmic events in Death Valley, geologically speaking. The huge Ubehebe Crater was created around 3,000 years ago when magma heated groundwater and the pressure from

The sharply defined rim of Little Hebe Crater is evidence of its youth, geologically speaking.

the resulting steam blew the overlying rock away. This explosion covered 6 square miles of desert with volcanic debris 150 feet deep. Called a maar volcano by geologists, Ubehebe is a crater without a cone. The rim has been eroding ever since the explosion, gradually filling the crater with alluvial fans.

Little Hebe, directly south, is much younger. Having exploded about 300 to 500 years ago, it is one of the newest geologic features of Death Valley. Little Hebe's rim is neat and well defined, exhibiting little of the erosion that has reduced Ubehebe's edge.

Pausing at the parking lot to read the information on the board and glancing at these monstrous holes in the earth might seem sufficient, but hiking all the way around this monumental display of volcanic power—then descending to the floor of the large crater—provides a much better understanding of the dimensions of the Ubehebe complex.

The first fourth of the hike takes you along the rim of the main crater. The size of the hole is overpowering. It is almost 0.5 mile across from rim to rim. Alluvial fans have formed on the walls as the rains tear down the crater's edges.

In the vicinity of Ubehebe there are an many as twelve additional craters, all examples of more maar activity. You will see numerous craters in various stages of eroding deterioration. Little Hebe stands out as a jewel of a crater. Neat and trim, this volcanic chasm is only 200 yards across. The younger, fresher rim has barely begun to weather. Volcanic materials are very durable. Clearly visible on the walls of Little Hebe are the layers beneath the earth's surface. Especially noticeable is a thick layer of viscous lava that had oozed from the earth's interior prior to the explosion of Little Hebe.

After the tour around Little Hebe, continue your hike around the main crater, which seems even larger after visiting its younger neighbor. A well-defined trail leads around Ubehebe. The trail down into the crater slopes downward from the rim at 1.3 miles. The volcanic cinder trail descends nearly 500 feet to the floor of the crater, where creosote bushes flourish. After major rainstorms the crater also features a small lake. Most of the time it is very dry. At the bottom you can imagine the force that blew off the earth to leave such a hole. The climb back to the parking area requires some exertion due to the skidding quality of the volcanic cinders.

The power of nature to modify the terrain via volcanic action stands in sharp contrast with the more gradual erosive forces that are demonstrated elsewhere in Death Valley. The earth has not finished rearranging its surface here in Death Valley. The forces that created Ubehebe and Little Hebe are merely dormant, not deceased.

111 EUREKA DUNES

General description:	A moderate loop or out-and-back day hike in the remote Eureka Valley to the tallest sand dunes in California.
Length:	3-mile loop or 1.5-mile out-and-back round-trip.
General location:	About 50 miles southeast of Big Pine, in northern Death Valley National Park, southeastern California.
Trail condition:	All-sand cross-country route.
Special attractions:	Remoteness, scenic backdrop of the colorful Last Chance Mountains, tallest sand dunes in California and possibly all of North America, endemic plants and animals.
Difficulty:	Moderate.
Best season:	October through April.
Starting elevation:	2,880 feet.
Maximum elevation:	3,480 feet (top of dunes).
Elevation gain/loss:	600 feet/none.
USGS topo map:	Last Chance Range SW-CA (1:24,000).
For more information:	Death Valley National Park (see Appendix D).

Key points:
- 0.0 Trail from either the picnic tables on the north or the monument in the parking area.
- 1.5 Begin climbing the east side of the dunes.
- 2.2 Top of the dunes.
- 3.0 Completion of loop back at the trailhead.

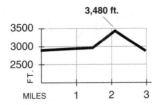

3,480 ft.

```
3500
3000
2500
F.T.
MILES    1    2    3
```

Finding the trailhead: From the south take Scotty's Castle Road to Grape-vine Junction and proceed northwest on the Ubehebe Crater Road for 2.8 miles to the Big Pine Road which is also known as the North Entrance Highway and Death Valley Road. The turnoff is signed "Eureka Dunes 45 miles". Turn north onto the washboard graded gravel Big Pine Road and drive 34 miles to the South Eureka Valley Road which is the road to the Eureka Dunes. Turn left (south) onto this road and drive 10 miles to the end-of-the-road picnic/parking area near the base of the dunes. From the north, Eureka Dunes can be reached from Big Pine via 28 miles of paved road and 11 miles of graded dirt road to the South Eureka Valley Road, turn right (south) and follow the narrow road for the final 10 miles to the base of the dunes.

The hike: The Eureka Dunes are a fascinating island of sand in a desert sea, within the recently expanded northern portion of the park. From a distance this 1- by 3-mile mountain of sand seems to hover over the remote Eureka Valley floor. Although not extensive, these dunes are the tallest in

The multi-banded Last Chance Mountains provide a colorful backdrop to the 3,440 foot summit of the Eureka Dunes.

EUREKA DUNES

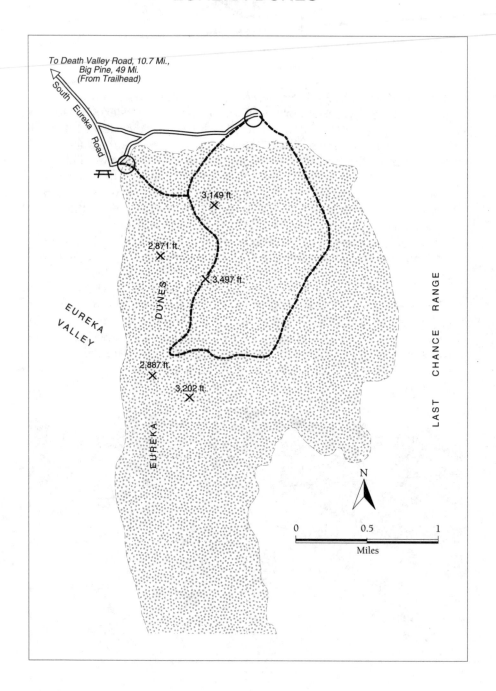

To Death Valley Road, 10.7 Mi.,
Big Pine, 49 Mi.
(From Trailhead)

South Eureka Road

3,149 ft.

2,871 ft.

3,497 ft.

EUREKA
VALLEY

DUNES

2,887 ft.

3,202 ft.

EUREKA

LAST CHANCE RANGE

N

0   0.5   1
Miles

California and likely the tallest in North America. From the dry lakebed at their western edge the Eureka Dunes rise abruptly more than 600 feet. Equally impressive is the sheer face of the Last Chance Mountains to the immediate east, with its colored striped bands of pink, black, and gray limestone.

If the sand here is completely dry you may hear one of the most unusual sounds in the desert: singing sand. When the sand cascades down the steepest pitch of the highest dune, a rumbling sound comparable to the bass note of a pipe organ emanates from the sand. No one knows exactly why this happens but the friction of smooth-textured sand grains sliding against each other probably has something to do with it.

These dunes receive more moisture than others in the park because they are positioned at the western foot of a high mountain range that intercepts passing storms. The isolation of the Eureka Dunes, far from any other dunes, has resulted in endemic species of animals and plants found nowhere else. For example, there are five species of beetles and three plants that have their entire range limited to these lofty mounds.

The three endemic plant species are shining locoweed, a candidate for Endangered Species listing, Eureka dune grass, and Eureka evening primrose, the latter two of which are listed as endangered species under the federal Endangered Species Act. Shining locoweed is a hummock-forming plant with root nodules that fix nitrogen from the air, a vital plant nutrient not available in the sand. When wind-blown sand covers the leafy flower shoots of the Eureka evening primrose, a new rosette of leaves forms at the tip. Large, white flowers bloom at night so that moths and other pollinators can avoid daytime heat. Usually Eureka dune grass is the only plant on the higher slopes of the dunes. Its thick roots hold shifting sand, forming hummocks. Stiff, spiny leaf tips discourage herbivores.

The Eureka Dunes are a small, ecologically unique place requiring our special care. Camp and keep vehicles a good distance from the base of the dunes, which is where most of the endemic plants and animals live. If possible, walk where others have in order to concentrate the impact away from pristine areas.

There are two basic choices for climbing the dunes, which can be hard work at times in the loose, shifting sand. The most direct route for the 600-plus-foot climb to the top is a 1.5 mile straight up and back route by way of a series of knife ridges. Because of the long driving distance to the trailhead a somewhat longer 3-mile loop is your better choice. In so choosing, you'll gain more intimacy with the dunes and their majestic Last Chance Mountains backdrop.

LOOP ROUTE

From the monument/parking/camping area head east cross-country along the base of the dunes toward the color-banded Last Chance Mountains which rise an impressive 4,000 feet above the Eureka Valley floor. Hiking along the base provides a constantly changing perspective of this unusual landscape

Teakettle Junction at the intersection of the Racetrack and Hunter Mountain roads in the remote northwestern region of Death Valley National Park.

as well as a good warm-up for climbing the steep backside of the dunes. A profusion of animal tracks will appear as well as the circular paths of grass tips in the sand from the ever-changing wind.

At 0.8 mile the initial flat stretch becomes laced with up and down gullies, with volcanic "bombs" embedded in the sand. At this point begin curving around the base of the dunes to the right (south). This wonderfully wide-open trek stands in startling contrast to the closed-in feeling one gets when exploring the deep canyons of Death Valley.

At around 1.5 miles begin climbing westward up any one of the several narrow knife-edge sand ridges that converge at the apex of the dunes. A vertical gain of about 600 feet to the 3,480-foot high point is spread over about 0.7 mile, with most of the climb during the final 0.2 mile. The dry lakebed, expansive Eureka Valley, colorful Last Chance Range, and the dunes themselves combine to form a stunning 360-degree panorama. To complete the 3 mile loop continue back down along narrow ridges and steep scooped-out bowls of sand in a north to northwesterly direction to the trailhead.

AFTERWORD

As seasoned hikers accustomed to the high snowy mountains of the Northern Rockies we were excited when the idea of exploring some of the California Desert was presented to us. It would be hard to find two more disparate regions—the California Desert and the Northern Rockies—within the Lower 48. We viewed the opportunity to learn more about such a different ecosystem as a tremendous challenge. And we foresaw many interim challenges along the way, such as the challenge of truly getting to know this splendid country and its hidden treasures beyond the roads. There would be the challenges of climbing rugged peaks, of safely traversing vast expanses of open desert, of navigating across alluvial fans to secluded canyons, of learning enough about the interconnected web of desert geology, flora, and fauna to be able to interpret some of its wonders for others to appreciate. These beckoned to us from blank spots on the park map.

But we each face a far greater challenge—the challenge of wilderness stewardship, which must be shared by all who venture into the wilderness of California's desert parks.

Wilderness stewardship can take many forms, from political advocacy to a leave-no-trace hiking and camping ethic to quietly setting the example of respect for wild country for others to follow. The political concessions that eventually brought about passage of the long awaited California Desert Protection Act have been made. Boundaries were gerrymandered, exclusions made, and nonconforming uses grandfathered. Still, the wilderness and park lines that have been drawn in these four great parks represent a tremendous step forward in the ongoing battle to save what little remains of our diminishing wilderness heritage.

But drawing lines is only the first step. Now, the great challenge is to take care of what we have. We can each demonstrate this care every time we set out on a hike. It comes down to respect for the untamed but fragile desert, for those wild creatures who have no place else to live, for other visitors, and for those yet unborn who will retrace our hikes into the next century and beyond.

We will be judged not by the mountains we climb but by what we pass onto others in an unimpaired condition. Happy hiking, and may your trails be clear with the wind and sun at your back.

APPENDIX A   OUR FAVORITE HIKES

FOR MOUNTAINS
Table Top Mountain Loop (75) Plateau with sweeping view of Mojave National Preserve

Telescope Peak (94) Central peak with magnificent view

FOR OPEN DESERT
Alcoholic Pass (20) Alluvial fan & ridge climb to low mountain pass

✳ CA Riding & Hiking Trail, Covington Flat to Keys View (61) Crosses varied terrain, includes sidetrip to Quail Peak *Joshua Tree (JT)*

Hole-in-the-Wall to Mid Hills (73) Dramatic features and views

Eureka Dunes (111) Highest dunes in North America, back drop of Last Chance Range

FOR CANYONS
Pine City Canyon (50) Dramatic canyon with boulder JT scrambling

Fort Piute/Piute Gorge (77) Gorge hike through heart of mountain range

Marble Canyon (100) Twisting walls with varied stripes and colors

Fall Canyon (106) Sheer walls above narrow canyon

FOR WATERFALLS & STREAMS
Sheep Canyon (24) Mountain valley with stream and fan palms

Caruthers Canyon (76) Seasonal brook with towering peaks

Surprise Canyon/ Panamint City (93) Spring-fed stream, chutes

Darwin Falls (98) Hideaway canyon with compound falls ✓
3/00

FOR OASES
Mountain Palm Springs (1) Series of palm groves, largest group of California fan palms

Borrego Palm Canyon (19) Falls, palm oasis in steep canyon

FOR OASES *(CONT'D)*

Lost Palm Oasis (26) Remote oasis, largest palm grove in Joshua Tree National Park

FOR INTERPRETIVE NATURE TRAILS

Borrego Palm Canyon (19) Excellent plant identification/ Bighorn Sheep country

Cottonwood Spring Nature Trail (29) Native American uses and processes for desert plants *JT*

Golden Canyon/ Gower Gulch Loop (85) Geology of Death Valley *part - 3/00*

Salt Creek Interpretive Trail (104) Geologic changes and pupfish *3/00*

FOR PRE-HISTORY AND HISTORY

Pictograph Trail (8) Native American sites

The Morteros (9) Native American sites

Barker Dam Nature Trail (57) Native American petroglyphs, ranching *JT*

Fort Piute/Piute Gorge (77) Petroglyphs, Mojave Road, Fort Piute

Hungry Bill's Ranch (92) Farm of 1880s

FOR MINES AND MILLS

Lost Horse Mine (41) Well-preserved historic mine structures *JT*

Wall Street Mill (55) Gold-processing mill *JT*

Ashford Canyon/Mine (78) Numerous mine buildings in scenic canyon

Keane Wonder Mine (88) Extraordinary tramway, mine, and mill

APPENDIX B RECOMMENDED EQUIPMENT

Use the following checklists as you assemble your gear for hiking the California desert.

DAY HIKE

- ☐ sturdy, well-broken-in, light-to-medium weight hiking boots
- ☐ broad-brimmed hat, which must be wind-proof
- ☐ long-sleeved shirt for sun protection
- ☐ long pants for protection against sun and brush
- ☐ water; 2 quarts to 1 gallon/day (depending on season), in sturdy screw-top plastic containers
- ☐ large-scale topo map and compass (adjusted for magnetic declination)
- ☐ whistle, mirror, and matches (for emergency signals)
- ☐ flashlight (in case your hike takes longer than you expect)
- ☐ sunblock and lip sunscreen
- ☐ insect repellent (in season)
- ☐ pocketknife
- ☐ small first-aid kit: tweezers, bandaids, antiseptic, moleskin, snakebite extractor kit
- ☐ bee sting kit (over the counter antihistamine or epinephrine by prescription) as needed for the season
- ☐ windbreaker (or raingear in season)
- ☐ lunch or snack, with baggie for your trash
- ☐ toilet paper, with a plastic zipper bag to pack it out
- ☐ your FalconGuide

WINTER HIGH-COUNTRY TRIPS

All of the above, plus:
- ☐ gaiters
- ☐ 2 gallon-size plastic food storage bags (wear them in your boots over your socks to keep feet dry in slushy conditions)
- ☐ warm ski-type hat and gloves
- ☐ warm jacket

Optional Gear

- ☐ camera and film
- ☐ binoculars
- ☐ bird and plant guidebooks
- ☐ notebook and pen/pencil

BACKPACKING TRIPS/OVERNIGHTS

All of the above, plus:

- ☐ backpack (internal or external frame)
- ☐ more water (at least a gallon a day, plus extra for cooking— cache or carry)
- ☐ clothing for the season
- ☐ sleeping bag and pad
- ☐ tent with fly
- ☐ toiletries
- ☐ stove with fuel bottle and repair kit
- ☐ pot, bowl, cup and eating utensils
- ☐ food (freeze dried meals require extra water)
- ☐ water filter designed and approved for backcountry use (if the route passes a water source)
- ☐ nylon cord (50 to 100 feet for hanging food, drying clothes etc.)
- ☐ additional plastic bags for carrying out trash
- ☐ your FalconGuide

APPENDIX C   OTHER INFORMATION SOURCES AND MAPS

NATURAL HISTORY ASSOCIATIONS

Anza-Borrego Desert Natural History Association
P.O. Box 310
Borrego Springs, CA 92004
(619) 767-3052

Joshua Tree National Park Association
74485 National Park Drive
Twentynine Palms, CA 92277
(619) 367-1488

Death Valley Natural History Association
& Mojave National Preserve
P.O. Box 188
Death Valley, CA 92328
(619) 786-3285

These associations are nonprofit membership organizations dedicated to the preservation and interpretation of the natural and human history of the parks for which they are named. Membership benefits include book discounts, educational programs, and periodic newsletters.

OTHER HANDY MAPS

Although the "At A Glance" chart lists only the detailed 7.5-minute topographic maps for each hike, the natural history associations also sell additional maps which are indispensible for overall trip planning, and for navigating around the park to and between hikes. These recommended maps are:

Anza-Borrego Desert State Park

- 1994 Anza-Borrego Region Recreation Map (color), 1:73,250 scale, Earthwalk Press, which includes all of ABDSP and surrounding lands.

- Topographic map set of 8 15-minute black & white maps covering the entire park, published by the Anza-Borrego Desert Natural History Association.

- AAA map of San Diego County published by the Automobile Club of Southern California

369

Joshua Tree National Park

- 1996 Joshua Tree National Park topographic backcountry & hiking map, 1:80,000 scale, published by Trails Illustrated.

- AAA map of Riverside County published by the Automobile Club of Southern California

Mojave National Preserve

- The Bureau of Land Management (BLM) managed the East Mojave National Scenic Area before Congress awarded it national preserve status. The BLM 1:100,000 scale Desert Access Guides are valuable, not only for roads but also for detemining land ownership. This is important because the preserve encompasses numerous private inholdings. The map guides covering the preserve are the New York Mountains (#9), Providence Mountains (#12), and Needles (#13). These maps, which are color-coded for ownership, can be purchased at the Information Center in Baker which is next to the giant thermometer.

- AAA map of San Bernadino County published by the Automobile Club of Southern California

Death Valley National Park

- 1996 Death Valley National Park topographic backcountry & hiking map, 1:160,000 scale, published by Trails Illustrated

- AAA map of Death Valley National Park published by the Automobile Club of Southern California

APPENDIX D STATE AND FEDERAL PARK MANAGEMENT AGENCIES

ANZA-BORREGO DESERT STATE PARK

District Superintendent
Anza-Borrego Desert State Park
200 Palm Canyon Drive
Borrego Springs, CA 92004
Park information, (619) 767-4684
Administrative office, (619) 767-5311
Camping reservations, Destinet,
1-800-444-7275

Agua Caliente County Park (surrounded
   by Anza-Borrego DSP)
c/o San Diego County Parks and
   Recreation Department
5201 Ruffin Road, Suite P
San Diego, CA 92123
Information, (619) 694-3049
Campground reservations, (619) 565-3600

For information about wilderness and
   other public lands adjacent to the
   park contact:
Bureau of Land Management
California Desert District
6221 Box Springs Boulevard
Riverside, CA 92507
(909) 697-5200

JOSHUA TREE NATIONAL PARK

Superintendent
Joshua Tree National Park
74485 National Park Drive
Twentynine Palms, CA 92277
(619) 367-7511
Camping reservations, Destinet,
1-800-365-2267

For information about wilderness and
   other public lands adjacent to the
   park contact:
Bureau of Land Management
California Desert District
6221 Box Springs Boulevard
Riverside, CA 92507
(909) 697-5200

MOJAVE NATIONAL PRESERVE

Superintendent
Mojave National Preserve
222 East Main Street, Suite 202
Barstow, CA 92311
(619) 255-8800

Mojave Desert Information Center
P.O. Box 241
Baker, CA 92309
(619) 733-4040

Hole-in-the-Wall Visitor Center (open
   irregular hours)
Black Canyon Road
Mojave National Preserve
(619) 928-2572

For information about wilderness and
   other public lands adjacent to the
   preserve contact:
Bureau of Land Management
California Desert District
6221 Box Springs Boulevard
Riverside, CA 92507
(909) 697-5200

MOJAVE NATIONAL PRESERVE *(CONT'D)*

Providence Mountains State Recreation
  Area & Mitchell Caverns Natural
  Preserve (within the boundaries of
  Mojave National Preserve)
P.O. Box 1
Essex, CA 92332-0001
(619) 928-2586
Campground reservations, Destinet,
1-800-444-7275

DEATH VALLEY NATIONAL PARK

Superintendent
Death Valley National Park
Death Valley, CA 92328
(619) 786-2331
Camping reservations, Destinet,
1-800-365-2267

For information about wilderness and
  other public lands adjacent to the
  park contact:
Bureau of Land Management
California Desert District
6221 Box Springs Boulevard
Riverside, CA 92507
(909) 697-5200

ABOUT THE AUTHORS

The authors on the summit of Kelso Dunes with the Granite Mountains in the background.

Bill Cunningham has been a lifelong "Wildernut," as a wildlands studies professor, an outfitter, a conservation activist and as a staffer for The Wilderness Society and Montana Wilderness Association from the mid-1970s to the mid-1980s, he worked toward passage of numerous wilderness bills for Montana and other parts of the country. Living in Missoula, Montana, Bill has written several books, most recently *Wild Montana* published by Falcon Press in 1995, and numerous articles about wilderness areas based on his extensive personal exploration.

Polly Burke, formerly a history teacher in St. Louis, Missouri, now makes her home in Montana and is pursuing a career as a freelance writer. Also, with Bill, an instructor with San Francisco State's Wildlands Studies program, she shares Bill's passion for wilderness.

Decades ago both Bill and Polly lived in California close to the desert— Bill in Bakersfield and Polly in San Diego. They enjoyed renewing their ties with California while exploring the state's desert regions. Months of driving, camping, and hiking, with laptop and camera, have increased their enthusiasm for California's desert wilderness. They want others to have as much fun exploring it as they did.